The Accountability Paradox in the Chinese Bureaucracy

Wenyan Tu

The Accountability Paradox in the Chinese Bureaucracy

palgrave
macmillan

Wenyan Tu
Institute for Global Public Policy,
The LSE-Fudan Research Centre for
Global Public Policy
Fudan University
Shanghai, China

ISBN 978-981-96-6391-0 ISBN 978-981-96-6392-7 (eBook)
https://doi.org/10.1007/978-981-96-6392-7

The research is supported by the National Natural Science Foundation of China (72304069) and the Shanghai Philosophy and Social Sciences Planning Project (2023ZGL008).

This Palgrave Macmillan imprint is published by the registered company Springer Nature Singapore Pte Ltd.
The registered company address is: 152 Beach Road, #21-01/04 Gateway East, Singapore 189721, Singapore

This book is dedicated to my mom

Preface

This book delves into the intricate dynamics of the accountability paradox within the Chinese bureaucracy, highlighting how enhanced accountability measures, while intended to promote compliance and responsiveness, instead lead to unintended negative consequences. The accountability systems have been unprecedentedly strengthened through comprehensive regulations and strict oversight of bureaucrats, profoundly shaping their motivations and behaviors. As a result, bureaucrats shift their focus from credit claiming to blame avoidance by engaging in subtle shirking behaviors, refraining from taking the initiative, and hindering innovation.

The book unpacks the accountability paradox into five sub-dimensions: the paradox of control, the paradox of agency, the paradox of responsibility, the paradox of structures, and the paradox of sources. To comprehensively analyze the dynamic interplay between accountability structures and bureaucratic agency, it employs a multifaceted approach. Specifically, it investigates the impacts of accountability on bureaucratic behavior through three lenses: the intensity of accountability, the components and configurations of accountability mechanisms, and the conflicts arising from various forms of accountability.

The findings suggest that intensified accountability does not necessarily lead to greater compliance among bureaucrats or improved governance. Specifically, sanction-based accountability, characterized by intensive monitoring and punitive measures, may prompt bureaucrats to engage in subtle shirking behaviors such as reframing responsibility and employing blame-avoidance strategies to manage work pressures and risks. Additionally, conflicts between hierarchical accountability from superiors and horizontal accountability from citizens, along with tensions between process-based and outcome-based accountability, place bureaucrats in a dilemma, leading to stagnation.

I have many people to thank. Three ladies play significant roles in my life, guiding me toward persistence, diligence, and strength. First and foremost, I want to express my deepest gratitude and love to my mother for her unconditional support. She has shaped me into a brave, honest, and resilient girl. While memories may fade, my love for her will never perish. The book is dedicated to her. The second lady to whom I want to express my sincere gratitude is my doctoral supervisor, Professor Ting Gong. This book is built on my doctoral thesis, which she meticulously revised word by word and sentence by sentence. The third lady I would like to extend my utmost appreciation to is my master's supervisor, Professor Xiajuan Guo. She guided me into the fabulous and dazzling world of academia, to which I am eager to devote myself for a lifetime.

During the writing of this book, the esteemed scholar Christopher Hood passed away, marking a significant loss for the academic community. I have cited many of his works in this book and have drawn considerable inspiration from them. I want to express my heartfelt gratitude to him; his contributions will endure forever. Last but not least, I am truly honored that this book is incorporated into the book series *Governing China in the 21st Century* edited by Professor Yijia Jing. Many thanks for him not only as the editor of this valuable book series but also as a supportive Dean of the Institute for Global Public Policy where I am affiliated.

Shanghai, China Wenyan Tu

Contents

Abbreviations

ABA	Anticipatory Blame Avoidance
CCDI	The Central Commission for Discipline Inspection
CCP	Chinese Communist Party
CCPCC	The Chinese Communist Party Central Committee
CDI	Commission for Discipline Inspection
ICTs	Information and Communication Technologies
KITA	Kick in The Ass
MPA	Master of Public Administration
NPA	New Public Administration
NPC	National People's Congress
NPM	New Public Management
NSC	National Supervisory Commission
OL	Organizational Learning
PAT	Principal-Agent Theory
PSM	Public Service Motivation
RBA	Reactive Blame Avoidance
SC	Supervisory Commission

List of Figures

List of Tables

CHAPTER 1

Introduction: The Accountability Paradox in the Chinese Bureaucracy

Accountability is promoted as a fundamental institution to regulate, rectify, and steer public officials. It is normally related to positive resonance and good governance (Bovens, 2007; Yang, 2012). Enhanced accountability may boost the fulfillment of responsibilities by creating greater answerability and transparency in the bureaucracy, curbing flagrant abuse of power, and ensuring compliance with superiors' mandates (Dubnick, 2003; Dunn & Legge, 2001). However, the potential for paradox or pathology within accountability mechanisms is concerning and puzzles both scholars and practitioners (Hood, 2014; Koppell, 2005; Ossege, 2012; Schillemans et al., 2013). Accountability overload is found to trigger its evil twin of blame avoidance and contributes to bureaucrats' evasion of responsibility (Christensen & Lægreid, 2015; Jos & Tompkins, 2004; Tu, 2024b). Dubnick (2005) and Jos and Tompkins (2004) remind us of the salience of the accountability paradox, which suggests that the frequent and intensive measurement of bureaucrats does not necessarily lead to a better government. Bureaucrats tend to prioritize blame avoidance and keep potentially blameworthy events off the agenda when they feel any mistake may be discovered and lead to punishment (Leland et al., 2021; Rajala, 2020; Tu, 2024).

The purpose of accountability is to foster compliance and responsiveness among bureaucrats, but instead, it causes bureaucrats' coping tactics, blame-avoiding strategies, and defensive behavior, which constitutes a

W. Tu, *The Accountability Paradox in the Chinese Bureaucracy*,
https://doi.org/10.1007/978-981-96-6392-7_1

paradox or pathology of accountability (Hood, 2014; Jos & Tompkins, 2004; Ossege, 2012; Schillemans et al., 2013). The accountability paradox is well documented in Western countries, but scarce attention has been paid to the accountability system in the Chinese context. In fact, until the beginning of the twenty-first century, the concept of accountability was introduced to China. In 2003, the central government held accountable some leaders for their poor performance in the fight against the SARS epidemic, marking the starting point of China's accountability system (Ran & Jian, 2021). However, the accountability system has been vague and weak, with only a small number of high-ranking officials being held accountable, which only occurred when large-scale safety incidents took place. This has been the case for nearly 10 years since the introduction of the system in 2003.

A significant turning point for the Chinese accountability system occurred when a set of transformations was initiated to overhaul the accountability framework after President Xi assumed the presidency at the end of 2012. The accountability mechanisms have been unprecedentedly strengthened by imposing comprehensive supervision and sanctions on bureaucrats, targeting their illegal acts, dereliction of duty, unsatisfactory performance, and various other malfeasance. The intention of the central government in enhancing accountability mechanisms is to prevent local authorities from abusing their delegated power and rectify their behavioral transgressions, thus building a system of governance that is accountable, responsive, and free of corruption. However, the intensified accountability has seemingly caused public officials to become risk-averse and to shirk responsibilities for fear of making mistakes and being implicated in investigations (Li et al., 2021; Tu & Gong, 2022b; Wang, 2022; Wang & Yan, 2020). In the face of intensified top-down accountability measures, local bureaucrats strategically shift their motivations from credit claiming to blame avoidance by refraining from taking the initiative in policy settings, over-conforming to rigid regulations, or creating bureaucratic barriers to decline unwanted demands (Li et al., 2021). The accountability paradox is evident in the Chinese context as well, but it displays certain distinctive features that are unique to China, shaped by its specific institutional backdrop and cultural context.

This book aims to provide a nuanced analysis of the accountability paradox that manifests in the Chinese context. It seeks to uncover the distinct characteristics of the accountability paradox unique to China. Furthermore, it delves into the institutional backdrop that has led to the transformation of the accountability system and examines its influence on bureaucratic behavior. This book attempts to provide answers to the following questions: What transformations do the Chinese accountability mechanisms undergo? What is the influence of these transformations on Chinese bureaucracy and bureaucratic behavior? How do public officials respond to increased accountability pressure? Why does the intensification of accountability fail to induce higher compliance and instead lead to shirking and blame avoidance among public officials? How does the configuration of accountability promote individuals' sense of responsibility without triggering their defensive motivations?

Accountability: A Contested Concept

Accountability, by itself, is an elusive, chameleon-like, and contested concept (Bovens et al., 2014; Dubnick & Yang, 2015; Han & Perry, 2020; Li et al., 2024). There are three aspects of debates regarding the conceptualization of accountability. First, scholars are divided on the concept of "accountability as a virtue" and "accountability as a mechanism" (Bovens, 2010). Some studies consider accountability a virtue and a desirable quality of states and governmental organizations. In this light, accountability can be regarded as synonymous with good governance, encompassing qualities such as responsiveness, a strong sense of responsibility, and a willingness to act transparently, fairly, compliantly, and equitably (Goodin et al., 2014). When it is considered a mechanism, accountability refers to the processes, structures, or practices that ensure individuals or organizations are held responsible for their actions and decisions to promote a transparency, integrity, and effective governance (Bovens, 2010; Brandsma & Schillemans, 2013; Tu, 2024b). Different from accountability as a virtue, accountability as a mechanism implies that it consists of a structured arrangement, and its misconfiguration may result in negative outcomes (Yang, 2012).

Second, scholars are divided on whether accountability connotates a dynamic relationship or a control tool imposed by the principal on the agent. The relational and communicative core of accountability is clearly evident in the social psychological literature on accountability. Here, many authors highlight the expectation that bureaucrats are required to explain and justify their actions to their superiors or significant others (Bovens, 2005). It signals dynamic interactions between actors and accountability forums where both sides exercise their advantages to gain the initiative and maximize self-interests. In the networks of accountability relationship, each party needs to consider "If I do this, how will others react?" (Tetlock, 1992, p. 337). For example, if an accountability forum wants the actor to prioritize its expectations over those of other forums, it needs to consider whether its strategies are effective and potent to influence the actor and the corresponding responses from the actor. The actor may also consider how to manage multiple or even conflicting expectations by weighing different accountability forums' capability to enforce consequences and the credibility of their commitments. Nevertheless, if accountability is positioned as a control tool meted out by the principal on the agent, it is more of a formal mechanism where the influence of power flows one-way and is imposed downwardly in a hierarchical chain. The agents are often portrayed as submissive and passive recipients of power pressure (Taylor, 1911; Weber, 1978). Compared to accountability as a relationship, accountability as a control tool often involves directing, regulating, or overseeing actions.

Third, scholars are contested on whether accountability represents a sanction-based consequence or a comprehensive process. Accountability, in various situational contexts and among numerous governments, normally centers around the imposition of punishment (Baldwin, 2004; Schillemans & Aleksovska, 2024; Tu & Gong, 2022a). Enforceability, considered a crucial condition of accountability, demonstrates "the ability of the overseeing actor(s) to impose sanction on the accountable actor(s) for failures and transgressions" (Brinkerhoff, 2001, p. 2). Accountability serves as an expedient punitive mechanism for those in positions of authority to maintain control and reinforce hierarchies, deter individuals from engaging in illegal or unethical behavior, and demonstrate to the public a commitment to integrity and justice (Dubnick & Yang, 2015; Fan, 2024; Schillemans, 2013). However, more and more scholars conceptualize accountability as a dynamic process involving various stages and phases (Pérez Durán, 2016). Based on the definition of accountability as a mechanism where "the actor has an obligation to explain and justify his or her conduct, the forum can pose questions and pass judgment, and the actor may face consequences" (Bovens, 2007, p. 450), Brandsma and Schillemans (2013) develop a model of the "accountability cube." It conceptualizes accountability as a process including three stages: information (information report and acquire), discussion (explain and inquire), and consequences (punishments or rewards). This process approach sheds light on the dynamic and comprehensive nature of accountability. The careful configuration of various accountability components is essential for an effective accountability system.

In this book, accountability is considered a dynamic relationship between account givers and forums in which the forums use various mechanisms to hold the actors accountable to their expectations, while the actors employ strategies to navigate diverse and sometimes conflicting expectations. In this relationship, a process-based approach is established between the actors and forums where information is exchanged, discussions take place, and consequences are enforced. In this light, this book regards accountability as a multidimensional mechanism consisting of a system of components working together and interacting with each other. It focuses on internal accountability within the Chinese government. Internal accountability in China refers to various sorts of checks and balances conducted by the bureaucracy or the Party to hold public officials accountable (Hu, 2017). Internal accountability is different from external accountability which involves supervision and oversight over public officials by actors outside the government, such as the media, citizens, or NGOs.

The Accountability Paradox

The accountability paradox refers to the phenomenon where the enforcement of accountability results in unintended negative consequences instead of the expected improvement in governance. The accountability paradox includes multiple dimensions, and the contradictions within its sub-dimensions contribute to the broader paradox of accountability. I outline five dimensions of paradox within accountability mechanisms (Table 1.1).

First, if the orientation of accountability is viewed as the control of the principal over the agent, there is an inherent paradox of control (In this book, when I mention the abstract terms "supervisor/politician/account holder" or "subordinate/bureaucrat/account giver," I designate the former as the principal using feminine pronouns, while the latter as the agent with masculine pronouns to avoid confusion). The core issue of the principal-agent relationship lies in balancing the conflict between the principal's control and the agent's professional autonomy. The delegation process inherently involves granting the agent the discretion to utilize their expertise, while also implementing control measures to prevent them from undermining the principal's interests (Bendor et al., 2001; Moe,

Table 1.1 Multifaceted dimensions of the accountability paradox

The accountability paradox	*Connotations*	*Countervailing meanings*
Paradox of control	The principal's control can mitigate agency problems. However, excessive control may restrict the agent's professional autonomy, reducing efficiency	Control vs. autonomy
Paradox of agency	Accountability is expected to induce bureaucrats' compliance. Alternatively, bureaucrats circumvent controls via various coping strategies	Compliance vs. Strategic coping
Paradox of responsibility	Accountability is expected to promote responsible and ethical behavior. Nevertheless, external control may crowd out bureaucrats' moral judgment	External standards vs. Responsible interpretations
Paradox of structures	The arrangement of various components of accountability is unbalanced	Punishment mechanism vs. a multidimensional structure
Paradox of sources	Multiple sources of accountability impose conflicting expectations on bureaucrats, resulting in a role dilemma	Hierarchical vs. horizontal expectations; outcome-based vs. Process-based demands

2012). The level of control indicates how much the principal can control the agent's administration to regulate, manage, or influence the actions and decisions of the agent. In contrast, autonomy shows the degree of independence and self-governance granted to the agent in making decisions and taking actions without external interference, allowing for decision-making based on professional judgment or organizational norms (Dahlström & Lapuente, 2022). While the principal's control can effectively curb the agent's malfeasance and corruption, excessive monitoring and sanction can stifle the agent's professional capabilities and efficiency (Christensen & Lægreid, 2015; Ji, 2022). Nevertheless, while the agent's autonomy may allow him to make the most of his expertise and information advantages to deliver matched public goods to citizens, excessive autonomy entails the risk of various agency problems, such as corruption, sabotage, and gaming (Panda & Leepsa, 2017). How to balance control and autonomy is an art of management.

Second, in relation to the positioning and role of the agent, there are two paradoxes: the paradox of agency and the paradox of responsibility. Whether bureaucrats should be hypothesized as an economic man or a responsible actor, a tool of policy implementation or a value bearer who is responsible for social justice are the deep sources of the two categories of paradox. Premised on the separation between politics and public administration, traditional public administration considers the bureaucracy a rational tool for implementing policies from the principal without personal preferences and emotions (Bendor, 1988; Gailmard & Patty, 2012; Olsen, 2006). Drawing on rational choice theory, principal-agent theory (PAT) considers the agent as an economic man who acts rationally and in their own self-interest to maximize utility or profit (Bennett & Naumann, 2005). Some observers argue that bureaucrats will either work or "shirk" depending on what generates the highest personal utility (Hayes & Wood, 1995; Rose-Ackerman, 1986). Therefore, supervision and sanctions should be imposed on them to increase their cost of shirking or drifting. However, departing from our expectation that the agent will automatically respond to the principal's intensified accountability mechanisms with responsiveness and compliance, bureaucrats are found to circumvent controls via various coping strategies, such as buck-passing, over-conforming, playing dumb, buffing, playing safe, resisting change, etc. (Ashforth & Lee, 1990; Hood, 2002; Ossege, 2012), leading to a paradox of agency.

If bureaucrats are viewed as value bearers who take responsibility for society and citizens' interests, as promoted by the New Public Administration (NPA), they are expected to exercise their discretionary power to make moral judgments in complicated administrative circumstances to uphold the broader common good (Frederickson, 1996; Sørensen, 2002; Lee, 2022; Waldo, 1952). In this regard, a bureaucrat's sense of responsibility and moral judgment are crucial for making the right decisions instead of mindlessly relying on regulations or directives from his superiors (Jos & Tompkins, 2004, 2009). The terms responsibility and accountability are often used interchangeably, which subtly implies that one of the purposes of accountability is to create responsible officials and governments. However, the paradox of responsibility emerges when good policy outcomes require bureaucrats' responsible interpretation, while the institutions and mechanisms of acountability designed to convey and enforce these external standards often crowd out the qualities or motivations necessary for responsible decision-making (Cooper, 2012; Harmon, 1995; Jos, 1988).

Third, accountability is considered a mechanism comprising a system of elements working together and interacting with each other. Information acquisition, discussion quality, and consequences focusing on punishment or rewards should be well configurated to promote "good" accountability. The unbalanced arrangement of these components of accountability is also a source of the accountability paradox. For example, accountability is often viewed as a fundamental mechanism to hold bureaucrats accountable for their wrongdoings, leading to greater emphasis on the consequence phase after malfeasance occurs, while scant attention is paid to the information and discussion phases. In this case, accountability may evolve as a mechanism for *post-hoc* sanction and fail to proactively prevent misconduct through systematic probes and discussion. Furthermore, if accountability prioritizes assessing and punishing actions without fostering dialogue among stakeholders or providing rewards to boost working morality, it may turn into a fault-finding and malignant mechanism, triggering risk aversion, blame avoidance, and a culture of low trust within the organization.

Fourth, the paradox of sources is increasingly a major problem faced by bureaucrats. Multiple sources of accountability impose conflicting expectations on bureaucrats, resulting in a role dilemma. Within the formal principal-agent relationship in the government, bureaucrats are obliged to meet multiple expectations from hierarchical accountability derived from the political, administrative, and legal directives (Bovens, Schillemans, & Hart, 2008; Romzek & Dubnick, 1987). On the other hand, they are also facing increasingly intensified horizontal accountability from the media, social organizations, and the public (Kenney, 2003; Reddick et al., 2020). As the state agent, they are acting on behalf of the government, responsible for strictly executing policies, regulations, and laws, while as the citizen agent, they should prioritize the needs and interests of citizens even via prosocial rule breaking (Dahling et al., 2012; Maynard-Moody & Musheno, 2000; Morrison, 2006; Sabbe et al., 2021).

In addition, some accountability forums emphasize outcome-based demands including efficiency, output, and performance, while others are process-based prioritizing compliance with input, rules, and process (Boussalis et al., 2018; Mattei, 2007). Each source of accountability establishes unique principles for suitable actions, making it challenging for bureaucrats to strike a balance among them, thereby leading to a considerable number of incidents from administrative decision-making errors (Klingner et al., 2002; Newman, 2004). It highlights the significance of developing bureaucrats' moral judgment in the context of increasingly complex administrative situations and governance networks.

In a nutshell, the paradox of accountability derives from internal conflicts of the five aspects. The five aspects point to the interactivity between accountability structure and human agency. Instead of regarding accountability as a static institutional setting exogenous to actors, this book seeks to explore the dynamic, complicated, and interaction between the constraints of accountability and the responses of bureaucrats. Different orientations, configurations, intensity, and sources of accountability may result in varying responses from bureaucrats—working, shirking, or gaming. Bureaucrats' different responses may, in turn, lead to the emergence of new forms of accountability structures. Specifically, agents' strategic actions are shaped and limited by the existing accountability frameworks, while these frameworks also adapt in response to the agents' strategic reactions (Courty & Marschke, 2007; Yang, 2012). There are always strategic moves and mutual adaptation between bureaucrats and their account holders (Tu & Gong, 2022b; Yang, 2012).

Yang (2012) suggests that it is important to develop actionable accountability knowledge, which requires answering three significant questions: "(a) Empirically, how exactly do actors of governance perceive, order, and deal with multiple accountability pressures and why? (b) empirically, what are the mechanisms or causal linkages that connect accountability institutions with actor behaviors and organizational/societal outcomes? and (c) empirically, exactly how are accountability institutions produced and reproduced by actors?" Guided by the three questions, this book aims to examine the influence of intensity, configurations, and conflicts within accountability structures on bureaucratic behavior. It also investigates how bureaucrats perceive and react to accountability pressures from various sources of authority, as well as how accountability structures adapt to bureaucratic actions in China.

Accountability and Bureaucratic Behavior

The accountability paradox is primarily rooted in the debate around the balance between institutional constraints and bureaucrats' discretionary power. Figure 1.1 illustrates how bureaucrats' behavior is influenced by the interaction between top-down control and their heterogeneous preferences and discretion. This framework is based on the principal-agent theory that is often used to address issues related to divergent preferences and information asymmetry between the principal and the agent. On the one hand, bureaucrats are under the control of their principals and are expected to behave strictly following their principal's demands. On the other hand, bureaucrats may hold different preferences from their superiors and considerable discretionary power, which enables them to drift away from their principals' directives and to work for their own benefit. Scholars who recognize the effectiveness of top-down control advocate externally imposed controls, such as monitoring, sanctions, and incentive mechanisms (Finer, 1941; McCubbins & Schwartz, 1984). Nevertheless, other scholars argue that internal control mechanisms within organizations, such as cultivating a cooperative culture and providing ethical training to foster bureaucrats' moral deliberation, is a more sustainable strategy to regulate the behavior of bureaucrats due to their bottom-up discretion to maneuver around the demands placed on them by superiors (Cooper, 2012; Friedlich, 1940; Jos & Tompkins, 2004).

Centered on the significance of external and internal controls, a classic debate between Carl Friedrich and Herman Finer was sparked in the later 1930s and early 1940s (Jackson, 2009; Plant, 2011). Finer (1941)

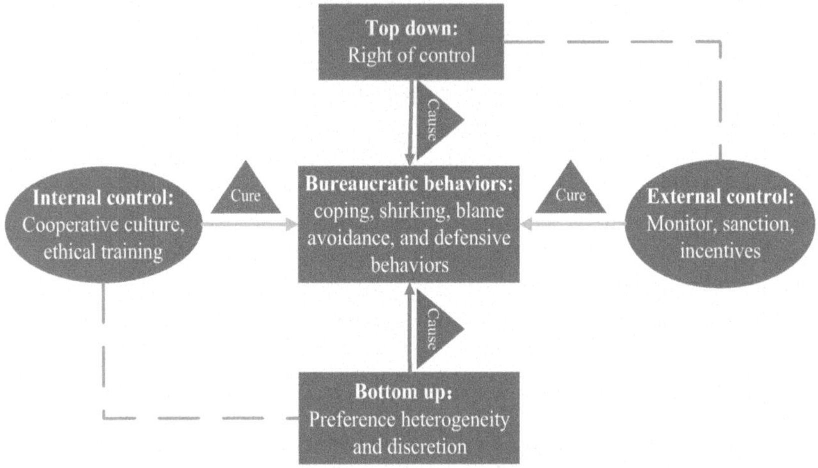

Fig. 1.1 Institutional constraints and bureaucratic behavior

emphasizes the primacy of external political control over bureaucrats, and considers that extrinsic constraints, such as oversight, punishment, or external laws should be equipped to hold bureaucrats accountable to politicians. Friedlich (1940), on the other hand, advocates that the inward responsibility and sense of personal morality of bureaucrats are more important drivers of their responsible behaviors to uphold broader public value. Thus, intrinsic motivation should not be replaced by restrictive formal legal controls, and the responsible judgment and moral reflection of bureaucrats should be encouraged (Cooper, 2012; Friedlich, 1940; Harmon, 1995).

The scientific management school considers bureaucracy a rational tool for implementing the commands and directives of the principal and emphasizes stringent supervision to ensure absolute compliance (Olsen, 2006). This paradigm prescribes a rigid and top-down command chain of authority from higher to lower levels, and a bureaucrat in the chain of command is regarded as a "robot" or a "cog in the machine," displaying absolute obedience without individual preferences and thoughts (Hasson & Goldberg, 1987; Sager & Rosser, 2009). Based on the presumption that bureaucrats respond passively to external control systems, accountability in the forms of monitoring and sanctions has been widely advocated as a mechanism to regulate public officials (Meier, 2009; Wood & Waterman, 1991).

However, a large volume of literature shows that bureaucrats are not passive to top-down control, and coercive or scientific management cannot force them to obey (Brehm & Gates, 1999; Meier & O'Toole, 2006; Tu & Gong, 2022a). This is because bureaucrats are not cogs in the machine, and they possess preferences, emotions, and interests that are not always consistent with those of their superiors (Brehm & Gates, 1999). Furthermore, according to the agency theory, discretion and information advantage inherent in power delegation offer agents a certain space to manipulate authority and circumvent control (Gailmard, 2002; Moe, 2006; Tummers & Bekkers, 2014). Coercive or scientific management cannot force subordinates to obey on account of their relative discretionary power and autonomy from organizational authority (Lipsky, 2010, pp. 13–18). Therefore, accountability does not necessarily foster bureaucrats' compliance and responsiveness, instead, bureaucrats may respond to "bad" accountability with a range of destructive strategies.

The preference heterogeneity between policymakers and policy enforcers or between supervisors and subordinates, as well as the discretion embedded in power delegation, combined to result in a "leakage of authority" (Downs, 1967, p. 134). Undeniably, the exertion of top-down control and oversight by superiors has a significant impact on the behavior of bureaucrats. Bureaucrats may rationally choose how to act based on the strength of supervision and potential sanctions from their superiors. However, bureaucrats may also leverage their discretionary power and informational advantages to outwardly display compliance but adopt a quiet, seemingly covert and disguised form of resistance to top-down authority, similar to the "everyday resistance" proposed by Scott (1985). For example, they may use coping strategies to divert pressure and subvert control mechanisms (De Bruijn, 2002). Furthermore, they may strategically shirk thorny responsibilities, preemptively evade risky tasks, and shift blame to scapegoats when problems arise (Gong & Tu, 2022). They may also adopt various blame-avoiding strategies, such as reducing policy innovation and formulation that contain a risk of failure (Howlett, 2014), refraining from taking the initiative in policy settings (Hood, 2002), or establishing a rigid protocol to obscure responsibility (Hood et al., 2016). In order to reduce a perceived threat or avoid an unwanted demand, they may defensively avoid action or change by playing dumb, stalling, and over-conforming to rigid bureaucratic procedures (Ashforth & Lee, 1990).

This book is based on the interactive game and equilibrium between top-down control and bottom-up defense. Superiors recognize that subordinates might employ coping or defensive strategies to manage the strict oversight and intense pressure they impose. Conversely, subordinates understand that their career advancement and departmental budgets are largely dependent on their supervisors, making excessive defensive behaviors unwise. The preferences of both sides are likely shaped by their interactions with one another. Subordinates may adopt adverse coping strategies in response to their superiors' preferences. In turn, supervisors may alter their personnel management approach based on the sometimes defensive and counterproductive reactions from subordinates, seeking more effective ways to encourage cooperation. Therefore, the key question is how to design accountability or control systems that foster a greater level of cooperation within organizations.

Why Increased Accountability Causes Bureaucratic Dysfunction in China?

This book is set against the backdrop of China, where an accountability paradox has become more evident since Xi came to power. This section provides an overview of the background leading to the emergence of this accountability paradox. The largest and most publicized anti-corruption campaign in the history of the Chinese Communist Party (CCP) was initiated by the Xi Jinping government following the 18th National Party Congress in 2012 and is still underway at full scale. Since the 18th Party Congress, the anti-corruption effort has been far-reaching in its unprecedented scope, length, depth, and mode to discipline the Party members and civil servants (Manion, 2016). Although the initial anti-corruption phase was guided by strong political will and executed in a campaign-style manner, the ongoing effort focuses on establishing legal and institutional foundations for the anti-corruption crackdown. It aims to build a comprehensive defense regime against corruption by strengthening institutions such as supervision, accountability, and punishment. Following this unprecedented sweeping anti-corruption crackdown, top-down accountability, as one of the major institutional structures, has undergone substantial transformation and intensification to comprehensively strengthen discipline across the system in tandem.

The substantial intensification of accountability is evident through the promulgation of static laws and regulations for overseeing bureaucrats and the systematic enforcement of these decrees. It is reported that the central government issued or amended more than 50 inner-party disciplinary regulations in the five years after the 18th National Congress of the CCP, in a bid to provide an institutional guarantee for comprehensively strengthening the party discipline over all cadres (Legal Daily, 2017). Some long-standing accountability mechanisms, such as public budgeting and auditing, inspections, performance appraisals, and codes of conduct, have been further strengthened at every level of the government to hold local authorities accountable. Stationing (*paizhu*, 派驻) and inspection tours (*xunshi*, 巡视), for example, have been launched as two major supervision measures intending to achieve full coverage of top-down inspections across all levels of the government, Party units, state organs, universities, and state-owned enterprises (Li, 2019). During the five years from 2013 to 2017, the central government conducted 12 rounds of inspections over 277 essential Party organizations, and from

2018 to 2022, the central government carried out 9 rounds of inspections (Tu & Gong, 2022b).

As shown in Table 1.2 and Fig. 1.2, both the number of filed cases and public officials who have been subjected to Party disciplinary and administrative sanctions by the Central Commissions for Discipline Inspection (CCDI) and local Commissions for Discipline Inspection (CDI) has witnessed a steady increase since 2013. The number of cases filed and officials prosecuted has increased significantly from 2013 to 2018, the first term of President Xi's administration, and the momentum on strengthening accountability has continued after 2018. The targets of inspections consist not only of corruption but also undesirable work styles, malfeasance or shirking in implementing upper-level policies, and unsatisfactory performance. The number of prosecuted officials at or above the county level has also seen a significant increase. For example, a total of 4,698 officials at or above the county level were punished in 2012, while over 20,776 officials at or above the county level were prosecuted in 2016.

According to the interviews conducted by correspondents of the China Comment (*banyuetan*, 半月谈), a township Party secretary complained that for his government, in 2018 alone, 200 days were spent on preparing

Table 1.2 Number of filed cases and prosecuted officials across ranks

Year	*Cases filed (10 thousand)*	*Prosecuted officials (10 thousand)*	*Officials at the provincial/ ministerial level*	*Officials at the department/ bureau level*	*Officials at county/ division level (10 thousand)*
2012	15.5	16.1	\	\	\
2013	17.2	18.2	31	\	\
2014	22.6	23.2	68	\	\
2015	33.0	33.6	90	\	\
2016	41.3	41.5	76	2700	1.8
2017	52.7	52.7	58	3300	2.1
2018	63.8	62.1	51	3500	2.6
2019	61.9	58.7	41	4000	2.4
2020	61.8	60.4	27	2859	2.2
2021	63.1	62.7	36	3024	2.5
2022	59.6	59.2	53	2450	2.1
2023	62.6	61.0	49	3144	2.4

Note Data released by the official website of the CCDI

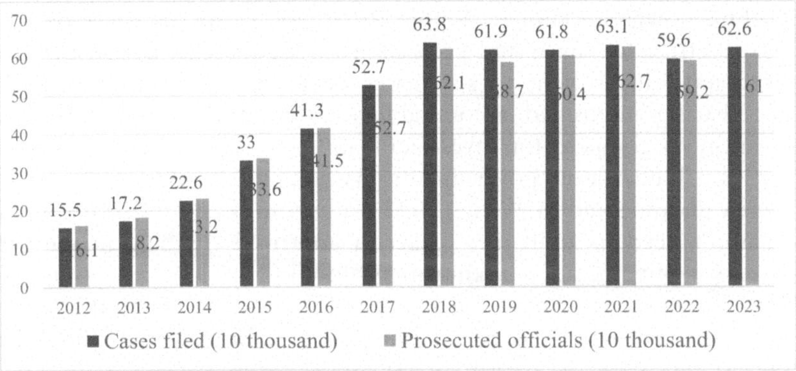

Fig. 1.2 Number of filed cases and prosecuted officials

for various inspections from upper-level authorities and accompanying the inspection teams when they were conducting checkups. A township official in an Eastern province received more than 50 inspection teams within half a year in 2018 (the China Comment, 2018). A public official was subject to disciplinary punishment for failing to answer a phone call from his supervisor after working hours when he was taking a shower (CCTV, 2018). An Education Bureau in Hunan province was subject to public reprimand (*tongbao piping,* 通报批评) for having snacks in the office (Pengpai News, 2018). Several teachers in Shanxi province were criticized for dining together on holiday (Pengpai News, 2018).

The intensification of accountability in China since 2012 has led to a series of unintended negative consequences, which can be viewed as an accountability paradox or pathology in the Chinese context. The intention of the central government in enhancing accountability mechanisms is to prevent local authorities from abusing their delegated power and to rectify their behavioral transgression. However, the intensification of accountability in China has led to a series of unintended negative consequences. Facing strengthened top-down accountability, local bureaucrats covertly adopt blame-avoiding strategies by shunning risky tasks, stifling innovation, and building blame-deflecting bureaucratic barriers (Wang, 2022; Wang & Yan, 2020).

It has been suggested that the extensive anti-graft initiative and intensified accountability have dampened the enthusiasm of government officials to boost local economic development due to the fear of being suspected of trading power for money. Before 2012, local officials exerted great efforts to strive for funds and projects from higher-level authorities and attract capital investment to stimulate the local economy (Nee et al., 2007). Facing intensified accountability, local officials have lost their motivation to compete for investment and have even rejected projects offered by higher-level governments (Wang, 2022). According to an interview documented by Wang (2022), a bureau head told an inspector, "You don't need to audit me. I haven't approved anything in the past two years." Bureaucratic shirking in promoting the local economy and dealing with businessmen has gained significant attention from the central government. Former Chinese Premier Keqiang Li stated in 2013 that failure to stay clean is a form of corruption, and slack is a disguised form of corruption (Chinese Government Website, 2014). An innovative mechanism—a fault-tolerance mechanism—was adopted by the central government to cushion the backfire of intensified accountability and encourage officials to be proactive in fulfilling their duties and taking initiatives.

The Limits of Existing Accounts for the Accountability Paradox

Scholars seek to provide plausible explanations for the accountability paradox. Overall, there are three major explanations for the accountability paradox. One popular argument is that the heightened accountability foments bureaucrats' defensive emotions and deviant behavior (Halachmi, 2014; Ossege, 2012). Scholars argue that while accountability deficit may trigger bureaucratic shirking, accountability overload in monitoring and sanction causes its evil twin of blame avoidance and contributes to bureaucrats' tactful evasion of daunting tasks (Christensen & Lægreid, 2015; Halachmi, 2014; Rabbi & Sabharwal, 2024). This explanation highlights how bureaucrats use tactical ploys to manipulate accountability procedures, processes, and narratives from the bottom up if the pressure to be accountable becomes unbearable for them (Kuipers & T Hart, 2014).

The second explanation is that some pivotal elements are absent in the accountability mechanism, leading to the pathology of accountability. Roberts (2002) suggests that unforced, reciprocal, and reflective dialogues between actors and accountability holders create a space for clarifying misunderstandings and fostering learning and deliberation.

Accountability without dialogues or communication may treat bureaucrats as passive subjects waiting to be evaluated and blamed, and thus leads to defensiveness and evasiveness among bureaucrats (O'Loughlin, 1990). In contrast to the approach of imposing sanctions by identifying faults, another crucial orientation of accountability being advocated by burgeoning research is to have account givers reflect on what caused problems and how to continuously promote learning and performance improvement through reflective dialogues and debates (Behn, 2001; Bovens, Schillemans, & Hart, 2008).

The third account challenges the profound orientation and intention related to accountability. The exercise of external accountability, on the one hand, requires bureaucrats to responsibly interpret and deliberate on the prescribed accountability requirements and standards. On the other hand, the very institutions, processes, and oversight mechanisms used to convey these external accountability standards and monitor compliance often end up undermining the moral deliberation, ethical reasoning, and sound professional judgment of the administrators tasked with carrying out the accountability mandates (Jos & Tompkins, 2004; Ossege, 2012). This tension suggests that a narrow, compliance-driven approach to accountability may come at the expense of the very ethical foundations and good governance that accountability is meant to uphold.

These explanations are plausible but suffer from a few crucial flaws. First, the established literature tends to conceptualize accountability as an aggregate term without unpacking it and explaining which parts are overloading and which are deficit. Furthermore, the configuration of accountability mechanisms is scarcely explored, leading to the over-fixation of specific elements of accountability. Third, the extant literature pays insufficient attention to the interaction between accountability constraints and bureaucrats' strategic responses to control. Fourth, the majority of the established research has been conducted within the context of Western, democratic countries, while insufficient attention has been paid to examining accountability in other non-democratic political and social contexts.

To advance the understanding of the accountability paradox, this book unpacks the internal mechanism of accountability to provide a more nuanced analysis of the relationship between accountability and bureaucratic behavior. Rather than regard accountability as an aggregate concept, I unpack it, considering it a mechanism with various components, and empirically explore the impacts of different components and configurations of accountability on bureaucratic behavior. Furthermore, rather than merely focus on accountability itself or examine individual bureaucrats in isolation, I scrutinize the dynamic interaction between the institutional constraints imposed on bureaucrats and individual bureaucrats' response to accountability pressures and conflicting expectations from multiple sources of accountability. Third, my study deploys a diverse range of both qualitative and quantitative data to support the explanations for the accountability paradox emerging in the Chinese context that has received insufficient attention from the extant literature.

Unpacking Accountability from Three Perspectives

Defined as a multifaceted mechanism composed of a system of elements working together and interacting with each other, accountability should not be treated as an aggregate term and should be unpacked to explore how the configuration and the interaction of different elements influence bureaucratic behavior. Unpacking the internal mechanism of accountability enables us to go beyond the general discussion of accountability and to provide a more nuanced understanding of the accountability paradox. To holistically examine the impact of accountability on bureaucratic behavior in China, this book adopts a comprehensive approach. It unpacks accountability by exploring its three key dimensions: the intensity of accountability mechanisms; the diverse components that constitute the accountability system; and the conflicts that arise between different expectations or demands of the accountability framework.

First, this book explores the impacts of accountability intensity on bureaucratic shirking. Scholars suggest that either accountability overload or deficit may cause bureaucratic dysfunction (Bovens et al., 2008; Rabbi & Sabharwal, 2024). Therefore, it is significant to examine how different levels of accountability intensity may exert impacts on bureaucratic behaviors. Accountability is a consequential undertaking, and the essence of accountability is ultimately about punishment—it means that the person being held accountable will face negative consequences for their actions or failures (Behn, 2001). The belief that accountability is synonymous with punishment or sanction persists among a significant number of scholars (Bovens et al., 2014). Therefore, this book gauges accountability intensity by the degree of monitoring and punishment imposed on bureaucrats. It seeks to explore how accountability intensity exerts impacts on bureaucrats and how bureaucrats conversely cope with accountability pressures. This book differentiates shirking into diverse types and examines the varying impacts of accountability intensity on bureaucrats' shirking behaviors. It indicates that intensive monitoring and punishment may inhibit bureaucrats from blatantly evading responsibility by, for example, being sloppy, inactive, or involved in non-work activities. However, they may induce bureaucrats to adopt some subtle defensive behaviors such as shifting and reframing responsibility to cope with work pressure and risks.

Second, this book delves into the elements or components that constitute the accountability system. Accountability is conceptualized by scholars as a dynamic, multi-stage process encompassing the entire practice of accountability, starting from the initial account-giving or reporting stage, and extending through questioning the adequacy of the reported information to the enforcement of consequences (Brandsma & Schillemans, 2013). Many authors who endorse this process-based approach have applied the model of the "accountability cube" developed by Brandsman and Schillemans (2013). This framework views accountability as a three-stage process: the information stage, where relevant information is provided or acquired by upper-level authorities; the discussion or debating stage, where the relevant information is discussed and debated; the consequences stage, where outcomes and impacts are determined (Han, 2020; Pérez Durán, 2016; Tu, 2024a). This book draws on the model of the "accountability cube" to capture the key elements and essence of accountability. Four indicators are generated from the cube: monitoring intensity, discussion quality, and reward- or punishment-based consequences. This book seeks to explore not only the respective impact of the four elements but also their different combinations on bureaucrats' blame avoidance, a behavior that is considered the opposite side of the same coin with accountability.

Third, this book explores how the conflicts arising from different expectations of the accountability framework influence bureaucratic behavior. A significant issue concerning accountability is the diverse expectations imposed on the agent by a large number of accountability holders within or outside the organization (Bovens, 2010; Busuioc & Lodge, 2016; Page, 2006). Nowadays, public sector employees worldwide are wrestling with a dense "web of accountability," where they need to fulfill the expectations from a set of accountability forums, such as political leaders, citizens, higher-level supervisors, peers, regulations, and professional codes (Koppell, 2005; Willems & Van Dooren,

2011; Ye et al., 2023). The conflicting expectations from multiple sources of accountability put agents under diverging pressure and then influence their behavioral choices. In China, bureaucrats are often caught between top-down and bottom-up accountability. The former holds them accountable to superiors, and the latter requires them to be responsive to local citizens' requests and interests. Policy priorities set by upper-level authorities are not always in the best interests of local citizens, which makes bureaucrats face expectation conflict. This book explores how much effort bureaucrats tend to put into a task when expectations of superiors and citizens for it are consistent, and the effort that they exert when expectations are divergent. Do they work in citizens' interests in defiance of their superiors' instructions or do they comply with top-down demands regardless of the preferences of local people?

Besides different sources of accountability, bureaucrats face varying logics of accountability. On one hand, they are required to comply with formal processes, standards, and protocols; on the other hand, they are expected to produce satisfactory performance, output, results, or outcomes. The conflicts between process-based accountability and outcome-based accountability can put bureaucrats in a dilemma. Strict adherence to procedures may fail to meet targets and undermine efficiency, while effectively attaining goals may entail the risk of violating rules. Xi's administration holds bureaucrats to high standards, demanding strict compliance with protocols while also expecting them to be proactive and effectively meet targets. This creates the risk of bureaucrats being blamed for either taking action or inaction. How do bureaucrats cope with these conflicting expectations? How does the government modify the accountability system to address these collisions? This book provides answers to these questions.

Data and Methodologies

This book combines qualitative methods and quantitative methods, which can be called mixed methods research, to shed light on the paradox of accountability. In general, mixed methods research is an approach that involves collecting, analyzing, and interpreting both quantitative data and qualitative data within a single research study (Almalki, 2016). Mixed methods research provides a way to bridge the gap between different research methods. Quantitative methods adopt numbers, statistical tests, and large-N datasets for causal reference, while qualitative methods use text, words, and small-N datasets to provide information about mechanisms and contexts (Lakshman et al., 2000). Quantitative methods include questionnaires, large-N case studies, and statistics. Qualitative methods consist of interviews, focus groups, participant observations, grounded theory, small-N case studies, and content analysis.

First, surveys were administered. Surveys involve the collection of quantitative data, such as people's opinions, feelings, and thoughts, from a sample selected from a specific segment of the population through a questionnaire. "A questionnaire enables quantitative data to be collected in a standardized way so that the data are internally consistent and coherent for analysis" (Malhotra, 2006, p. 83). The major data source of this book derived from 870 questionnaires among Chinese civil servants administered by the author in 2019. The questionnaire comprises items related to the respondents' perception of accountability and their propensity for shirking behavior and blame-avoidance strategies (Chapters 4–6).

Second, text data about the bureaucratic shirking phenomena and accountability schemes from official documents and media reports were collected. 432 shirking cases publicized on the official website of the CCDI from 2012 to 2018 were used to classify the different types of bureaucratic shirking (Chapter 4). Laws, policies, rules, regulations, and circulars about accountability promulgated by the central and local governments were collected. This book also utilizes media reports on accountability. It collected reports from newspapers, official websites, and magazines, including the official websites of the CCDI and local CDIs, official newspapers like the Procuratorate Daily and China Discipline Inspection News, as well as influential media outlets such as the China Comment, China Youth Daily, Xinhua Net, Sohu Net, Pengpai News, People's Daily, Beijing Times, and CCTV. By analyzing reports from various media sources, the study can compile in-depth information and gain a comprehensive understanding of the implementation and impact of accountability mechanisms. Policy documents related to the fault-tolerance mechanism promulgated in 19 provinces were collected to explore the intention, characteristics, and conditions of the initiation of the fault-tolerance mechanism (Chapter 7).

Third, this book conducts 36 interviews with Chinese public officials to complement the quantitative data and gain a deeper understanding of the context in which the accountability paradox arises. The interviewees are employed in various departments, including local governments, the Department of Finance, local CDIs, the Social Security Administration, and the Public Security Bureau across the provinces of Guangdong, Jiangxi, Hunan, Jiangsu, Anhui, Sichuan, Hubei, and Guizhou. Interviews, one of the major qualitative research methods, are employed to obtain thick and rich data that offer information about mechanisms and contexts (Schultze & Avital, 2011). I employed semi-structured in-depth interviews to capture government officials' views on the effectiveness of accountability and how they deal with pressures from accountability mechanisms. Interviews comprise the following questions: "How is your job enthusiasm?" "Are you motivated? If yes, what motivates you to work hard, and if not, why and what strategies will you adopt to handle job tasks?" "What is the major accountability that you face?" "Who holds you accountable?" "Do you see any flaw in the accountability system and can you give specific examples?" "How do you deal with the pressure of accountability?".

Fourth, case study was utilized. A case study is a research method that involves an in-depth examination of a specific instance, event, or phenomenon within its real-life context to provide a detailed and comprehensive view of the subject. I collected 66 typical cases that were publicly reported by official media and websites from 2012 to 2023 to identify patterns and characteristics of cases that receive the fault-tolerance mechanism (Chapter 7). In-depth analyses were conducted on these cases to explore the specific circumstances and conditions of the mechanism.

This book utilized multiple linear regression models to explore the causal relationship between accountability intensity and shirking phenomena. Second, K-means algorithm cluster analysis was employed to classify forms of accountability based on the cluster of the elements of accountability. Third, a between-subjects survey experiment is applied to explore the interaction of diverse expectations and accountability intensity on bureaucrats' working efforts. Last but not least, content analysis, interviews, and typical case studies were also adopted.

Significance

This book has theoretical and practical implications. Theoretically, it contributes to the established literature by considering accountability as a complex mechanism that has multifaceted effects on bureaucratic behaviors. Different from the established literature, which generally considers accountability as an abstract concept, this book disaggregates accountability and treats it as a mechanism with different components. The respective impact of the four elements of accountability and their configuration on shirking and blame avoidance are explored to gain a better understanding of the internal mechanism of accountability. This book sheds light on an often neglected issue in accountability studies; that is, a "bad" configuration of accountability may produce unintended negative consequences. For example, sanction-based accountability may induce defensive emotions and behaviors among bureaucrats.

Second, the dynamic interaction between accountability structure and bureaucratic agency is explored. How bureaucrats respond to accountability intensity and diverse expectations imposed by multiple accountability are worth studying to reveal their personal preferences, motivations, and value judgments. While the existing literature focuses on accountability itself, this book explores the variation in bureaucrats' responses to accountability. Bureaucrats may respond to accountability with compliance or diverse defensive strategies, depending on the configuration of accountability and the nature of the tasks they face. Furthermore, the configuration of accountability may also be modified in response to bureaucrats' reactions.

Third, this book makes methodological contributions. The existing empirical research on accountability is fragmented and scarce. A large volume of the established literature on accountability is conceptual, focusing on the connotations and types of the term itself (Brandsma & Schillemans, 2012). By adopting the accountability cube, this book develops more specific indicators for the empirical measurement of accountability as a mechanism. Furthermore, this book sheds light on the empirical relationship between accountability and performance. The relationship between accountability and performance is still an institutionalized myth that requires attention (Dubnick, 2005; Meyer & Rowan, 1977). This book contributes to a better understanding of the impacts of accountability on bureaucratic shirking, blame avoidance, and working efforts.

This book has practical implications, as well. Designing effective accountability systems to generate a responsible government and bureaucracy is essential to every country. It sheds light on the complexity of the accountability mechanism and the importance of the interaction between institutions and individuals in a bureaucracy. It suggests that the purpose and design of accountability should foster a sense of responsibility for citizens and promote learning from others and mistakes among bureaucrats rather than centering on allocating blame. Thus, the accountability mechanism should focus more on engaging civil servants in participation, dialogue, and learning in different phases of the accountability process.

Roadmap

The rest of The *Accountability Paradox in the Chinese Bureaucracy* is divided into seven chapters described below.

Chapter 2: *The Control of Bureaucracy.* This chapter introduces different perspectives on the rationality of bureaucracy. It summarizes varying forms of external and internal controls. Additionally, this chapter analyzes the different classifications of the Chinese bureaucracy and explores its distinct characteristics.

Chapter 3: *Accountability Transformation in the Chinese Bureaucracy.* This chapter delves into the institutional background of accountability transformation. It conducts a comprehensive analysis of the transformation of accountability since Xi took power in 2012. It suggests that the Chinese accountability system has been substantially intensified and institutionalized. Furthermore, political accountability takes precedence over bureaucratic accountability in terms of status and authority.

Chapter 4: *Accountability Intensity and Bureaucratic Shirking.* This chapter explores the impact of accountability intensity on bureaucratic shirking. It classified bureaucratic shirking into three types, namely, evade responsibility, shift responsibility, and reframe responsibility. Then, it explores how monitoring intensity and punishment-based consequence exert impacts on the three forms of shirking. It indicates that intensive monitoring and punishment may inhibit bureaucrats from blatantly evading responsibility. However, they may induce bureaucrats to adopt some subtle coping strategies to deal with work pressure and risks.

Chapter 5: *The Accountability Cube and Blame Avoidance.* This chapter draws on a conceptual model of "accountability cube" to capture the key elements and essence of accountability (Brandsma & Schillemans, 2013; Han, 2020). Four indicators are generated from the cube: monitoring intensity, discussion quality, and reward- or punishment-based consequences. This chapter first explores the respective impact of the four elements of accountability on blame avoidance. Besides, four types of accountability were generated by cluster analysis, and the impact of different configurations of accountability on blame avoidance was examined.

Chapter 6: *Accountability Conflicts and Bureaucrats' Working Effort.* This Chapter investigates bureaucrats' responses to the conflict between hierarchical accountability and horizontal accountability by using a between-subjects experimental design. The findings suggest that bureaucrats' moral judgment and personal preferences do matter when they are confronted with divergent expectations from superiors and citizens. Intensified hierarchical accountability does not necessarily lead to greater compliance and may cause bad outcomes.

Chapter 7: *Fault-Tolerance Mechanism: A Compromise between Outcome-Based Accountability and Process-Based Accountability.* This chapter explores how the fault-tolerance mechanism implemented by the Chinese government functions as a strategy to mitigate the adverse effects of heightened sanction-based accountability and to reconcile the conflict between process-based and outcome-based accountability. Analyzing 66 cases that received the fault-tolerance mechanism, this chapter suggests that the fault-tolerance mechanism is a compromising instrument that attempts to strike a balance between bureaucratic discretion and political control by alleviating the conflict between procedural compliance and managerial performance.

Chapter 8: *Promoting Good Accountability: What Should Be Done.* This chapter engages in a discussion of the relationship between accountability constraints and bureaucratic responses. It explores the contested relationship of accountability with responsibility, trust, and organizational learning. Next, it analyzes the advantages of felt accountability and dialogue accountability and conditions for a good accountability system.

References

Almalki, S. (2016). Integrating quantitative and qualitative data in mixed methods research—Challenges and benefits. *Journal of Education and Learning*, 5(3), 288–296.

Ashforth, B. E., & Lee, R. T. (1990). Defensive behavior in organizations: A preliminary model. *Human Relations, 43*(7), 621–648.

Baldwin, R. (2004). The new punitive regulation. *The Modern Law Review, 67*(3), 351–383.

Behn, R. D. (2001). *Rethinking democratic accountability*. Brookings Institution Press.

Bendor, J. (1988). Formal models of bureaucracy. *British Journal of Political Science, 18*(3), 353–395.

Bendor, J., Glazer, A., & Hammond, T. (2001). Theories of delegation. *Annual Review of Political Science, 4*(1), 235–269.

Bennett, N., & Naumann, S. E. (2005). Understanding and preventing shirking, job neglect, social loafing, and free riding. In Kidwell, R. E., & Martin, C. L. (Eds.), *Managing Organizational Deviance* (pp. 113–126). Sage Publications.

Boussalis, C., Feldman, Y., & Smith, H. E. (2018). Experimental analysis of the effect of standards on compliance and performance. *Regulation & Governance, 12*(2), 277–298.

Bovens, M. (2007). Analysing and assessing accountability: A conceptual framework. *European Law Journal, 13*(4), 447–468.

Bovens, M. (2010). Two concepts of accountability: Accountability as a virtue and as a mechanism. *West European Politics, 33*(5), 946–967.

Bovens, M., Schillemans, T., & Hart, P. 'T. (2008). Does public accountability work? An assessment tool. *Public Administration, 86*(1), 225–242.

Brandsma, G. J., & Schillemans, T. (2013). The accountability cube: Measuring accountability. *Journal of Public Administration Research and Theory, 23*(4), 953–975.

Brehm, J. O., & Gates, S. (1999). *Working, shirking, and sabotage: Bureaucratic response to a democratic public*. University of Michigan Press.

Brinkerhoff, D. W. (2001). Taking account of accountability: A conceptual overview and strategic options. *Draft Report, US Agency for International Development, Center for Democracy and Governance, Implementing Policy Change Project, Phase, 2.*

Busuioc, E. M., & Lodge, M. (2016). The reputational basis of public accountability. *Governance, 29*(2), 247–263.

CCTV. (2018, November 16). *A deputy director reprimanded for not answering phone call from the inspection team while bathing in the evening*. Viewed July 8, 2024. https://baijiahao.baidu.com/s?id=1617258831995708694&wfr=spider&for=pc

Chinese Government Website. (2014, October 9). *Li Keqiang: Shirking is another form of corruption*. Viewed July 8, 2024. https://www.gov.cn/xinwen/2014-10/09/content_2761524.htm

Christensen, T., & Lægreid, P. (2015). Performance and accountability—A theoretical discussion and an empirical assessment. *Public Organization Review, 15*(2), 207–225.

Cooper, T. L. (2012). *The responsible administrator: An approach to ethics for the administrative role*. Wiley.

Cooper, T. (2019). *Handbook of administrative ethics*. Routledge.

Courty, P., & Marschke, G. (2007). Making government accountable: Lessons from a federal job training program. *Public Administration Review, 67*(5), 904–916.

Dahling, J. J., Chau, S. L., Mayer, D. M., & Gregory, J. B. (2012). Breaking rules for the right reasons? An investigation of pro-social rule breaking. *Journal of Organizational Behavior, 33*(1), 21–42.

Dahlström, C., & Lapuente, V. (2022). Comparative Bureaucratic Politics. *Annual Review of Political Science, 25*(1), 43–63.

De Bruijn, H. (2002). Performance measurement in the public sector: Strategies to cope with the risks of performance measurement. *International Journal of Public Sector Management, 15*(7), 578–594.

Downs, Anthony. (1967). *Inside Bureaucracy*. New York: Harper-Collins.

Dubnick, M. J. (2003). Accountability and ethics: Reconsidering the relationships. *International Journal of Organization Theory & Behavior, 6*(3), 405–441.

Dubnick, M. (2005). Accountability and the promise of performance: In search of the mechanisms. *Public Performance & Management Review, 28*(3), 376–417.

Dubnick, M. J., & Yang, K. (2015). The pursuit of accountability: Promises, problems, and prospects. In Menzel, D. C., & White, J. D. (Eds.), *The state of public administration* (pp. 171–186). Routledge.

Dunn, D. D., & Legge, J. S., Jr. (2001). US local government managers and the complexity of responsibility and accountability in democratic governance. *Journal of Public Administration Research and Theory, 11*(1), 73–88.

Fan, Y. (2024). Accountability in public organization: A systematic literature review and future research agenda. *Public Organization Review*, 1–16.

Finer, H. (1941). Administrative responsibility in democratic government. *Public Administration Review, 1*(4), 335–350.

Frederickson, H. G. (1996). Comparing the reinventing government movement with the new public administration. *Public Administration Review, 56*(3), 263–270.

Friedlich, C. J. (1940). Public policy and the nature of administrative responsibility. *Public Policy, 1*, 1–20.

Gailmard, S. (2002). Expertise, subversion, and bureaucratic discretion. *Journal of Law, Economics, and Organization, 18*(2), 536–555.

Gailmard, S., & Patty, J. W. (2012). Formal models of bureaucracy. *Annual Review of Political Science, 15*(1), 353–377.

Gong, T., & Tu, W. (2022). Fighting corruption in China: Trajectory, dynamics, and impact. *China Review, 22*(2), 1–19.

Goodin, R., Bovens, M., & Schillemans, T. (2014). Public accountability. In M. A. P. Bovens, R. E. Goodin, & T. Schillemans (Eds.), *The Oxford handbook public accountability* (pp.1–22). Oxford Handbooks.

Halachmi, A. (2014). *Accountability overloads*. In M. A. P. Bovens, R. E. Goodin, & T. Schillemans (Eds.), *The Oxford handbook public accountability* (pp. 560–573). Oxford Handbooks.

Han, Y. (2020). The impact of accountability deficit on agency performance: Performance-accountability regime. *Public Management Review, 22*(6), 927–948.

Han, Y., & Perry, J. L. (2020). Employee accountability: Development of a multidimensional scale. *International Public Management Journal, 23*(2), 224–251.

Harmon, M. M. (1995). *Responsibility as paradox: A critique of rational discourse on government*. Thousand Oaks, CA: Sage.

Hayes, K., & Wood, L. L. (1995). Utility maximizing bureaucrats: The bureaucrat's point of view. *Public Choice, 82*(1–2), 69–83.

Hood, C. (2002). The risk game and the blame game. *Government and Opposition, 37*(1), 15–37.

Hood, C. (2014). Accountability and blame–avoidance. In M. A. P. Bovens, R. E. Goodin, & T. Schillemans (Eds.), *The Oxford handbook public accountability* (pp. 603–616). Oxford Handbooks.

Hood, C., Jennings, W., & Copeland, P. (2016). Blame avoidance in comparative perspective: Reactivity, staged retreat and efficacy. *Public Administration, 94*(2), 542–562.

Howlett, M. (2014). Why are policy innovations rare and so often negative? Blame avoidance and problem denial in climate change policy-making. *Global Environmental Change, 29*, 395–403.

Hu, C. (2017). Accountability of public servants under dominant political settlements of China: Effects, challenges, and issues. *International Journal of Public Administration, 40*(3), 240–255.

Jackson, M. (2009). Responsibility versus accountability in the Friedrich-Finer debate. *Journal of Management History, 15*(1), 66–77.

Ji, S. (2022). Role of managerial and political accountability in improving performance of local governments. *Public Performance & Management Review, 45*(3), 499–531.

Jos, P. H. (1988). Moral autonomy & the modern organization. *Polity, 21*(2), 321–343.

Jos, P. H., & Tompkins, M. E. (2004). The accountability paradox in an age of reinvention: The perennial problem of preserving character and judgment. *Administration & Society, 36*(3), 255–281.

Jos, P. H., & Tompkins, M. E. (2009). Keeping it public: Defending public service values in a customer service age. *Public Administration Review, 69*(6), 1077–1086.

Kenney, C. D. (2003). Horizontal accountability: Concepts and conflicts. In Mainwaring, S., & Welna, C. (Eds.), *Democratic Accountability in Latin America* (pp. 55–76). OUP Oxford.

Klingner, D. E., Nalbandian, J., & Romzek, B. S. (2002). Politics, administration, and markets: Conflicting expectations and accountability. *The American Review of Public Administration, 32*(2), 117–144.

Koppell, J. G. (2005). Pathologies of accountability: ICANN and the challenge of "Multiple Accountabilities Disorder." *Public Administration Review, 65*(1), 94–108.

Kuipers, S., & t Hart, P. (2014). Accounting for crises. In M. A. P. Bovens, R. E. Goodin, & T. Schillemans (Eds.), *The Oxford handbook public accountability.* Oxford Handbooks.

Lee, S. (2022). When tensions become opportunities: Managing accountability demands in collaborative governance. *Journal of Public Administration Research and Theory, 32*(4), 641–655.

Legal Daily. (2017, July 7). *The inner-Party regulations provide an institutional guarantee for strengthening the Party discipline.* Viewed July 23, 2020. https://www.chinacourt.org/article/detail/2017/07/id/2907982.shtml

Leland, S., Mohr, Z., & Piatak, J. (2021). Accountability in government contracting arrangements: Experimental analysis of blame attribution across levels of government. *The American Review of Public Administration, 51*(4), 251–262.

Lipsky, M. (2010). *Street-level bureaucracy: Dilemmas of the individual in public service.* Russell sage foundation.

Li, J., Ni, X., & Wang, R. (2021). Blame avoidance in China's cadre responsibility system. *The China Quarterly, 247*, 681–702.

Li, L. (2019). Politics of anticorruption in China: Paradigm change of the Party's Disciplinary Regime 2012–2017. *Journal of Contemporary China, 28*(115), 47–63.

Li, Y., Koppenjan, J., & Wang, H. (2024). Individual, organizational, and institutional accountability: A systematic literature review in public administration. *Public Management Review*, 1–31.

Manion, M. (2016). Taking China's anticorruption campaign seriously. *Economic and Political Studies, 4*(1), 3–18.

Mattei, P. (2007). Managerial and political accountability: The widening gap in the organization of welfare. *International Review of Administrative Sciences, 73*(3), 365–387.

Maynard-Moody, S., & Musheno, M. (2000). State agent or citizen agent: Two narratives of discretion. *Journal of Public Administration Research and Theory, 10*(2), 329–358.

McCubbins, M. D., & Schwartz, T. (1984). Congressional oversight overlooked: Police patrols versus fire alarms. *American Journal of Political Science*, 28(1), 165–179.

Meier, K. J. (2009). The scientific study of bureaucracy: An overview. In G. A. Krause & K. J. Meier (Eds.), *Politics, policy, and organizations: Frontiers in the scientific study of bureaucracy* (pp. 1–19). University of Michigan Press.

Meier, K. J., & O'Toole, L. J. (2006). Political control versus bureaucratic values: Reframing the debate. *Public Administration Review, 66*(2), 177–192.

Moe, T. M. (2006). Political control and the power of the agent. *Journal of Law, Economics, and Organization, 22*(1), 1–29.

Moe, T. M. (2012). Delegation, control, and the study of public bureaucracy. *The Forum, 10*(2), 1–45.

Morrison, E. W. (2006). Doing the Job Well: An Investigation of Pro-Social Rule Breaking. *Journal of Management, 32*(1), 5–28.

Nee, V., Opper, S., & Wong, S. (2007). Developmental state and corporate governance in China. *Management and Organization Review, 3*(1), 19–53.

Newman, J. (2004). Constructing Accountability: Network Governance and Managerial Agency. *Public Policy and Administration, 19*(4), 17–33.

O'Loughlin, M. G. (1990). What is bureaucratic accountability and how can we measure it? *Administration & Society, 22*(3), 275–302.

Olsen, J. P. (2006). Maybe it is time to rediscover bureaucracy. *Journal of Public Administration Research and Theory, 16*(1), 1–24.

Ossege, C. (2012). Accountability—Are we better off without it?: An empirical study on the effects of accountability on public managers' work behaviour. *Public Management Review, 14*(5), 585–607.

Page, S. (2006). The Web of Managerial Accountability: The Impact of Reinventing Government. *Administration & Society, 38*(2), 166–197.

Panda, B., & Leepsa, N. M. (2017). Agency theory: Review of theory and evidence on problems and perspectives. *Indian Journal of Corporate Governance, 10*(1), 74–95.

Pengpai News. (2018, April 27). *The presence of snacks and novels in the office has been public reprimanded*. Viewed July 8, 2024. https://www.thepaper.cn/newsDetail_forward_2100958.

Pérez Durán, I. (2016). Accountability from the perspective of the forum: Citizens' attitudes towards accountability in Europe. *West European Politics, 39*(4), 835–858.

Plant, J. F. (2011). Carl J. Friedrich on Responsibility and Authority. *Public Administration Review, 71*(3), 471–482.

Rabbi, M. F., & Sabharwal, M. (2024). Understanding accountability overload: Concept and consequences in public sector organizations. *International Journal of Public Administration*, 1–19.

Rajala, T. (2020). Blame avoidance strategies in governmental performance measurement. *Financial Accountability & Management, 36*(3), 278–299.

Ran, R., & Jian, Y. (2021). When transparency meets accountability. *China Review, 21*(1), 7–36.

Reddick, C. G., Demir, T., & Perlman, B. (2020). Horizontal, vertical, and hybrid: An empirical look at the forms of accountability. *Administration & Society, 52*(9), 1410–1438.

Roberts, N. C. (2002). Keeping public officials accountable through dialogue: Resolving the accountability paradox. *Public Administration Review, 62*(6), 658–669.

Romzek, B. S., & Dubnick, M. J. (1987). Accountability in the public sector: Lessons from the challenger tragedy. *Public Administration Review, 47*(3), 227–238.

Rose-Ackerman, S. (1986). Reforming public bureaucracy through economic incentives? *The Journal of Law, Economics, and Organization, 2*(1), 131–161.

Sabbe, M., Moyson, S., & Schiffino, N. (2021). Citizen-agency versus state-agency at the frontline in prisons and probation services: A systematic literature review. *Social Policy & Administration, 55*(1), 206–225.

Sager, F., & Rosser, C. (2009). Weber, Wilson, and Hegel: Theories of modern bureaucracy. *Public Administration Review, 69*(6), 1136–1147.

Schillemans, T. (2013). *The public accountability review. A meta-analysis of public accountability research in six academic disciplines* (working paper).

Schillemans, T., & Aleksovska, M. (2024). Making nonpunitive accountability matter: Exploring behavioral effects of nonpunitive accountability in a conjoint experiment. *Public Administration*, padm.13024.

Schillemans, T., Van Twist, M., & Vanhommerig, I. (2013). Innovations in accountability: Learning through interactive, dynamic, and citizen-initiated forms of accountability. *Public Performance & Management Review, 36*(3), 407–435.

Scott, J. C. (1985). *Weapons of the weak: Everyday forms of peasant resistance*. Yale University P.

Sørensen, E. (2002). Democratic theory and network governance. *Administrative Theory & Praxis, 24*(4), 693–720.

Taylor, F. W. (1911). *The principles of scientific management*. Noton & Company.

Tetlock, P. E. (1992). The impact of accountability on judgment and choice: Toward a social contingency model. In *Advances in experimental social psychology*, 25: 331–376.

The China Comment. (2018, August 28). Township cadres: More people come to supervise us than to help us with our work. Viewed July 23, 2020. http://m.people.cn/n4/2018/0828/c203-11514661.html

Tu, W. (2024a). Unpacking the accountability cube and its relationship with blame avoidance. *Public Management Review, 26*(3), 701–723.

Tu, W. (2024b). The interactive effect of extrinsic controls and public service motivation on blame avoidance. *Public Personnel Management*, 00910260241283549.

Tu, W., & Gong, T. (2022a). Accountability intensity and bureaucrats' response to conflicting expectations: A survey experiment in China. *Public Management Review, 24*(11), 1779–1801.

Tu, W., & Gong, T. (2022b). Bureaucratic shirking in China: Is sanction-based accountability a cure? *The China Quarterly, 249*, 259–274.

Tummers, L., & Bekkers, V. (2014). Policy implementation, street-level bureaucracy, and the importance of discretion. *Public Management Review, 16*(4), 527–547.

Waldo, D. (1952). Development of theory of democratic administration. *American Political Science Review, 46*(1), 81–103.

Wang, E. H. (2022). Frightened mandarins: The adverse effects of fighting corruption on local bureaucracy. *Comparative Political Studies, 55*(11), 1807–1843.

Wang, P., & Yan, X. (2020). Bureaucratic slack in China: The anti-corruption campaign and the decline of patronage networks in developing local economies. *The China Quarterly, 243*, 611–634.

Weber, M. (1978). *Economy and society: An outline of interpretive sociology, 1.* University of California press.

Willems, T., & Van Dooren, W. (2011). Lost in diffusion? How collaborative arrangements lead to an accountability paradox. *International Review of Administrative Sciences, 77*(3), 505–530.

Wood, B. D., & Waterman, R. W. (1991). The dynamics of political control of the bureaucracy. *American Political Science Review, 85*(3), 801–828.

Yang, K. (2012). Further understanding accountability in public organizations: Actionable knowledge and the structure–agency duality. *Administration & Society, 44*(3), 255–284.

Ye, Z., Ma, B., & Li, Y. (2023). Wrestling with multiple accountabilities in times of crisis: Findings from the experiences of Chinese local governments in responding to COVID -19. *Review of Policy Research*, ropr.12573.

CHAPTER 2

The Control of Bureaucracy

One paramount concern in the study of administration is the control of bureaucrats. Questions such as "are bureaucrats accountable," "are bureaucrats responsive," and "who, or what controls their behavioral choices" remain salient and fundamental. Some scholars argue that bureaucrats should be subjected to top-down control to manage their discretion, while others believe that internal motivation is crucial, advocating for the granting of discretion to help them adapt policies to local conditions. This chapter begins by exploring various viewpoints on the rationality of the bureaucracy and the motivation hypothesis of bureaucrats, which results in differing preferences for bureaucratic control approaches. It summarizes different types of external and internal controls. Additionally, the chapter outlines three conceptualizations of the Chinese bureaucracy and highlights its unique traits. Unlike in Western countries, the separation between politics and administration in China is not based on elections. A major challenge facing both scholars lies in differentiating the roles of the party and the government, as well as clarifying their respective functions.

W. Tu, *The Accountability Paradox in the Chinese Bureaucracy*,
https://doi.org/10.1007/978-981-96-6392-7_2

Bureaucracy as Instrumental Rationality vs. Value Rationality

The sociologist and pivotal scholar of bureaucracies Weber (1978, pp. 24–25) made a distinction between instrumental rationality and value rationality. Instrumental rationality focuses on selecting the most effective means to achieve specific ends. In contrast, value-rational action is rooted in a commitment to fundamental values and entails a conscious belief in the specific significance that those values hold in particular circumstances (Monteiro & Adler, 2022). Specifically, instrumental rationality is about the means and efficiency, while value rationality is about the ends and moral justification. No matter regarded as the administrative branch of government or as a form of organization, bureaucracy in traditional public administration was characterized by instrumental rationality.

As the administrative branch of government, the bureaucracy is responsible for the efficient implementation of policies promulgated by politicians. "Wilson's advocacy of the separation of politics (policy formulation) from administration (implementation) paralleled Weber's distinction between ends and means implied by the legal/technical mode of rationality embodied in the bureaucratic form of social organization" (Harmon, 1995, p. 165). Goodnow (2017) draws a clear line between politics and administration where the democratically elected politicians represent "the will of the state," while the professional government is in charge of neutrally "executing the will of the state" (17). Specifically, legislative representatives and chief executives voted by citizens are responsible for promulgating public policies; then the administrative body figures out the most effective methods to strictly execute the policies. Political actors hold bureaucrats accountable for policy implementation and citizens hold politicians accountable for policy-making (West, 2004). The underlying logic is that by separating administration from politics and by utilizing scientific management to optimize work processes, the bureaucracy can be a rational tool for implementing the commands and directives of the state, and its performance is based on the instrumental efficiency in achieving predetermined goals (Olsen, 2006). As they are not democratically elected, bureaucrats are not legitimated to impose their values, preferences, and judgments in the implementation of policies.

As a form of organization, bureaucracy is considered an ideal type of model—the most instrumentally rational and the most efficient in achieving the goals of the organization (Monteiro & Adler, 2022).

The scientific management school prescribes a rigid and top-down command chain of authority from higher to lower levels, and an individual in the chain of command is fitted as a "robot" or a "cog in the machine," displaying absolute obedience without individual preferences and thoughts (Gulick, 1937; Taylor, 1919). Taylor (1911), known as the father of scientific management, introduced principles for effective management. He emphasized that every employee should be carefully selected, trained, and developed through scientific methods. Taylor emphasizes the enforced standardization of implementation and working conditions and the compliance of employers with these rules. He also claims that all workers are motivated by material incentives and should be imposed by external control. Scholars of the classical school of management emphasize strict principles and supervision over subordinates and their absolute compliance.

Max Weber's (1978) elaboration of "ideal-type" bureaucracy exerts a significant impact on public sector management. According to Weber, a rational bureaucracy in its fundamental form is characterized by (a) clear chains of command and hierarchy; (b) rules and regulations govern every decision and action; (c) specialization or a clear division of labor; (d) managed through written and traceable directives; (e) impersonality; (f) professional management with merit-based recruitment and promotion. The principle of impersonality stipulates that decisions and actions should be based on formal rules and regulations rather than the personal interests, emotions, or preferences of bureaucrats (Dahlström & Lapuente, 2022). As impersonal agents guided by political impartiality, Weber suggests that bureaucrats should strictly implement policies or orders from politicians or supervisors without any hesitation or reservation.

However, a burgeoning number of researchers within the field of public administration emphasize the value rationality of bureaucracy and the ethical foundation of public administration (Frederickson, 1996; Waldo, 1952). Simon (2013) asserts that administration is decision-making, indicating implementation is inherently political. Citizens increasingly demand a more effective and efficient government that provides flexible and personalized services. Emerged in the late twentieth century as a response to the limitations of traditional public administration, the NPA suggests that bureaucrats should and are able to speak on behalf of the "people" and promote social justice. The NPA shows more interest in the active role than the passive non-actor role that public administrators play in democracy (Bourgon, 2007; Denhardt &

Denhardt, 2015; Dunleavy & Hood, 1994). Public administrators are no longer regarded as neutral in processes of democratic government; instead, they are expected to incorporate public interests and social justice into their decision-making and make the broad common good their ultimate objective (Fox & Miller, 1994; Kelly, 1998; Meier, 2023). Value rationality highlights the importance of motivations that extend beyond mere self-interest, focusing instead on the greater good and commitment to public service.

Michael Lipsky's influential book, *Street Level Bureaucracy: Dilemmas of the Individual in Public Service* (2010), encouraged scholars to focus on the role of front-line bureaucrats in shaping policies. Street-level bureaucrats are "public service workers who interact directly with citizens in the course of their jobs, and who have substantial discretion in the execution of their work" such as police officers, firefighters, social workers, teachers, and health workers. Lipsky argues that public policies are not merely implemented as intended from the top down; instead, they are shaped and modified at the street level. The interpretations and decisions made by street-level bureaucrats can significantly alter the intentions and outcomes of policies. The paradigm of NPM advocates decentralization that allows local managers and agencies who are more familiar with the specific situations to make decisions to be more closely aligned with the specific needs and circumstances of their communities (Christensen & Lægreid, 2001). A controversial concept "pro-social rule breaking" is further proposed to depict the act of violating established rules or norms in a way that benefits citizens or serves a greater social good (Dahling et al., 2012; Morrison, 2006). Bureaucrats, especially the front-line ones, are considered to play a significant role in bridging the gap between top-down policies and local circumstances or citizens' demands. This stream of literature graphically highlights the importance of value rationality of bureaucracy and bureaucrats' moral exercise of their discretion.

Motivation Hypothesis of Bureaucrats

The varying viewpoints on control stem from different hypotheses about the motivations of bureaucrats. The hypothesis of rational man posits that individuals make decisions based on rational calculations to maximize their utility. The hypothesis of rational man considers bureaucrats as opportunistic actors and denounces them as passive, lazy, and calculative (Cook & Wood, 1989). Bureaucrats primarily act out of self-interest and will either work or shirk depending on which generates the highest personal utility (Huber, 2002). Therefore, discretion should be reduced to prevent bureaucrats from using to pursue their own, private goals.

Value rationality tends to see bureaucrats as intrinsically motivated to serve the public. Scholars believe that public institutions may help nurture and preserve prosocial and altruistic values (Pierre & Peters, 2017), and many have noted the presence of public service motivation (PSM) in the public sector. It is suggested, for example, that public sector managers exhibit a greater interest in serving the society than do private managers (Crewson, 1997). The concept of PSM is notably articulated by Perry and Wise (1990) in their seminal article, *The Motivational Bases of Public Service*. They define PSM as "an individual's predisposition to respond to motives grounded primarily or uniquely in public institutions and organizations" (Perry & Wise, 1990, p. 368).

PSM is regarded as a special type of intrinsic motivation among public employees who are attracted to public service because of their intrinsic interests and altruistic predisposition to serve the public interest (Houston, 2006; Jacobson, 2011). It is characterized as altruistic or prosocial intentions to serve the interests of a community of people, a state, or humankind (Bright, 2008; Schott et al., 2019). Perry (1996) proposes six dimensions of PSM: attraction to public policy-making, commitment to the public interest/civic duty, social justice, civic duty, compassion, and self-sacrifice. A bulk of empirical evidence supports the assertion that these prosocial values have a strong positive effect on civil servants' job performance (Bellé, 2013; Bright, 2008), organizational commitment (Awan et al., 2020), citizenship behavior (Pandey et al., 2008), and job satisfaction (Tu et al., 2024). Laboratory experiments conducted by Banuri and Keefer (2013) in Indonesia find that if civil servants have higher prosocial preferences, they tend to put more effort into prosocial tasks.

Control and Discretion

Different assumptions about the rationality of bureaucracy present differing perspectives on control and discretion. Emphasizing instrumental rationality and rational actor assumption tends to support stronger top-down control over the bureaucracy, whereas the perspective of value rationality and PSM views discretion as an essential aspect of the operation of the bureaucracy, encouraging bureaucrats to use their judgment to enhance the public goods of policy programs.

Evans (2010) suggests that discretion refers to the degree of freedom employees can exercise in a particular context. Lipsky (2010) defines discretion as the autonomy street-level bureaucrats possess in deciding the type, amount, and quality of sanctions and rewards during the implementation of policies. Tummers and Bekkers (2014) distinguish the top-down and bottom-up perspectives of discretion. From a top-down perspective, discretion is often not welcomed. Discretion is regarded as a potential threat, as bureaucrats might utilize it to chase their personal goals rather than the principal's objectives (Epstein & O'halloran, 1994). This can adversely affect the implementation of policy programs, undermining the effectiveness and democratic legitimacy (La Palombara, 2006). In this regard, control mechanisms should be equipped to ensure the compliance of bureaucrats and curb agency drifting (Wood & Waterman, 1991; Adler & Borys, 1996).

From a bottom-up perspective, discretion is viewed differently; it is considered essential for applying general rules, regulations, and norms to specific situations, thereby enhancing the effectiveness of policy programs and fostering democratic support (Tummers & Bekkers, 2014). Additionally, bureaucrats, especially the street-level ones, often face daunting tasks that involve divergent expectations from multiple stakeholders and regulations (Hupe & Buffat, 2014; Tu et al., 2024) and the constraints of time, funding, and resources (Tummers & Bekkers, 2014). It is crucial for them to prioritize which expectations and rules based on their moral deliberation and professionalism in specific circumstances (Maynard-Moody & Musheno, 2000; Tu & Gong, 2022). From a bottom-up perspective, discretion can enhance the value and significance of a policy for citizens, as it allows policy programs to be tailored to the particular circumstances (Hupe, 2019; Tummers et al., 2012).

Difficulties in Controlling Bureaucrats

Both instrumental rationality and value rationality represent scholars' normative views on how bureaucracy should function and the extent and types of control that should be imposed on bureaucrats. However, when it comes to the actual control of bureaucrats, various challenges arise. According to the principal-agent theory, the difficulty in controlling bureaucrats primarily stems from preference heterogeneity between principals and agents (politicians and bureaucrats, or superior bureaucrats and subordinate bureaucrats) and the inherent discretion embedded in delegation (Calvert et al., 1989; Tamm & Snidal, 2014). The unquestioning obedience to orders advocated by the scientific management school is impossible because bureaucrats possess preferences, emotions, and interests that are not always consistent with those of their superiors. In addition, coercive or scientific management cannot force subordinates to obey on account of their relative discretionary power and autonomy from organizational authority (Lipsky, 2010, pp. 13–18).

Preference heterogeneity is typical between principals and agents, indicating that agents often have diverging preferences from their principals. A bureaucracy's failure to accomplish specific formal objectives usually arises from these divergent preferences. No one can function as an impartial machine devoid of emotions and values. In Inside Bureaucracy (1967), Downs identifies five types of bureaucrats based on their differing preferences: climbers, conservers, zealots, advocates, and statesmen. The first two types are entirely self-serving: climbers seek to enhance their own power, income, and prestige, while conservers aim to preserve their existing power and status. The last three types represent bureaucrats with mixed motivations, combining self-interest with "altruistic loyalty to larger values." Zealots are committed to specific policies or concepts, advocates focus on broader policies or organizations, and statesmen prioritize the welfare of society as a whole. Downs' typology illustrates that bureaucrats have their own preferences and are often not committed to the goals of their supervisors or politicians.

Brehm and Gates (1997) refute the absolute control of supervisors over bureaucrats and argue that choices about the allocation of effort depend in part on subordinates' own preferences for policies. If subordinates oppose a policy, they may engage in dissent-shirking by doing only the bare minimum or trying to sabotage it. Nevertheless, they are likely to put in more effort for a policy they support, even without oversight. By studying street-level bureaucrats, Lipsky (2010) also notes that subordinates in organizations are often in conflict with their superiors in perspectives and preferences and thus, in some respects, cannot be thought to adhere to principals' goals consistently. As Rose-Ackerman (1978, p. 6) states, "agents generally have some freedom to put their individual interests ahead of their principal's and will do so if perceived benefits outweigh possible costs."

In addition to preference heterogeneity, bureaucrats have significant discretionary power that allows them to choose behaviors that may not align with their superiors' preferences. The discretion that comes with delegation provides agents with the latitude to exercise authority and make decisions independently of their principals (Hawkins & Jacoby, 2006). Factors such as the nature of bureaucrats' jobs, their work environment, and the challenges of monitoring contribute to the level of discretion they have in relation to their supervisors' authority.

First, the complex working environments and direct interactions with citizens provide bureaucrats with the discretion to shape the nature, quantity, and quality of services. Civil servants often face intricate situations involving diverse citizen demands and conflicting stakeholder expectations, making general policy guidelines insufficient for providing precise instructions (Lipsky, 2010). While political actors typically establish broad goals or principles for a policy, it is bureaucrats who develop specific strategies and detailed implementation processes (Feldman & Khademian, 2002; Kaufman, 2001). Consequently, the success of policy implementation largely hinges on administrators' professional expertise and their understanding of the actual circumstances.

Bureaucrats also possess the ability to exercise judgment and considerable latitude in choosing among alternatives. In his influential work Administrative Behavior, Simon (2013) emphasizes that "decision-making is the heart of administration, and the vocabulary of administrative theory must stem from the logic and psychology of human choice" (p. xi). This challenges the notion of absolute supervisory control and highlights the significant discretion that bureaucrats have in policy implementation. Similarly, Lipsky (2010) supports a bottom-up perspective in public administration, arguing that front-line workers play a crucial role in shaping public policy outcomes, which is equal in importance to the contributions of policymakers at higher levels.

Second, the high costs and other challenges in controlling bureaucrats further enhance their discretion and autonomy. Numerous studies demonstrate that implementing a monitoring system or incentive scheme that effectively encourages everyone to work and prevents shirking is costly (Brehm & Gates, 1997; Holmström, 1979). Due to these high costs, supervisors often overlook minor misconduct by subordinates. Additionally, information asymmetry gives subordinates an advantage over their supervisors, complicating oversight even when documentation appears complete (Briscoe, 2007). For instance, when reporting to supervisors, subordinates might exploit their professional knowledge and understanding of real situations to misrepresent, obscure, or withhold information (Brehm & Gates, 1997). Furthermore, the interdependence among bureaucrats and the presence of informal networks within organizations enable them to cover up and protect one another, exacerbating the difficulty of identifying who is responsible for specific actions. This issue is intensified in governmental systems with multiple hierarchical levels, such as in China, where low-level officials may collude to withhold or fabricate information required by higher authorities.

In conclusion, the differences in preferences between policymakers and policy implementers, as well as between supervisors and subordinates, combined with the discretion inherent in power delegation, lead to a phenomenon known as "leakage of authority." Two key concepts highlight the challenges in ensuring bureaucratic compliance: adverse selection (hidden information) and moral hazard (hidden actions). The two types of asymmetric information significantly impact principal-agent relationships. Adverse selection occurs when principals are unable to ascertain their agents' true preferences and capabilities (Sobol, 2016). Moreover, principals cannot observe their subordinates' actions, allowing the latter to conceal information and acts without the former's knowledge, a scenario referred to as "moral hazard" (Hölmstrom, 1979; Nielson & Tierney, 2003). This dynamic creates a situation where "the principal does not know the precise preferences and skills of the agent, and therefore cannot determine how effective the agent will be, how diligently they will work, or whether they align with the principal's objectives" (Thompson, 2007, p. 6). In that case, agents may "slack" by engaging in independent actions that contradict their principals' intentions.

Control and Coping Strategies

Bureaucrats, especially those at the street level, who have divergent preferences and discretionary power, tend to use coping strategies to relieve pressure and undermine control mechanisms (Lotta et al., 2024; Vedung, 2015). Lazarus (1984, p. 141) define coping broadly as "constantly changing cognitive and behavioral efforts to manage specific external and/or internal demands that are appraised as taxing or exceeding the resources of the person." Lipsky (2010) employs the concept of "coping" to describe the strategic measures or "management of work stresses" used by street-level bureaucrats—such as police officers, social workers, teachers, and physicians—when they confront various demands and workloads. He considers the coping mechanisms adopted by street-level bureaucrats a form of self-defense "to make their jobs psychologically easier to manage," "as responses to job stress," and "to avoid confrontations with work failures" (Lipsky, 2010, pp. 141, 144).

A burgeoning number of scholars engage in the study of coping during public service delivery (Loon & Jakobsen, 2018; Tummers et al., 2015). Bureaucrats must implement policies under challenging conditions, such as divergent expectations from policy rules or multiple stakeholders, and the gap between demands and available resources (Brodkin, 2011; Hupe & Buffat, 2014), which can cause tremendous stress. Furthermore, street-level bureaucrats feel that "personal and organizational resources are chronically and severely limited in relation to the tasks that they are asked to perform" (Weatherley & Lipsky, 1977, p. 172). Due to these scarce resources and the demanding requirements of the job, bureaucrats may respond to pressure by employing a variety of conscious or subconscious coping strategies.

Tummers et al. (2015) classify coping into three categories based on bureaucrats' interactions with clients: moving toward clients, moving away from clients, and moving against clients. "Moving toward clients" refers to coping strategies that benefit the clients. For example, front-line workers may bend or break the rules or use their personal resources to meet clients' demands. The latter two categories can be seen as coping for the convenience of bureaucrats and against clients' interests. Loon and Jakobsen (2018) describe these two as passive client-oriented coping, which reduces meaningful interactions with clients and may provoke confrontations.

Moving away from clients consists of three typical coping strategies: routinizing, rationing, and creaming. These terms are identified by Lipsky (2010). The most frequently employed method of coping in bureaucracy is routinizing. Bureaucrats typically establish routines to minimize the need for making individual decisions while handling tasks or clients in challenging and complex settings (Wu et al., 2019). Instead of treating clients on an individual or humanistic basis or handling tasks according to different circumstances, bureaucrats standardize and routinize their work to decrease their workload. Rationing services refers to the practice where bureaucrats offer limited services to citizens rather than an optimal amount. They attempt to reduce demand for their services by restricting information, making access challenging, controlling agendas, or selectively enforcing simple policies with a high likelihood of success (Lipsky, 2010). Creaming suggests that "street-level bureaucrats often choose those clients who seem most likely to succeed in terms of bureaucratic success criteria" (Lipsky, 2010).

Tummers et al. (2015) categorize rigid rule-following and aggression as forms of "moving against clients." Rigid rule-following refers to bureaucrats adhering to rules in an inflexible manner that may contradict clients' demands. They argue that strict adherence to rules allows frontline workers to manage clients, particularly those who are demanding. Common phrases used by bureaucrats—such as "the rules clearly say...," "it has always been done this way," or "I did not make the rules"—illustrate their strategic use of regulations as excuses to deny citizens' requests (Ashforth & Lee, 1990). The coping strategy of aggression is employed by bureaucrats to vent their anger or as a way to relieve their frustrations when clients are aggressive toward them (Hershcovis & Reich, 2013).

Who and What Control Bureaucrats

In Brehm and Gates's seminal book *Working, Shirking, and Sabotage: Bureaucratic Response to a Democratic Public* (1999), they pose several significant questions worth deep pondering.

> Who influences bureaucrats' choices? Is it the supervisor, the fellow bureaucrat, the clientele, political leaders, or the bureaucratic environment? How do these actors influence bureaucrats? Is it by wielding sanctions and rewards, appointments, budgetary control, or by constricting the flow of information?

They identify four potential factors that may influence a bureaucrat's decisions to either work, shirk, or sabotage: the bureaucrat's preferences, peer bureaucrats, supervisors, and the clients they serve. Romzek and Dubnick (1987) propose four diverging forms of accountability that may exert control on bureaucrats. Based on the variation in the source and degree of control in public agencies, four types of accountability systems are generated: legal accountability, bureaucratic accountability, political accountability, and professional accountability. Political and legal accountability puts bureaucrats under expectation or control outside the bureaucracy. Political accountability is central to democratic pressure, where public agencies should be responsive to their major constituencies such as citizens, elected politicians, advocacy groups, and the community (Brandsma & Adriaensen, 2017; Kim, 2018). As for legal accountability, particularly the "lawmaker," imposes legal sanctions or formal contracts on public agencies. Bureaucratic and professional accountability are pressures from internal sources of control within the bureaucracy. Bureaucratic accountability involves supervision from a higher level of authority, which utilizes a set of strategies, including organizational rules or regulations, performance management, and supervisory directives to regulate subordinates. Professional accountability is defined as "deference to expertise and performance standards derived from professional norms and prevailing practices of one's peer or work group" (Johnston & Romzek, 1999, p. 387). Scholars also propose diverse sources of control over the bureaucracy, such as accountability imposed by elections, bureaucracy, judiciary, market, and social (Bovens, 2007; Willems & Van Dooren, 2011). In a nutshell, bureaucrats may face control from three sources. First, they face top-down control from elected politicians, higher-level superiors, and legal overseers, which can be regarded as hierarchical accountability (Vlaicu & Whalley, 2016). Second, bureaucrats face bottom-up or social control from citizens, clients, or interest groups when they engage in interactions with them. Third, they are influenced by their peer bureaucrats and organizational culture.

The classic debate between Carl Friedrich and Herman Finer was sparked on the primacy of external and internal controls on bureaucrats (Plant, 2011). Finer (1941) argues that in contrast to the soft control of public ethical training, external control—such as implementing new legislation, promulgating new regulations, reorganizing structures, or imposing stricter oversight—is more effective and powerful in managing bureaucrats. Friedlich (1940) contends that neither the electorate nor the legislative assemblies can effectively bring out responsible conduct by close supervision. Friedrich emphasizes the importance of professional ethics and standards within the bureaucracy, arguing that trained and skilled administrators could self-regulate effectively while maintaining accountability to the organization. Different perspectives on the rationality of bureaucracy may lead to varying approaches to control. When viewing bureaucracy as instrumental rationality, external controls are often favored. In contrast, when seen as value rationality, internal controls are more likely to be preferred. The following part introduces specific measures of external and internal control over bureaucrats.

External Controls

Organizations can lower agency problems either by aligning preferences or by minimizing information asymmetry between the principal and the agent. Therefore, exterior control mechanisms, such as monitoring, punishment, promotion, and material rewards imposed by supervisors, should be equipped in administration to monitor bureaucrats' performance and prevent them from drifting.

Monitoring and sanctioning mechanisms. Monitoring mechanisms are often used by principals to control and influence agents' behavior. They are categorized into "police patrol" and "fire alarm" (Lupia & McCubbins, 1994). Police control is a metaphor referring to centralized or top-down monitoring mechanisms designed for principals to scrutinize agents directly to detect and discourage any violations of the principals' preferences (McCubbins & Schwartz, 1984). Principals may examine agents' work by assessing work reports filed regularly by their agents, holding hearings to question agents, and conducting patrols in person. Police patrol practice is costly for principals who need to spend considerable time and money on detecting and remedying violations that their agents try to conceal.

Under a decentralized fire alarm system, principals rely on external monitoring of third parties, such as citizens, interest groups, and media. For example, the US Congress establishes various procedures (e.g., access to information) that enable individual citizens and organized interest groups to monitor bureaucrats and report to principals in the case of any violation of agency discretion (McCubbins & Schwartz, 1984). When bureaucrats fail to supply qualified services, constituents may complain fiercely to their congressmen and bring violations to their attention. A fire alarm practice like this helps the principal save energy and time in controlling the agent.

In addition to monitoring mechanisms, principals may try to reduce agency problems by imposing punishment on their agents' transgression. Various sanction mechanisms may be adopted by the principal to constrain the actions of the agent. Weingast and Moran (1983) suggest that adequate sanctions are effective deterrents for agents. The study by Weingast (1984) indicates that, in the United States, Congress exerts a massive influence on the appointment of top bureaucratic officials and poses a formidable threat of ex-post sanctions on bureaucrats, which gives them considerable authority to control bureaucrats and motivate them to work hard (Weingast, 1984). According to Pollack (2003), principals can use three types of sanctions against errant agents. First, politicians may dismiss or refuse to reappoint agents whom they perceive to be drifting away from their preferences. Second, in response to agency problems, politicians may cut their budgets. Third, politicians may restrict or revise the authority that they have delegated to the agents.

Incentive schemes. Besides the various oversight and sanction mechanisms to control agents, incentive mechanisms can be adopted to stir up agents' enthusiasm and motivate them to put more efforts into work even without close monitoring from principals. Incentive mechanisms are designed to overcome preference divergence and information asymmetry between principals and agents. When the goals of a principal and an agent align, the principal does not need to invest in costly incentive mechanisms because the agent will behave according to their preferences. Furthermore, if the principal can fully observe the agent's actions, then the incentive issue becomes moot, as the principal can accurately provide remuneration that reflects the agent's level of effort. Unfortunately, agents' preferences may be considerably different from those of their principals, and principals may fail to observe the extent of the efforts that the agents put into their work (Hölmstrom, 1979; Nielson & Tierney, 2003; Thompson, 2007, p. 6). Thus, incentive mechanisms need to be in place to motivate agents to act in accordance with principals' preferences. Scholars identify three types of incentive mechanisms that are commonly adopted in the public sector.

First, incentive contracts are schemes designed to tie agents' compensation to their performance, thereby inducing them to work harder. These contracts replace the unobserved information regarding agents' efforts with verifiable information related to their job outcomes (outputs, profits, etc.). However, closely linking agents' compensation to their outputs presents challenges in designing effective incentive contracts. Various types of incentive contracts exist to connect agents' compensation to their performance, such as linear compensation schemes (Baker, 2002), rank-order tournaments (Lazear & Rosen, 1981), and elimination tournaments.

In the first type, incentive contracts are normally linear, meaning that the relationship between compensation and agents' performance demonstrates a positive linear correlation, as seen in piece-rate systems. A linear incentive contract is a high-powered incentive mechanism that can sometimes achieve optimal incentive effects in the private sector (Holmstrom & Milgrom, 1987). However, high-powered incentives may not be a desirable choice in the public sector. Scholars argue that a high-powered linear compensation contract may distort the agent's incentives when performance is difficult to identify and quantify, when the agent engages in multitasking, when the output is highly dependent on external random factors, or when the agent is highly risk-averse (Lazear, 1989).

The second type is the efficiency wage, which refers to an incentive wage offered to agents that is higher than the market salary. The efficiency wage posits that workers' productivity is positively correlated with their wages and that higher wages can motivate employees to enhance their effort and reduce malfeasance. Leibenstein (1963) underscores the link between wages, nutrition, and health, suggesting that higher wages enable workers to afford nutritious food, thereby making them healthier and increasing productivity. Solow (1979) proposes a similar explanation, stating that increased wages improve morale and commitment, which directly affects productivity.

Shapiro and Stiglitz (1984) provide another explanation for efficiency wages. They argue that an agent is more likely to engage in shirking if their firm offers a salary that matches the market wage, as there are no consequences for such behavior; if they are terminated, they can easily secure another job at a similar pay. On the other hand, if employees receive a salary above the market rate, they are less inclined to shirk because they fear losing their higher compensation if they are caught (Mühlau & Lindenberg, 2003). For agents receiving efficiency wages, the cost of shirking becomes prohibitively high. Additionally, efficiency wages can help attract highly skilled employees to a firm, leading to enhanced productivity. This practice is commonly implemented in Singapore's public sector.

The third incentive mechanism revolves around career concerns, as agents are often motivated by their promotion opportunities and the likelihood of being transferred to other organizations (Fama, 1980; Holmström, 1999). Fama (1980) suggests that the career concerns can effectively mitigate agency problems, as public managers are invested in their reputation within the organizations. There are several reasons why officials aim for promotions. First, officials are motivated to perform well to secure promotions, which typically come with salary increases and enhanced job benefits. Second, many positions include up-or-out agreements, which create pressure to achieve promotions within a specific timeframe (Ghosh & Waldman, 2010). Failure to do so can result in diminished career prospects. While dismissals are rare in the public sector, it is not uncommon in the Chinese government for an official to miss the opportunity to compete for higher positions if they are not promoted in the initial round (Gao, 2017). Holmström (1999) illustrates how an individual's concern for their future career profoundly influences their work incentives. Scholars also note that government officials prioritize maintaining their positions or seeking promotions (Cai, 2014; Weaver, 1986).

Internal Controls

Building on Barnard's work, Simon introduced the concept of the "zone of acceptance" to describe the extent to which bureaucrats choose to accept or reject hierarchical authority (Nielsen & Jacobsen, 2018). According to Simon (2013, p. 196), authority is defined as "the acceptance by the subordinate of the decisions of the superior" rather than the superior's ability to impose sanctions for noncompliance. The existence of credible threats of sanctions can broaden employees' zone of acceptance. However, Simon also notes that this zone is shaped by employees' bargaining power and societal norms regarding what requests are appropriate for employers to make of their employees (Nielsen & Jacobsen, 2018). He views the relationship between superiors and subordinates as reciprocal, emphasizing that both parties affect the dynamics of their interactions, thereby challenging the notion of coercive and dominant power held by supervisors (Meier & O'Toole Jr, 2006).

An increasing body of literature advocates for administrative ethics that prioritize internal control and the public good (Cooper, 2012). Scholars who favor internal or intrinsic control challenge the effectiveness of coercive supervision, arguing that extrinsic incentives imposed by supervisors are inadequate for motivating bureaucrats to perform well (Kuvaas et al., 2017). For instance, Adler (1983) suggests that only individuals with low self-esteem are swayed by the coercive power of supervisors. Instead, intrinsic motivation—developed through the internalization of norms and values associated with professionalism and public service—plays a more significant role in guiding bureaucrats' moral behavior (Pierre & Peters, 2017; Tu, 2024).

Research indicates that public sector employees place less value on economic rewards compared to their private sector counterparts (Bullock et al., 2015; Houston, 2000). This suggests that public organizations are less reliant on utilitarian incentives to motivate their workforce. Scholars argue that public employees tend to exhibit higher PSM than those in the private sector. Additionally, they propose that the public sector can cultivate bureaucrats' prosocial values and altruistic behaviors, moving beyond mere rational choice logic (Ritz et al., 2016).

From the perspective of social learning theory (Krohn, 1999), it is believed that individuals acquire norms and values through training and interactions with colleagues within their organizations. This internalization results from professional indoctrination and training that foster loyalty, integrity, and diligence among employees (Ginsburg, 2002). The socialization process within the public sector's organizational culture instills the intrinsic motivation and ethical standards expected of civil servants (Bellé, 2015; Buelens & van den Broeck, 2007). Consequently, scholars advocate for a transformation of the public sector's organizational culture, promoting PSM as a guiding mechanism for bureaucratic behavior. Organizations that encourage PSM are more likely to inspire their members to embrace altruistic behaviors rather than engage in shirking or loafing.

Brehm and Gates (1997) also refute the absolute control of supervisors over bureaucrats due to constraints on supervisory resources and asymmetric information. Instead, bureaucrats themselves and the organizational culture play a more significant role in determining whether they will shirk or work than material rewards and punishments from their supervisors. First, whether subordinates shirk or work depends on their own preference toward the policy being implemented. If they dislike the policy, they will adopt dissent-shirking, which is quite different from being merely lazy. Nevertheless, the subordinates may invest more energy in a policy that they support even without supervision from their supervisors. Second, "bureaucrats control the behavior of one another" (Brehm & Gates, 1999, p. 196). They interact with one another through networks and learn from others in the organization; thus, solitary preference is a major influencing factor determining whether they will work or shirk (Brehm & Gates, 1999, p. 74). Pierre and Peters (2017) argue that public servants are driven by professional values and often carry out their responsibilities without the need for supervision. They contend that trust-based administrative systems, which focus on shared professional values and a spirit of cooperation, lead to lower transaction and monitoring costs compared to contract-based systems that rely on hierarchical control.

Some economists highlight the significance of cultivating the "right" type of culture to address productivity and agency problems through economic theories. They stress the importance of creating a corporate culture that promotes cooperation among employees to minimize shirking and boost work ethic (Kreps, 1990; Rob & Zemsky, 2002). According to Rob and Zemsky (2002), workers encounter a prisoner's dilemma: without assurance that their colleagues will also put in effort or that their lack of cooperation will be noticed by supervisors, they are likely to shirk or loaf. They propose that a viable solution is to encourage a preference for cooperation among workers and to design incentive structures that increase the benefits of collaborative efforts.

Kreps (1990) and Miller (1992) offer important perspectives on how corporate culture influences the relationship between supervisors and subordinates. Kreps (1990) considers that repeated games and the desire to preserve their reputation promote employees to sustain cooperative behavior to safeguard future beneficial transactions. The reputation argument comes into play as potential future partners observe how well the actor currently adheres to their contracts when deciding whether to collaborate with them later (Kreps, 1990). Therefore, the manager's job is to create proper incentives and a cooperative organizational culture to address the control problem (Miller, 1992).

Who Are the Bureaucrats in China

Unlike democratic states, there is no clear and explicit separation between administration and politics in China. The authority of administrative agencies and Party organizations appears to be intertwined in the process of national governance, making them often regarded as an integrated organization. However, when analyzing Chinese politics, we may find that there is indeed a separation between the ruling party—who hold the highest national power—and the bureaucratic organizations that operate under the leadership of the ruling Party, despite the blurry division of functions between them. Chairman Mao's repeated criticisms of the bureaucratic system and the frequent rectification movements within and outside the Party indicate a recurring tension between the highest political will and the bureaucratic system that carries out specific operations.

The Communist Party of China (CPC) is the sole governing party, integrating political authority with administrative functions. Politicians and bureaucrats often belong to the same party, blurring the lines between political decisions and administrative execution. Administrative apparatuses and Party organizations coexist at each level of the Chinese government and are jointly responsible for implementing policies mandated by higher authorities. As a result, there is no clear agreement on the identification of political principals and public agents in China. I present three possible explanations for determining who bureaucrats are. First, some scholars argue that the central government functions as the political principal, while the various local levels serve as the bureaucracy (Huang, 2002). The Chinese government is structured into central and local tiers. According to Huang (2002), the central level, which includes Party organs like the Politburo and the organization department, as well as administrative bodies such as the State Council, Commissions, and Ministries, represents the controlling authority. Conversely, the local levels encompass provincial, municipal, county, and village agencies. He outlines two primary reasons for this distinction.

The controlling level holds personnel authority over the agencies at the controlled level and is tasked with making critical decisions. The Politburo, positioned at the pinnacle of the political hierarchy, serves as the ultimate decision-making body where all significant strategic choices are formulated. The State Council then translates these strategic decisions into specific policies. Furthermore, the differences in preferences are particularly pronounced between these two levels. Local governments naturally have well-defined areas of focus and often prioritize their specific sectoral or regional objectives over the broader interests of the entire system (Huang, 2002). The tension between central authority and local authority is significant. In an interview conducted in 2005, former Vice Minister of Education Baoqing Zhang remarked, "the biggest problem in China right now is that policies cannot be effectively implemented. Sometimes, policies issued in Zhongnanhai (the central) often fail to reach beyond its walls" (Sina News, 2005).

Second, some scholars classify Chinese officials into two types: "floating" and "native" officials (***liuguan / tuguan,*** 流官/土官) (Liao et al., 2020). Floating officials, who are appointed and transferred by the Party across different regions, can be viewed as political elites, while native officials, who are stationed for life in one location and overseen by the personnel departments of the administrative branch, are seen as bureaucrats (Ang, 2020). The top one percent—approximately 500,000 officials at the division level (*chuji*, 处级) and above—constitute China's "political elites" (Walder, 2006; Wilson, 2019). A middle layer of civil servants, about 19 percent of the total personnel, carries out management roles within party or state agencies (Ang, 2020). "The remaining 80 percent are non-civil service public employees, such as clerks, inspectors, police officers, health-care workers, and township cadres, who directly deliver services to citizens" (Ang, 2020, p. 90). Elite officials are evidently powerful figures in China's authoritarian hierarchy, as they determine various economic and social policies during their term in the jurisdiction. A considerable number of literature explores the impact of official rotation on local development (Chen et al., 2024; Jiang & Mei, 2020; Zhang & Gao, 2008). Rotation is a strategy to converge preferences and supply local information to the central level (Huang, 2002). However, the importance of the remaining unrotated rank-and-file officers in shaping policies should not be underestimated. This group runs the daily machinery of governance and implements policies at the grassroots level, significantly influencing the execution of national policies and the relationship between local government and society (Ang, 2020; Zhan et al., 2014; Zhang et al., 2021). However, research on low-level local bureaucrats within local government is still relatively scarce.

Third, the Party apparatus embodies the will of the state, whereas the administrative apparatus functions as the bureaucracy responsible for implementing policies. Political scientists describe the unique form of governance in China as the "party-government system" (Edin, 2003; Snape & Wang, 2020; Zhou et al., 2021). At each level of the administrative jurisdictions, both the party committees and the government maintain their own organizational structures. However, there is a distinct hierarchical order in which the party headquarters hold authority over the government. The relationship between the party and government is historically evolving in terms of the relative weight of the party versus administrative authority (Zhou et al., 2021). During the reform and opening-up era, the party-government relationship had to be recalibrated to accommodate the new economic landscape marked by market-oriented reforms and mixed property rights. The party aimed to maintain its authority while introducing greater flexibility in governance to promote economic growth. This adjustment involved redefining roles and responsibilities as a developmental state, resulting in relatively loose control of the

Party over the government. Deng Xiaoping repeatedly stressed the importance of separating Party functions from government duties in various contexts. In 1980, he stated that party organizations at all levels should, in principle, delegate a substantial portion of daily administrative and management tasks to the government and relevant departments whenever possible. Besides formulating policies and making decisions about key personnel appointments, party leaders should devote the majority of their time and energy to ideological and political work (Beijing News, 2013).

Xi's administration adjusts the party-government relationship, with greater emphasis placed on the primacy of party organizations in guiding and directing all aspects of governance and organizational activities (Gong & Tu, 2022; Lee, 2017). This approach is intended to create a more unified governance framework, where party directives take precedence and ensure that all levels of government operate in harmony with party goals. Some political apparatus, such as the CDIs and the SCs, have experienced a bolstering of their roles and influence within the governance structure. Therefore, the centralization of power within the party has been significantly institutionalized.

In conclusion, researchers suggest three classifications to distinguish between politicians and bureaucrats within the Chinese government (Table 2.1). This book explores the motivations, preferences, and behaviors of Chinese bureaucrats, as well as the different forms of accountability applied to them within the party-government framework. Most of the survey participants and interviewees in this study are non-leading officials at or below the division level, primarily tasked with policy implementation. Many of these respondents are similar to the street-level bureaucrats identified by Lipsky (2010) in the American context.

As we have made a distinction between politics and public administration in China, it is significant to distinguish political accountability and bureaucratic accountability. In China, political accountability primarily refers to the responsibility imposed on party and government leaders for political errors, decision-making failures, or misconduct in the performance of their duties. The core of political accountability is to ensure that party and government leaders align with the party's principles, policies, and guidelines in their political stance, policy implementation, and leadership conduct, thereby upholding the party's leadership and the stability of the nation. Administrative or bureaucratic accountability primarily refers to the responsibility for the negligence, dereliction of duty,

Table 2.1 Three types of classification between politicians and bureaucrats in China

Classifications	*Politics or politicians*	*Bureaucracy or bureaucrats*
The central-local level	Apparatus and officials at the central level	Apparatus and officials at the local level
Rotated-native officials	Leaders and elite officials rotated across places by the Party	Non-leading officials who are stationed in one location
Party-government system	Party organs	Administrative branch

inaction, and improper actions of administrative agencies and bureaucrats during the performance of their duties. The core of bureaucratic accountability is to ensure that administrative agencies and their personnel perform their responsibilities in accordance with the law, efficiently, and with integrity, thereby safeguarding public interests and the legitimate rights of the people. Table 2.2 illustrates the differences between political accountability and bureaucratic accountability in the subjects, scope, mechanisms, and objectives in China. This book primarily focuses on the two predominant accountability systems in the Chinese bureaucracy, which are integrated into a hierarchical accountability framework.

Table 2.2 The differences between political and bureaucratic accountability

	Political accountability	*Bureaucratic accountability*
Subjects	Party and government leaders or organizations	Administrative agencies or agents
Scope	Political stance, decision-making failures, responsibility for major incidents	Policy implementation, public management, public services
Mechanisms	Intra-party disciplinary inspection, supervisory accountability	Internal audits, administrative penalties
Objectives	Ensuring leaders are accountable to the party and the people	Ensuring efficiency and compliance of administrative agencies

The Organization of the Chinese Bureaucracy

The operation of the Chinese bureaucracy shares some similarities with the Weberian bureaucracy, but also presents the distinct characteristics of China's party-government system. Similar to the Weberian bureaucracy, the Chinese bureaucracy depends on hierarchical authority, specialized functions, and established procedures to deal with routine duties. However, campaign-style enforcement is frequently adopted to overcome bureaucratic ossification and invigorate public officials' initiative (Wang et al., 2022; Zhou, 2021). Campaign-style enforcement involves temporarily disrupting formal institutions, standard bureaucratic routines, and professional practices, while implementing top-down political mobilization to concentrate all resources on a specific core task (Cai & Tang, 2023; Zhou, 2022). The procedures of campaign-style governance typically include: first, politicizing a routine task as a primary objective; second, organizing mobilization meetings to encourage entire bureaucratic organizations and their members to actively engage in the task; and third, utilizing performance management to monitor, evaluate, and assess the progress of the task (Zhou, 2022).

Campaign-style enforcement is considered a flexible approach to address bureaucratic inertia and encourage officials' initiative. While rational bureaucracy is typically viewed as the most effective method for maintaining order and enhancing efficiency, its structural traits also lead to organizational rigidity and sluggishness (Wilson, 2019). The Chinese bureaucracy suffers significantly from ineffectiveness and inertia due to its large-scale organizational system and complex principal-agent structure (Wedeman, 2001).

In the Chinese party-government system, it is a politicized bureaucracy rather than a rational one, in which politicized officials are often granted arbitrary power to transcend bureaucratic boundaries and mobilize resources from various sources to facilitate social transformation (Whyte, 1973; Zhou, 2022). The CCP's revolutionary tradition encourages breaking from routine power and existing institutional frameworks to enhance bureaucratic effectiveness (Harding, 1981). When routine bureaucracy falls short and urgent goals arise, higher authorities implement campaign-style enforcement through specialized rectifications (*zhuanxiang zhili*, 专项治理), centralized treatments (*jizhong zhengzhi*, 集中整治), and specialized struggles (*zhuanxiang douzheng*, 专项斗争) to mobilize lower-level officials (Biddulph et al., 2012).

Campaign-style enforcement is evolving from a radical mass mobilization approach to being integrated into routine bureaucratic processes, resulting in a hybrid known as "institutionalized mobilization" (White, 1990) or "managed campaign" (Perry, 2011; Zeng, 2020). During Mao's era, this approach primarily manifested as radical mass mobilization and ongoing political campaigns. The numerous campaigns from that time reflected the belief that "bureaucratic performance could be improved by temporarily reducing an organization's level of hierarchy, routine, formalism, and specialization" (Harding, 1981, p. 22).

As modernization proceeds, "revolutionary" campaigns in the Mao period inevitably give way to the post-revolutionary politics of "rational" bureaucratic modes and party institutionalization (Lowenthal, 1970). However, the legacy of campaigns has remained a well-recognized approach to overcoming bureaucratic hurdles to cope with sudden and unexpected challenges or to achieve urgent goals in post-Mao China (Perry, 2011; White, 1990). For example, the one-child policy and investment attraction policy mobilized almost all government departments and officials, regardless of their specific roles, to implement these initiatives through mobilization. While campaigns remain a crucial method for addressing bureaucratic inertia and encouraging officials' initiative, they differ significantly from Maoist campaigns. Scholars consider that managed campaigns have become a common and pragmatic mechanism under the routine bureaucracy for public officials (Zeng, 2020). The sources of inspiration and strength are now more eclectic and widely recognized, as reflected in the use of terms like "mechanisms" (*jizhi,* 机制), "dynamics" (*lidu,* 力度), and "fixed time" (*qixian,* 期限). Additionally, it is grassroots officials, rather than ordinary peasants, who typically take on the primary roles in these managed campaigns (Perry, 2011).

Why can campaign-style enforcement be adopted in China as a strategy to address the rigidity and sluggishness of rational bureaucracy? Who has the capability to mobilize the bureaucracy? Zhou et al. (2021) suggest that at each hierarchical level, the party system follows top-down mobilization orders and plays a dominant role in campaign-style mobilization, whereas the administrative offices are organized in a conventional Weberian bureaucracy. Such a structure allows the Party apparatus to mobilize and dominate the government apparatus. The highest authority can disrupt the routine governance processes of the bureaucratic system using the party's apparatus, initiating political mobilizations to effectively implement the leader's directives. The central authority possesses "arbitrary power," allowing it to intervene at any level or stage of the bureaucratic system, with the authority to assess, judge, disrupt, or expedite bureaucratic activities whenever necessary. This dynamic explains why bureaucrats place significant emphasis on political tasks and political accountability.

Conclusion

Instrumental rationality views bureaucracy as a rational tool for policy implementation, portraying bureaucrats as rational actors driven by external controls. In contrast, value rationality emphasizes the bureaucracy's role in promoting the broader common good, suggesting that bureaucrats are motivated by intrinsic values. These differing views on bureaucracy's rationality can result in various control approaches and accountability configurations. The instrumental rationality perspective may lead to a top-down accountability system focused on rigorous monitoring and sanctions, whereas the value rationality perspective may encourage the development of cooperative organizational culture, ethical training, and internal checks.

In many countries, external controls take precedence over internal controls in regulating bureaucrats. However, a paradox arises: the increased emphasis on top-down control does not guarantee absolute compliance from bureaucrats. The discretionary power of bureaucrats embedded in delegation and their work nature provides them latitude to subvert or cope with institutional pressure. Therefore, the design of external controls should take into account bureaucrats' preferences, motivations, and influences. The central question is how to create accountability or control systems that foster better cooperation within the bureaucracy, which is the main issue I intend to address in this book.

The Chinese bureaucracy displays traits typical of Weberian bureaucracy, but these traits are shaped and modified by the unique party-government system. The presence of both Party and government structures at every hierarchical level enables Party organs to interrupt the normal functioning of the bureaucracy and mobilize all governmental resources to achieve key policy goals. This dynamic effectively mitigates bureaucratic rigidity, stagnation, and resistance. With the reinforcement of Party organs under Xi's administration, political accountability is significantly strengthened. Chapter 3 will scrutinize the dynamic status and relationship between political accountability and bureaucratic accountability.

References

Ackerman, S. R. (1978). *Corruption: A study in political economy*. Academic Press.

Adler, N. J. (1983). Cross-cultural management research: The ostrich and the trend. *Academy of Management Review, 8*(2), 226–232.

Adler, P. S., & Borys, B. (1996). Two types of bureaucracy: Enabling and coercive. *Administrative Science Quarterly*, *41*(1), 61–89.

Ang, Y. Y. (2020). *China's gilded age: The paradox of economic boom and vast corruption*. Cambridge University Press.

Ashforth, B. E., & Lee, R. T. (1990). Defensive behavior in organizations: A preliminary model. *Human Relations, 43*(7), 621–648.

Awan, S., Bel, G., & Esteve, M. (2020). The benefits of PSM: An oasis or a mirage? *Journal of Public Administration Research and Theory*, *30*(4), 619–635.

Baker, G. (2002). Distortion and risk in optimal incentive contracts. *Journal of Human Resources, 37*, 728–751.

Banuri, S., & Keefer, P. (2013). Intrinsic motivation, effort and the call to public service. *World Bank Policy Research Working Paper*, 6729.

Beijing News. (2013, March 25). *Accurately grasp the connotation of "separation between party and government"*. Viewed November 20, 2024. http://theory.people.com.cn/n/2013/0325/c49150-20899102.html

Bellé, N. (2013). Experimental evidence on the relationship between public service motivation and job performance. *Public Administration Review, 73*, 143–153.

Bellé, N. (2015). Performance-related pay and the crowding out of motivation in the public sector: A randomized field experiment. *Public Administration Review, 75*(2), 230–241.

Biddulph, S., Cooney, S., & Zhu, Y. (2012). Rule of law with Chinese characteristics: The role of campaigns in lawmaking. *Law & Policy, 34*(4), 373–401.

Brehm, J. O., & Gates, S. (1999). *Working, shirking, and sabotage: Bureaucratic response to a democratic public*. University of Michigan Press.

Bourgon, J. (2007). Responsive, responsible and respected government: Towards a New Public Administration theory. *International Review of Administrative Sciences, 73*(1), 7–26.

Bovens, M. (2007). Analysing and assessing accountability: A conceptual framework. *European Law Journal, 13*(4), 447–468.

Brandsma, G. J., & Adriaensen, J. (2017). The principal–agent model, accountability and democratic legitimacy. In T. Delreux & J. Adriaensen (Eds.), *The principal agent model and the European Union* (pp. 35–54). Springer International Publishing.

Bright, L. (2008). Does public service motivation really make a difference on the job satisfaction and turnover intentions of public employees? *The American Review of Public Administration, 38*(2), 149–166.

Briscoe, F. (2007). From iron cage to iron shield? How bureaucracy enables temporal flexibility for professional service workers. *Organization Science, 18*(2), 297–314.

Brodkin, E. Z. (2011). Policy work: Street-level organizations under new managerialism. *Journal of Public Administration Research and Theory, 21*(suppl_2), i253–i277.

Buelens, M., & Van Den Broeck, H. (2007). An analysis of differences in work motivation between public and private sector organizations. *Public Administration Review, 67*(1), 65–74.

Bullock, J. B., Stritch, J. M., & Rainey, H. G. (2015). International comparison of public and private employees' work motives, attitudes, and perceived rewards. *Public Administration Review, 75*(3), 479–489.

Cai, C., & Tang, N. (2023). China's campaign-style implementation regime: How is "Targeted poverty Alleviation" being achieved locally? *Journal of Chinese Political Science, 28*(4), 645–669.

Cai, Y. (2014). *State and agents in China: Disciplining government officials*. Stanford University Press.

Calvert, R. L., McCubbins, M. D., & Weingast, B. R. (1989). A theory of political control and agency discretion. *American Journal of Political Science, 33*(3), 588–611.

Chen, Y., Liu, X., & Liu, Y. (2024). 'The assisting hand' or 'the grabbing hand': Experimental evidence from PPP investments in the implementation of official rotation systems. *Journal of Chinese Governance, 10* (2), 1–36.

Christensen, T., & Lægreid, P. (2001). NEW PUBLIC MANAGEMENT: The effects of contractualism and devolution on political control. *Public Management Review, 3*(1), 73–94.

Cook, B. J., & Wood, B. D. (1989). Principal-agent models of political control of bureaucracy. *American Political Science Review, 83*(3), 965–978.

Cooper, T. L. (2012). *The responsible administrator: An approach to ethics for the administrative role*. Wiley.

Crewson, P. E. (1997). Public-service motivation: Building empirical evidence of incidence and effect. *Journal of Public Administration Research and Theory, 7*(4), 499–518.

Dahling, J. J., Chau, S. L., Mayer, D. M., & Gregory, J. B. (2012). Breaking rules for the right reasons? An investigation of pro-social rule breaking. *Journal of Organizational Behavior, 33*(1), 21–42.

Dahlström, C., & Lapuente, V. (2022). Comparative bureaucratic politics. *Annual Review of Political Science, 25*(1), 43–63.

Denhardt, J. V., & Denhardt, R. B. (2015). The new public service revisited. *Public Administration Review, 75*(5), 664–672.

Dunleavy, P., & Hood, C. (1994). From old public administration to new public management. *Public Money & Management, 14*(3), 9–16.

Edin, M. (2003). Remaking the communist party-state: The cadre responsibility system at the local level in China. *China: An International Journal, 1*(01), 1–15.

Epstein, D., & O'halloran, S. (1994). Administrative procedures, information, and agency discretion. *American Journal of Political Science, 38*(3), 697–722.

Evans, T. (2010). Professionals, managers and discretion: Critiquing street-level bureaucracy. *The British Journal of Social Work, 41*(2), 368–386.

Fama, E. F. (1980). Agency problems and the theory of the firm. *Journal of Political Economy, 88*(2), 288–307.

Feldman, M. S., & Khademian, A. M. (2002). To manage is to govern. *Public Administration Review, 62*(5), 541–554.

Finer, H. (1941). Administrative responsibility in democratic government. *Public Administration Review, 1*(4), 335–350.

Fox, C. J., & Miller, H. T. (1994). *Postmodern public administration: Toward discourse*. SAGE Publications

Friedlich, C. J. (1940). Public policy and the nature of administrative responsibility. *Public Policy, 1*, 1–20.

Gao, X. (2017). Promotion prospects and career paths of local party-government leaders in China. *Journal of Chinese Governance, 2*(2), 223–234.

Ghosh, S., & Waldman, M. (2010). Standard promotion practices versus up-or-out contracts. *The RAND Journal of Economics, 41*(2), 301–325.

Ginsburg, T. (2002). Comparative administrative procedure: Evidence from Northeast Asia. *Constitutional Political Economy, 13*(3), 247–264.

Gong, T., & Tu, W. (2022). Fighting Corruption in China. *China Review, 22*(2), 1–19.

Gulick, L. (1937). Notes on the theory of organization. In *Classics of organizational theory* (4th ed.). Harcourt Brace College Publishers.

Harding, H. (1981). *Organizing China: The problem of bureaucracy, 1949–1976*. Stanford University Press.

Harmon, M. M. (1995). *Responsibility as paradox: A critique of rational discourse on government*. Thousand Oaks, CA: Sage.

Hawkins, D. G., & Jacoby, W. (2006). How agents matter. *Delegation and Agency in International Organizations, 1*, 199–228.

Hershcovis, M. S., & Reich, T. C. (2013). Integrating workplace aggression research: Relational, contextual, and method considerations. *Journal of Organizational Behavior, 34*(S1), S26-S42.
Holmström, B. (1979). Moral hazard and observability. *The Bell Journal of Economics, 10*(1), 1074–1091.
Holmström, B. (1999). Managerial incentive problems: A dynamic perspective. *The Review of Economic Studies, 66*(1), 169–182.
Holmstrom, B., & Milgrom, P. (1987). Aggregation and linearity in the provision of intertemporal incentives. *Econometrica: Journal of the Econometric Society, 55*, 303–328.
Houston, D. J. (2000). Public-service motivation: A multivariate test. *Journal of Public Administration Research and Theory, 10*(4), 713–728.
Houston, D. J. (2006). "Walking the walk" of public service motivation: Public employees and charitable gifts of time, blood, and money. *Journal of Public Administration Research and Theory, 16*(1), 67–86.
Huang, Y. (2002). Managing Chinese bureaucrats: An institutional economics perspective. *Political Studies, 50*(1), 61–79.
Huber, J. D. (2002). *Deliberate discretion: The institutional foundations of bureaucratic autonomy*. Cambridge University Press.
Hupe, P. (2019). *Research handbook on street-level bureaucracy*. Edward Elgar Publishing.
Hupe, P., & Buffat, A. (2014). A public service gap: Capturing contexts in a comparative approach of street-level bureaucracy. *Public Management Review, 16*(4), 548–569.
Jacobson, W. S. (2011). Creating a motivated workforce: How organizations can enhance and develop public service motivation (PSM). *Public Personnel Management, 40*(3), 215–238.
Jiang, J., & Mei, Y. (2020). Mandarins make markets: Leadership rotations and inter-provincial trade in China. *Journal of Development Economics, 147*, 102524.
Johnston, J. M., & Romzek, B. S. (1999). Contracting and accountability in state Medicaid reform: Rhetoric, theories, and reality. *Public Administration Review, 59*, 383–399.
Kaufman, H. (2001). Major players: Bureaucracies In American Government. *Public Administration Review, 61*(1), 18–42.
Kelly, R. M. (1998). An inclusive democratic polity, representative bureaucracies, and the new public management. *Public Administration Review, 58*(3), 201–208.
Kim, Y. (2018). Analyzing accountability relationships in a crisis: Lessons from the Fukushima disaster. *The American Review of Public Administration, 48*(7), 743–760.

Kreps, D. M. (1990). Corporate culture and economic theory. In Alt, J. E., & Shepsle, K. A. (Eds.), *Perspectives on Positive Political Economy* (pp. 90–143). Cambridge University Press.

Kuvaas, B., Buch, R., Weibel, A., Dysvik, A., & Nerstad, C. G. (2017). Do intrinsic and extrinsic motivation relate differently to employee outcomes? *Journal of Economic Psychology, 61*, 244–258.

La Palombara, J. (2006). An overview of bureaucracy and political development. *Comparative Public Administration*, 15, 193–220.

Lazarus, R. S. (1984). *Stress, appraisal, and coping* (Vol. 464). Springer.

Lazear, E. P. (1989). Incentive contracts. In J. Eatwell, M. Milgate, & P. Newman (Eds.), *Allocation, information and markets* (pp. 152–162). Palgrave Macmillan UK.

Lazear, E. P., & Rosen, S. (1981). Rank-order tournaments as optimum labor contracts. *Journal of Political Economy, 89*(5), 841–864.

Lee, S. (2017). An institutional analysis of Xi Jinping's centralization of power. *Journal of Contemporary China, 26*(105), 325–336.

Leibenstein, H. (1963). Technical progress, the production function, and development. In W. W. Rostow (Ed.), *The economics of take-off into sustained growth* (pp. 185–200). Palgrave Macmillan UK.

Liao, X., Tsai, W.-H., & Lin, Z.-W. (2020). Penetrating the grassroots: First-secretaries-in-residence and rural politics in contemporary China. *Problems of Post-Communism, 67*(2), 169–179.

Lipsky, M. (2010). *Street-level bureaucracy: Dilemmas of the individual in public service*. Russell sage foundation.

Lotta, G., Krieger, M. G. M., Cohen, N., & Kirschbaum, C. (2024). Not separate, but certainly unequal: The burdens and coping strategies of low-status street-level bureaucrats. *Governance, 37*(3), 907–926.

Lowenthal, R. (1970). Russia and China: Controlled conflict. *Foreign Affairs, 49*, 507.

Lupia, A., & McCubbins, M. D. (1994). Who controls? Information and the structure of legislative decision making. *Legislative Studies Quarterly, 19*, 361–384.

Maynard-Moody, S., & Musheno, M. (2000). State agent or citizen agent: Two narratives of discretion. *Journal of Public Administration Research and Theory, 10*(2), 329–358.

McCubbins, M. D., & Schwartz, T. (1984). Congressional oversight overlooked: Police patrols versus fire alarms. *American Journal of Political Science, 28*, 165–179.

Meier, K. J. (2023). Representative bureaucracy and social equity: Bias, perceived fairness and efficacy. *Journal of Social Equity and Public Administration, 1*(1), 23–38.

Meier, K. J., & O'Toole, L. J. (2006). Political control versus bureaucratic values: Reframing the debate. *Public Administration Review, 66*(2), 177–192.

Miller, G. (1992). *Managerial dilemmas: The political economy of hierarchy*. Cambridge University.

Monteiro, P., & Adler, P. S. (2022). Bureaucracy for the 21st Century: Clarifying and expanding our view of bureaucratic organization. *Academy of Management Annals, 16*(2), 427–475.

Morrison, E. W. (2006). Doing the job well: An investigation of pro-social rule breaking. *Journal of Management, 32*(1), 5–28.

Mühlau, P., & Lindenberg, S. (2003). Efficiency wages: Signals or incentives an empirical study of the relationship between wage and commitment. *Journal of Management and Governance, 7*, 385–400.

Nielsen, P. A., & Jacobsen, C. B. (2018). Zone of acceptance under performance measurement: Does performance information affect employee acceptance of management authority? *Public Administration Review, 78*(5), 684–693.

Nielson, D. L., & Tierney, M. J. (2003). Delegation to international organizations: Agency theory and World Bank environmental reform. *International Organization, 57*(2), 241–276.

Olsen, J. P. (2006). Maybe it is time to rediscover bureaucracy. *Journal of Public Administration Research and Theory, 16*(1), 1–24.

Pandey, S. K., Wright, B. E., & Moynihan, D. P. (2008). Public service motivation and interpersonal citizenship behavior in public organizations: Testing a preliminary model. *International Public Management Journal, 11*(1), 89–108.

Perry, E. J. (2011). From mass campaigns to managed campaigns: "Constructing a new socialist countryside." In Heilmann, S., & Perry, E. J. (Eds.), *Mao's invisible hand* (pp. 30–61). Harvard University Asia Center.

Perry, J. L. (1996). Measuring public service motivation: An assessment of construct reliability and validity. *Journal of Public Administration Research and Theory, 6*(1), 5–22.

Perry, J. L., & Wise, L. R. (1990). The motivational bases of public service. *Public Administration Review, 50*, 367–373.

Pierre, J., & Peters, B. G. (2017). The shirking bureaucrat: A theory in search of evidence? *Policy & Politics, 45*(2), 157–172.

Plant, J. F. (2011). Carl J. Friedrich on responsibility and authority. *Public Administration Review, 71*(3), 471–482.

Pollack, M. A. (2003). Control mechanism or deliberative democracy?: Two images of comitology. *Comparative Political Studies, 36*(1–2), 125–155.

Ritz, A., Brewer, G. A., & Neumann, O. (2016). Public service motivation: A systematic literature review and outlook. *Public Administration Review, 76*(3), 414–426.

Rob, R., & Zemsky, P. (2002). Social capital, corporate culture, and incentive intensity. *RAND Journal of Economics, 33*, 243–257.

Romzek, B. S., & Dubnick, M. J. (1987). Accountability in the public sector: Lessons from the challenger tragedy. *Public Administration Review, 47*(3), 227–238.

Schott, C., Neumann, O., Baertschi, M., & Ritz, A. (2019). Public service motivation, prosocial motivation and altruism: Towards disentanglement and conceptual clarity. *International Journal of Public Administration, 42*(14), 1200–1211.

Shapiro, C., & Stiglitz, J. E. (1984). Equilibrium unemployment as a worker discipline device. *The American Economic Review, 74*(3), 433–444.

Simon, H. A. (2013). *Administrative behavior*. Simon and Schuster.

Sina News. (2005, November 17). *Why do central government orders sometimes not reach out of Zhongnanhai?* Viewed November 15, 2024. https://news.sina.com.cn/c/2005-11-17/05097459370s.shtml

Snape, H., & Wang, W. (2020). Finding a place for the Party: Debunking the "party-state" and rethinking the state-society relationship in China's one-party system. *Journal of Chinese Governance, 5*(4), 477–502.

Sobol, M. (2016). Principal–agent analysis and pathological delegation: The (almost) untold story. *Governance, 29*(3), 335–350.

Solow, R. M. (1979). Another possible source of wage stickiness. *Journal of Macroeconomics, 1*(1), 79–82.

Tamm, H., & Snidal, D. (2014). Rational choice and principal-agent theory. In Weiss, T. G., & Wilkinson, R. (Eds.), *International Organization and Global Governance* (pp. 132–143). Routledge.

Taylor, F. W. (1911). *The principles of scientific management*. Noton & Company.

Taylor, F. W. (1919). *The principles of scientific management*. Harper & Brothers.

Thompson, A. (2007). *Principal problems: UN weapons inspections in Iraq and beyond*. Alexander Thompson.

Tu, W. (2024). The interactive effect of extrinsic controls and public service motivation on blame avoidance. *Public Personnel Management*, 00910260241283549.

Tu, W., & Gong, T. (2022). Accountability intensity and bureaucrats' response to conflicting expectations: A survey experiment in China. *Public Management Review, 24*(11), 1779–1801.

Tu, W., Hsieh, C.-W., Chen, C.-A., & Wen, B. (2024). Public service motivation, performance-contingent pay, and job satisfaction of street-level bureaucrats. *Public Personnel Management, 53*(2), 256–280.

Tummers, L., & Bekkers, V. (2014). Policy implementation, street-level bureaucracy, and the importance of discretion. *Public Management Review, 16*(4), 527–547.

Tummers, L. L., Bekkers, V., Vink, E., & Musheno, M. (2015). Coping during public service delivery: A conceptualization and systematic review of

the literature. *Journal of Public Administration Research and Theory, 25*(4), 1099–1126.
Tummers, L., Steijn, B., & Bekkers, V. (2012). Explaining the willingness of public professionals to implement public policies: Content, context, and personality characteristics. *Public Administration, 90*(3), 716–736.
Van Loon, N. M., & Jakobsen, M. L. (2018). Connecting governance and the front lines: How work pressure and autonomy matter for coping in different performance regimes. *Public Administration, 96*(3), 435–451.
Vedung, E. (2015). Autonomy and street-level bureaucrats' coping strategies. *Nordic Journal of Studies in Educational Policy, 2015*(2), 28643.
Vlaicu, R., & Whalley, A. (2016). Hierarchical accountability in government. *Journal of Public Economics, 134*, 85–99.
Walder, A. G. (2006). The party elite and China's trajectory of change. In Brødsgaard, K. E., & Yongnian, Z. (Eds.), *The Chinese communist party in reform* (pp. 25–42). Routledge.
Waldo, D. (1952). Development of theory of democratic administration. *American Political Science Review, 46*(1), 81–103.
Wang, F., Wang, M., & Yin, H. (2022). Can campaign-style enforcement work: When and how? Evidence from straw burning control in China. *Governance, 35*(2), 545–564.
Weatherley, R., & Lipsky, M. (1977). Street-level bureaucrats and institutional innovation: Implementing special-education reform. *Harvard Educational Review, 47*(2), 171–197.
Weaver, R. K. (1986). The politics of blame avoidance. *Journal of Public Policy, 6*(4), 371–398.
Weber, M. (1978). *Economy and society: An outline of interpretive sociology (Vol. 1).* University of California press.
Wedeman, A. (2001). Incompetence, noise, and fear in central-local relations in China. *Studies in Comparative International Development, 35*, 59–83.
Weingast, B. R. (1984). The congressional-bureaucratic system: A principal agent perspective (with applications to the SEC). *Public Choice, 44*(1), 147–191.
Weingast, B. R., & Moran, M. J. (1983). Bureaucratic Discretion or Congressional Control? Regulatory Policymaking by the Federal Trade Commission. *Journal of Political Economy, 91*(5), 765–800.
West, W. F. (2004). Formal procedures, informal processes, accountability, and responsiveness in bureaucratic policy making: An institutional policy analysis. *Public Administration Review, 64*(1), 66–80.
White, T. (1990). Postrevolutionary mobilization in China: The one-child policy reconsidered. *World Politics, 43*(1), 53–76.
Whyte, M. K. (1973). Bureaucracy and modernization in China: The Maoist critique. *American Sociological Review, 38*, 149–163.

Willems, T., & Van Dooren, W. (2011). Lost in diffusion? How collaborative arrangements lead to an accountability paradox. *International Review of Administrative Sciences, 77*(3), 505–530.

Wilson, J. Q. (2019). *Bureaucracy: What government agencies do and why they do it*. Hachette UK.

Wood, B. D., & Waterman, R. W. (1991). The dynamics of political control of the bureaucracy. *American Political Science Review, 85*(3), 801–828.

Wu, H., Wang, X., & Chen, P. (2019). Coping with customer mistreatment: Joining job routinization and proactive personality. *Journal of Managerial Psychology, 34*(8), 519–532.

Zeng, Q. (2020). Managed campaign and bureaucratic institutions in China: Evidence from the targeted poverty alleviation program. *Journal of Contemporary China, 29*(123), 400–415.

Zhan, X., Lo, C.W.-H., & Tang, S.-Y. (2014). Contextual changes and environmental policy implementation: A longitudinal study of street-level bureaucrats in Guangzhou, China. *Journal of Public Administration Research and Theory, 24*(4), 1005–1035.

Zhang, J., & Gao, Y. (2008). Term limits and rotation of Chinese governors: Do they matter to economic growth? *Journal of the Asia Pacific Economy, 13*(3), 274–297.

Zhang, L., Zhao, J., & Dong, W. (2021). Street-level bureaucrats as policy entrepreneurs: Action strategies for flexible community governance in China. *Public Administration, 99*(3), 469–483.

Zhou, X. (2021). Chinese bureaucracy through three lenses: Weberian, Confucian, and Marchian. *Management and Organization Review, 17*(4), 655–682.

Zhou, X. (2022). *The logic of governance in China: An organizational approach*. Cambridge University Press.

Zhou, X., Ai, Y., Ge, J., Gu, H., Li, D., Li, L., Lu, Q., Zhao, W., & Zhu, L. (2021). The party–government relationship in the Chinese bureaucracy: Evidence from patterns of personnel flow. *Chinese Journal of Sociology, 7*(3), 315–346.

CHAPTER 3

Accountability Transformation in the Chinese Bureaucracy

The conventional conceptualization of accountability tends to associate accountability with electoral democracy, in which elections serve as the primary mechanism that allows the (powerless) public to hold (powerful) politicians accountable. "Accountability usually means that voters know, or can make good inferences about, what parties have done in office and reward or punish them conditional on these actions" (Stokes, 2005, p. 316). Under democratic arrangements, the citizens can remove corrupt politicians from office by voting, which constrains state power and enhances accountability (Ferraz & Finan, 2007; Held, 2004; Olsen, 2013). Elected politicians are thus legitimated to hold the unelected bureaucracy accountable for the implementation of policies, which is referred to as political accountability over the bureaucracy. Some scholars, thus, even claim that "no parliament means no accountability" (Jabbra & Dwivedi, 1988, p. 255).

China is characterized as a dominant political settlement in which one group or party maintains a prevailing influence over governance, policy-making, and institutional processes (Hu, 2017). In a dominant settlement, there is a significant gap between the power of the rulers and that of the ruled, suggesting that the accountability mechanisms in these countries are either inadequate or ineffective (Di John & Putzel, 2009; Khan, 2010). Since the check of power in China is not grounded on electoral politics, scholars view the country as lacking genuine accountability

W. Tu, *The Accountability Paradox in the Chinese Bureaucracy*,
https://doi.org/10.1007/978-981-96-6392-7_3

for its politicians and thus the bureaucracy. In a dominant political settlement without general elections, how does China hold its bureaucracy accountable? What forms of accountability does it employ? This chapter seeks to address these questions.

From a management perspective, democratic accountability is not the only institutional device to hold the government accountable. Scholars propose increasing forms of accountability in governance networks, for example, legal accountability, bureaucratic accountability, political accountability, professional accountability, market accountability, social accountability, and others (Bovens, 2007; Dowdle, 2006; Romzek & Dubnick, 2018). Some scholars suggest that, in the absence of a democratic mechanism, accountability in China can still be realized through alternative means, such as Party and state accountability (Hu, 2017), social or participatory accountability (Ma, 2012; Li et al., 2022), village-election accountability (Martinez-Bravo et al., 2011), and informal accountability through solidarity groups (Tsai, 2007).

This chapter sheds light on it from a macro-historical viewpoint, analyzing the accountability systems implemented from the Mao era to Xi's administration. Xi's leadership marks a turning point for the institutionalization of the accountability system, as it initiates a series of comprehensive reforms on the existing accountability framework. The Xi Era can be portrayed as a sanction-based political accountability system in which the Party plays a dominant role in controlling the bureaucracy. Four shifts are witnessed, that is, a shift from positive incentive to sanction-based incentive, a shift from campaign-style rectification to regulation-based accountability, a shift from internal, bureaucratic accountability to external political accountability, and a shift from one-level-down inspections to the central and skip-level inspections. In a nutshell, the Chinese accountability system has experienced a drastic transformation that substantially reshapes the whole institutional structure and bureaucratic behavior.

The Early Periods: A Campaign-Driven Moral Education

The primary approach to regulating bureaucrats during the Mao era is characterized by campaign-driven moral and ideological education. After the establishment of the new Chinese government, Mao recognized that the prevalence of bureaucratic inertia, excessive formalism, and bureaucratism within the government apparatus was undermining the revolutionary spirit and goals that he had envisioned for the new political system. Consequently, the CCP moved away from rationalizing political organizations and bureaucracy, as they believed that a regularized, bureaucratic structure dampened the enthusiasm of both the masses and public officials (Whyte, 1973). Through his revolutionary career, Mao gradually developed a novel understanding of moralism, focusing on the importance of morality and ideology in shaping the thoughts and actions of cadres. "Ideology provides the moral cement that not only arouses commitment but creates the cohesive forces which prevent the struggle from turning into disintegration" (Schurmann, 2022, p. xlii). To build a professional revolutionary party, Mao deployed ideological education as a major means of ensuring discipline, loyalty, and commitment among public officials and promoting self-sacrifice, commitment, and hard work for the cause of revolution and socialism (Gong, 2008; Li, 2001). Mao firmly believed that motivation is the driving force of moral energies, such as dedication, devotion, determination, faith, frugality, industry, and simplicity. Consciousness and motivation were mutually reinforced to motivate bureaucrats to work hard.

Recurrent political studies, criticism and self-criticism, moral education, and rectification campaigns were launched to foster revolutionary passions, moral ideals, and ideological values and thus to rectify bureaucratism, waste, commandism, and corruption (Zeng, 2020). Between 1949 and 1976, there were almost 67 political campaigns initiated, averaging 2.5 campaigns per year (C. Hu, 2017; G. Hu 2017). Holding bureaucrats accountable and disrupting the sluggish bureaucracy were the major goals of these numerous immense motivational reforms and organizational purges. For example, there are the "Rectification Campaigns" in the 1940s and 1950s, "the San-fan Campaign" in 1951–1952, the "New San-fan Campaign" in 1953, the "Wu-fan Campaign" in the 1960s, the "Socialist Education Movement under Revised Later Ten Points" in 1964, and the "Ideological Study Campaign" in 1965–1966 (Harding, 1981). The goal of these campaigns was to rectify ideological consciousness and traditional values to mobilize the whole nation's enthusiasm for the cause of revolution and socialism. At the same time, high moral standards, such as diligence, courage, altruism, self-discipline, and heroic sacrifice, were indoctrinated to inspire Party members and bureaucrats to work hard (Gong, 2008).

In terms of the specific modes of controlling bureaucracy, two primary approaches of control were adopted. One is criticism and self-criticism within the bureaucratic system (Harding, 1981). This involved encouraging bureaucrats to openly critique and reflect on their own shortcomings and mistakes, fostering a culture of accountability and continuous improvement within the government apparatus. The other is the mass mobilization of the public outside the bureaucracy to participate in criticizing and exposing malfeasance of bureaucrats (Gao & Su, 2018). This allowed the revolutionary leadership to harness the energy and participation of the masses to put pressure on the bureaucracy and hold officials accountable. Harding (1981) classifies four remedial approaches to address the problems of the bureaucracy in Mao's era along two-dimensional matrices of rationalization versus radicalism and internal versus external. Regularized internal remedialism refers to rational and routinized procedures implemented within the bureaucratic system to indoctrinate and train government cadres. Regular political rituals and group criticisms launched within organizations maximize the involvement of employees and help maintain comradely relations (Whyte, 1973). Radical internal remedialism broke the formal organizational structure and procedures and threw away writing rules and regulations to fuel bureaucrats' revolutionary zeal. Regularized external remedialism refers to "limited mass supervision of the bureaucracy within a formal organizational framework," such as the petition system (Harding, 1981, p. 331), while radical external remedialism gives the mass greater authority to monitor bureaucrats. Harding considers internal remedialism the core mechanism to reform the bureaucracy, while external remedialism is viewed as a complementary tactic. This is because the public's right to monitor the administrative apparatus was "not a right inherent in the people but one given them by the authority" (Meisner, 1999, p. 333).

In conclusion, due to the constraints of limited material resources and poor economic development in Mao's era, the primary accountability and control mechanisms employed to address bureaucratic problems did not rely on material incentives or institutional reforms. Instead, the focus was on ideological and moral education, achieved through disrupting the formal bureaucratic structure and mobilizing citizens in a campaign-style approach. However, the campaign-style mobilization during this period was overly radical, largely discarding rules and regulations, which exerts detrimental effects on the overall governmental system.

The Reform Years: Incentive-Based Bureaucratic Accountability

Due to the tendency to target an excessive number of cadres, the mass campaign-style accountability mechanisms in Mao's era caused disastrous organizational problems (Cai, 2014, p. 52). The scale of radical mass mobilization campaigns and ideological education in regulating bureaucrats' deviant behaviors has gradually waned since the reform and opening up initiated in the late 1970s. The Deng leadership recognized that the inspirational and motivational power of revolutionary ideology had diminished over time, and that formal bureaucratic institutions remained the indispensable mechanism for controlling and managing the bureaucracy (Lieberthal, 1995). Deng stressed that "rely on the masses, but do not launch campaign," and the replacement of "red" and revolutionary cadres by bureaucratic technocrats or experts signified an end to the campaign era (Lee, 1991). The process of disciplining officials became institutionalized and was handled systematically by specialized anti-corruption agencies following the reinstatement of the Ministry of Supervision and the CDIs.

China has experienced a significant and sustained economic boom for nearly three decades since the implementation of the reform and opening-up policies. Some scholars attribute the rapid rise of the Chinese economy to bureaucratic initiative and efficiency in policy implementation (Jing et al., 2015). After abandoning its primary reliance on ideological education, what measures did the Party utilize to incentivize bureaucrats and hold them accountable for their behavior? A significant change took place in the accountability system when the focus of the central government shifted from political loyalty to economic performance during the post-Mao era. The government since then put more emphasis on material and promotion incentives rather than ideological motivation, and local governments gained substantial discretionary power in boosting the local economy. The cadre management of this period is featured by a high-powered incentive model that closely ties officials' performance to material rewards and promotion incentives.

Fiscal Incentive

From the reform and opening-up period until 1993, the fiscal contracting system (*caizheng baogan*, 财政包干) is regarded as the main incentive for local officials to boost local economic development in order to increase revenue collection (Jin et al., 2005; Lin & Liu, 2000). During the 1980s, the Chinese fiscal arrangement shifted from a unitary system, where the central government had absolute control over revenue collection and budget allocation, to a more decentralized system that allowed for revenue sharing between central and local governments (Lin & Liu, 2000). From then on, the central and local governments began to "eat in separate kitchens" (*fenzao chifan,* 分灶吃饭) with fiscal revenue and expenditure being clearly divided into the sub-national and central levels. Local governments were allowed to retain a portion of the revenues they collected to afford local investment, remuneration, and the delivery of public goods and services (Shen et al., 2012; Wong, 1992).

Although the control from the center has been impaired, many studies and considerable empirical evidence indicate that local governments, as the residual claimants of revenues in the fiscal contracting system, have strong incentives to invest in infrastructure construction and preserve the market rather than rent-seeking (Montinola et al., 1995; Oi, 1992; Qian & Weingast, 1997). While the central government's share of the total revenue decreased from 40.5 percent to 22 percent over the period 1984–1993 (Zhang, 2006), the Chinese economy has increased at a rate of about 10% annually since the launching of the economic reforms in 1978 (Lin & Liu, 2000).

Oi (1992) proposes the term "local state corporatism" to describe the role of local governments as akin to that of a board of directors in a business corporation. Qian and Weingast (1997) argue that Chinese local governments capture the features of "market-preserving" federalism, enabling sub-national governments to limit state revenue predation and therefore retain financial resources for economic growth. Fiscal decentralization has granted local governments discretion to establish strong incentives for local officials to prioritize economic development within their jurisdictions (Oi, 1992, p. 100).

The retention of a portion of the increased revenues also means that local governments have more financial flexibility to allocate funds for compensation and bonuses. Based on Ang's (2020, pp. 107–108) study of Shandong province, formal wages remained relatively stable, while fringe compensation nearly doubled between 1979 and 1993, during the implementation of the fiscal contracting system. There is a much greater regional variation in fringe compensation, with the maximum disparity reaching 26 times. Wealthier local governments, which have higher tax revenues, significantly compensate their staff more. A profit-sharing practice is established in which the taxes paid by enterprises are directly linked to the benefits received by bureaucrats, which effectively shows local officials that increasing economic growth and tax revenue is the most reliable way to ensure substantial compensation (Ang, 2020, pp. 100–101).

Therefore, although the control of the center over local officials was undermined in this period, by tying local officials' financial incentives to revenue generation, the system enhances local cadres' entrepreneurship and work morale in boosting economic prosperity. Local officials were granted substantial autonomy to carry out fiscal functions, and successful revenue generation and economic performance can result in bonuses or salary increases, aligning their interests with accountability.

Political Tournament Among Party and State Leaders

The tax-sharing system replaced the fiscal contracting system in 1994 to recentralize fiscal management, which undermines local governments' share of fiscal revenue. However, as the fiscal incentives decline, the momentum of local officials to boost economic development does not wane. Scholars consider that a promotion tournament based on the growth of GDP has become the primary incentive for officials, especially those in leadership positions (Li et al., 2019; Zhou, 2022). Specifically, the promotion tournament system incentivizes local officials to launch initiatives and work diligently to boost the local economy by directly linking their career advancement to their economic achievements.

This system encourages local leaders of the same rank across different regions to engage in fierce competition with each other in terms of their economic performance in order to secure promotion (Cai & Treisman, 2006; Landry et al., 2018; Sachs & Woo, 2001). While some scholars have questioned the validity of the tournament model, there is abundant empirical evidence confirming the validity of the political tournament around GDP growth (Bai & Li, 2022; Choi, 2012; Li & Zhou, 2005). Scholars reveal that GDP growth among cadres, the average economic performance over their tenure, the relative economic performance compared with their counterparts, and the relative economic performance in comparison with the former leader are positively related to the local leader's promotion (Landry et al., 2018; Li & Zhou, 2005; Yao & Zhang, 2015). The promotion incentives effectively aligned the central government's preferences with those of local authorities, which ensured the implementation of the central directives and boosted their entrepreneurial spirit in boosting local prosperity.

Cadre Responsibility System

Within the bureaucratic framework, the government also introduced various administrative measures and institutional reforms to improve top-down accountability among low-level governments or ordinary officials. An influential accountability mechanism was deployed to ensure the effective operation of bureaucracy, that is, the "target-based performance management" (*mubiao zerenzhi, 目标责任制*) or cadre responsibility system. Echoing the NPM paradigm promoting performance measurement systems, the Chinese bureaucracy has adopted the cadre responsibility system since the mid-1980s. The central Chinese authorities have decentralized many government functions to local agencies while focusing primarily on setting macro-level reform objectives (Edin, 2003). Within the performance measurement system, the goals of the central government are converted into specific policy objectives and distributed downwards through the administrative hierarchy and local governments sign performance contracts with subordinate government organizations (Gao, 2009; Jing et al., 2015). These contracts charted by the upper-level authority outline concreted targets, indicators, and points used to evaluate the performance of the lower-level agencies, and the leaders of each organization are held accountable for their performance accordingly (Gao, 2015).

The cadre responsibility system endows higher-level agencies the authority to nominate, appoint, transfer, and remove cadres at lower levels, leading to compliance and the active attainment of targets from subordinates (Chan & Gao, 2008; Gao, 2009). Whiting (2017) describes township and village officials' strong motives to boost the rural industry on account of political and pecuniary incentives. She underscores the primacy of economic indicators in the cadre evaluation system and the subsequent material rewards in the form of a bonus if the targets are attained successfully. Both the budget of an organization and the remuneration of cadres are closely associated with their organizational performance (Zhou, 2017).

Besides "carrots," "sticks" are paired to strengthen the potency of the cadre responsibility system. Normally, low-level governments are required to complete targets within a specified time and are subject to random inspections from upper-level authorities and punishment if targets are not accomplished (Gao, 2010). For example, some of the targets in responsibility contracts are hard targets (*yingzhibiao,* 硬指标) with veto power, and failure to accomplish any of them would negate all the other fulfilled achievements. Once a veto is issued, the organization may face negative consequences. Some punishments are light, such as pay deductions and benefit cuts; others are moderate, such as criticism, notification, and demerits; and still others are very severe, such as demotion and even dismissal. The veto measure was first applied in the 1980s to the implementation of the one-child policy. For example, Guizhou province stipulated that units subjected to the vote in the implementation of the one-child policy directives would face the following consequences: Revocation of the unit's honorary titles and qualification for commendations and awards; individuals would be barred from receiving honorary titles, being considered for commendations and awards, and from promotions for the party secretary and the head in the unit. For units that have been vetoed for two consecutive years, the party secretary and the head would be subject to dismissal or demotion (Chinese Government Website, 2007). Thus, Establishing clear objectives along with strong incentives, whether through rewards or penalties, motivates grassroots officials to diligently achieve the targets set by higher authorities.

Although the cadre responsibility system seems to enforce harsh penalties on government officials, its actual application is mainly driven by reward-based outcomes and lenient punishments. In China, the interests and responsibilities of the superior governments and the immediate lower-level agencies are closely connected. The high reliance of the superior government on the collaboration and expertises of their lower-level agencies to accomplish tasks makes them cautious in meting out punitive measures (Zang, 2017; Zhou et al., 2013). Scholars identify a phenomenon of "collusion" between local governments and their direct superior authorities, where the latter conceals the poor performance of the former and strategically collaborates with them to navigate and respond to policies, laws, regulations, and inspections from the next higher level (Zhou, 2010). Therefore, in the bureaucratic system, very few officials are actually subject to administrative sanction unless they fail to achieve critical hard targets or cause serious consequences for the society, while the accomplishment of tasks indeed ensures material rewards and potential career advancement.

Despite the hierarchical downward pressure from the central government, local bureaucratic agencies and officials still maintain a significant degree of discretion and autonomy in how they interpret, implement, and achieve the prescribed policy targets (Edin, 2003). Local officials are reported to selectively execute tasks that are more quantitatively measurable and prominent in the eye of superior authority (O'Brien & Li, 2017), to "muddle through" by adopting improvised coping strategies and focusing on short-term, incremental gains (Zhou et al., 2013), and to symbolic implement policies by establishing image projects (Cai, 2004).

Weak Legal and Regulatory Framework for Accountability

The cadre responsibility system functions as an actual mechanism to hold government officials accountable for their performance within the bureaucracy during this period. It is more of a management and maneuverable mechanism of accountability, while a formal legal and regulatory framework for accountability has not been established. The concept of accountability was not formally introduced in China until the start of the twenty-first century. CDIs primarily investigated crimes regarding economic corruption and serious dereliction of duty. Therefore, a large number of administrative actions that breached laws or regulations but did not constitute crimes went unpunished during the 1980s and 1990s.

In 2003, the central government held accountable some cadres in leadership positions for their poor performance in the fight against the SARS epidemic, marking the starting point of China's accountability system. After SARS, a series of disastrous social incidents occurred continuously, such as the 2005 Songhua River pollution incident, the 2008 melamine-tainted milk powder scandal, the 2010 Shanghai Jing'an fire incident, and the 2011 Wenzhou train collision. These high-profile incidents generated sustained public outcry, imposing pressure on the government to take action and ensure that the officials involved face consequences for their poor performance, bad decisions, or negligence. Within 10 years since 2003, almost 20 officials at the vice ministerial-level officials or above were held accountable for the occurrence of grand disastrous accidents or mass incidents. Most of them were subject to bureaucratic accountability (*xingzheng wenze,* 行政问责), such as administrative warning, demerit, or dismissal.

Both the central government and local governments have expedited the establishment of accountability systems. In 2005, the General Office of the State Council issued the "*Several Opinions of the State Council on Pushing Forward the Administrative Law Enforcement Responsibility System*" (《国务院办公厅关于推行行政执法责任制的若干意见》). In 2009, the Chinese Communist Party Central Committee (CCPCC) and the General Office of the State Council jointly released the "*Interim Provision on the Implementation of the Accountability System for the Leaders of the Party and Government*" (《关于实行党政领导干部问责的暂行规定》, *IPIAS*), which is the first official regulation on accountability system issued by the central government. The regulation applies to the leadership members of the departments and their internal institutions of the CCPCC and the State Council; leadership members of the departments of the local party committees and governments at or above the county level. Accountability measures would be imposed on party and government leaders in any of the seven situations, including serious decision-making errors, negligence leading to major accidents within the jurisdiction, and improper handling of mass incidents or emergencies. The provision seeks to enhance the sense of leadership responsibility among Party and state leaders, holding them accountable for significant accidents within their jurisdiction. In 2008, Hu Jintao stressed the importance of speeding up the adoption of performance management systems and accountability measures for government officials, calling for stricter investigations and accountability for dereliction of duty and abuse of power (Zhang & Wang, 2023).

Many local governments, including Changsha City, Tianjin City, Chongqing City, Hainan City, and Shenzhen City, have issued interim measures for bureaucratic accountability to ensure that bureaucrats are held responsible for their administrative actions. The regulations regarding accountability include those that directly target the local chief executives, such as the "Interim Measures on Accountability of Chief Executives of Government Departments in Chongqing" (《重庆市政府部门行政首长问责暂行办法》) and those that target ordinary civil servants, such as the "Measures on Accountability of the Administrative Inaction of State Organs and Their Personnel in Taiyuan City" (《太原市国家机关及其工作人员行政不作为问责办法》). Some regulations targeted specific areas, such as the "Interim Measures on the Accountability for Work Safety Production in Foshan City" (《佛山市安全生产问责制暂行

办法》). While these measures emphasize rule compliance, they also highlight the importance of administrative efficiency and performance. In 2005, the "Measures for Holding Accountable the Actions Affecting the Efficiency of Government Agencies in Zhejiang Province" (《浙江省影响机关工作效能行为责任追究办法》) was introduced, institutionalizing an "efficiency revolution." The peak period for local governments and departments to issue regulations regarding accountability was between 2004 and 2007, with the number of policies introduced reaching nearly a hundred (Zhang & Wang, 2023).

The promulgation of these accountability regulations is a response to citizens' dissatisfaction with the serious misconduct and inaction of public officials concerning public interests, prompting the central government to recognize the severity of agency problems. Within the cadre responsibility system, public officials tend to prioritize satisfying their immediate superiors over being accountable to the demands of the public. Faced with pressure to meet various performance indicators from higher-ups, some lower-level governments even resort to illegal tactics or harsh measures to enforce citizen compliance, significantly eroding public trust in the government.

During this period, bureaucratic accountability was a key focus, operating alongside intra-party accountability systems. Although the accountability regulations and policies appear strong in theory, their actual implementation is often limited. These regulations primarily target cadres in leadership positions, while the everyday misconduct of regular officials often goes unpunished. Additionally, accountability mechanisms are typically activated only after significant safety crises or large-scale incidents, holding specific leaders and officials responsible for managing the crisis. In comparison to the severity and negative outcomes of these high-profile incidents, the resulting punishments tend to be quite lenient. Occasionally, cadres who had previously been held accountable were reinstated or promoted to new positions, leading to widespread public outrage. For example, Junkai Bao, the former Deputy Director of the Food Production Supervision Department of the General Administration of Quality Supervision, Inspection and Quarantine (AQSIQ), received a serious reprimand from the local CDI for being the key responsible official in the 2008 melamine-tainted milk powder scandal. Following this reprimand, he was reported by the media to have been transferred to serve as the Director and Party Secretary of the Anhui Entry-Exit Inspection and Quarantine Bureau, with an administrative rank elevated by half a level. Following heated discussions and public dissatisfaction, the AQSIQ then reassigned him back to the headquarters as Deputy Director of the Science and Technology Department, just under two months after the punishment was issued.

In summary, over the past three decades since China's reform and opening up, the central government has primarily concentrated on achieving rapid economic growth and fulfilling various development targets. To support this economic agenda, local officials were given considerable discretion to apply their expertise and knowledge in interpreting and implementing policies at the local level. Local officials faced inadequate oversight and accountability for misconduct or malpractice, while they were generally assured of material rewards as long as they achieved the objectives set by their superiors, regardless of the means employed to reach those goals. With strong positive incentives, such as financial rewards and opportunities for career advancement, along with relatively weak supervision and penalties, local government bureaucrats exhibited significant enthusiasm and entrepreneurial spirit in fostering economic development within their jurisdictions (Jing et al., 2015).

However, within this performance-driven system, some local government officials even resort to illegal tactics to ensure the completion of tasks and directives from higher authorities, ignoring the grievances and concerns of citizens (Cai, 2014; O'Brien & Li, 2017). This leads to selective enforcement or aggressive law enforcement that undermines citizens' interests. For example, when land acquisition and demolition were the primary "hard target" of local governments, local officials resorted to almost all possible means, including water stoppage, power outages, threats, intimidation, and the forced demolition of residential houses, to complete their task of demolition (*Beijing Times*, 2014). Rampant corruption and various types of malfeasance among local authorities caused growing social tensions (Cai, 2014; Sun, 2001). A considerable number of collective actions burst out, and leapfrog petitions were sparked by local agents' misconduct (Cai, 2008). Reportedly, the number of collective actions increased ten times from 8700 in 1993 and 87,000 in 2005 to 187,000 in 2012 (Wedeman, 2016).

The Xi Era: Sanction-Based Political Accountability

The Deng period was characterized by cycles of decentralization and loosening up, and the subsequent Jiang and Hu administrations have also granted local authorities substantial discretionary power. The rise of Xi to power has been marked by a series of efforts by the political center to re-tighten the reins of power to overcome the fragmentation and social unrest that arose from excessive decentralization (Schubert & Alpermann, 2019). The Third Plenum of the 18th Central Committee of the CCP (2013) marked a turning point where the Chinese leadership acknowledged the need to move away from the previous high-speed, GDP-driven development approach, and instead sought to reorient the governance framework by placing more emphasis on social and political imperatives (People's Daily Online, 2013).

Since then, Xi's administration mainly concentrated on preserving its unitary leadership and strengthening the command-and-control capacity of the central government (Guo, 2017). Agenda-setting and policy-making processes have become centralized at the central government evidenced by the rhetoric "top-down design" and an "overall plan." Furthermore, "implementation has been subject to stricter control at each level by the superior authorities, with considerable interference - 'hard steering,' as we call it - from the center" (Schubert & Alpermann, 2019, p. 200). The accountability system has undergone substantial transformation, with the aim of empowering the party committees and political-legal institutions to oversee and discipline the bureaucracy.

A Shift from Positive Incentives to Sanction-Based Consequences

Both the role of promotion and material incentives in influencing bureaucratic behavior have been weakened in Xi's administration. First, Xi emphasizes many times and in various situations that a high-speed, GDP-driven development approach should be forsaken. At the national work conference in June 2013, Xi called for a more comprehensive approach to performance evaluation and assessment at the national work conference. He emphasized the need to look beyond just economic development and visible results, and also consider the underlying foundation and potential performance. Specifically, he stated that metrics related to improving people's livelihoods, social progress, and environmental sustainability should be included as important indicators, rather than relying solely on GDP growth rate as the primary measure of distinguished cadres (People's Daily Online, 2014). Although he stressed that GDP growth should not be the sole or primary measure used to assess performance, he also acknowledged that GDP cannot be completely disregarded. However, in the year following the Third Plenary Session of the 18th CPC Central Committee, more than 70 municipalities or counties across China canceled the use of GDP evaluation altogether (China National Radio Website, 2014). It is quite typical in China for local governments to take more radical action in advancing specific policy priorities set by the central leadership, a phenomenon characterized as "downward acceleration of implementation pressures level by level" (*cengceng jiama,* 层层加码) (Zhou & Lian, 2020).

Under Xi's leadership, the abandonment of economic performance as the primary indicator for evaluating officials has made the political tournament system and cadre responsibility system less clear-cut, reducing the direct link between officials' measurable performance and their promotion prospects. Furthermore, the introduction of additional important indicators centered on people's livelihoods and social progress is challenging to measure accurately and is more susceptible to manipulation.

The role of material incentives is also largely attenuated by Xi's anti-corruption rectification. The wage structure of Chinese public officials primarily consists of two parts: formal wages and fringe compensation (Ang, 2020). Formal wage is paid according to the standardized wage system that is primarily based on their official positions and ranks, which varies little across departments and regions. By contrast, fringe compensation that is determined by local government tax revenue and each agency's "small coffers" (*xiaojinku,* 小金库) varies widely across regions and departments. Under the tax-sharing system in China, local governments are permitted to retain a portion of the tax revenue, and the majority of China's taxes come from business-related taxes. As a result, expanding the tax base for local governments primarily involves attracting and incentivizing businesses to operate within their jurisdictions to secure generous compensation and perks for local officials.

Corrupt transactions between the government and business became a major target under Xi's powerful anti-corruption storm. In this circumstance, bureaucrats were deterred away from government-business cooperation and even avoided meeting with entrepreneurs in case of being implicated in corruption investigations (Wang, 2022). The relationship between public officials and businessmen was reported to have shifted from a "shoulder to shoulder" (*goujian dabei,* 勾肩搭背) dynamic to a "back against back" (*beiduibei,* 背对背) dynamic, a metaphor suggesting an adversarial, disconnected engagement between government officials and businessmen (CPC News, 2015). Furthermore, the anti-corruption campaign has led to a more standardized and regulated use of government funds, as officials will be held accountable for not using up the funds within the prescribed time, but they may risk making mistakes or being investigated for corruption if they perform too much (Hope et al., 2020). In this regard, local officials' enthusiasm for promoting the local economy has dampened, leading to a decrease in local government revenue and officials' compensation.

The "eight-point code" (*baxiang guiding,* 八项规定) initiated by the Political Bureau of the Central Committee of the CPC in 2012 further comprehensively regulates the use of government funds. Numerous small coffers regarded as "organizational corruption" were cracked down. In May 2013, the Ministry of Supervision issued the "*Provisions on Disciplinary Actions for the Granting of Allowances and Subsidies in Violation of Regulations*" (《违规发放津贴补贴行为处分规定》). Since then, many local governments have suspended performance-based rewards for civil servants, and some even required officials to return previously issued bonuses (CB-2021-31). In 2018, the General Office of the CCPCC and the General Office of the State Council issued the "*Notice on Strictly Prohibiting the Self-Issuance of Policies to Distribute Salaries, Allowances and Subsidies*" (《关于严禁自行出台政策发放工资津贴补贴有关问题的通知》). The notice stipulates that 12 categories of allowances and subsidies for civil servants will be canceled, including overtime pay, on-duty allowances, and free vacation.

As a result, the source of funds originally used to boost officials' compensation was completely severed, and the fringe compensation was officially defined as organizational corruption. The tacit profit-sharing model suggested by Ang (2020) has been abolished. Since the 1980s, various perks, including overtime pay, bonuses, free meals, free vacations, subsidized housing, entertainment allowances, and daily necessities such as food, electricity, and gas, have served as implicit practices to supplement bureaucrats' paltry formal salaries and also aligned financial incentives with their performance. Eliminating perks is a significant step to control the previously excessive position-related consumption (*sangong xiaofei,* 三公消费) and curb organizational corruption. However, this move also dampens bureaucrats' work morale. A department leader said, "after the overtime pay was canceled, public employees left as soon as they clocked out" (CB-2024-31). The anti-corruption campaign has diminished bureaucrats' morale due to the removal of certain welfare and bonus benefits.

As the promotion and material incentive mechanisms have become increasingly weakened, higher-level authorities can only rely on stricter monitoring and punishment to mobilize their subordinates. This implies that the high-powered incentive mechanism closely linking officials' economic performance with their compensation and career advancement has been replaced by sanction-based mechanisms. The shift in the assessment and accountability system disrupts the established career development paths for officials within the bureaucratic system. Officials tend to shift the focus from administrative tasks and economic development to political objectives and tasks, resulting in lower administrative efficiency.

A Shift from Campaign-Style Rectification to Regulation-Based Accountability

The increased monitoring and punishment of officials' malfeasance were primarily implemented through Party disciplinary mechanisms rather than through the legal or administrative systems. The CCP leaders put much emphasis on Party building and proposed to comprehensively strengthen the discipline of the Party (*quanmian congyan zhidang*, 全面从严治党) (People's Daily Online, 2015). The measures, such as the "eight-point code" and the "clean-up of four undesirable work styles" (*fan sifeng*, 反四风) in the form of formalism, bureaucratism, hedonism, and extravagance were introduced by the Party Central Committee rather than by the supreme legislative body, the National People's Congress (NPC), as an additional set of Party disciplinary codes (Yuen, 2014), and the CCDI is in charge of enforcing them. In China, the Ministry of Supervision (MS) and the CCDI work jointly and share the same staffs under separate titles (*heshu bangong*, 合署办公), while the MS as a department of the State Council is responsible for fighting corruption and malfeasance among civil servants, and the CCDI as a Party organ is in charge of disciplining the Party members. Since the majority of civil servants are members of the CCP, strengthening Party discipline means reinforcing the Party's control over the entire bureaucratic system.

The first endeavor of the central authority to improve the disciplinary mechanisms was to amend a series of critical regulations. In October 2014, the Fourth Plenary Session of the Eighteenth Central Committee proposed to comprehensively advance the rule of law and required the Party to govern in accordance with the laws. In 2015, the CCP leadership amended three significant regulations, as follows: *the CCP Regulation Regarding On-Site Inspections* (《中国共产党巡视工作条例》), *the CCP Principles on Integrity and Self-Discipline* (《中国共产党廉洁自律准则》), and *the Chinese Communist Party Regulation on Party Discipline* (《中国共产党纪律处分条例》), which lay the foundation and provide guidance for disciplining officials.

The *On-Site Inspection* provides institutional guidance for the responsibility allocation of inspections and enhances the leading position of the Central Inspection Groups over the local inspection work (Chinese Government Website, 2015). The *Integrity and Self-Discipline* extends its scope of application from leading cadres to all the Party members, indicating the effort to comprehensively strengthen the discipline of the whole Party. It is the first basic rule that faces all the Party members and strengthens the integrity and self-discipline of the whole Party (CCDI Website, 2015). The amended *Regulation on Party Discipline* added six "negative lists" (*fumian qingdan,* 负面清单), which specifies the types of misconduct that Party members are prohibited from engaging in, across six key disciplinary areas: political discipline, organizational discipline, integrity discipline, mass discipline, work discipline, and daily life discipline (CPC Member Website, 2015). It also institutionalizes certain practices that have been used to strengthen Party discipline, such as the eight-point code and the purging of four undesirable work styles. It represents the most comprehensive and stringent set of Party rules since the reform and opening up.

In 2016, two amended regulations further strengthened supervision and accountability among the Party. The first is the *Regulations on intra-party supervision* (《中国共产党党内监督条例》). It clearly establishes the significant role of the central Party organizations in strengthening the supervision of the Party. It also clarifies the responsibilities of the CCDI in carrying out internal Party supervision, and the supervision and management relationship between the local CDIs, the local Party committees, and the upper-level disciplinary bodies. This regulation, on the whole, serves to consolidate the power of supervision and oversight firmly within the Politburo and the CCDI. The other one is the *Regulation of the Chinese Communist Party on Accountability* (《中国共产党问责条例》, *RCCPA*). This regulation, developed from the *Interim Provisions on the Implementation of Accountability of the Party and Government Leading Cadres*, is a more authoritative and systematic regulation within the Party. It provides institutional guidance for the Party's accountability mechanisms, stipulating that any dereliction of duty or negligence must be held accountable, and the punishment must be strict. Notably, the regulation introduces a "lifelong accountability" mechanism (*zhongshen zhuize*, 终身追责), stipulating that those who are responsible for serious dereliction of duty and grave consequences should be held accountable indefinitely, even if they have been transferred to other positions, promoted, or retired.

I conducted a word cloud analysis by conducting a comparison between the RCCPA regulation and the IPIAS. The former is the most significant regulation related to accountability in Xi's era, while the latter was in effect before Xi. A word cloud is a method of visualizing word frequency in a corpus of texts, where the size of the words represents the frequency of mentions, and the most dominant words are placed at the center. Word clouds help identify the focus and priorities of the accountability system during different periods. The left side of Fig. 3.1 displays the word cloud of the RCCPA, while the right side shows the IPIAS. The most frequent words of the RCCPA include Party organizations (*dang zuzhi,* 党组织), responsibility (*zeren,* 责任), and discipline (*jilv,* 纪律). The most frequent words of the IPIAS consist of Party and government (*dangzheng,* 党政), personnel organizations (*renshi bumen,* 人事部门), and management (*guanli,* 管理). It shows that political accountability imposed by Party organizations, which focuses on discipline, outweighs bureaucratic accountability carried out by administrative branches that emphasizes managerial performance under Xi's administration.

Besides these basic and critical regulations, the central government issued other important decrees to regulate and discipline public officials, including the *Chinese Communist Party Regulations on the Draft of Laws and Regulations within the Party* (《中国共产党党内法规制定条例》), *Regulations on the Selecting and Appointing of Party and Government Leading Cadres* (《党政领导干部选拔任用工作条例》), and *Provisions on the Reporting of Individual Matters of Leading Cadres* (《领导干部报告个人有关事项规定》). By 2021, a total of 146 intra-party regulations had been issued or amended, including those mentioned above (Gong & Tu, 2022). The sheer volume and detail of these new and amended Party

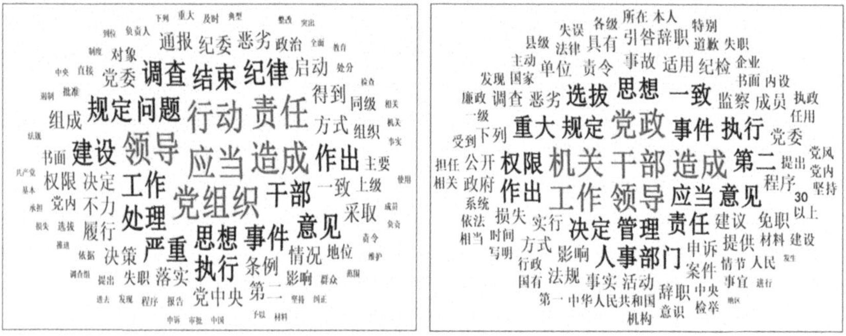

Fig. 3.1 Word cloud of official regulations on accountability

regulations indicate that the CCP leadership is making a concerted effort to exert tighter control and more heightened accountability over its Party members and local authorities. The following part elaborates on the transformation of organizational settings and the implementation of these decrees. Through this, the CCP tightens its grip on the bureaucracy as a whole.

A Shift from Internal Bureaucratic Accountability to External Political Accountability

The supervisory agencies have been restructured in order to strengthen the Party's absolute leadership in combating officials' malfeasance and to centralize supervisory authority over cadres. The reorganization was achieved by transforming the multi-agency structure into a single centralized anti-corruption agency model, with the establishment of the National Supervisory Commission system (*guojia jiancha weiyuanhu, 国家监察委员会, NSC*) as an overarching state organ to oversee all individuals who exercise public power. Before 2018, China had a multi-track anti-corruption and supervisory system, characterized by the coexistence of several major systems tackling corruption, including the discipline inspection system of the CCP, the state supervision system under the Ministry of Supervision, and the anti-corruption force of the People's Procuratorate. Frictions and conflicts among these disciplinary and legal institutions were rife, and overlapping or redundant investigations undermined the efficiency of anti-corruption work. After the structural reform, the NSC absorbed the anti-corruption forces of the procuratorate system and the Ministry of Supervision and became the dominant supervisory body. As a matter of fact, the NSC conducts collaborative operations and shares personnel resources with the CCDI (*heshu bangong,* 合署办公).

The restructuring of supervisory agencies is not merely an organizational reshuffling, but rather a much more fundamental transformation in the position and nature of supervisory agencies within the broader state apparatus. The NSC is listed as a state organ in Chapter Three of the constitutional amendment passed in March 2018, which established the legal status of the Supervisory Commission and provided a constitutional basis for it to exercise its supervisory powers in accordance with the law. The first supervision law titled *the Supervision Law of the People's Republic of China (《中华人民共和国监察法》)* was enacted in the same year that substantially transformed the landscape of Chinese accountability. The law clearly stipulates that the supervision and accountability of public officials in administrative agencies falls under the purview and responsibilities of the supervisory agencies. The crucial change is the addition of the NSC as the fourth pillar alongside the existing State Council (the administrative branch), the Supreme People's Court, and the Supreme People's Procuratorate, forming China's overarching institutional framework as "one government with one commission and two courts" (*yifu liangyuan yiwei,* 一府两院一委), replacing the previous "one government with two courts" (*yifu liangyuan,*一府两院). This new institutional configuration elevates the status of the National SC as the highest-level supervisory agency, placing it on par with the State Council, reflecting the enhanced supervisory and investigative power granted to this new anti-corruption agency.

The CCP leaders position the NSC and local Supervisory Commissions (SC) as political institutions specialized in oversight and supervisory accountability (*jiancha wenze,* 监察问责). Crucially, these supervisory bodies are designed to be independent from the administrative apparatus of the government. This structural change led to a transformation in China's accountability system, shifting it from being primarily an internal bureaucratic issue managed within the administrative branch to an externally imposed political accountability mechanism. The politically oriented SCs now serve as dominant, independent watchdogs with the power to scrutinize, investigate, and discipline officials across the entire government structure. While the NSC is officially a state organ elected by the National People's Congress (NPC), in practice it is accountable to and reports directly to the CCP Central Committee and only reports its special work to the NPC due to it works jointly with the Party's internal disciplinary body, CCDI. Therefore, in essence, the restructuring is a strategic move to consolidate and centralize the Party's grip over the bureaucratic machinery, while also potentially creating new tensions between the various state organs. The discretionary power of the administrative branch has been significantly undermined under the supervision of SCs.

Officials in SCs are required to apply the "four forms of supervision and discipline enforcement" (*jiandu zhiji sizhong xingtai*, 监督执纪四种形态) in their routine work (Li & Wang, 2019). The first form involves the regular conduct of criticism and self-criticism, including timely reminders, advisory conversations, educational criticism, and self-reflection to effectively ensure daily supervision. The second form is mild disciplinary punishments including warnings and serious warnings. The third form is heavy disciplinary punishments and significant position adjustments including the revocation of party positions, probation within the party, and expulsion from the party, which applies to serious disciplinary violations. The fourth form is serious disciplinary violations involving criminal charges. This form is the most serious punishment including expulsion from the party, termination of public office, and referral to judicial authorities for criminal prosecution when involves alleged criminal charges. The four forms of working mechanism aim to enhance daily supervision and prevent officials from engaging in serious disciplinary violations and duty crimes, thereby gradually reducing the application of form three and four punishments (Li, 2019). It also indicates that the supervisory scope is not limited to duty crimes such as bribery, dereliction of duty, and abuse of power, but is expanded to certain minor breaches of Party discipline, rules, and regulations.

Besides the establishment of the national supervisory organ, the dual-leadership structure of local CDIs is also transformed, which further strengthens the centralization of supervisory authority. Prior to the reform, local CDIs were subject to the authority of both the Party Committees in their localities and the upper-level discipline inspection organs. They relied significantly on the local Party Committees for personnel and financial support, which may hamper their independence and efficacy in monitoring the activities of local party officials. Since the Third Plenum of the 18th Party Congress resolved to amend the dual-leadership structure in 2013, the influence of local Party Committees over disciplinary agencies has waned, while the vertical control of higher-up anti-corruption agencies over CDIs has been strengthened. The authority of upper-level CDIs takes precedence over that of local Party Committees in investigations of corruption and the selection and promotion of CDI officials (Yuen, 2014). Specifically, local CDIs are now required to report ongoing investigations mainly to the higher-level anti-corruption agencies. The adoption of the system of vertical appointment of CDI officials has reduced the interference of local Party Committees with anti-corruption work.

With the institutionalization and reinforcement of intra-party accountability and supervisory accountability, the status of administrative power and bureaucratic accountability has been weakened. The number of officials or cases held accountable within the administrative bureaucracy has shown a significant downward trend, while local SCs play an increasingly dominant role in holding bureaucrats accountable for their violation of rules, dereliction of duty, and infringement of public interests. In a word, political accountability in the form of intra-party accountability and supervisory accountability is highly strengthened with more focus on compliance with Party discipline, regulations, and rules.

A Shift from One-Level-Down Inspections to Central and Skip-Level Inspections

The Xi's administration has pushed the Party and Central's supervisory tentacles downward the government hierarchy. Top-down supervision has swept across all parts of the Party-state bureaucracy. The Party committee uses inspection tours (巡视, *xunshi*) and stationing teams (派驻, *paizhu*) as tools to detect and investigate suspected corruption and other malfeasance in government institutions and public organizations including state-owned enterprises, universities, and public hospitals (Gong & Tu, 2022). Inspection tours are organized periodically by the Central Committee of the Party and the provincial, autonomous region, and municipal committees to oversee the party organizations in the localities, departments, enterprises, and public institutions under its management. The central government conducted 12 rounds of inspections of some centrally managed enterprises and provinces from 2013 to 2017 (Carothers & Zhang, 2023). At the same time, stationing teams have been dispatched by the CCDI and NSC to central Party and state organs to inspect discipline. It has been reported that the CCDI and NSC achieved full coverage of inspection over the 140 Party and state organs at the central level, with 52 stationing teams (Gong & Tu, 2022). Local CDIs and SCs have also dispatched their own inspection teams to detect and rectify wrongdoing in the Party and government organs at the same or lower levels. These top-down inspections have a deterrent effect, as the inspecting teams are empowered to launch full-scale investigations and can recommend penalties in cases of corruption or other political and administrative misconduct.

Furthermore, the municipal and county Party committees also dispatch inspection and supervision teams to conduct inspection tours (*xuncha*, 巡察) of the lower-level Party and government organs on a regular basis. Such inspections have led to the exposure of collective corruption among high-ranking officials in Shanxi province, for example. Some innovative approaches were adopted to boost the efficiency of supervision. For example, skip-level inspections (*tiji xuncha*, 提级巡察) deployed by some municipal party committees allow the inspection teams to directly oversee and investigate two levels down party and government entities. In 2023, the Xi'an municipal party committee comprehensively launched skip-level inspections of the party organizations in some of the districts, counties, villages, and communities.

Skip-level inspections serve as a proactive attempt to overcome the information asymmetry in monitoring grassroots officials. The cadre management of the Chinese government has been characterized by "one-level-down management" since the decentralization of personnel appointments in 1984 (O'Brien & Li, 2017). Under this arrangement, officials at each level of the bureaucracy gained full authority over appointing, evaluating, and disciplining their next level down of subordinates, which has incentivized officials to "be hyperresponsive to their immediate superiors at the expense of other interests" (O'Brien & Li, 2017, p. 171) and carried out orders from their superiors "too zealously, regardless of objective limitations and popular reaction" (Harding, 1981, p. 351). This arrangement can also explain the collusion between higher-level officials and their immediate subordinates. Superiors may cover up their subordinates' transgressions, encroachments on citizens' interests, or even deviations from central policies in exchange for their loyalty and compliance. Inspection tours directly launched by the central committee and skip-level inspections curb the likelihood of collusion between officials of adjacent levels of government. Rather than engaging in collusion, officials at each level now tend to protect themselves by shifting blame to others.

Besides skip-level inspections, the crossing inspection *(jiaocha xuncha,* 交叉巡察*)* model is also widely adopted, where inspection teams are sent from location A to inspect location B, and vice versa, or from B to C. This approach seeks to alleviate the negative impacts of patronage relationships and networks on the efficiency of inspections.

A Summary of the Trajectory of Accountability Transformation

To sum up, the four shifts mentioned highlight a significant transformation in accountability systems under Xi's administration compared to previous periods. Table 3.1 summarizes the characteristics of accountability mechanisms across different time frames. Prior to Xi's era, there were no systematic regulations governing accountability, leading to a vague legal understanding of the concept. In the pre-reform period, campaign-style criticism and self-criticism served as the primary approaches for addressing bureaucrats' moral and behavioral degeneration. The post-reform period introduced a series of institutional overhauls and reforms, yet it still lacked systematic establishment of accountability regulations, resulting in an unclear legal framework. The development and implementation of accountability systems were in their early stages. During this time, bureaucratic accountability, along with intra-party accountability, held officials accountable for illegal actions, negligence, inadequate duty performance, or poor results. Various personnel management mechanisms, such as cadre responsibility contracts and fiscal decentralization, were utilized to incentivize bureaucrats.

Xi's administration initiated a comprehensive reform of the accountability system, positioning accountability as a prominent issue for both practitioners and scholars (Tu, 2024; Tu & Gong, 2022a). An integrated accountability framework has been established, primarily driven by intra-party (political) accountability and is supported by bureaucratic accountability. The focus of accountability has shifted significantly. Intra-party accountability mainly addresses deficiencies in political construction, ideological development, organizational structure, and the rectification of work styles among Party organs and leaders. The prominence of intra-party or political accountability indicates a prioritization of efforts related to Party building, discipline, and regulatory compliance, while administrative efficiency, economic development, and ouputs have become less emphasized.

Table 3.1 The trajectory of accountability transformation in China

Period	*Years*	*Forms of accountability*	*Features*
Pre-reform	1949–1970s	Campaign-driven moral education	Recurrent political studies, criticism and self-criticism, moral education, and rectification campaigns
Post-reform	1980s–1990s	Incentive-based bureaucratic accountability	Internal bureaucracy; link fiscal, material, and promotion with economic performance
Xi era	since 2012	Sanction-based political accountability	External bureaucracy; stringent supervision and punishments to deter bureaucrats

CCP leaders aim to create a collaborative and comprehensive supervision system for the Party and State to enhance constraints and oversight over power. This system includes four supervisory mechanisms: CDIs, SCs, stationed teams, and inspection teams. The leadership has committed to ensuring that no areas are exempt from supervision (*jiandu wu jinqu,* 监督无禁区) and seeks extensive inspection coverage across major Party and state bodies. Moreover, bureaucrats who committed minor regulatory violations faced severe and sometimes arbitrary sanctions during the early stage of intensified accountability.

In summary, the previous incentive-based bureaucratic accountability, which tied material rewards and promotion opportunities to performance, has been supplanted by sanction-based political accountability characterized by stringent supervision and punishment. Additionally, the assessment system has transitioned from a focus on results to an emphasis on procedures, prioritizing strict compliance with rules, regulations, and directives. This shift in the accountability framework reshapes the political and bureaucratic structure, significantly affecting bureaucrats' motivations and behaviors.

Conclusion

Accountability mechanisms in China have undergone a systematic overhaul since President Xi came into office in late 2012. The Mao era is marked by a campaign-driven approach to moral education and recurrent political studies aimed at instilling the bureaucracy with a revolutionary spirit. The reform years, beginning with the economic reforms, are characterized by bureaucratic accountability based on material incentives. During this phase, the cadre responsibility system closely links bureaucrats' material compensation to their attainment of performance indicators, acting as a key driver to motivate the bureaucracy to enhance the local economy and carry out directives from higher-level authorities.

The systematic intensification of accountability following an unprecedented top-down anti-corruption crackdown under Xi's administration is a vehicle to strengthen the Central and ruling party's political control over the local bureaucracy. Political accountability in China has considerably strengthened through centralization and formalization, primarily targeting violations of specific rules and procedures. Heightened political accountability, characterized by the tight supervision of bureaucratic agents to ensure adherence to procedures, integrity, and responsiveness to the interests and concerns of the politicians. The rise of sanction-based political accountability has coincided with a decline in the relative significance of the reward-based bureaucratic accountability.

Although the intensified accountability has effectively constrained bureaucrats' flagrant abuse of power and corruption, it has a downside, as it undermines bureaucrats' entrepreneurship and efficiency (Li et al., 2021; Tu & Gong, 2022b). There is a potential dilemma faced by local cadres, caught between demands for taking initiatives to achieve managerial performance and risks of being blamed for violating regulations or making unintended mistakes, which may render them incapable of taking any action. Facing political risks and uncertainties exerted by heightened accountability, bureaucrats strategically redefine their responsibilities and employ various blame-avoidance tactics, leading to systemic bureaucratic slack or standstill at the local level. Chapters 4–7 will delve into the unintended negative consequences brought about by the intensified sanction-based accountability to the bureaucracy.

References

Ang, Y. Y. (2020). *China's gilded age: The paradox of economic boom and vast corruption*. Cambridge University Press.

Bai, Y., & Li, Y. (2022). Political tournaments and regional growth-enhancing policies: Evidence from Chinese prefectures. *Journal of Regional Science, 62*(5), 1358–1385.

Beijing Times. (2014, March 30). Forced demolition accidents: Half violence and half profiteering. Viewed June 9, 2024. https://www.gov.cn/test/2007-10/10/content_773198.htm

Bovens, M. (2007). Analysing and assessing accountability: A conceptual framework. *European Law Journal, 13*(4), 447–468.

Cai, H., & Treisman, D. (2006). Did government decentralization cause China's economic miracle? *World Politics, 58*(4), 505–535.

Cai, Y. (2004). Irresponsible state: Local cadres and image-building in China. *Journal of Communist Studies and Transition Politics, 20*(4), 20–41.

Cai, Y. (2008). Local governments and the suppression of popular resistance in China. *The China Quarterly, 193*, 24–42.

Cai, Y. (2014). *State and agents in China: Disciplining government officials*. Stanford University Press.

Carothers, C., & Zhang, Z. (2023). From corruption control to everything control: The widening use of inspections in Xi's China. *Journal of Contemporary China, 32*(140), 225–242.

CCDI. (2015, October 21). *The central committee of the CPC issued the "The CCP Principles on Integrity and Self-Discipline."* Viewed July 8, https://www.ccdi.gov.cn/toutiaon/201510/t20151022_91274_m.html

Chan, H. S., & Gao, J. (2008). Performance measurement in Chinese local governments: Guest editors' introduction. *Chinese Law & Government, 41*(2–3), 4–9.

China National Radio Website. (2014, August 13). *Over 70 counties and cities have abolished GDP assessments: China is moving away from the sole focus on GDP*. Viewed June 9, 2024. https://finance.cnr.cn/gundong/201408/t20140813_516199875.shtml

Chinese Government Website. (2007, August 21). *Guizhou implements a 'one-vote veto' system for the implementation of one-child policy for Party and government leaders*. Viewed July 8, 2024. https://www.gov.cn/gzdt/2007-08/21/content_722546.htm

Chinese Government Website. (2007, October 10). *The Political Bureau of the Central Committee of the Communist Party of China conducted its fourth collective study session, chaired by Hu Jintao*. Viewed July 8, 2024. https://www.gov.cn/test/2007-10/10/content_773198.htm

Chinese Government Website. (2015, August 13). *The Central Committee of the CPC issued the "CCP Regulation Regarding On-Site Inspections."* Viewed July 8, 2024. https://www.gov.cn/zhengce/2015-08/13/content_2912512.htm

Choi, E. K. (2012). Patronage and performance: Factors in the political mobility of provincial leaders in post-Deng China. *The China Quarterly, 212*, 965–981.

CPC Member Website. (2015, October 21). *The Central Committee of the CPC issued the "CCP Regulation on Party Discipline."* Viewed July 8, 2024. https://news.12371.cn/2015/10/21/ARTI1445435033479869.shtml

CPC News. (2015, September 6). *Government and business should not be 'shoulder to shoulder,' but they also shouldn't be 'back against back.* Viewed June 9, 2024. https://finance.cnr.cn/gundong/201408/t20140813_516199875.shtml

Di John, J., & Putzel, J. (2009). *Political settlements: Issues paper*. Birmingham, UK: Governance and Social Development Resource Centre.

Dowdle, M. D. (2006). *Public accountability: Designs, dilemmas and experiences*. Cambridge University Press.

Edin, M. (2003). State capacity and local agent control in China: CCP cadre management from a township perspective. *The China Quarterly, 173*, 35–52.

Ferraz, C., & Finan, F. (2007). *Electoral accountability and corruption in local governments: Evidence from audit reports (No. 2843). IZA Discussion Papers.*

Gao, J. (2009). Governing by goals and numbers: A case study in the use of performance measurement to build state capacity in China. *Public Administration and Development, 29*(1), 21–31.

Gao, J. (2010). Hitting the target but missing the point: The rise of non-mission-based targets in performance measurement of Chinese local governments. *Administration & Society*, 42(1_suppl), 56S–76S.

Gao, J. (2015). Performance measurement and management in the public sector: Some lessons from research evidence. *Public Administration and Development, 35*(2), 86–96.

Gao, J., & Su, Y. (2018). Social mobilization in a changing China: A critical review of the literature. *Current Sociology, 66*(6), 929–949.

Gong, T. (2008). The party discipline inspection in China: Its evolving trajectory and embedded dilemmas. *Crime, Law and Social Change, 49*, 139–152.

Gong, T., & Tu, W. (2022). Fighting corruption in China. *China Review, 22*(2), 1–19.

Guo, B. (2017). China's administrative governance reform in the era of "new normal." *Journal of Chinese Political Science, 22*, 357–373.

Harding, H. (1981). *Organizing China: The problem of bureaucracy, 1949–1976*. Stanford University Press.

Held, D. (2004). Democratic accountability and political effectiveness from a cosmopolitan perspective. *Government and Opposition, 39*(2), 364–391.

Hope, O., Yue, H., & Zhong, Q. (2020). China's anti-corruption campaign and financial reporting quality. *Contemporary Accounting Research, 37*(2), 1015–1043.

Hu, C. (2017). Accountability of public servants under dominant political settlements of China: Effects, challenges, and issues. *International Journal of Public Administration, 40*(3), 240–255.

Hu, G. (2017). Political reform cost in China. In G. Hu (Ed.), *The cost of development in China* (pp. 101–120). Springer Singapore.

Jabbra, J. G., & Dwivedi, O. P. (1988). *Public service accountability: A comparative perspective*. West Hartford, CT: Kumarian Press.

Jin, H., Qian, Y., & Weingast, B. R. (2005). Regional decentralization and fiscal incentives: Federalism, Chinese style. *Journal of Public Economics, 89*(9–10), 1719–1742.

Jing, Y., Cui, Y., & Li, D. (2015). The politics of performance measurement in China. *Policy and Society, 34*(1), 49–61.

Landry, P. F., Lü, X., & Duan, H. (2018). Does performance matter? Evaluating political selection along the Chinese administrative ladder. *Comparative Political Studies, 51*(8), 1074–1105.

Lee, H. Y. (1991). *From revolutionary cadres to party technocrats in socialist China* (Vol. 31). University of California Press.

Li, H., & Zhou, L.-A. (2005). Political turnover and economic performance: The incentive role of personnel control in China. *Journal of Public Economics, 89*(9–10), 1743–1762.

Li, J., Ni, X., & Wang, R. (2021). Blame avoidance in China's cadre responsibility system. *The China Quarterly, 247*, 681–702.

Li, L. (2019). Politics of anticorruption in China: Paradigm change of the party's disciplinary regime 2012–2017. *Journal of Contemporary China, 28*(115), 47–63.

Li, L., & Wang, P. (2019). From institutional interaction to institutional integration: The national supervisory commission and china's new anti-corruption model. *The China Quarterly, 240*, 967–989.

Li, X. (2001). The Chinese cultural revolution revisited. *China Review*, 137–165.

Li, X., Liu, C., Weng, X., & Zhou, L.-A. (2019). Target setting in tournaments: Theory and evidence from China. *The Economic Journal, 129*(623), 2888–2915.

Li, Y., Qin, X., & Koppenjan, J. (2022). Accountability through public participation? Experiences from the ten-thousand-citizen review in Nanjing China. *Journal of Public Policy, 42*(1), 43–62.

Lieberthal, K. (1995). A new China strategy. *Foreign Affairs, 74*(46), 35–49.

Lin, J. Y., & Liu, Z. (2000). Fiscal decentralization and economic growth in China. *Economic Development and Cultural Change, 49*(1), 1–21.

Ma, J. (2012). The rise of social accountability in China. *Australian Journal of Public Administration, 71*(2), 111–121.

Martinez-Bravo, M., i Miquel, G. P., Qian, N., & Yao, Y. (2011). *Do local elections in non-democracies increase accountability? Evidence from rural China*. National Bureau of Economic Research.

Meisner, M. (1999). *Mao's China and after: A history of the People's Republic*. Simon and Schuster.

Montinola, G., Qian, Y., & Weingast, B. R. (1995). Federalism, Chinese style: The political basis for economic success in China. *World Politics, 48*(1), 50–81.

O'brien, K. J., & Li, L. (2017). Selective policy implementation in rural China. In Brodsgaard, K. E. (Ed.), *Critical readings on the communist party of China (4 Vols. Set)* (pp. 437–460). Brill.

Oi, J. C. (1992). Fiscal reform and the economic foundations of local state corporatism in China. *World Politics, 45*(1), 99–126.

Olsen, J. P. (2013). The institutional basis of democratic accountability. *West European Politics, 36*(3), 447–473.

People's Daily Online. (2013, November 15). *Chinese Central Communist's decisions on several important issues about deepening the overall reform.* Viewed June 9, 2024. http://finance.people.com.cn/n/2013/1115/c1004-23559387.html

People's Daily Online. (2014, August 14). *How Xi Jinping views GDP: One should not simply assess performance based on GDP.* Viewed June 9, 2024. http://politics.people.com.cn/BIG5/n/2014/0814/c1001-25462153.html

People's Daily Online. (2015, February 27). *Xi Jinping's strategic though of the "Four Comprehensives."* Viewed June 10, 2024. http://politics.people.com.cn/n/2015/0227/c1001-26603910.html

Qian, Y., & Weingast, B. R. (1997). Federalism as a commitment to preserving market incentives. *Journal of Economic Perspectives, 11*(4), 83–92.

Romzek, B. S., & Dubnick, M. J. (2018). Accountability in the public sector: Lessons from the Challenger tragedy. In Stivers, C. (Ed.), *Democracy, bureaucracy, and the study of administration* (pp. 182–204). Routledge.

Sachs, J. D., & Woo, W. T. (2001). Understanding china's economic performance. *The Journal of Policy Reform, 4*(1), 1–50.

Schubert, G., & Alpermann, B. (2019). Studying the Chinese policy process in the era of 'top-level design': The contribution of 'political steering' theory. *Journal of Chinese Political Science, 24*, 199–224.

Schurmann, F. (2022). *Ideology and organization in communist China* (Vol. 3). University of California Press.

Shen, C., Jin, J., & Zou, H. (2012). Fiscal decentralization in China: History, impact, challenges and next steps. *Annals of Economics & Finance, 13*(1), 1–51.

Stokes, S. C. (2005). Perverse accountability: A formal model of machine politics with evidence from Argentina. *American Political Science Review, 99*(3), 315–325.

Sun, Y. (2001). The politics of conceptualizing corruption in reform China. *Crime, Law and Social Change, 35*, 245–270.

Tsai, L. L. (2007). Solidary groups, informal accountability, and local public goods provision in rural China. *American Political Science Review, 101*(2), 355–372.

Tu, W. (2024). Unpacking the accountability cube and its relationship with blame avoidance. *Public Management Review, 26*(3), 701–723.

Tu, W., & Gong, T. (2022a). Bureaucratic shirking in China: Is sanction-based accountability a cure? *The China Quarterly, 249*, 259–274.

Tu, W., & Gong, T. (2022b). Accountability intensity and bureaucrats' response to conflicting expectations: A survey experiment in China. *Public Management Review, 24*(11), 1779–1801.

Wang, E. H. (2022). Frightened Mandarins: The adverse effects of fighting corruption on local bureaucracy. *Comparative Political Studies, 55*(11), 1807–1843.

Wedeman, A. (2016). Corruption and collective protest in China. In Gong, T., & Scott, I. (Eds.), *Routledge handbook of corruption in Asia* (pp. 195–211). Routledge.

Whiting, S. H. (2017). The cadre evaluation system at the grass roots: The paradox of party rule. In Brodsgaard, K. E. (Ed.), *Critical readings on the Communist Party of China (4 Vols. Set)* (pp. 461–478). Brill.

Whyte, M. K. (1973). Bureaucracy and modernization in China: The Maoist critique. *American Sociological Review, 38*(2), 149–163.

Wong, C. P. W. (1992). Fiscal reform and local industrialization: The problematic sequencing of reform in Post-Mao China. *Modern China, 18*(2), 197–226.

Yao, Y., & Zhang, M. (2015). Subnational leaders and economic growth: Evidence from Chinese cities. *Journal of Economic Growth, 20*, 405–436.

Yuen, S. (2014). Disciplining the party. Xi Jinping's anti-corruption campaign and its limits. *China Perspectives, 2014*(3), 41–47.

Zang, X. (2017). How cohesive is the Chinese bureaucracy? A case study of street-level bureaucrats in China. *Public Administration and Development, 37*(3), 217–226.

Zeng, Q. (2020). Managed campaign and bureaucratic institutions in China: Evidence from the targeted poverty alleviation program. *Journal of Contemporary China, 29*(123), 400–415.

Zhang, H., & Wang, X. (2023). Political accountability for major safety incidents in China: Influencing factors and their significance. *Journal of Tsinghua University (Philosophy and Social Sciences), 31*(2): 170–184. (张欢,王新松. 中国特大安全事故政治问责:影响因素及其意义. 清华大学学报(哲学社会科学版).

Zhou, X. (2010). The institutional logic of collusion among local governments in China. *Modern China, 36*(1), 47–78.

Zhou, L. (2022). Promotion Tournaments—Literature Review and Future Directions. *Quarterly Journal of Economics and Management*, *1*(1), 1–34.

Zhou, X., & Lian, H. (2020). Modes of governance in the Chinese bureaucracy: A "control rights" theory. *The China Journal, 84*, 51–75.

Zhou, X., Lian, H., Ortolano, L., & Ye, Y. (2013). A behavioral model of "muddling through" in the Chinese bureaucracy: The case of environmental protection. *The China Journal, 70*, 120–147.

Zhou, Z. (2017). Performance management reforms in mainland China. In Berman, E. M. (Ed.), *Public administration in East Asia* (pp. 117–144). Routledge.

CHAPTER 4

Accountability Intensity and Bureaucratic Shirking

Whether the intensification of accountability curbs agency shirking is a question that puzzles many scholars and practitioners. According to the principal-agency theory, agency shirking occurs when the agent minimizes his efforts to serve the principal's interests, which is more likely to occur when he believes that more leisure time can be created without facing negative consequences (Hawkins & Jacoby, 2006). Therefore, agency shirking can be curbed by imposing stronger accountability to increase the cost of shirking. However, a burgeoning body of research documents that the intensification of accountability fails to induce compliance among bureaucrats; rather, it provokes defensive emotions and destructive behaviors, which points to the sub-dimension paradox of agency.

By differentiating forms of bureaucratic shirking, this chapter sheds light on this question. Chapter 3 indicates that the sanction-based accountability mechanism featured by stringent monitoring and sanction has been strengthened to regulate the bureaucracy in China. This chapter takes a further step to explore the impact of sanction-based accountability on bureaucratic shirking. The results show that the increase in monitoring and punishment may inhibit bureaucrats from blatantly evading responsibility by, for example, being sloppy, inactive, or involved in non-work activities. However, they may induce bureaucrats to adopt some subtle coping strategies such as shifting and reframing responsibility to deal with work pressure.

W. Tu, *The Accountability Paradox in the Chinese Bureaucracy*, https://doi.org/10.1007/978-981-96-6392-7_4

Accountability Intensity: Deficit or Overload

Deficit and overload are two opposite ends of a continuum of accountability intensity. A bulk of literature commonly links an accountability deficit with the absence of control over the bureaucracy. The significant growth in the number of staff and organizational complexity of the executive branch exacerbates the concern that bureaucracy may be out of control of political representatives (Bovens et al., 2008; Stephenson, 2008; Wood & Waterman, 1991). The accountability deficit emerges when the accountability forum faces serious obstacles in gaining insight into and exercising meaningful control over the bureaucratic agency (Behn, 2001, p. 76; Han, 2020; Mulgan 2003, p. 74; van Osch et al., 2023). Weingast and Moran (1983) summarize four concrete aspects of accountability deficit: "(1) the lack of oversight hearings; (2) the infrequency of congressional investigations and policy resolutions; (3) the perfunctory nature of confirmation hearings of agency heads; (4) the lack of ostensible congressional attention to or knowledge about the ongoing operation and policy consequences of agency choice; and (5) the superficiality of annual appropriations hearings" (p. 767).

Besides, some scholars suggest that the credible threat of sanction is essential for ensuring meaningful accountability (Schillemans & Smulders, 2015), and a moderate level of sanction is required to motivate actors to make improvements in response to performance feedback (De Bruijn, 2002). In a nutshell, accountability deficit primarily derives from the lack, infrequency, or superficiality of investigations or hearings, the insufficiency of knowledge related to public administration, and the lack of necessary sanction for transgressions on the part of accountability holders. Without effective mechanisms for obtaining information from the agent, the information asymmetry between the principal and the agent worsens. Additionally, lacking the credible capability to enforce consequences may diminish the principal's authority to effectively regulate the agent.

On the other spectrum of accountability intensity is "accountability overload." Accountability overload involves double connotations. The first refers to the increasingly dense web of different forms of accountability imposed by political, legal, professional, bureaucratic, and social sources of authority, which may exert a comparatively large number of mutually contradictory expectations on bureaucrats (Koppell, 2005; Romzek & Dubnick, 1987). The second form of overload refers to the stringent strength of demand, monitoring, and sanction that a principal imposes on her agents. The audit society devotes too much attention to the "rituals of verification" (Power, 1997). Bovens et al. (2008) identify several attributes of accountability overload. The primary characteristic is that the accountability forum places unreasonably high demands on the restricted energy and resources of bureaucrats, such as excessive reporting requirements or highly stringent performance standards. Furthermore, the frequent inspections and punitive measures for unsatisfactory performance add to the overload of accountability (Tu & Gong, 2022a). Some scholars consider that accountability has gradually come to primarily signify the imposition of sanctions following a monitoring process, leading to what is known as accountability overload (Mansbridge, 2014; Tu & Gong, 2022b).

In contrast to democratic systems embedded in the web of diverse accountability, the Chinese administrative system is primarily characterized by a hierarchical and top-down accountability system (Hou et al., 2022; Li et al., 2022; Tu, 2024). The major accountability mechanisms faced by bureaucrats are political accountability and bureaucratic accountability. In China, there is no clear division between political forces and administrative authority. Therefore, the distinction between political and bureaucratic accountability is blurred for low-level officials, and both types of accountability are characterized by a hierarchical dynamic, where public employees report to and are accountable to their higher-level supervisors (Almén, 2018). Thus, this chapter uses the intensity of hierarchical accountability to capture the strength of political and bureaucratic accountability.

Prior to 2012, the accountability deficit was the major problem of the accountability system within the Chinese bureaucracy. Although the cadre responsibility system put much emphasis on efficiency, both bureaucratic and political accountability for the violation of rules were weak, leading to widespread corruption and the misuse of power. The deficit of accountability is vividly captured by a Chinese saying that "top-down supervision is too remote, bottom-up supervision too difficult, and CDI action too late" (*shangji jiandu taiyuan, xiaji jiandu tainan, jiwei jiandu taiwan,* 上级监督太远，下级监督太难，纪委监督太晚). Since Xi assumed power, accountability, especially political accountability, has been unprecedentedly intensified. Several forms of top-down monitoring mechanisms as "police patrol" are initiated. As forms of political accountability within the Party, numerous inspection tours (*xunshi and xuncha,* 巡视和巡察) have been organized by the Central Committee of the Party and the committees of each level to launch full-scale investigations and can impose penalties in cases of corruption or other political and administrative misconduct. As forms of bureaucratic accountability, inspection teams (*ducha zu,* 督查组), supervision teams (*ducha zu,* 督察组), and guidance teams (*dudao zu,* 督导组) are established to reinforce oversight. The inspection teams are responsible for routine inspections, where the higher-level checks the implementation of policies and problems faced by the lower-level officials. The supervision teams, on the other hand, conduct inspections to check illegal or disciplinary violations when carrying out tasks at the local level. The guidance teams are tasked with specifically promoting a particular piece of work, for example, the crackdown on organized crime and mafia.

While bureaucrats are effectively controlled, they complain about the accountability overload. Many local officials complained that the current working situation features "one person does the job, and a group of people supervise it" (CB-2019-21). There is a widespread saying among grassroots officials, "there are thousands of knives above, but only one head below, so eventually one of the knives will strike the head" [that is, many upper-level agencies oversee the lower-level officials who are responsible for various tasks and may eventually make mistakes and be held accountable] (CB-2023-22). Some punishments are arbitrary and excessive. For example, an official was criticized by the government for having two punctuation errors in a poverty alleviation handbook (CPC News, 2019). Several teachers were criticized by the local CDI for organizing a self-funded dinner during the holiday (Netease News, 2020). In a certain southwestern region, a mass incident occurred, and the responsible departments received punishment. However, the county leaders believed that the range of punishments was insufficient, so they added departments with no direct connection to the incident to the blame list (Netease News, 2020). In an institutional setting characterized by heightened accountability, grassroots officials in a disadvantaged position within the power hierarchy are vulnerable to becoming "scapegoats." For instance, in a city of Northeast China, over 40 officials were held accountable for poor performance when carrying out special epidemic prevention work in the livestock industry. Of these, 90% are public employees at the township level or lower, including over 20 personnel at the village level (Netease News, 2020).

Evidently, China's accountability system has been greatly strengthened to tackle accountability deficits. Higher-level officials possess substantial power and mechanisms to ensure lower-level officials are held accountable. However, as the high-level officials willfully exercise the accountability system, it fails to gain authority and recognition within the bureaucracy, resulting in a lack of genuine compliance. Bureaucrats strategically cope with the accountability system with a series of tactics, including refraining from making initiatives, over-conforming to paperwork, and resisting changes to deprecate innovation. In the eye of the central government, local officials lose entrepreneurship and become shirking (*buzuowei,* 不作为或懒政). Since 2012, the shirking phenomenon has attracted extensive attention from China's top leaders, who consider it "another form of corruption."

Recognizing the seriousness of blame avoidance and shirking problem among local officials, the central government highlighted it for the first time in the Chinese Government Work Report of 2015 and urged public officials to shoulder their responsibilities enthusiastically. The report emphasized that governments at all levels should enhance the personnel management system by ensuring that well-performing officials are rewarded while those who fail to fulfill their duties should face punishments. A considerable number of regulations were promulgated to curb bureaucratic shirking among government officials. These include, for example, *special Plans on Further Deepening the Treatment of Shirking and Malfeasance* (《关于进一步深化"为官不为""为官乱为"问题专项治理的工作方案》) issued by the Beijing Municipal CDI in 2017; *Accountability Measures against Shirking of the Party and Government Cadres* (《党政领导干部不作为不担当问责办法》) issued by the CDI of Liaoning Province in 2014, and *Special Plans on Dealing with the Problem of Shirking and lack of responsibility* (《关于开展不作为不担当问题专项治理方案》) published by the Tianjin Municipal Committee in 2017.

Furthermore, both the CCDI and the State Council launched regular inspections to address shirking behaviors across various government departments. Local governments attempt to crack down on shirking in a variety of ways. For example, Chenzhou City in Hunan province held hearings concerning public officials' shirking behaviors on television and broadcast them live to the public (The CCDI Website, 2014). Kunming City in Yunnan province established supervision and reporting mechanisms targeting the working style of officials by encouraging the public to report shirking behaviors of officials through telephones, the Internet, and petition letters (Xinhua News, 2015).

Bureaucratic Shirking

Definition

Bureaucratic shirking is a severe and notorious problem in governments. It exerts a pernicious impact on effective governance and prohibits governments from developing prompt and necessary responses to public needs. Brehm & Gates (1999) suggest that bureaucrats' behaviors can be categorized into three forms based on the extent of effort that they put into work: working by putting efforts in accomplishing the policy goals of the principal; shirking as the bureaucrat is opposed to a particular policy or just wants to seek more leisure time; and sabotage by devoting energy to undermine the policy goals. Scholars further put forth three types of errors that bureaucrats usually commit. The first type of error occurs when bureaucrats intend to perform their tasks but do so poorly or inefficiently. The second type involves public sector employees abusing or overreaching their delegated authority. The third type is inadequate action or inaction at all, which can be regarded as shirking (Peters, 2014, p. 211). The difference between the first type of error and shirking lies in that the former is committed unintentionally while the latter is intended to minimize working efforts.

The term shirking can be traced to the economics and managerial literature and is defined as the tendency of workers to exert less effort in order to create more leisure time for a given wage (Judge & Chandler, 1996; Leibowitz & Tollison, 1980). It is suggested that employees prefer larger amounts of leisure time for a given wage and will shirk when the utility gained from shirking exceeds that obtained from working (Bennett & Naumann, 2005). Therefore, when employees can create more on-the-job free time without facing negative consequences, they are more likely to shirk by increasing absenteeism, lateness, and stalling (Adler & Golan, 1981; Angle & Perry, 1981). This concept was then adopted by the agency theory to describe public agents who, as rational economic men, seek to maximize their self-interest or minimize their efforts to serve the principal's interests (Hawkins & Jacoby, 2006; Pollack, 1997).

The established definitions of shirking are slightly obscure. Minimizing work efforts does not adequately capture the connotation and attributes of shirking. A plausible definition of a term should consist of a set of necessary conditions and encompass the essential features of the term (Rosch & Mervis, 1975). The prevalence of shirking phenomena in the Chinese government offers a valuable opportunity to dive deep into the connotations, characteristics, and forms of shirking. The common shirking behaviors adopted by Chinese bureaucrats include but are not limited to, stalling, idling, buck-passing, and playing it safe in carrying out public duties. The central government has promulgated *the Opinions on Further Encouraging Cadres to Embrace a New Era, Take on New Responsibilities, and Make New Achievements* (《关于进一步激励广大干部新时代新担当新作为的意见》) to encourage cadres to take initiatives and refrain from shirking. Almost all provincial governments have also enacted regulations to promote the elimination of shirking behaviors among government officials. There are some typical definitions of shirking in these official decrees:

> Shirking refers to the phenomenon in which leading cadres fail to perform or fulfill their duties poorly because of inaction, slow action, or not daring to take action, causing adverse effects and consequences. (Chenzhou Municipal Government Website, 2014)

> Shirking refers to public officials' misconduct in the process of fulfilling their duties, such as decision-making errors, poor implementation, inadequate supervision, prevarication, laziness, inefficiency, and lax work discipline. (Pingxiang Municipal Government Website, 2015)

> Shirking refers to public officials' behaviors, such as inadequate duty fulfillment, weak implementation, lack of initiative, and lax work discipline, which causes detrimental influences and consequences. (Jiyuan Municipal Government Website, 2016)

Based on the established literature on shirking and Chinese official decrees' definition, this book defines bureaucratic shirking as follows: *bureaucrats intentionally minimize efforts in performing public responsibilities to satisfy personal interests.* The conceptualization emphasizes bureaucrats' intentional minimization of their efforts in fulfilling public responsibilities, rather than unintentionally performing these duties poorly due to incompetence. Furthermore, responsibility is the key element of the concept of bureaucrat shirking. Only by clearly defining what constitutes the responsibilities of public officials can we determine which behaviors should be regarded as bureaucratic shirking. Barry and Shaw (1979, p. 27) defines responsibility as "a sphere of duty or obligation assigned to a person by the nature of that person's position, function, or work." Based on the major roles played by Chinese local officials, I classify their public responsibilities into three types.

The first aspect is policy responsibility, which pertains to the execution of directives from higher authorities and is likely the main duty of Chinese public officials. The work of these officials revolves around the policy instructions from high-level authorities and their direct superiors, which can change rapidly based on the priorities of the national agenda. For example, when the one-child policy was a key priority for the central government, nearly all public officials in township governments took on the responsibility for birth control, irrespective of their departments and official job duties (Kennedy & Chen, 2018).

The second is social responsibility, which implies that public officials should serve the interests of citizens, a significant objective of the CCP leadership according to the Party Constitution. Besides implementing upper-level directives in accordance with central guidelines, local officials are required to solve local problems, deliver services to local citizens, and maintain social stability. However, since Chinese citizens lack the channels and means to hold officials accountable for their neglect of social responsibilities, officials tend to prioritize top-down accountability over the expectations of the public. Consequently, the public may turn to social protests and petition higher authorities to voice their concerns and draw attention from the higher-ups or even the central government (Cai, 2014). If mass incidents or major conflicts between the government and citizens arise within their jurisdiction, local leaders will be held accountable by higher authorities. As a result, local officials strategically manage their interactions with citizens, responding to their needs by judging the timing and circumstances.

Third, bureaucrats need to shoulder post-related responsibilities. These responsibilities often receive inadequate attention because they are typically not under close oversight from higher-level officials and do not garner much public attention. However, neglecting these responsibilities can lead to significant damage to public welfare and national interests. For instance, officials' failure to thoroughly conduct regular inspections of public facilities and manufacturing plants has led to a rise in public safety incidents.

Types and Characteristics

Shirking is a complicated and multifaceted phenomenon that takes different forms. To identify its patterns and characteristics, I collected 432 shirking cases reported by the CCDI on its official website from 2012 to 2019. These cases were identified by searching three terms that have been officially used to describe shirking in China: ***buzuowei* 不作为, *weiguan buwei* 为官不为, and *lanzheng*** 懒政. The CCDI's website is the most authoritative source reporting shirking cases in China, and it has regularly and widely publicized such cases collected nationwide since 2012. The broad coverage and considerable diversity of the CCDI-reported cases allow us to pinpoint the major patterns of bureaucratic shirking.

Content analysis was employed to analyze the text data. Content analysis is a major method for analyzing text data. It provides knowledge and understanding of the patterns, characteristics, and factors of the phenomenon under study (Downe-Wamboldt, 1992). Regarding coding of the text, I followed the coding approach proposed by Corbin and Strauss (1990). With the help of the software NVivo 11, this research coded the data in three steps. The first step is open coding, which is based on the original and literal meaning emerging from the data. The second step is axial coding, which identifies connections among the categories generated in the open codes. Some categories will be included in one group. The third step is selective coding, which further groups the categories generated in the second step. This step conceptualizes the codes, enabling the analytical story more theoretical.

Based on a content analysis of the 432 cases, I identified six major types of shirking: buck-passing, bluffing, playing it safe, stalling and inaction, idling, and negligence, which can be further grouped into three core categories, namely shifting responsibility, reframing responsibility, and evading responsibility shown in Table 4.1. Most of the cases display only one type of shirking strategy. Only a few cases involve two types, and I classify them into both categories.

Evading responsibility refers to the practice whereby bureaucrats are completely unwilling to shoulder responsibility and flagrantly display an intention toward inaction by stalling, idling at work, or working carelessly. *Stalling* describes a situation where officials take minimal or no action

Table 4.1 A classification of shirking behaviors

Selective coding	*Axial coding*	*Open code*	*Cases*
Evading responsibility	Stalling and inaction	Slow or no response to public demands	38
		Slow or no implementation of state policies	64
		Slow or no performance in routine duties	107
	Idling	Engaging in non-work-related activities during working hours	67
		Absenteeism or late arrivals and early departures	25
	Negligence	Failure to take proper care of assigned duties	80
Shifting responsibility	Buck-passing	Shifting responsibilities to subordinates	7
		Shifting responsibilities to other departments	7
		Shifting responsibilities to superiors	3
Reframing responsibility	Bluffing	Launching fake or specious projects	3
		Beautifying paperwork or fabricating numbers to present an image of accomplishment	26
	Playing it safe	Aversion to risks and innovations in decision-making	5
		Dogmatism and rigidly sticking to regulations regardless of reality	4

while waiting for the momentum of an action to fade away (Ashforth & Lee, 1990). *Idling* occurs when officials engage in recreational activities during working hours, such as chatting with coworkers, surfing online, playing cards, absenteeism, and taking more frequent or longer breaks than allowed while working. *Negligence* means that officials undertake work without care. Evading responsibility was prevalent in the Chinese bureaucracy, characterized by absenteeism, tardiness, early departures, and playing cards or mahjong during work hours, especially prior to 2012 when accountability measures were less stringent. For example, some officials try to evade responsibilities by turning off or not answering phone calls from superiors (The CCDI Website, 2018). Numerous cases of that nature were uncovered and punished with the intensification of accountability. Consequently, flagrant evasion of responsibility has been significantly reduced.

Shifting responsibility refers to the way in which bureaucrats pass the buck or responsibility to others, such as their colleagues, superiors, subordinates, other departments, or whoever else possible. It is a typical strategy for public officials in China to shift workloads or the implementation of unpopular policies to others. The fragmented structure of lines and blocks (*tiaotiao kuaikuai*, 条条块块), along with its five-tier hierarchy, blurs the boundaries of responsibilities and allows officials to shift responsibility upward, downward, or horizontally. It is convenient for higher-level authorities to shift heavy workloads and thorny duties to lower-level officials by forcing them to sign responsibility contracts, thereby placing grassroots officials under piling-up working pressure (Liu & Li, 2024). Making low-level officials sign responsibility contracts has become a commond approach for upper-level agencies to shift responsibilities downward. As accountability intensified, upper-level officials gained stronger motivation to push pressures downward and impose stricter inspections on their subordinates to avoid blame from the next higher authority. According to a survey conducted by Wensheng Chen, chief expert of the Hunan Rural Development Research Institute, the township that signed the most responsibility contracts reached 51 copies, and the one with the least signed 36 copies among the places he investigated in 2018 (The China Comment, 2018). The autonomous village governments have become the last stop of pressure and blame passing (CB-2019-18; CB-2019-28).

According to Hood (2010), top managers are well-placed to shift responsibilities by employing various strategies, such as appointing the right individuals to positions where blame is likely to fall if issues arise, utilizing different rhetorical approaches when presenting themselves to the public, and designing organizational structures that enable blame to be diffused throughout complex frameworks. This is also applicable within the Chinese government. In the Chinese government, the "first hands" (*yibashou,* 一把手*)* including both the secretary of the Party committee and the Chief Executive of the government at each hierarchical level, possess absolute power within their tiers. As a result, they can wield power to reduce and disperse their own responsibilities, leading to an unbalanced power-responsibility relationship, where their power exceeds the responsibilities they shoulder, resulting in a situation of "power overload." Conversely, grassroots officials find themselves in a situation where their responsibilities outweigh their power, causing "responsibility overload" (Deng, 2020). The division of responsibilities within organizations is also unclear. Department heads are more likely to assign additional tasks to individuals who are cooperative and competent rather than to those who are careless in their work. Those who take on more work are more likely to face a higher risk of making mistakes, yet they do not receive a higher salary (CB-2019-10; CB-2019-26). A widely circulated idiom in the Chinese bureaucracy is that "do less work, make fewer mistakes; do no work, make no mistakes" (*shaozuo shaocuo, buzuo bucuo,* 少做少错, 不做不错).

On the other hand, lower-level officials will not passively wait to be treated as scapegoats; instead, they also seek to shift responsibilities upwards to higher levels. By involving their superiors in tough decision-making and consistently reporting their work progress to superiors, they avoid making any risky decisions and bearing liability. According to the fieldwork conducted by Deng (2020), in various tasks, particularly those related to innovations and reforms, lower-level officials often seek to engage their superiors by inviting them to participate in working meetings. This approach is based on two main considerations: first, it allows them to shift responsibility and also transfer benefits; second, it enables them to leverage the power and resources of higher-level officials to push forward reforms. If the reforms fail, they can seek protection from their superiors. Another common tacit practice for passing the buck is to attribute any subsequent outcomes to the individual who signs the document approving the project (*shui qianming shui fuze,* 谁签名, 谁负责). As a result, "smart" officials often avoid signing documents or trying to obtain multiple signatures on a work document to blur and disperse responsibility. According to an official in a department of a southern city, a project is required to be signed for approval by almost everyone in the department from sector staff to sector director and from deputy-bureau directors to the bureau director in charge in order to disperse responsibility (CB-2019-6).

Reframing responsibility refers to the ways in which bureaucrats distort their responsibilities to make them less stressful and risky, or easier to implement, through two distinct strategies: playing it safe and bluffing. Reframing responsibility indicates a significant distortion and deviation of policies from their original intent and becomes a means to serve or protect bureaucrats themselves. To play it safe, for example, some officials try to stay away from innovative and risky tasks, and others mechanically follow common practices whenever possible to avoid making mistakes or rigidify regulations to hide behind rules. According to investigations by correspondents of the China Comment, when there are no clear directives and detailed implementation procedures from superiors, grassroots officials are reluctant to take any action (The China Comment, 2018).

But still, some officials try to bluff their way out of accountability pressure. They play tricks to create a misleading image of success in achieving targets and manage strict top-down evaluations by beautifying paperwork, making up statistics, and exaggerating accomplishments (Tu & Gong, 2022a, b). For example, in order to deal with provincial inspections on the afforestation task, some local governments in Jiangxi province "generate forest in one night" (*yiye chenglin,* 一夜成林). Specifically, local officials did not pave the suitable soil on roads and instead planted trees directly on cement and asphalt roads (People's Daily Online, 2019). Some officials focus on beautifying paperwork or fabricating numbers to exaggerate accomplishments. According to Gao (2016, p. 950), "the deliberate distortion of the work accomplishments of local governments is a growing concern for China's leaders." An interviewee said, "the higher the stack of reporting files, the safer I feel. In fact, there isn't much substantive work in it" (CB-2019-10).

Generally speaking, shifting and reframing responsibilities are more covert and difficult to detect, while evading responsibility is more obvious and easier to be detected. This explains why the number of officially reported cases of evading responsibility is substantially larger than those of shifting and reframing responsibility. The following parts examine the impacts of intensified accountability on the three forms of shirking.

Does Intensified Accountability Curb Shirking

Based on different assumptions of who controls bureaucrats' behavior, scholars are divided on the impacts of accountability. Rational choice theory predicts that greater monitoring and punishment mechanisms prohibit opportunistic behavior by making it more "costly" (Alchian & Demsetz, 1972; McCubbins & Schwartz, 1984). Facing strict monitoring and threat of punishment, bureaucrats may tend to comply with basic regulations and dare not to evade or distort their responsibilities.

Accordingly, behavioral transgressions may be inhibited, and appropriate practices of public officials are ensured. Scholars argue that oversight plays an essential role in curbing power abuse and maintaining the appropriate conduct of public officials, who will comply with work procedures and fulfill their responsibilities more faithfully if they know that they are being closely monitored (De Bruijn, 2002).

Grounded on the bureaucracy's inherent discretionary power, other scholars argue that excessive accountability intensity in the form of oversight and sanction may backfire. The more frequent and stricter the evaluations, the greater the pressure for officials to meet the requirements, and the more likely they will adopt defensive and self-protective strategies to game the system (Ashforth & Lee, 1990; Terman & Yang, 2016). Under the sanction-oriented logic of accountability, bureaucrats may become risk-averse and thus adopt a variety of adverse coping strategies, such as deprecating risky agendas, passing the buck, and sticking to excessive proceduralism, to avoid the hazard of being blamed (Ashforth & Lee, 1990; Mansbridge, 2014). Besides passing the buck, bureaucrats may try to reframe their responsibilities; for example, they may spend more time and energy on preparing and beautifying reports or launching image projects to impress their supervisors, but they do not necessarily perform better in the policy-making and public service delivery (Bovens et al., 2008; Ossege, 2012). Due to severe punishments for procedural violations of public officials after the 18th National Congress of the CCP, many public officials chose to play it safe by refusing to approve or launch new projects (Wang, 2022).

De Bruijn (2002) shows in great detail how the various means of assessment and control mechanisms become subverted by subordinates' strategic managerial behavior, including ritualization, mutual stereotyping, defensive routines, and hostile behavior. In this light, the success of accountability relies on account givers' cooperation, support, and compliance with the accountability system, as they may cope with accountability pressure by strategic behaviors. Scholars warn about the salience of the accountability paradox; that is, stringent monitoring of bureaucrats may repel bureaucrats' responsible judgment and moral deliberation (Jos & Tompkins, 2004). In other words, accountability in the form of monitoring and sanction is a double-edged sword: It may help curb bureaucratic shirking but may also contribute to it under certain

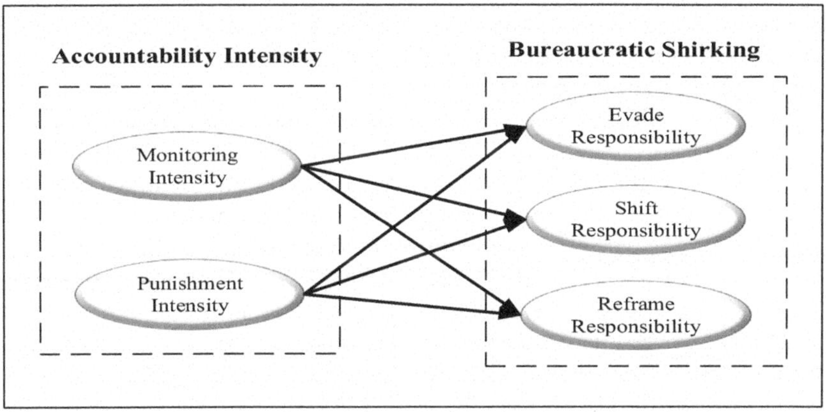

Fig. 4.1 The impacts of accountability intensity on bureaucratic shirking

circumstances. This chapter explores the impacts of accountability intensity on three forms of bureaucratic shirking. Figure 4.1 illustrates the research framework.

Data and Analysis

To show the relationship between accountability intensity and different forms of bureaucratic shirking, I draw on a large-N original survey among Chinese officials. The respondents are full-time public officials enrolled as part-time students in Master of Public Administration (MPA) programs at universities. In recent decades, a considerable number of universities launched MPA programs tailoring curriculum for public officials. These programs, especially those set up by prestigious universities, are quite popular among officials who seek to upgrade their education degrees. I chose MPA students as respondents because doing so allowed me to access a considerable number of officials from different government posts and with diverse backgrounds.

Given China's vast territory and regional diversity, I tried to broaden the geographical coverage of the sample by selecting one or two MPA programs in each of the western, central, and eastern regions, respectively. A total of 1100 anonymous questionnaires were collected, of which 870 were valid. The respondents are from 19 different provinces and work for a diverse group of public organizations, including environmental protection, tax collection, education, public safety, and personnel agencies. The design of the questionnaire was based on the results of the content analysis and interviews.

The data, collected from MPA students, may cause some concerns about their representativeness. One goal of the survey methodology is to minimize the random differences between the sample and the survey population and thus provide statistical estimates of the characteristics of the targeted population. Probability or random sampling procedures can guarantee the representativeness of a sample. However, it is almost impossible to collect a random sample among bureaucrats in the Chinese government due to various budget and political constraints. Although the respondents were not randomly selected from the total population of officials, the sample size (870) is relatively large, and the respondents are from various public organizations and regions. "In situations where a non-probability procedure is the only choice, researchers are advised to describe the sample in sufficient detail so that others can understand to whom, where, and when the findings are generalizable" (O'Dwyer & Bernauer, 2013, p. 7). This book will provide detailed information on the respondents to alleviate concerns about generalization.

Self-reported questionnaires may encounter the problem of social desirability bias in that respondents tend to conform to social norms or expectations and answer questions in a manner that will be viewed positively by others (Krumpal, 2013). Shirking is a sensitive issue, and it is crucial to ensure that respondents provide honest answers to the questionnaire rather than responses they believe would be socially desirable. It is therefore important to make respondents comfortable about sharing their views. First, the respondents were assured repeatedly that the questionnaire was anonymous, their answers would not be classified as right or wrong, and the information collected would be kept strictly confidential and used for academic purposes only. Second, Officials appear to be more inclined to express their genuine opinions in classroom settings rather than at work, as the school environment is more relaxed.

Dependent variable. The dependent variable is bureaucratic shirking, which consists of three different types of shirking behavior: evading responsibility, shifting responsibility, and reframing responsibility. For each type of shirking, I used two or three items to gauge respondents' attitudes toward them. The purpose was to measure their perceptions of bureaucratic shirking rather than their actual engagement in shirking. The sensitivity of the questionnaire was thus reduced. Evading responsibility was measured with three items: "It is no big deal to delay tasks for two or three days," "it is ok to surf the internet or watch videos occasionally during working hours," and "one does not have to handle work with great care." The three items are highly correlated, and factor analysis was used to aggregate them into one factor (Eigenvalue = 1.75, Cronbach's a = 0.72), which cumulatively explains 65.58%. Shifting responsibility was gauged by two items, consisting of "more responsibilities lead to more mistakes, so one should get involved as little as possible" and "one should avoid risk and give difficult tasks to others." The validity and reliability of the factor are acceptable (Eigenvalue = 1.63, Cronbach's a = 0.77). Reframing responsibility consists of two kinds of behavior, buffing and playing safe, and was gauged with a reliable four-item measure comprising "well-written reports are more important than well-done jobs," "trophy projects demonstrate good political performance and please superiors," "I tend to comply strictly with written rules, even though they are not in line with reality," "One should stick to routines and avoid making any change and innovation." The factor analysis aggregated the four items into one factor, with Eigenvalue being 1.85 larger than criterion 1 and Cronbach's alpha being 0.70, presenting acceptable reliability of the scale. A five-point Likert scale was adopted for each item, with 1 being "completely disagree" and 5 "completely agree" and a higher score indicating a stronger propensity toward shirking.

Explanatory variable. The independent variable, accountability intensity, is measured by six items that reflect the monitoring and punishment intensity imposed by superiors. An exploratory factor analysis of the six items presented in Table 4.2 shows that they can be aggregated into two major factors. Factor 1 reflects the intensity of monitoring, which gauges whether or not respondents perceive their superiors' supervision as very strict. Factor 2 demonstrates the severity of punitive consequences, measuring whether and to what extent respondents consider they may be punished if they perform poorly. I further performed a confirmatory factor analysis (CFA) on the two factors. CFA is often used to view the construct validity of the scales. The CFI and TLI indicate a good fit above 0.95, and the RMSEA and SRMR should be below 0.08 (Hu & Bentler, 1999). The CFA model fits well (CFI = 0.997, TLI = 0.994, RMSEA = 0.027, PCLOSE = 0.892, SRMR = 0.019), and all factor loadings are significant. For the explanatory variable, we also used a five-point

Table 4.2 Factor loading of the sanction-based accountability

Question items	*Factor 1 loading*	*Factor 2 loading*
Upper-level departments impose strict supervision over my work	0.733	
I need to report my work to upper-level departments frequently	0.866	
Upper-level departments check and evaluate my work frequently	0.800	
Poor performance will be severely criticized		0.814
The possibility of being punished is very high if I do not perform well		0.870
Punishment is severe enough to deter me		0.746

Likert scale, by which a higher score indicates a higher level of monitoring intensity and more stringent punishment.

Control variables. Other confounding variables that may influence the dependent variable are included as controls. First, responsibility clarity is controlled because it gives actors in the accountability chain a clear sense of who has what responsibilities, how, and why, so that shirking can be prevented. For that purpose, I included in the survey such questions as whether respondents consider their responsibilities to be clearly defined. Second, resource constraint, referring to the shortage of manpower and material support for bureaucrats, is also controlled because officials may feel particularly stressed and are more likely to reframe responsibilities if they don't have sufficient resources to fulfill them (Hupe & Buffat, 2014). Third, peer pressure measured by whether colleagues are working hard is also controlled because bureaucrats interact with and learn from each other in an organization, and their solidary preference is a major factor influencing their decision on whether they should work or shirk (Brehm & Gates, 1999).

A third control variable is PSM. Scholars believe that PSM exerts strong positive effects on organizational performance by promoting a strong sense of citizenship and a high level of job involvement among officials (Pandey et al., 2008; Tu et al., 2024). Following Perry (1996), I adopt three items to measure bureaucrats' commitment to the public interest by asking the respondents to indicate to what extent they agree with the statements that "meaningful public service is very important to me," "doing what is best for society is more important than my own interests," and "I am willing to go to great lengths to fulfill my public responsibilities." All the four major control variables are gauged by a five-point Likert-type scale, with higher scores indicating greater responsibility clarity, more severe resource constraint, higher PSM, and stronger peer influence to work hard.

Basic demographic information was also controlled, including gender, age, administrative rank, and monthly income. Gender was set as a dichotomous variable coded as male = 0 and female = 1. Age was measured across six levels ("≤30" = 1, "31–35" = 2, "36–40" = 3, "41–45" = 4, "46–50" = 5, and "50" = 6) and recoded as a dummy variable in regression models with "≤30" = 0 and ">30" = 1. Administrative rank was treated as an ordinal variable with six levels: section staff (*keyuan*, 科员) or below = 1, deputy-section grade (*fukeji*, 副科级) = 2, section grade (科级, *keji*) = 3, deputy-division grade (*fuchuji*, 副处级) = 4, division grade (*chuji*, 处级) = 5, and deputy-bureau grade (*fujuji*, 副局级) or above = 6. Monthly income was also set as an ordinal variable with 5 scales: "≤5000¥" = 1, "5001–7500¥" = 2, "7501–10,000¥" = 3, "10,001–12,500¥" = 4, "12,500¥" = 5. To account for unobservable factors, such as culture, institutions, politics, and policies that vary across provinces, province-fixed effects were controlled.

One major problem of the same data source is the common source bias (CSB), suggesting that correlations between independent and dependent variables are inflated and inaccurate (Jakobsen & Jensen, 2015). Harman's single-factor test was adopted to assess if CSB was a concern (Tehseen et al., 2017). I ran exploratory factor analyses on all items of the four independent latent constructs and one dependent latent construct. The principal component analysis generated 5 common factors (Eigenvalue > 1) accounting for 70.31% of the total variance, and the first rotated factor captured only 23.44% of the variance in the data. The results provide evidence against the severity of common method bias as there is no single factor that accounts for a majority of the total variance.

Descriptive Analysis

Table 4.3 presents the demographic distribution of the sample, in which 45.95% are male, and 54.05% are female. The majority of respondents are young public officials with 87.14% being at or under the age of 35. Of the respondents, 11.87% work in organs directly under provincial governments, 22.72% in organs directly under municipal governments,

34.46% in district (county or city) governments, and 28.41% in township (street) governments, indicating that about two-thirds of the respondents work at district (county) or township (street) institutions. As for the administrative rank, 70.56% of the respondents are section personnel or below, and about 20.44% are at the deputy-section level or section level, demonstrating that the rank of the officials in the sample is not very high.

The sample predominantly consists of relatively young, lower- or middle-level grassroots bureaucrats who resemble Western street-level bureaucrats and serve as key actors subject to accountability pressures and are likely to resort to shirking strategies. Consequently, the findings might not be representative of the entire civil service in China. However, since the Chinese bureaucracy shows structural isomorphism across all hierarchical levels, insights gained from lower-level officials can still offer

Table 4.3 Demographic distribution

Demographics	*Groups*	*Frequency*	*Percent*
Gender	Male	397	45.95
	Female	467	54.05
Age	≤30	533	61.76
	31 ~ 35	219	25.38
	36 ~ 40	62	7.18
	41 ~ 45	27	3.13
	46 ~ 50	7	0.81
	>50	15	1.74
Workplace	Provincial-level units	102	11.87
	Municipal-level units	178	20.72
	District or county-level units	296	34.46
	Township or street-level units	244	28.41
	Others	39	4.54
Administrative rank	Section staff (*keyuan*) or below	604	70.56
	Deputy-section grade (*fukeji*)	126	14.72
	Section grade (*keji*)	49	5.72
	Deputy-division grade (*fuchuji*)	4	0.47
	Division grade (*chuji*)	54	6.31
	Deputy-bureau grade (*fujuji*) or above	19	2.22
Monthly income	≤5000 ¥	203	23.63
	5001 ~ 7500	336	39.12
	7501 ~ 10,000	176	20.49
	10,001 ~ 12,500	82	9.55
	>12,500	62	7.22

valuable perspectives on the broader context of officialdom, including higher-level officials.

Descriptive statistics of all the variables are reported in Table 4.4. As shown in the table, the average value of monitoring intensity is 3.75, indicating that the monitoring imposed by superiors is relatively strong. More than 60% of the respondents "agree" or "strongly agree" that oversight imposed by their superior departments is intensive. This result is consistent with the findings from the interviews, which also indicate intensive monitoring imposed by upper-level governments. An interviewee, working in a township government, said that "we sometimes receive seven or eight task documents and three notices of inspection in a day" (CB-2019-1). An interviewee who is responsible for water protection expressed that the work has been repeatedly inspected by the central, provincial, and municipal departments of environmental protection, departments of water resources, and CDIs. They spend a large amount of time making preparations for the inspections imposed by different departments each month (CB-2019-4). The problem with frequent inspections is that the data or information needed by different upper-level departments overlap, which wastes grassroots officials considerable time preparing duplicated documents for each inspection (CB-2019-1; CB-2019-2; CB-2019-4; CB-2019-19).

Punishment-based consequences are prominent in the public sector, with its mean being 3.51. The interviewees revealed that the punishment has become much more severe since Xi assumed office. Verbal warnings, writing self-critical reports, and circulating criticism (*tongbao pingpi*, 通报批评) have been widely used by local CDIs (CB-2019-5; CB-2019-17). An interviewee responsible for front-line urban management said that whenever the local CDI received a complaint about her department from citizens, CDI officials would came to investigate, issue verbal warnings, and require them to write self-critical reports regardless of the reasons (CB-2019-5).

The results suggest that the respondents' propensity to evade and shift responsibility is not very strong, with average values being 2.11 and 2.82 respectively. Nevertheless, the likelihood of reframing responsibility is higher, with an average value of 3.66; 71.6% of the respondents scored above 3-point, the neutral point.

Figure 4.2 shows the frequency and kernel density of the three types of shirking behavior. The figure of kernel density also indicates that more observations lie on the left side of 3-point in the distribution of evading

Table 4.4 Descriptive statistics of key variables

	N	*Mean*	*SD*	*Min*	*Max*
Bureaucratic shirking					
Evading responsibility	856	2.11	0.86	1	5
Shifting responsibility	855	2.82	0.98	1	5
Reframing responsibility	855	3.66	0.75	1	5
Accountability intensity					
Monitoring intensity	859	3.75	0.81	1	5
Punishment intensity	855	3.51	0.83	1	5
Control variables					
Responsibility clarity	855	3.01	1.07	1	5
Resources constraint	861	2.91	1.07	1	5
Public service motivation	857	3.87	0.84	1	5
Peer pressure	855	3.53	0.99	1	5
Gender (male = 0)	867	0.54	0.50	0	1
Age	866	1.61	1.01	1	6
Administrative rank	859	1.66	1.26	1	6
Monthly income	862	2.38	1.16	1	5

responsibility, while more respondents are located on the right side of 3-point in the distribution of reframing responsibility. The growing strictness of supervision within the government hierarchy may have made it difficult for officials to easily evade their responsibilities. Consequently, they might respond to monitoring pressures by employing strategies to reframe or distort their accountability.

Some interviewees indicated that rigorous monitoring effectively reduced officials' nonfeasance and misfeasance, resulting in notable improvements in work discipline and service attitudes toward citizens (CB-2019-23; CB-2019-5). However, a downside of intensive monitoring is that some officials focus more on avoiding criticism and blame rather than dedicating themselves to their work and boosting the interests of citizens (CB-2019-1). "We do not proactively address issues or perform duties that our superiors do not pay much attention to. Some officials even conceal problems as long as they remain undetected, ensuring that negative information about minor incidents stays within the village, while news of more serious issues does not spread beyond the town" (CB-2019-21).

Figure 4.3 presents respondents' attitudes toward the three behaviors classified as evading responsibility. It shows officials' low acceptance of the

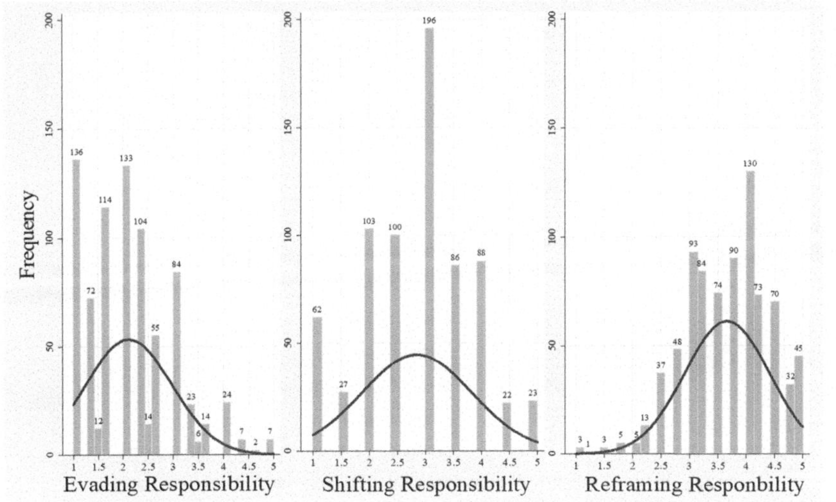

Fig. 4.2 Frequency and kernel density of shirking behaviors

statements: "It is fine to engage in non-work activities during working hours such as surfing online or watching videos," "it is no big deal to delay tasks for two or three days," and "it is fine to deal with work carelessly." More than 60% of the respondents chose "strongly disagree" or "slightly disagree" for all three items. More than 40% of the respondents strongly opposed focusing on non-work interests during office hours or working carelessly.

With regard to shifting responsibility, when asked for their opinion regarding the statement "more responsibilities lead to more mistakes, so one should get involved as little as possible," 33.52% of the respondents agreed, while 27.72% disagreed, as shown in Fig. 4.4. In response to the statement "one should avoid risk and give difficult tasks to others," 17.68% of the respondents agree, while 43.42% disagree. The results of the two items indicate that officials tend to assume less responsibility but are less likely to shift risks to others, although the responsibility inevitably falls to others if they try to do as little as possible. The unclear distribution of responsibilities is one reason bureaucrats can evade accountability, even with close supervision. As some interviewees complained, it is quite common in the public sector that bureaucrats undertake more tasks while

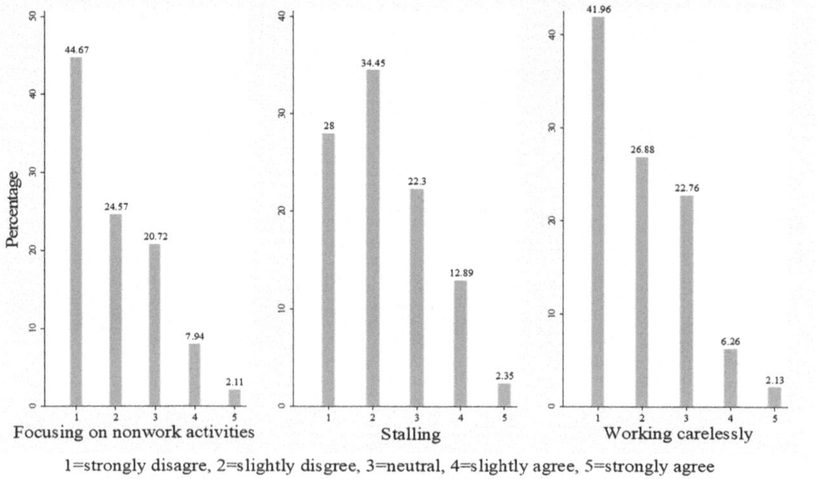

Fig. 4.3 Attitudes toward evading responsibility

receiving the same salary as those who perform fewer or even none, and even worse, the former is more likely to make mistakes than the latter (CB-2019-2; CB-2019-16; CB-2019-17).

Reframing responsibility consists of two types of strategies, that is, buffing and playing safe. As shown in Fig. 4.5, the respondents demonstrate a higher level of acceptance of reframing responsibility. Regarding buffing, only 10.42% of the respondents "strongly disagree" or "slightly disagree" with the statements that "trophy projects demonstrate good political performance and please superiors," and 13.65% of the respondents disagree that "well-written reports are more important than well-done jobs." The respondents also display a strong propensity to play safe. A total of 62.03% of the respondents agree with the statement "I tend to comply strictly with written rules, even though they are not in line with reality," and 53.47% agree with the statement "I stick to routines and do not want to make any change or innovation." One of the interviewees pointed out that "if a leader intends to launch any reform or innovation, it is inevitable that they will violate existing regulations and upset those with vested interests, as many rules are often vague. Thus, the more initiatives you undertake, the greater the likelihood of making

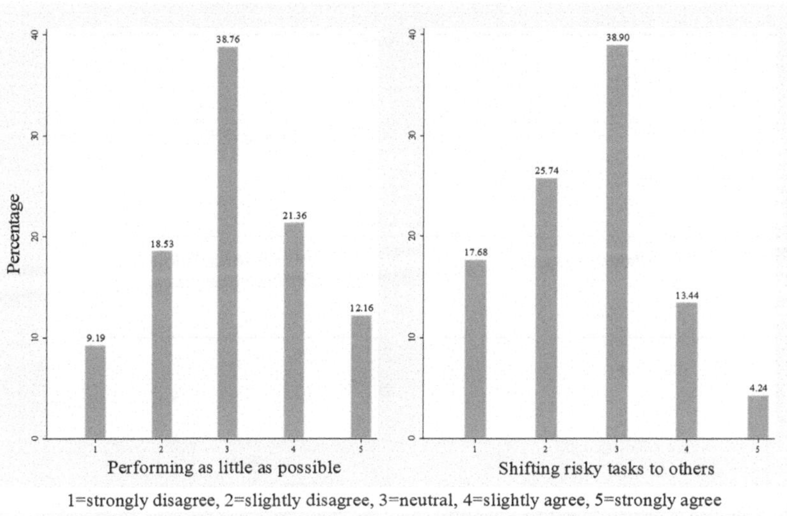

Fig. 4.4 Attitudes toward shifting responsibility

mistakes, which provides others more excuses to attack you. Amid the anti-corruption crackdown, no one is willing to take initiative" (CB-2019-8). Several interviewees suggested that the increased emphasis on compliance with rules and regulations discourages officials from carrying out policies proactively and innovatively (CB-2019-21; CB-2019-29; CB-2019-30).

The results indicate that shifting and reframing responsibility are more tolerated by the respondents, while evading responsibility is less acceptable to them. When officials perceive a certain type of shirking as widespread enough to be considered "normal," they are more likely to accept it or even engage in it by themselves.

Regression Results

The results of the multiple linear regression analysis of the three types of shirking are reported in Table 4.5. The variance inflation factor (VIF) of each variable in the six models is much lower than the usual diagnosis criterion (10), demonstrating that there are no multicollinearity problems in these models. Models 1, 3, and 5 include only control variables,

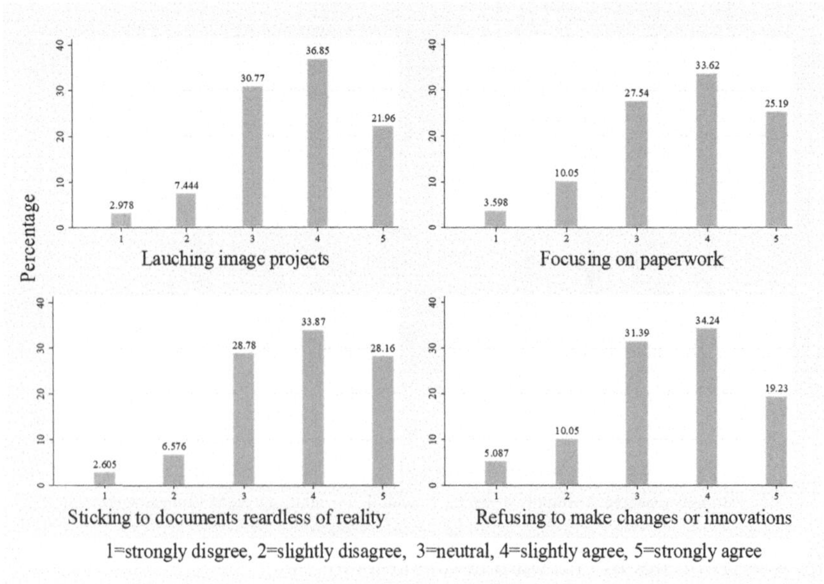

Fig. 4.5 Attitudes toward reframing responsibility

such as gender, age, administrative rank, monthly income, responsibility clarity, and resource constraint, while independent variables are introduced in Models 2, 4, and 6. To account for all unobserved time-invariant province-level confounders, province-fixed effects are included in all models.

The results show that accountability exerts different impacts on the three types of shirking. Monitoring intensity is negatively related to evading responsibility ($\beta = -0.10$, $p < 0.05$) in Model 2, but it has a positive impact on reframing responsibility ($\beta = 0.16$, $p < 0.01$) in Model 6. The effects of punishment intensity are in the same direction as that of monitoring intensity. Specifically, punishment intensity shows a significant negative correlation with evading responsibility ($\beta = -0.12$, $p < 0.01$) but has a positive relationship with reframing responsibility ($\beta = 0.11$, $p < 0.05$). In other words, the greater the respondents perceive the monitoring and punishment intensity to be, the less likely they will be to evade responsibility, but the more likely they are to reframe responsibility.

Table 4.5 Regression results of the three types of shirking

	Evade responsibility		*Shift responsibility*		*Reframe responsibility*	
	Model 1	*Model 2*	*Model 3*	*Model 4*	*Model 5*	*Model 6*
Control variables						
Gender	−0.11*	−0.12**	0.04	0.04	−0.02	−0.00
	(0.06)	(0.06)	(0.07)	(0.07)	(0.05)	(0.05)
Age	0.03	0.02	0.16**	0.17**	0.12**	0.14**
	(0.07)	(0.07)	(0.08)	(0.08)	(0.06)	(0.06)
Administrative rank	0.00	0.00	−0.06*	−0.06*	−0.01	−0.01
	(0.03)	(0.03)	(0.03)	(0.03)	(0.02)	(0.02)
Monthly income	0.04	0.04	0.09**	0.09**	0.05*	0.05*
	(0.03)	(0.03)	(0.04)	(0.04)	(0.03)	(0.03)
PSM	−0.24***	−0.21***	−0.27***	−0.28***	0.01	−0.04
	(0.04)	(0.04)	(0.04)	(0.04)	(0.03)	(0.03)
Peer pressure	−0.12***	−0.10***	−0.11***	−0.11***	−0.05*	−0.08***
	(0.03)	(0.03)	(0.04)	(0.04)	(0.03)	(0.03)
Responsibility clarity	−0.10***	−0.12***	−0.19***	−0.18***	−0.20***	−0.16***
	(0.03)	(0.03)	(0.03)	(0.03)	(0.03)	(0.03)
Resource constraint	−0.06**	−0.04	0.08**	0.08**	0.12***	0.09***
	(0.03)	(0.03)	(0.04)	(0.04)	(0.03)	(0.03)
Accountability Intensity						
Monitor intensity		−0.10**		0.10		0.16***
		(0.05)		(0.07)		(0.04)
Punishment intensity		−0.12***		−0.06		0.11***
		(0.04)		(0.05)		(0.03)
Province fixed effects	√	√	√	√	√	√
Adj R-squared	0.11	0.15	0.17	0.16	0.18	0.22

Note Standard errors in parentheses; *** $p < 0.01$, ** $p < 0.05$, * $p < 0.1$

This suggests that intensified accountability intensity may deter bureaucrats from evading responsibility, which is the more obvious and flagrant type of shirking, but it may induce some more subtle shirking strategies, such as reframing responsibility, to enable bureaucrats to cope with accountability pressure. The effects of monitoring and punishment intensity on shifting responsibility (namely, buck-passing) yield no statistical significance. This may be because when facing stringent accountability, although officials may attempt to shift thorny responsibilities to others, it would be practically difficult to do so since other officials would also avoid becoming scapegoats.

The regression results in Table 4.5 show some interesting effects of the control variables. Age, responsibility clarity, peer pressure, resource constraint, and PSM have significant impacts on the propensity for shirking. The respondents over 30 years old are more likely to shift responsibility and reframe responsibility than those under 30 years old. A possible reason for this is that as their work experience increases, officials may know better how to deal with work pressures by implementing various intricate strategies. Furthermore, responsibility clarity is negatively related to all three shirking behaviors, indicating that when responsibilities are clearly stated and assigned, it will be more difficult for officials to shirk their duties by shifting them to others or distorting them. If responsibilities remain obscure, sanction-based accountability can only cause more buck-passing or safe-playing to avoid being blamed. Peer pressure is also negatively associated with the three shirking behaviors, demonstrating that if other colleagues are all dedicated to working, it is less likely for one to shirk his or her responsibility. Resource constraint shows a positive correlation with shifting responsibility and reframing responsibility. Hence, without an adequate supply of work-related resources, officials are more likely to shift workloads to others or distort tasks to make them easier to implement. PSM presents a negative association with evading responsibility and shifting responsibility. This means that bureaucrats with higher prosocial values are less inclined to be sloppy and inactive or pass the buck to others. Some interviewees said that, as their salary is not incentive enough, their personal sense of responsibility is the major driving force to work hard (CB-2019-5; CB-2019-14).

Reasons for Shirking

Job Motivation

What motivates bureaucrats to work hard? Scholars categorize employees based on their motivations into three types: "social man," who places greater emphasis on good relationships with clients, colleagues, or superiors; "economic man," who is primarily motivated by monetary incentives, promotions, or leisure time; and "self-realization man," who is inspired more by work-related values and needs, such as the importance of tasks and the fulfillment derived from work (Nielsen, 2006). Similarly, Brehm & Gates (1999) categorize rewards into two types: pecuniary and nonpecuniary rewards. Pecuniary rewards typically include material gains, promotions, job security, and leisure, while nonpecuniary rewards encompass, but are not limited to, a personal sense of achievement, job satisfaction, the challenge of the job, and a preference for solidarity. In this survey, respondents were asked to choose two out of five items in response to the question, "What aspects of the job could motivate you to work hard?" as shown in Table 4.6.

The results show that nonpecuniary motives are the primary reasons for public officials' motivation to work hard. Among the respondents, 67.21% believe that feeling a sense of accomplishment from their work could encourage them to work diligently. Some interviewees suggested that "the strong work morale in my department comes from a sense of pride and professionalism, particularly in specialized roles that demand specific expertise" (CB-2019-13). Civil servants also show strong preferences for pecuniary motives: 56.83% of the respondents indicated that "getting a promotion or better career prospects" boosts their work morale. Additionally, 34.88% prefer receiving pecuniary rewards as compensation for good performance. Furthermore, 25.85% of the respondents value recognition from their colleagues. Only 3.41% identified "strict punishment mechanisms" as a key factor in enhancing their work enthusiasm. One interviewee pointed out, "Under frequent and rigorous top-down inspections, we feel passive and unmotivated when handling routine and basic tasks. We tend to focus on the tasks assigned by the department that is checking us today" (CB-2019-16). This indicates that increasing monitoring and punishment is not an effective way to boost officials' work efforts; instead, it may provoke defensive emotions and behaviors.

Table 4.6 Motivations for work

Options	*Number of people*	*Percentage*
Feeling accomplished	552	67.21
Promotion or better career prospects	466	56.83
Pecuniary rewards	286	34.88
Respect from colleagues	212	25.85
Strict punishment mechanisms	28	3.41

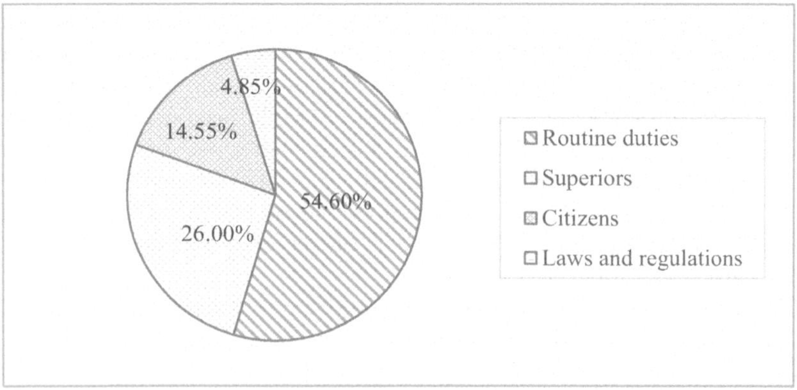

Fig. 4.6 Perceptions of responsibility

Perceptions of Responsibility

Bureaucrats operate within webs of accountability, where they are accountable to multiple internal and external stakeholders with diverse expectations. The survey asked respondents to indicate what or whom they should primarily be responsible for, including citizens, superiors, job-related duties, and laws or regulations. As shown in Fig. 4.6, up to 50% of the respondents believe that they are responsible for routine duties, while 26% consider themselves mainly accountable to their superiors. Additionally, 14.55% view serving citizens' interests as their major responsibility, and only 4.85% consider themselves primarily accountable to laws and regulations.

Perceived Causes of Shirking

Respondents were asked to identify the reasons bureaucrats shirk their responsibilities. The survey provided six options, from which respondents could select three. As shown in Table 4.7, more than 81.1% of bureaucrats consider that "incentive mechanisms are ineffective, meaning that hard work does not guarantee promotion or material gains" as the primary reason. Many interviewees pointed out that the chances of being promoted are slim, especially for grassroots officials, and that personal connections (*guanxi*, 关系) with higher-level authorities are more crucial for career advancement (CB-2019-2; CB-2019-4; CB-2019-18; CB-2019-23). "The more personal connections you have, the more secure your position will be" (CB-2019-20). Regarding material gains, another question related to merit pay in the survey revealed that about 70% of respondents believe their salary is not performance-based, with only 24.7% receiving merit pay.

One interviewee complained, "Before the 18th National Congress of the CCP, we could receive some overtime pay. The inspection team called off this stipulation and even required us to return the allowances we had previously received. Now we have to pay for our own board expenses and commuting fees. Who would be willing to work overtime?" (CB-2019-2). Another interviewee noted, "In the past, officials did not take the basic salary seriously because it was negligible compared to the bonuses they received. Now, the basic salary has become the major source of income, so even a small increase motivates them to work hard" (CB-2019-23).

Furthermore, nearly half of the respondents believe that strict accountability is a reason officials hesitate to take the initiative. Specifically, 42.44% believe that tight supervision restricts bureaucrats' discretion to act proactively, while 42.68% consider "heavy workloads and limited resources" as reasons for shirking responsibilities. Some scholars suggest that the anti-corruption campaign makes officials risk-averse and undermines their entrepreneurial spirit (Wang, 2022; Wang & Yan, 2020). However, the survey shows that very few respondents view combating corruption as a factor of shirking. The results demonstrate that incentive mechanisms are crucial for motivating bureaucrats, while the current accountability system focuses more on monitoring and punishment.

Table 4.7 Causes of shirking

Options	*Number of people*	*Percentage*
Incentive mechanisms are not effective	665	81.10
Accountability is so intensive that officials do not dare to take the initiative	362	44.15
Heavy workload, and limited resources	350	42.68
Too strict control from supervisors leaves less discretion to act proactively	348	42.44
Supervision is not strong enough to control officials	319	38.90
Anti-corruption reduces work morale	41	5.00

Conclusion

This chapter addresses the under-explored question of whether accountability intensity can reduce bureaucratic shirking and serve as an effective cure for official malfeasance and nonfeasance. In the scholarly literature, the concept of accountability is often positively associated with the appropriate exercise of discretionary power (Brandsma & Schillemans, 2013). Accountability is expected to play a significant role in promoting strict compliance among bureaucrats and refraining them from shirking responsibilities. This chapter displays a paradox of agency that the intensification of accountability does not necessarily lead to compliance among bureaucrats, who may strategically cope with accountability pressures. It first provided a nuanced picture of bureaucratic shirking by disaggregating it into three types: evading responsibility, shifting responsibility, and reframing responsibility. This was followed by an examination of the impact of accountability intensity in the form of monitoring and punishment on each of the three types of shirking.

The findings reveal that intensified monitoring and severe punishment may deter bureaucrats from blatantly evading responsibility but may also induce more subtle types of shirking, such as reframing responsibility. Specifically, under heavy accountability pressure, bureaucrats may move away from conventional shirking behavior, such as being sloppy, inactive, idle at work, and slacking off, to engage in more covert shirking activities. Some may stick to the status quo and avoid making innovations or changes so as to play it safe; others may fabricate an image of success in fulfilling their responsibilities in order to disguise their irresponsible behavior. All this indicates that the intensification of sanction-based accountability may have deterrent effects on some types of shirking but not on others. It makes bureaucrats dare not to flagrantly evade responsibility and prevents abuse of power to some degree, but accountability pressure does not necessarily raise bureaucrats' responsibility awareness, and they may respond negatively by developing coping strategies.

The Chinese government has gradually become aware of the potential problems of accountability overload in recent years. It began to call for the establishment of fault-tolerance mechanisms and incentive mechanisms in 2016 to encourage reformers and innovators to put more effort into work, take the initiative, and strive for achievements. The frequency of top-down inspections and assessments of local work has decreased since the central government issued the *Circular on the Coordination of Inspection, Checking, and Assessment Work* (《关于统筹规范督查检查考核工作的通知》) in August 2018. However, accountability pressure within the Chinese bureaucracy won't vanish easily, as it takes time to institutionalize fault-tolerance mechanisms and to ensure their effective implementation.

This chapter contributes to a better understanding of the complex patterns and causes of bureaucratic shirking in China. It illustrates that accountability is by no means a panacea for bureaucratic shirking and may even backfire, causing opportunistic behaviors among bureaucrats. Practically, the analysis of the responses of public officials to accountability overload and their attitudes toward shirking proves that externally imposed control is not a cure for shirking because it does not help public officials develop an inner sense of responsibility. To deal with bureaucratic shirking, the Chinese government should put more emphasis on promoting high-level public service motivation, value-based compliance, and a strong awareness of public interests among its officials.

References

Adler, S., & Golan, J. (1981). Lateness as a withdrawal behavior. *Journal of Applied Psychology, 66*(5), 544–554.

Alchian, A. A., & Demsetz, H. (1972). Production, information costs, and economic organization. *The American Economic Review, 62*(5), 777–795.

Almén, O. (2018). Participatory innovations under authoritarianism: Accountability and responsiveness in Hangzhou's social assessment of government performance. *Journal of Contemporary China, 27*(110), 165–179.

Angle, H. L., & Perry, J. L. (1981). An empirical assessment of organizational commitment and organizational effectiveness. *Administrative Science Quarterly, 26*(1), 1–14.

Ashforth, B. E., & Lee, R. T. (1990). Defensive behavior in organizations: A preliminary model. *Human Relations, 43*(7), 621–648.

Barry, V., & Shaw, W. H. (1979). *Moral issues in business*. Wadsworth.

Behn, R. D. (2001). *Rethinking democratic accountability*. Brookings Institution Press.

Bennett, N., & Naumann, S. E. (2005). Understanding and preventing shirking, job neglect, social loafing, and free riding. In Kidwell, R. E., & Martin, C. L. (Eds.), *Managing Organizational Deviance* (pp. 113–126). Sage Publications.

Bovens, M., Schillemans, T., & 't Hart, P. (2008). Does public accountability work? An assessment tool. *Public Administration, 86*(1), 225–242.

Brandsma, G. J., & Schillemans, T. (2013). The accountability cube: Measuring accountability. *Journal of Public Administration Research and Theory, 23*(4), 953–975.

Brehm, J. O., & Gates, S. (1999). *Working, shirking, and sabotage: Bureaucratic response to a democratic public*. University of Michigan Press.

Cai, Y. (2014). *State and agents in China: Disciplining government officials*. Stanford University Press.

Chenzhou Municipal Government Website. (2014, September 22). *Implementation Rules for Accountability of Leading Cadres' Five Types of Shirking Behaviors (《领导干部 "为官不为" 五个一律问责实施细则》) promulgated by Chenzhou city, Hunan province in 2014*. http://www.czs.gov.cn/html/zwgk/ztbd/zfdzd/xgwj/content_486888.html

Corbin, J. M., & Strauss, A. (1990). Grounded theory research: Procedures, canons, and evaluative criteria. *Qualitative Sociology, 13*(1), 3–21.

CPC News. (2019, April 1). "*Accountability" also requires "responsibility."* Viewed October 9, 2024. http://theory.people.com.cn/n1/2019/0401/c40531-31005644.html

De Bruijn, H. (2002). Performance measurement in the public sector: Strategies to cope with the risks of performance measurement. *International Journal of Public Sector Management, 15*(7), 578–594.

Deng, D. (2020). Shift blame upward and transfer responsibility layer by layer. *Theoretical Investigation* (2), 157–162. (邓大才. 反向避责:上位转嫁与逐层移责——以地方政府改革创新过程为分析对象.理论探讨).

Downe-Wamboldt, B. (1992). Content analysis: Method, applications, and issues. *Health Care for Women International, 13*(3), 313–321.

Gao, J. (2016). "Bypass the lying mouths": How does the CCP tackle information distortion at local levels? *The China Quarterly, 228*, 950–969.

Han, Y. (2020). The impact of accountability deficit on agency performance: Performance-accountability regime. *Public Management Review, 22*(6), 927–948.

Hawkins, D. G., & Jacoby, W. (2006). How agents matter. *Delegation and Agency in International Organizations, 1*, 199–228.

Hood, C. (2010). The blame game: Spin, bureaucracy, and self-preservation in government. Princeton University Press.

Hou, L., Liu, M., & Zhang, D. (2022). Top-down accountability, social unrest, and anticorruption in China. *The American Review of Public Administration, 52*(6), 423–438.

Hu, L. T., & Bentler, P. M. (1999). Cutoff criteria for fit indexes in covariance structure analysis: Conventional criteria versus new alternatives. *Structural equation modeling: a multidisciplinary journal, 6*(1), 1–55.

Hupe, P., & Buffat, A. (2014). A Public Service Gap: Capturing contexts in a comparative approach of street-level bureaucracy. *Public Management Review, 16*(4), 548–569.

Jakobsen, M., & Jensen, R. (2015). Common method bias in public management studies. *International Public Management Journal, 18*(1), 3–30.

Jiyuan Municipal Government Website. (2016, June 22). *Measures to Hold Officials Accountable for Shirking in Jiyuan City (《济源市懒政怠政为官不为责任追究办法》) promulgated by Jiyuan city, Henan province in 2016*. https://www.jiyuan.gov.cn/zwgk/zcwjk/jzb1/t814047.html

Jos, P. H., & Tompkins, M. E. (2004). The accountability paradox in an age of reinvention: The perennial problem of preserving character and judgment. *Administration & Society, 36*(3), 255–281.

Judge, T. A., & Chandler, T. D. (1996). Individual-level determinants of employee shirking. *Relations Industrielles, 51*(3), 468–487.

Kennedy, J. J., & Chen, D. (2018). State capacity and cadre mobilization in China: The elasticity of policy implementation. *Journal of Contemporary China, 27*(111), 393–405.

Koppell, J. G. (2005). Pathologies of accountability: ICANN and the challenge of "multiple accountabilities disorder." *Public Administration Review, 65*(1), 94–108.

Krumpal, I. (2013). Determinants of social desirability bias in sensitive surveys: A literature review. *Quality & Quantity, 47*(4), 2025–2047.

Leibowitz, A., & Tollison, R. (1980). Free riding, shirking, and team production in legal partnerships. *Economic Inquiry, 18*(3), 380–394.

Liu, L., & Li, Q. (2024). Target and performance: evidence from China's air quality management. *Public Performance & Management Review, 47*(1), 174–203.

Li, Y., Qin, X., & Koppenjan, J. (2022). Accountability through public participation? Experiences from the tenthousand- citizen review in Nanjing, China. *Journal of Public Policy, 42*(1), 43–62.

Mansbridge, J. (2014). A contingency theory of accountability. In M. Bovens, R. E. Goodin, & T. Schillemans (Eds.), *The Oxford handbook of public accountability* (pp. 55–68). Oxford University Press.

McCubbins, M. D., & Schwartz, T. (1984). Congressional oversight overlooked: Police patrols versus fire alarms. *American Journal of Political Science, 28*, 165–179.

Mulgan, R. (2003). *Holding power to account: Accountability in modern democracies*. Springer.

Netease News. (2020, May 7). *The official media of the CCDI criticized arbitrary accountability*. Viewed October 9, 2024. https://www.163.com/dy/article/FC0U39R805439A3X.html

Nielsen, V. L. (2006). Are street-level bureaucrats compelled or enticed to cope?. *Public administration, 84*(4), 861–889.

O'Dwyer, L. M., & Bernauer, J. A. (2013). *Quantitative research for the qualitative researcher*. Sage.

Ossege, C. (2012). Accountability—Are we better off without it?: An empirical study on the effects of accountability on public managers' work behaviour. *Public Management Review, 14*(5), 585–607.

Pandey, S. K., Wright, B. E., & Moynihan, D. P. (2008). Public service motivation and interpersonal citizenship behavior in public organizations: Testing a preliminary model. *International Public Management Journal, 11*(1), 89–108.

People's Daily Online. (2019, December 6). *Strict rectification of vanity projects and image projects*. Viewed October 11, 2024. http://news.china.com.cn/2018-02/10/content_50474208.htm

Perry, J. L. (1996). Measuring public service motivation: An assessment of construct reliability and validity. *Journal of Public Administration Research and Theory, 6*(1), 5–22.

Peters, B. G. (2014). Accountability in public administration. In M. Bovens, R. E. Goodin, & T. Schillemans (Eds.), *The Oxford handbook of public accountability* (pp. 211–225). Oxford University Press.

Pingxiang Municipal Government Website. (2015, August 21). *Temporary measures for the accountability of shirking of the party and state staffs (《党和国家工作人员履职不力行为问责暂行办法》) promulgated by Pingxiang city, Jiangxi province in 2014*. http://jx.people.com.cn/n/2015/0403/c360836-24379536.html

Pollack, M. A. (1997). Delegation, agency, and agenda setting in the European Community. *International Organization, 51*(1), 99–134.

Power, M. (1997). *The audit society: Rituals of verification*. Oxford University Press.

Romzek, B. S., & Dubnick, M. J. (1987). Accountability in the public sector: Lessons from the challenger tragedy. *Public Administration Review, 47*(3), 227–238.

Rosch, E., & Mervis, C. B. (1975). Family resemblances: Studies in the internal structure of categories. *Cognitive Psychology, 7*(4), 573–605.

Schillemans, T., & Smulders, R. (2015). Learning from accountability?! Whether, what, and when. *Public Performance & Management Review, 39*(1), 248–271.

Stephenson, M. C. (2008). Optimal political control of the bureaucracy. *Mich. L. Rev., 107*, 53.

Tehseen, S., Ramayah, T., & Sajilan, S. (2017). Testing and controlling for common method variance: A review of available methods. *Journal of Management Sciences, 4*(2), 142–168.

Terman, J. N., & Yang, K. (2016). Reconsidering gaming in an accountability relationship: The case of minority purchasing in Florida. *Public Performance & Management Review, 40*(2), 281–309.

The CCDI Website. (2014, October 25). *The third televised political inquiry in Chenzhou, Hunan, examines the issue of bureaucratic shirking*. Viewed October 9, 2024. https://www.ccdi.gov.cn/tjts/jingtou/201511/t20151116_155452.html

The CCDI Website. (2018, August 17). *Nine cases tell you: Failure to answer phone calls is a serious problem under these situations*. Viewed October 10, 2024. https://www.ccdi.gov.cn/toutiao/201808/t20180817_177913.html?from=singlemessage

The China Comment. (2018, August 17). *It's easy to find scapegoats, but hard to find someone responsible*. Viewed October 10, 2024. https://baijiahao.baidu.com/s?id=1614465967434285895&wfr=spider&for=pc

The China Comment. (2018, February 10). *"Red-tapism" at the grassroots level: Work won't be done without leaders' directive*. Viewed October 10, 2024. http://news.china.com.cn/2018-02/10/content_50474208.htm

Tu, W. (2024). Unpacking the accountability cube and its relationship with blame avoidance. *Public Management Review, 26*(3), 701–723.

Tu, W., & Gong, T. (2022a). Accountability intensity and bureaucrats' response to conflicting expectations: A survey experiment in China. *Public Management Review, 24*(11), 1779–1801.

Tu, W., & Gong, T. (2022b). Bureaucratic shirking in China: Is Sanction-based accountability a cure? *The China Quarterly, 249*, 259–274.

Tu, W., Hsieh, C. W., Chen, C. A., & Wen, B. (2024). Public service motivation, performance-contingent pay, and job satisfaction of street-level bureaucrats. *Public Personnel Management, 53*(2), 256–280.

Van Osch, D., De Ruiter, R., & Yesilkagit, K. (2023). An accountability deficit? Holding transgovernmental networks to account. *Journal of European Public Policy, 30*(2), 315–333.

Wang, E. H. (2022). Frightened mandarins: The adverse effects of fighting corruption on local bureaucracy. *Comparative Political Studies, 55*(11), 1807–1843.

Weingast, B. R., & Moran, M. J. (1983). Bureaucratic discretion or congressional control? Regulatory policymaking by the federal trade commission. *Journal of Political Economy, 91*(5), 765–800.

Wood, B. D., & Waterman, R. W. (1991). The dynamics of political control of the bureaucracy. *A merican Political Science Review, 85*(3), 801–828.

Xinhua News. (2015, May 21). *File a complaint through a dedicated hotline if If you encounter bureaucratic shirking*. Viewed October 10, 2024. http://www.xinhuanet.com/politics/2015-05/21/c_127824354.htm

CHAPTER 5

The Accountability Cube and Blame Avoidance

This chapter explores the relationship between accountability and its evil twin—blame avoidance. Some scholars relate accountability to positive resonance and good governance (Bovens, 2010; Gamble, 2023). They suggest that enhanced accountability may boost the fulfillment of responsibilities by creating greater answerability and transparency in the bureaucracy, curbing flagrant abuse of power, and ensuring compliance with superiors' mandates (Dubnick, 2003; Dunn & Legge, 2001). However, a burgeoning strand of literature cautions that accountability may trigger its evil twin—blame avoidance—and contribute to the evasion of responsibility (Halachmi, 2014; Hood, 2014; Jos & Tompkins, 2004; Tu, 2024b).

What is the impact of accountability on blame avoidance? Are accountability and blame avoidance opposite sides of the same coin? How does the configuration of hierarchical accountability promote individuals' sense of responsibility without triggering their defensive motivation? Bureaucrats may react to a good accountability design with cooperation and compliance and respond to a bad accountability configuration with coping or defensive behaviors.

This chapter examines the sub-paradox of accountability structure. The paradox of structures examines the configuration of various components of accountability and how unbalanced arrangements of different elements may lead to negative consequences. By drawing on the cube

W. Tu, *The Accountability Paradox in the Chinese Bureaucracy*, https://doi.org/10.1007/978-981-96-6392-7_5

model to unpack accountability and holistically measuring accountability with concrete indicators, It advances the understanding of the internal mechanism of accountability and reconciles the competing theoretical expectations about its relationship with blame avoidance. The results show that sanction-based accountability that fixates on supervision and sanctions may yield unintended adverse consequences and result in strong blame-avoidance intention among bureaucrats, while trust-based accountability emphasizing discussion quality and reward-based consequences is more likely to foster a supportive and cooperative organizational culture, thus reducing blame avoidance.

The Accountability Cube

This chapter considers accountability a multifaceted mechanism instead of an aggregate concept and examines the impacts of its components on blame avoidance. The accountability cube, proposed by Brandsma and Schillemans (2013), is an informative model to unpack accountability as a mechanism. The accountability cube with a three-dimensional phase, includes information, discussion, and consequences phases, capturing the key elements of accountability (Blind, 2014; Brandsma & Schillemans, 2013; Schillemans & Busuioc, 2015). The cube attempts to gauge the intensity of the three phases, that is, the level of information (little ↔ much), the intensity of discussions (non-intensive ↔ intensive), and the reach of sanctions (few ↔ many).

I enhance this model by emphasizing the interaction between account holders and givers, as well as by adding additional measurement dimensions beyond intensity. As to the information phase, many scholars focus on the account giver's reporting of performance-related information (Koop, 2011; Wang, 2002). I argue that the account holder's active acquisition of information from the account giver through inspections and auditing is also significant during the information phase. Information reports by the account giver and information acquisition by the account holder are complementary strategies to ensure the accuracy of information. During the discussion phase, besides the intensity of discussions, the quality of discussions should be taken into consideration as a monologic style of dialogue cannot produce effective communication. Numerous conferences and discussions lacking genuine dialogues fail to achieve consensus and instead increase the workload. As to the consequence phase, instead of merely focusing on the reach of sanctions, I

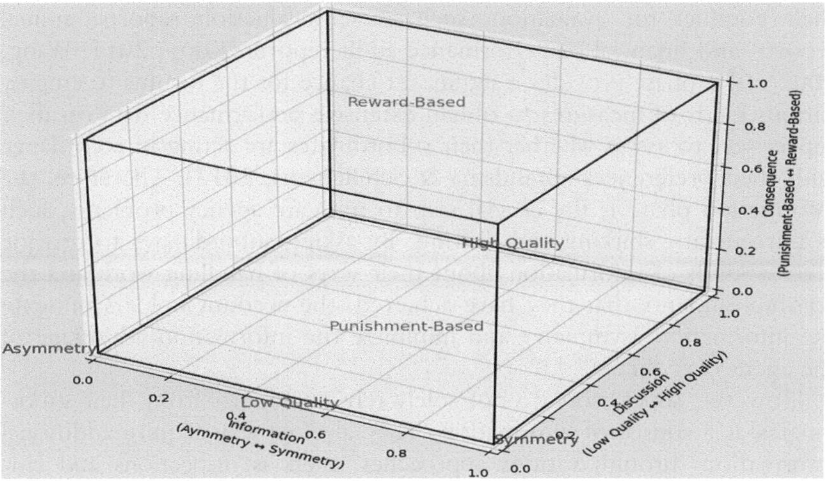

Fig. 5.1 The accountability cube (*Source* Adapted from Brandsma and Schillemans [2013])

classify consequences into two forms: reward-based consequences and punishment-based consequences, and examine how bureaucrats respond to the different consequences. Account holders need to communicate the consequences or necessary actions to be taken. Interactions help the account giver grasp the reasons and importance of the consequences, while also allowing for reflection and improvement. Overall, interactions in the three phases promote understanding, communication, and enhancement, ensuring the effectiveness and fairness of the accountability process.

Figure 5.1 shows the accountability cube adapted from Brandsma and Schillemans (2013). The X-axis represents the information phase (Asymmetry ↔ Symmetry). The Y-axis represents the discussion phase (High Quality ↔ Low Quality). The Z-axis represents the consequence phase (Reward-Based ↔ Punishment-Based).

Information Phase

In the information phase of an accountability scheme, the actors are required by accountability forums to provide documents or data about their conduct for evaluation, such as self-evaluation reports, annual reports, and financial or performance audit reports (Koop, 2011; Wang, 2002). The phase provides a significant chance for the forums to employ various kinds of measures to obtain extensive performance data on their supervisees to assess whether their subordinates are acting in accordance with their preferences (Brandsma & Schillemans, 2013). Therefore, the information phase is the crucial step to mitigate agency problems, such as bureaucratic shirking and drifting. By asking subordinates to provide various kinds of information about their ways of handling work and the accomplishments that they have achieved, the account holders mitigate the information asymmetry and minimize the information advantage of the agent over them.

However, supervisors do not solely rely on reports from their subordinates as a source of information. They also actively acquire additional information through various approaches, such as inspections and citizens' whistle-blowing (Acs, 2018; McCubbins & Schwartz, 1984). The common approaches to information collection continue to be government audits and inspections (Finan et al., 2017). In this regard, the extent of monitoring is crucial during the information phase, as the account holders determine what materials should be submitted and initiate various inspections or evaluations to assess bureaucratic performance. Monitoring is not only the start of enforcing consequences (punishments or rewards) based on the collected information but also by itself serves as an important credible deterrent.

Discussion Phase

The information phase is normally followed by a discussion phase, in which accountability forums assess performance information and may pose follow-up questions (Brandsma & Schillemans, 2013). The importance of the discussion phase is grounded in three facets of reasons. First, the discussion phase enables the supervisor to assess the credibility of the information. Subordinates, by virtue of their professional expertise and more intimate knowledge of actual circumstances, may exploit this advantage to misrepresent, obscure, or withhold information when reporting to their supervisors (Brehm & Gates, 1999; Gao, 2015). Second, the discussion phase offers the subordinate opportunities to explain, justify, and defend their actions (Brandsma & Schillemans, 2013). A dialogue between account holders and givers, using a shared "language of justification" (Day & Klein, 1987, p. 5), is the core of accountability (Harmon, 1995, pp. 191–197). Third, a high-quality discussion offers a mutual communication opportunity for an exchange of views to clarify misunderstandings and forge a consensus. Through candid dialogues, the agent may gain a deep understanding of the principal's preferences and intentions, and the principal also obtain more information from the agent about the practical situations and the difficulties encountered in the implementation of policies (Meier & O'Toole, 2006, p. 178). Ideally, superiors may modify policy goals and designs based on the agent's suggestions. Effective communication, in particular, significantly enhances cooperation (Orbell et al., 1988).

Discussions can take a variety of forms, from formal job discussions or conferences to informal ways such as a private chat over the phone or a face-to-face meeting. Discussions also vary in frequency and quality. The frequency centers on how often principals and agents actually engage in discussions. More specifically, the focus is on whether principals and agents have a feedback discussion regularly, frequently, or only after a problem arises (Brandsma, 2013, p. 131). Discussion quality depends on whether the discussion merely touches on superficial operational details or allows the actor and forum to fully articulate their concerns, clarify misunderstandings, and forge a consensus (Mulgan, 2000). Discussion with low-quality leads to feedback that "will only touch on minor details of operation and hardly give actor and forum the opportunity to fully express their views on the task at hand and the (lack of) progress made" (Brandsma & Schillemans, 2013, p. 955), while discussion with high quality "allows both parties in the accountability relationship to share their deepest concerns and thoughts about the way a given task is executed" (Brandsma & Schillemans, 2013, p. 957).

Consequence Phase

In the consequence phase, supervisors make judgments on their subordinates and then either impose punishments if their performance is unsatisfactory or give rewards if they meet expectations (Brandsma & Schillemans, 2013). The consequence should be deterrent or incentive enough to ensure bureaucrats' compliance in the next rounds of implementation.

Reward-based consequences can be categorized as positive incentives, which seek to motivate subordinates by promising a reward, whereas punishment-based consequences are negative incentives, aiming to control subordinates by threatening punishment. Reward-based consequences have a wide variety of forms, such as performance pay, bonuses, promotion or position transfers, open compliments, and honorary titles. Punishment-based consequences comprise a broad array of sanctions, ranging from formal to informal. Formal sanctions, enforced through laws and regulations, also take different forms, such as dismissal, degradation, demerit, and deduction of salary, bonuses, or budget. Although it is sporadic for bureaucrats to face dismissal or demotion, punishment-based consequences still seem to be more adopted than reward-based consequences in the public sector in the form of criticism or bonus reduction. Informal sanctions cannot be enforced through regulations, but can put pressure on the misbehaving agent by exposing his wrongdoings or unethical behavior ("naming and shaming") (Hafner-Burton, 2008; Wei et al., 2023).

The three phases often occur in a sequential order, but sometimes they may occur simultaneously or skip one of the phases (Brandsma & Schillemans, 2013). In an organization or a bureaucracy, the principal and agent are involved in repeated games in which the results in the first round exert an impact on the actions of both sides in the next round. The deterrent effect of accountability consequences may also influence the behavior of bureaucrats in the information and discussion phases. Sometimes, the agent may be asked to submit information without the opportunity to explain and justify what has happened. Principal-agent models are primarily concerned with whether the principal can acquire information about her agent's behavior and the positive or negative consequences the principal can impose on the agent based on the information. At other times, the negative consequence phase may not necessarily be invoked by principals for fear of jeopardizing the intimate personal relationship with their agents (Zhou, 2010). Under some circumstances, those in charge of collecting performance information may engage in corrupt practices and misuse the information, which may undermine the accountability system (Finan et al., 2017).

Four components are generated from the three phases of the cube: monitoring intensity, discussion quality, reward-based consequences, and punishment-based consequences. This chapter seeks to explore not only the respective impact of the four elements but also their different combinations on blame avoidance.

Blame Avoidance—The Evil Twin of Accountability

Blame avoidance is a prevailing and powerful incentive for public agents in an increasingly risky society (Hood, 2010; Weaver, 1986). It refers to "ways of trying to minimize, evade, or transfer culpability for harm or loss perceived to have been avoidable" (Hood, 2014, p. 2). Sulitzeanu-Kenan and Hood (2005) classify blame-avoidance behavior into anticipatory blame avoidance (ABA) and reactive blame avoidance (RBA). ABA is characterized by keeping potential problems and pitfalls off the agenda before they arise and become the sources of blame, while RBA refers to the presentational approaches used to mitigate culpability after blame has been raised (Hinterleitner & Sager, 2017; Hood, 2002; Ran, 2017). In the administrative literature, more attention has been paid to RBA, while ABA receives insufficient attention. ABA has become a pressing problem with an increasing number of bureaucrats responding to uncertainty and accountability pressures with an array of blame management strategies, such as shifting thorny tasks, self-limitation of discretion, and dispelling creative thinking (Hood, 2010; Tu, 2024a; Tu & Gong, 2022a). In this regard, ABA can be considered as an unintended perverse consequence of accountability that is meant to encourage officials to take responsibility. ABA is a destructive and disreputable activity within a bureaucracy, and it deserves more scholarly attention. This chapter focuses on the impacts of accountability cube on ABA.

Public officials adopt various strategies to avoid blame. Weaver (1986) proposes eight specific strategies that politicians frequently employ to avoid or mitigate public blame. They may keep potential blame-generating issues from the agenda regardless of the importance of the issues, redefine issues to reduce their own culpability if the issues cannot be kept from the agenda, delay bad outcomes by committing extra resources, pass the buck to let others make decisions, support popular policy alternatives, diffuse blame by dispersing it among other policymakers, constrain discretion to avoid making decisions, and find a scapegoat for bad outcomes.

Hood (2002) identifies three strategies employed by individuals, groups, or organizations to avoid blame, namely, presentational strategies, policy strategies, and agency (or delegation) strategies. Presentational strategies are impression management and attempts to shape the public's perceptions. It involves four tactics: maintaining a low profile until the trouble fades away over time, changing the subject to redirect public focus and bury bad news, winning the argument by offering convincing justifications, or drawing a line with a preemptive apology to neutralize critics and gain sympathy. Policy strategies are ways to control policies agenda or operate routines to minimize the risk of institutional or individual liability or blame. It comprises four approaches: Abstinence by rejecting any advice, protocolization by sticking to the rules, individualization by putting the onus on users, operators, or victims, and herding by employing collective decision. Agency strategies are efforts to diffuse formal duties or jurisdiction among institutions and other colleagues to shift responsibilities and find "scapegoat." It consists of static and dynamic strategies. The static strategies involve creating organizational structures that pass unpopular responsibilities down the hierarchy or establishing public–private and intergovernmental partnerships to disperse responsibility. The dynamic strategies include frequent reorganizations and the utilization of market forces to shift blame.

The three strategies are not mutually exclusive and have overlaps. Top-level officeholders usually possess significant resources at their disposal to employ all three types of strategies. Bartling and Fischbacher (2012) demonstrate in a set of experiments that supervisors can strategically use delegation as a way to offload accountability for contentious decisions and policies onto someone else. Although front-line officials have limited resources, they can leverage collective decision-making as a rationale to win the argument, skillfully manage various forms of accountability to shift blame, and creatively interpret policies and operations. Public officials make predominant use of presentational strategies during reactive blame games, while ABA relies more on policy strategies and agency strategies.

As to the driving forces of increased blame-avoiding intention in the public sector, the established literature attributes it to a "risk society," a modern society increasingly filled with newly occurred hazards and insecurities (Beck, 2009; Hood, 2002). Public actors are aware of their constituents' negativity bias, a tendency to outweigh real or potential losses over gains, which makes them prioritize blame avoidance and adopt risk management strategies (Weaver, 1986). The rise of public opinion has forced public officials to be more cautious and risk-averse. Moreover, as increased accountability and evaluation mechanisms are being introduced into the public sector, blame avoidance is a widely adopted strategy for bureaucrats to cope with uncertainty, blame risk, and work pressures (Mortensen, 2013; Ossege, 2012). Blame avoidance can be considered the evil twin of accountability that is meant to encourage officials to take responsibility.

In the face of diminished opportunities for claiming credit and intensified accountability, the easiest way for public officials to avoid blame is to reduce policy formulation and innovation that contain a risk of failure (Howlett, 2014), and to refrain from taking the initiative in policy settings (Hood, 2002). Moreover, protocolization becomes an excuse for inaction, which leads to burdensome and rigidity of administrative procedures (Zollo et al., 2002). Public officials may try to build complex and ambiguous administrative turf and procedures to obscure responsibilities (Hood, 2010, p. 170). What is more, blame is more likely to be imposed on street-level bureaucrats, diverting the public's attention from the negligence of the top and middle-level officials. The front-line bureaucrats may also strategically circumvent the predicament by distorting or blurring responsibilities to protect themselves. In a word, blame avoidance can greatly hinder an organization by fostering rigidity and cumbersome, ultimately resulting in inefficiency and inaction.

Blame Avoidance Among Grassroots Bureaucrats in China

Hierarchical accountability dominates the Chinese government with upper-tier authority exercising utmost control over lower-tier agencies (Shi & Ni, 2017). The Chinese government is more of an inward-looking hierarchy where blame avoidance is likely to surge when higher-level governments strengthen sanction-based accountability over lower-ranking officials. According to Hood (2002), in certain social contexts, the public has an inclination to blame those in leadership for various issues, whether they are significant or minor. Conversely, in other social environments, blame is often directed at individuals at a low level who are perceived as incompetent or clumsy. In China, the government structure is set up in such a way that places grassroots bureaucrats in vulnerable positions, as they are responsible for implementing the majority of policies and tasks, and often become scapegoats for higher-level officials when problems occur. The organizational structure of the Chinese government can be described by three key characteristics that transfer workload and liability downward.

First, the operation of the Chinese government is guided by the principle of "localized management" (*shudi guanli*, 属地管理). It is a "clever" organizational structure for higher authorities to transfer tasks and blame to lower levels. This system mandates that local governments manage social matters comprehensively and take responsibility for any incidents that occur within their jurisdictions. Interviewees working in township governments expressed concerns about this system, as it obscures responsibilities between superiors and subordinates (CB-2019-7; CB-2019-21). Upper-level governments wield this arrangement to pass on many challenging tasks to township governments that lack relevant professional expertise and resources to handle them (CB-2019-7).

Another characteristic of the organizational design is a "pressure-centered system" (*yalixing tizhi*, 压力型体制), where performance indicators and implementation pressure intensify as they move down through each level (*cengceng jiama*, 层层加码) (Han & Wang, 2023; Zhou & Lian, 2020). Specifically, during the policy implementation process, the standards become increasingly stringent at each level, leading to tight the execution. Grassroots officials face strong pressure to meet highly demanding targets and are required to complete these objectives within a specified timeframe. For example, the central government sets the GDP growth target at a 6% increase, provinces will aim for 8%, and cities are required to strive for 10% (Beijing News, 2021). In the process of delegating tasks, each level sets its own deadline. Initially, a week is allotted, but it is often reduced to three days during transmission, and at the grassroots level, officials are sometimes required to submit materials within just a few hours (CB-2019-3). There are two reasons underlying this system. First, the upper-level authorities want to surpass their counterparts to gain greater career advancement. Second, the higher-ups tend to retain the privileges and latitude for themselves while passing the stress and workload down to their subordinates. Grassroots officials with limited resources and manpower have to strategically deal with the intensified workload and pressure. Research identifies substantial efforts made by local officials to cope with these pressures through various strategies, including selective implementation, evasion, distortion, sabotage, and collusion (Kung et al., 2009; Chung, 2016; Zhou, 2010).

Third, the Chinese government is characterized by extended hierarchical structures consisting of five levels of administration. The stretch principal-agent chains make it difficult for higher-level officials to obtain accurate information related to local circumstances. Therefore, policies made by the higher-ups are usually at odds with the local contexts. Previously, the lower-level officials were endowed with considerable latitude to flexibly implement policies according to local conditions. However, in the last decade, power has largely been centralized, with agenda-setting and policy-making processes shifted to the central government (Lee, 2018; Schubert & Alpermann, 2019). The authority for setting goals, coordinating personnel, and distributing incentives at the grassroots level has been continuously centralized. "In the past, policy documents issued by upper-level governments usually included a statement indicating that lower-level officials could adapt policies to local conditions during implementation. However, with the rise in accountability intensity, many governments remove this statement for fear of making mistakes and being blamed" (CB-2024-10). Under power centralization and intensified sanction-based accountability, local officials lose considerable latitude to negotiate and bargin with higher-level officials, who are also under pressure from their superiors and forced to implement unpopular policies. The pressure from upper-levels and resistance from citizens puts grassroots officials in a dilemma and have to take various blame-avoiding strategies to cope with the pressure.

This kind of organizational structure is portrayed as "a small horse pulls a big cart" (*xima la dache,* 小马拉大车) where grassroots governments take on tasks that exceed their resources and capabilities, thus leading to a certain degree of organizational dysfunction. In the context of local governance, the excessive burden primarily manifests in three forms. The first is task overload. A large number of tasks are shifted to grassroots levels, including core tasks such as Party building, petition management, emergency responses, rural revitalization, ecological protection, and production safety. The second is responsibility overload. In some regions, higher-level departments can easily pass the buck to grassroots organizations by holding meetings or issuing documents. For example, in a certain county, the Market Supervision Bureau delegated responsibilities related to food safety and counterfeit drug detection to townships, despite the fact that these townships lack the necessary capacity and resources for drug identification (Renmin Luntan, 2024). The third is pressure overload. The tasks assigned by higher authorities are not only numerous but also come with tight deadlines and strict demands.

Besides top-down accountability, grassroots officials are also more susceptible to criticism from citizens. In China, citizens' trust in the government is hierarchical, with greater trust placed in central authorities than in local governments (Su et al., 2016). This pattern of hierarchical government trust is attributed to economic performance, cultural traditions, and institutionalized propaganda programs that uphold the legitimacy of the central government (Shi, 2001; Zhong, 2014). In fact, the attribution of blame among Chinese citizens is also hierarchical, as they tend to blame lower-level officials more than higher-level officials when problems occur. This hierarchical blame attribution is intentionally constructed by higher authorities through a series of institutional designs, including the localized management system, pressure-centered system, and the extended hierarchical structure, which strengthen the central government's authority and divert citizens' dissent to local governments. As grassroots officials are responsible for implementing many unpopular and contentious policies and engaging in daily interactions with citizens, they often bear the brunt of public blame. There is a famous saying among rural citizens: "The policies above are all good; the problem is that officials below implement them inappropriately" (*上面的政策都是好的, 只是下面的人执行歪了*). Faced with both top-down and bottom-up blame, it becomes the most rational choice for grassroots officials to employ various blame-avoiding strategies.

As for the blame-avoidance strategies adopted by grassroots officials, I would like to cite interesting findings from a Chinese scholar based on his fieldwork in a county in 2021 (Tian, 2023). In 2020, Province S mandated all regions to enhance the early rice production. However, constrained by local resource endowments, County X is better suited for a unique medium rice planting, making the large-scale promotion of early rice cultivation unsuitable for the area. As a result, the policy faced strong resistance from the public.

Three blame-avoiding tactics were adopted by the grassroots officials in County X. The first is mechanical execution. Faced with strong oversight and accountability pressure from higher authorities, grassroots officials tend to prioritize superiors' directives over citizens' demands and strictly adhere to the orders from above. For example, some village officials were aware that certain plots of land were not suitable for early rice cultivation, yet they planted early rice on them without considering the actual condition. The second strategy is creating a façade. Some grassroots officials planted bamboo shoots in areas unsuitable for rice cultivation to "cheat" technical oversight from higher authorities. On lands that are more likely to be inspected by superiors (such as plots along major roads), they planted early rice regardless of the suitability of the land to cope with superiors' inspections. The third tactic is formalism. This involves considerable superficial work to ostensibly fulfill responsibilities through formal procedures, including meticulously keeping records, preparing documentation, and following established protocols. In a nutshell, the institutional design of the Chinese government places grassroots bureaucrats in positions that are vulnerable to the intensification of accountability.

The hierarchical accountability in China is synonymous with monitoring and punishment, where opportunities for equal dialogues between higher-level authorities and subordinates are absent (Tu & Gong, 2022a). Power centralization leaves a small latitude for lower-level officials to challenge or even negotiate with the high-ups. Grassroots officials must implement policies rigorously without hesitation and may face sanctions if they fail to do so. Therefore, the strengthened accountability in recent years has prompted grassroots officials to adopt various blame-avoiding strategies rather than fostering constructive compliance and achieving good governance outcomes.

The Accountability Cube and Blame Avoidance

The four elements of accountability can be classified into two categories: positive reinforcement and negative reinforcement. According to Herzberg (2008), there are two different ways to motivate employees: a negative or a positive "kick in the ass" (KITA). The negative KITA is the use of threats, close monitoring, and poor performance evaluations to gain compliance. The positive KITA motivates employees by promising rewards, communication, and job participation. Positive and negative reinforcement are two major organizational approaches to regulating employees (Herzberg, 2008; Hilbe & Sigmund, 2010). Discussion and reward-based consequences are positive reinforcement that seeks to motivate bureaucrats by promising incentive measures to promote cooperative behaviors. Monitoring intensity and punishment-based consequences are categorized into negative reinforcement that exerts deterrent effects on bureaucrats and thus prevents them from committing deviant behavior. This chapter explores the impacts of the accountability cube on blame avoidance. Figure 5.2 illustrates the research framework.

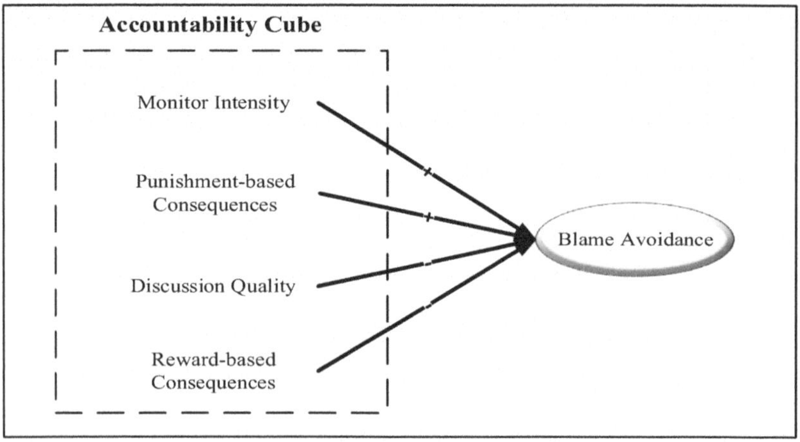

Fig. 5.2 The impacts of accountability cube on blame avoidance

Negative Reinforcement

Monitoring intensity and punishment-based consequences can be classified into negative reinforcement that constructs a sanction-imposing sense of accountability. A growing body of literature laments how intensive monitoring and punishment sometimes backfire (Hood, 2014; Ossege, 2012). A presumption that bureaucrats respond mechanically to top-down control is unfounded; coercive or scientific management cannot force subordinates to obey (Brehm & Gates, 1999; Meier & O'Toole, 2006; Tu & Gong, 2022b). Under the sanction-oriented logic of accountability, bureaucrats tend to prioritize blame avoidance and keep potentially blameworthy events off the agenda when they feel any mistake may be discovered and lead to punishment (Leland et al., 2021; Rajala, 2020). They may become risk-averse and adopt a variety of gaming strategies, such as deprecating risky agendas, passing the buck, and sticking to excessive proceduralism, to avoid the hazard of being blamed (Ashforth & Lee, 1990; Mansbridge, 2014).

Furthermore, an excessive focus on control and sanction is found to thwart the fundamental forms of innovation as well as to force out professionalism and moral deliberation (De Bruijn, 2002; Jos & Tompkins, 2004; Lindkvist & Llewellyn, 2003). Howlett (2014) reveals that out of fear of being held accountable for a policy failure, policymakers in the domain of climate change are less likely to launch novel policy inventions and refrain from taking the initiative in policy settings. It seems that public accountability in a low-trust and fault-finding environment is likely to elicit defensive emotions and blame avoidance (Hood, 2010; Ossege, 2012). In this light, stringent monitoring and punishment may not necessarily enhance bureaucrats' sense of responsibility. Instead, they tend to induce bureaucrats to cope with accountability pressures by repelling any potential blame-generating service. Given the foregoing discussion, I put forth the following proposition.

Proposition 1 Negative reinforcement including monitoring and punishment may increase ABA.

Positive Reinforcement

A burgeoning volume of literature considers that traditional accountability arrangements fixating on control and punishment of uncooperative behavior are likely to induce undesirable consequences such as goal displacement and gaming (Jakobsen et al., 2018; Lewis & Triantafillou, 2012). Public management academics increasingly advocate that accountability should be more attuned to learning and rewarding good behavior rather than controlling bureaucrats (Bovens et al., 2008). Accountability focusing on fault-looking might be inward-looking and closed, while accountability as learning promotes openness and reflexivity in the administrative process (Baxter et al., 2017; Schillemans & Smulders, 2015).

Policy learning and exchanges of best practices require extensive participation and dialogue between superior authorities and affected stakeholders (Lewis & Triantafillou, 2012). It is significant for those who are assessed to engage in the process of decision-making and consultation rather than being treated as passive subjects waiting to be evaluated and blamed (O'Loughlin, 1990). Continuous improvement and exchanges of best practices are possible through unforced, reciprocal, and reflective dialogues between relevant stakeholders (Rashman & Radnor, 2005; Schillemans & Smulders, 2015). Constructing accountability as a process of dialogue contributes to mutual understanding and, thus a sense of trust and a shared identity (Roberts, 2002). The effective forms of accountability should engage employees in discussion to learn from failure rather than focusing on the allocation of blame.

Similar to discussion, rewards for good performance also increase subordinates' perceptions of being trusted and subsequently strengthen their commitment to the organization (Podsakoff & Todor, 1985). Reward-based consequences may help build a more positive and appreciative atmosphere instead of a culture of fear and anxiety created by the constant threat of punishment (Gürerk et al., 2009). Compared with punishment techniques, positive reinforcement is more likely to be positively associated with higher levels of job satisfaction and performance because subordinates normally perceive rewards as symbols of support and recognition from superiors (Wayne et al., 2002). Corduneanu et al. (2020) suggest that if extrinsic rewards are conducted without crowding out individuals' basic psychological needs for autonomy, competence, and relatedness, they can effectively sustain public service motivation and thus enhance performance.

A supportive and equitable work environment is particularly required for bureaucrats, especially front-line workers, who are usually subject to tremendous workloads from superiors and constantly experience strain in dealing with the stressful demands and complaints of citizens (Lipsky, 2010). Public services are not always intrinsically interesting and enjoyable but are often riddled with tensions deriving from expectations collision, scarce resources, and intensive accountability (Brodkin, 2011; Hupe & Buffat, 2014). By conveying information about competence, fairness, and support, contingent rewards recognize public employees' competence and their dedication to serving the public (Eisenberger et al., 1999). Therefore, I propose that discussion and reward-based consequences may promote a more trusting and cooperative organizational climate in which blame-avoiding strategies are adopted less frequently. Thus, it is reasonable to put forth the following proposition.

Proposition 2 Positive reinforcement including discussion and rewards may curb ABA.

Interaction Effect in the Accountability Cube

One significant goal of accountability mechanisms is to mitigate information asymmetry between public principals and agents, which guarantees that principals are informed about their agents' behavior and are able to hold them accountable. Both monitoring and discussion are pivotal strategies for obtaining performance information, and they may interact with each other in the process of information acquisition to exert impacts on bureaucrats' propensity for blame avoidance.

Monitoring is thought to be essential in curbing agents' information advantages over their principals and thus makes it difficult for agents to deny their responsibilities (Miller, 2005). However, if bureaucrats are subjected to intensive oversight, they may perniciously manipulate performance measures and misrepresent their performance information to avoid accountability pressures (Gao, 2015). By providing bureaucrats a chance to explain their ways of handling tasks, the hardships they face, and their job outcomes, supervisors are more likely to obtain accurate performance information than mechanical supervision. Misunderstandings and tension arising from monitoring may also be mitigated through communication and dialogues, which contain bureaucrats' propensity to adopt blame-avoiding strategies (Harmon, 1995, p. 196). Discussion or dialogue is increasingly regarded as a solution to the pathologies of accountability derived from its improper configurations and implementation (Hood, 2014; Roberts, 2002). Therefore, discussion quality may moderate the effects of monitoring intensity on ABA, which leads to the third proposition.

Proposition 3 Discussion quality moderates the effect of monitoring intensity on ABA such that the positive association between monitoring intensity and ABA will be weakened with more qualified discussions.

Accountability Types and Anticipatory Blame Avoidance

This study further explores the impacts of different combinations of the four elements of accountability on blame avoidance. An expanding body of research proposes diverse forms of accountability, such as sanction-based, trust-based, dynamic, process-focused, and outcome-focused accountability (Bovens et al., 2008; Mansbridge, 2014; Zhang & Mittal, 2005). This study generates four types of accountability approaches based on variations in the two critical dimensions: (1) negative reinforcement centering on monitoring and potential punitive consequences, and (2) positive reinforcement centering on discussion and potential rewarding consequences.

As shown in Table 5.1, the laissez-faire style is defined by a combination of a low level of negative reinforcement and a low degree of positive reinforcement. Specifically, the information, discussion, and consequences

Table 5.1 Matrix of four types of accountability

		Negative reinforcement: monitoring and potential punitive consequences	
		Low	*High*
Positive reinforcement: discussion and potential rewarding consequences	Low	Laissez-faire style	Sanction-based style
	High	Trust-based style	Carrot and stick style

phases are almost absent in the accountability system, which is equivalent to accountability deficits and can be characterized as a "laissez-faire" type. Conversely, a relatively high level of both negative and positive reinforcement defines the "carrot and stick" style of accountability, which wields both carrot (incentives) and stick (punitive measures) approaches to regulate public agents' conduct. This type is also called benevolent paternalism and has long been found to be an effective management approach in Asian organizations (Cheng et al., 2004).

The "sanction-based" type combines a relatively low level of positive reinforcement and a high level of negative reinforcement. This type of accountability tries to control bureaucrats by keeping a close watch over them and threatening punishment for behavioral deviations. It is assumed that monitoring and sanction against violation of obligations are sufficient to deter agents from any deviant behavior (Finan et al., 2017; McCubbins & Schwartz, 1984). In contrast, the "trust-based" style is characterized by a combination of a high level of positive reinforcement and a relatively low degree of negative reinforcement. This type of accountability encourages participation, dialogue, and rewards for good behavior instead of repressive personnel management. The premise of this type of accountability is that public agents are well motivated in a supportive environment in which they tend to engage in cooperative behaviors even without monitoring (Pierre & Peters, 2017).

The typology of negative and positive reinforcement was inspired by the organizational control modes in the management literature. Within it are outlined a variety of management approaches and their links with organizational performance (Walton, 1985). Two general modes of control have been proposed. One mode depends on hierarchical command and control to enforce the compliance of bureaucrats; the other mode engages employees in decision-making processes to nurture shared values and commitment (Arthur, 1994; Heinsman et al., 2006). The sanction-based and trust-based styles of accountability bear some resemblances with the two modes of organizational control.

This study further examines the respective impacts of the four accountability types on blame avoidance and identifies which one is the most effective in curbing blame avoidance. Although sanction-based accountability may be appropriate in organizations with low trust, it aggravates distrust and creates a vicious circle as distrust generates a thirst for continuous monitoring and assessment (Ehren et al., 2020). By breeding distrust and risk aversion, a sanction-imposing sense of accountability may perniciously affect the public sector by impeding change and innovation and undermining the responsible judgments of individuals (Ebrahim, 2005; Jos & Tompkins, 2004). Nevertheless, trust-based accountability creates a less stressful and defensive climate by allowing subordinates to give an account of their behaviors (Mansbridge, 2014). For Pierre and Peters (2017), trust-based administrative systems, centering on shared professional values and cooperative spirits, may lower monitoring costs. This leads to the fourth proposition.

Proposition 4 Trust-based accountability is more likely to reduce ABA than sanction-based accountability.

Data and Analysis

Dependent variable: anticipatory blame avoidance. Hood (2002) distinguishes between three major approaches public agents adopt to avoid or mitigate blame, namely, presentational strategies, policy strategies, and agency strategies. Agency and policy strategies keep potentially blame-attracting tasks off the agenda. Deployed in advance of potential blame, the two approaches can be categorized as anticipatory forms of blame avoidance. To contain considerable blame risks, some officeholders refrain from taking the initiative in policy settings, over-conform to rigid regulations, or create bureaucratic barriers to decline unwanted demands (Li et al., 2021). Others try to shift workloads and thorny tasks to others including their colleagues, subordinates, or high-ranking authorities by various strategies (Hood, 2010).

Referring to the existing scholarly work, this study gauged ABA by a three-item structure comprising representative forms of agency and policy strategies on a five-point Likert scale (1 = Strongly disagree; 5 = Strongly agree). The three items include "more responsibilities lead to more mistakes, so one should get involved as little as possible," "One should avoid risk and give difficult tasks to others," and "One should stick to routines and avoid making any change and innovation." It measured respondents' intentions toward blame avoidance rather than their actual engagement in it. The sensitivity of the questionnaire was therefore reduced. The principal component factor analysis aggregated the three items into one factor, with the eigenvalue being larger than 1 and the cumulative explanation being 69%. The Cronbach's alpha is 0.68, presenting satisfactory reliability. A higher score indicates a stronger propensity for civil servants to skillfully adopt blame-avoiding strategies.

Independent variable: The accountability cube includes four indicators: monitoring intensity, discussion quality, reward-based consequences, and punishment-based consequences. Referring to the extant literature (Brandsma, 2013; Brandsma & Schillemans, 2013), I adopted a total of 13 items to measure the four accountability elements by a five-point Likert scale with 1 being "completely disagree" and 5 "completely agree." The measurement scales of monitoring intensity and punishment-based consequence are the same as in Chapter 3. Drawing on the scales of interactional justice (Skarlicki & Folger, 1997) and discussion (Brandsma & Schillemans, 2013), I used three items to gauge discussion quality between supervisors and subordinates. Respondents were asked whether the upper-level authorities allowed them to express their views on a job or a job assessment and communicate with them regularly. Inspired by Brandsma's (2013) scale of different types of consequences in the accountability cube, I formulated six items focused on reward-based and punishment-based consequences.

In order to confirm the dimensionality of these items, I conducted an exploratory factor analysis using varimax rotation. Table 5.2 shows that four components emerged with the Eigenvalue values larger than 1, accounting for 64.71% of the total variance. In factor analysis, item loadings above 0.6 (in bold) suggest that the item contributes significantly to that factor and is regarded as part of the construct. Four common factors were generated, and their Cronbach's alphas are: monitoring intensity (4 items, α = 0.79), discussion quality (3 items, α =

0.78), reward-based consequence (3 items, $\alpha = 0.71$), punishment-based consequence (2 items, $\alpha = 0.74$). I further performed a confirmatory factor analysis to evaluate the validity of the positive pressure and negative pressure dimensions. The goodness-of-fit indices for the whole construct of accountability are: CFI = 0.974, TLI = 0.960, RMSEA = 0.051, and SRMR = 0.04. The goodness-of-fit indices for the dimension of positive reinforcement show that CFI = 0.996, TLI = 0.978, RMSEA = 0.064, and SRMR = 0.010. The goodness-of-fit indices for the CFA on the dimension of negative reinforcement are CFI = 0.998, TLI = 0.996, RMSEA = 0.022, and SRMR = 0.019.

Table 5.2 Principal component analysis of the accountability cube

	Item loadings			
	Monitoring intensity	*Discussion quality*	*Reward-based*	*Punishment-based*
M1: Upper-level departments impose strict supervision over my work	**0.673**	0.110	0.144	0.170
M2: I need to report my work to upper-level departments frequently	**0.858**	0.049	−0.017	0.096
M3: Upper-level departments check and evaluate my work frequently	**0.797**	−0.095	0.017	0.156
M4: Any detail of the tasks must be recorded in the paperwork	**0.722**	−0.181	−0.092	0.132
D1: The higher authorities will listen to my explanations if my performance is not satisfying	−0.071	**0.832**	0.116	0.039

(continued)

Table 5.2 (continued)

	Item loadings			
	Monitoring intensity	*Discussion quality*	*Reward-based*	*Punishment-based*
D2: The upper authorities are willing to listen to our suggestions on work	−0.072	**0.853**	0.173	0.017
D3: The higher authorities communicate with me regularly	0.218	**0.612**	0.248	−0.018
R1: Performance evaluation in our department is fair	0.043	0.360	**0.710**	−0.028
R2: Chances for getting a promotion or better transfer is large if I perform well	0.067	0.239	**0.807**	−0.019
R3: Good performance will be rewarded with incentive material gains	−0.114	−0.008	**0.790**	0.093
P1: Poor performance will be severely criticized	0.136	0.003	−0.005	**0.884**
P2: The possibility of being punished is very high if I do not perform well	0.149	−0.008	0.040	**0.870**
Model statistics				
Eigenvalue	2.428	2.637	1.902	1.596
Cronbach's alpha	0.78	0.79	0.71	0.74

Basic demographic information was controlled for, including gender, age, administrative rank, and monthly income. Four key variables that are thought to exert impacts on ABA are also controlled for, that is, responsibility clarity, resources constraint, PSM, and peer pressure. To account for unobservable factors, such as culture, institutions, politics, and policies that vary across provinces, province-fixed effects were controlled. Mid-point response style was also controlled in the models. Mid-point response style is a common problem in a self-report survey in which respondents tend to choose the middle point regardless of content (Baumgartner & Steenkamp, 2001). I constructed a mid-point response style variable by counting the proportion of mid-points in 31 random heterogeneous items in the survey to capture this bias.

Table 5.3 provides the descriptive statistics of key variables. The average value of monitoring intensity is 3.75. Punishment-based consequences also present a relatively high score with a mean of 3.51. The mean of reward-based consequences is 2.96, and the mean of discussion quality is 3.12. The results demonstrate that the Chinese government has imposed intense monitoring and punishments to discipline public officials since Xi took office in 2012. Negative reinforcement was more likely to be used than positive reinforcement to regulate civil servants. As for the dependent variable, civil servants' propensity to wield blame-avoiding strategies is relatively strong with an average value of 3.49.

Table 5.3 Descriptive statistics and correlations

Variables	*Mean*	*SD*	*(1)*	*(2)*	*(3)*	*(4)*	*(5)*	*(6)*	*(7)*	*(8)*	*(9)*	*(10)*	*(11)*	*(12)*	*(13)*
(1) Monitoring intensity	3.75	0.88	1.00												
(2) Punishment-based	3.51	0.83	0.32***	1.00											
(3) Discussion quality	3.12	0.94	0.02	0.04	1.00										
(4) Reward-based	2.96	0.96	0.02	0.06	0.48*	1.00									
ABA	3.49	0.84	0.20***	0.25*	−0.27*	−0.31*	1.00								
(6) Responsibility clarity	3.01	1.07	0.24***	0.12*	−0.29*	−0.26*	0.36*	1.00							
(7) PSM	3.87	0.84	0.19***	0.17*	0.34*	0.20*	−0.02	−0.04	1.00						
(8) Peer pressure	3.53	0.99	0.06	0.06	0.43*	0.41*	−0.19*	−0.28*	0.22*	1.00					
(9) Resource constraint	3.09	1.07	0.14***	0.12*	−0.36*	−0.43*	0.29*	0.30*	−0.08*	−0.41*	1.00				
(10) Gender (male = 0)	0.54	0.50	−0.06	−0.08*	0.09*	−0.03	−0.07*	−0.06	−0.01	0.01	0.00	1.00			
(11) Age	1.61	1.01	−0.04	0.05	0.02	0.00	0.05	−0.02	0.08*	0.03	0.01	−0.10*	1.00		
(12) Administrative rank	1.64	1.26	−0.03	0.05	0.05	0.12*	0.01	−0.05	0.07*	0.02	−0.01	−0.09*	0.52*	1.00	
(13) Monthly income	2.38	1.16	0.04	0.06	0.04	0.04	0.09*	−0.02	0.10*	−0.04	−0.03	−0.09*	0.21*	0.29*	1.00

Note ****$p < 0.01$, **$p < 0.05$, *$p < 0.1$

Relationship Between the Accountability Cube and ABA

I employed multiple linear regressions to analyze the relationship between accountability and ABA. Table 5.4 presents the results of regression analyses. The control variables such as basic demographic factors, responsibility clarity, resource constraint, and peer pressure were included in Model 1 to form a benchmark for comparison. Holding constant all control variables, Models 2, 3, 4, and 5 were constructed to reveal the respective impact of the four accountability elements on the dependent variable. The four components were introduced together in Model 6, and an interaction term between monitoring intensity and discussion quality was included in Model 7. The variance inflation factor (VIF) test did not detect any multicollinearity problem in these models as VIF values were all below 2.

Table 5.4 Multiple linear regression results of accountability on ABA

	ABA						
	Model 1	*Model 2*	*Model 3*	*Model 4*	*Model 5*	*Model 6*	*Model 7*
Gender	0.03	0.03	0.03	0.06	0.01	0.05	0.05
	(0.06)	(0.06)	(0.06)	(0.06)	(0.06)	(0.06)	(0.06)
Administrative rank	−0.03	−0.03	−0.03	−0.02	−0.01	−0.01	−0.01
	(0.03)	(0.03)	(0.03)	(0.02)	(0.03)	(0.02)	(0.02)
Age	0.12*	0.13*	0.12*	0.12*	0.07	0.09	0.10
	(0.07)	(0.07)	(0.07)	(0.07)	(0.07)	(0.07)	(0.06)
Monthly income	0.04	0.03	0.04	0.03	0.03	0.03	0.03
	(0.03)	(0.03)	(0.03)	(0.03)	(0.03)	(0.03)	(0.03)
Responsibility clarity	−0.18***	−0.17***	−0.18***	−0.16***	−0.17***	−0.13***	−0.13***
	(0.03)	(0.03)	(0.03)	(0.03)	(0.03)	(0.03)	(0.03)
PSM	−0.12***	−0.13***	−0.12***	−0.06*	−0.09***	−0.08**	−0.10***
	(0.04)	(0.04)	(0.04)	(0.04)	(0.04)	(0.04)	(0.04)
Resource constraint	0.13***	0.12***	0.13***	0.09***	0.08**	0.05	0.05
	(0.03)	(0.03)	(0.03)	(0.03)	(0.03)	(0.03)	(0.03)
Peer pressure	−0.08**	−0.09***	−0.08**	−0.03	−0.03	−0.02	−0.03
	(0.03)	(0.03)	(0.03)	(0.03)	(0.03)	(0.03)	(0.03)
Accountability cube							

(continued)

Table 5.4 (continued)

	ABA						
	Model 1	*Model 2*	*Model 3*	*Model 4*	*Model 5*	*Model 6*	*Model 7*
Monitoring intensity		0.11***				0.10***	0.11***
		(0.04)				(0.04)	(0.04)
Punishment–based consequences			0.07*			0.06	0.05
			(0.04)			(0.04)	(0.04)
Discussion quality				−0.24***		−0.17***	−0.16***
				(0.04)		(0.04)	(0.04)
Reward-based consequences					−0.20***	−0.16***	−0.15***
					(0.04)	(0.04)	(0.04)
Monitoring intensity *Discussion quality							−0.15***
							(0.04)
Mid-point responses	−0.74***	−0.64***	−0.70***	−0.84***	−0.68***	−0.63***	−0.61***
	(0.17)	(0.17)	(0.17)	(0.16)	(0.16)	(0.17)	(0.17)
Province fixed effects	√	√	√	√	√	√	√
Constant	4.18***	3.89***	4.03***	4.58***	4.36***	4.21***	4.05***
	(0.37)	(0.38)	(0.39)	(0.37)	(0.36)	(0.39)	(0.39)
F	6.241	6.353	6.102	7.256	7.100	7.508	7.903
Adj R-squared	0.189	0.197	0.189	0.223	0.218	0.246	0.262

Note *** $p < 0.01$, ** $p < 0.05$, * $p < 0.1$

As shown in Model 2, monitoring intensity is positively related to ABA ($\beta = 0.11$, $p < 0.01$). Punishment-based consequence also presents a significant positive correlation with ABA ($\beta = 0.07$, $p < 0.1$) in Model 3. Therefore, Proposition 1 about the positive effects of monitoring and punishment intensity on ABA is supported. Models 4 and 5 indicate that positive reinforcement exerts opposite impacts on ABA in comparison with negative reinforcement. Specifically, discussion quality shows a significant negative correlation with ABA ($\beta = -0.24$, $p < 0.01$), and the reward-based consequence is also negatively associated with ABA ($\beta = -0.20$, $p < 0.01$). The significant relationships still hold after introducing all the explanatory variables in Models 5 and 6. As a result, Proposition 2 is supported. In a nutshell, the results demonstrate that intensive monitoring and punishment may lead civil servants to adopt various blame management strategies, such as blurring responsibility among institutions and officeholders and refraining from policy formulation. In contrast, high-quality discussion and reward-based consequences seem to effectively contain civil servants' incentives to avoid blame.

This study took one step further to explore the interaction between monitoring intensity and discussion quality on blame-avoiding intention. Model 6 reports a significant interaction between the intensity of monitoring and the effectiveness of discussion for ABA ($\beta = -0.15$, $p < 0.01$). Figure 5.3 shows the moderating effect of discussion quality on the relationship between monitoring intensity and ABA. It plots two regression lines with the blue one indicating low discussion quality and the red signifying high discussion quality. The blue line shows that if civil servants have fewer effective dialogues with their superior departments, they are more likely to respond to intensified monitoring with blame-avoiding activities. The red line demonstrates that if discussion quality is high, monitoring intensity is less likely to trigger bureaucrats' propensity to shift blame. Thus, discussion quality can undermine the positive impact of

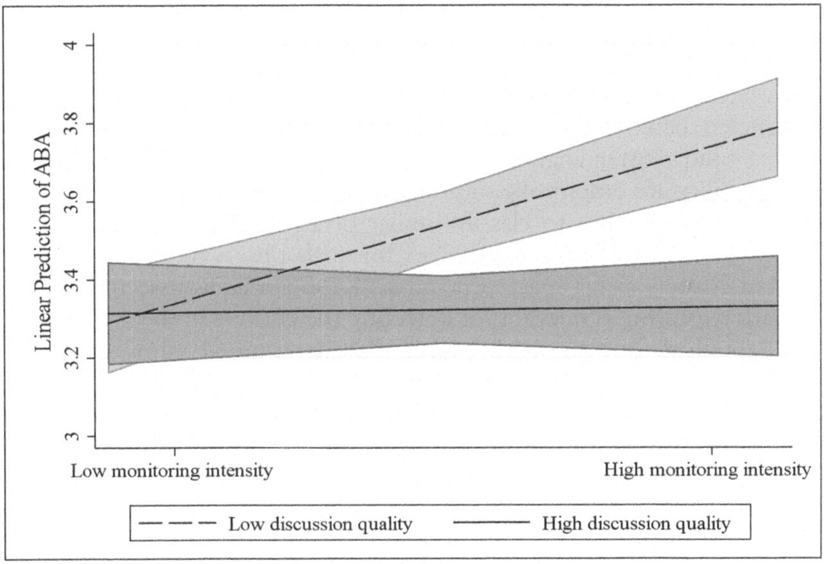

Fig. 5.3 Interaction between monitoring and discussion

monitoring intensity on ABA, which supports Proposition 3. This implies that effective discussion between subordinates and superiors may mitigate the tension and defensive emotions caused by intensive monitoring. As a result, the process of monitoring should be accompanied by more opportunities for subordinates to express their views.

The regression results also reveal some interesting findings about the control variables. Responsibility clarity is negatively associated with bureaucrats' ABA across the seven models. This indicates that if responsibilities are clearly stated and assigned, it will be difficult for officials to seek loopholes to distort their responsibilities. Bureaucrats with a higher level of PSM are also found to be less likely to adopt blame management strategies, indicating that PSM is a significant prosocial disposition in inhibiting bureaucrats' propensity for resorting to blame-avoiding strategies. Resource constraint shows a positive correlation with ABA, while peer pressure is negatively associated with ABA. However, the significant effects of resource constraint do not hold in Models 6 and 7, and the significant effects of peer pressure do not hold in Models 4, 5, 6, and 7.

Relationship Between Different Accountability Types and ABA

Four types of accountability mechanisms have been theoretically constructed based on the variations in negative and positive reinforcement. I used cluster analysis to explore whether the four categories of accountability are empirically meaningful and interpretable. Cluster analysis uses an algorithm to classify similar observations into clusters with the nearest mean of several variables for each observation and to keep different clusters as far apart as possible (Kaufman & Rousseeuw, 2009). K-means clustering is relevant for detecting the clusters in the data if there is a theoretical foundation to expect a predetermined number of clusters (Audenaert et al., 2019). Therefore, the K-means algorithm requires advanced knowledge of the number of clusters and uses a predefined cluster. As this study has theoretically proposed a four-category model of accountability, the K-means clustering procedure in the SPSS 23 was used and specified four clusters. As shown in Fig. 5.4, the K-means clustering corresponds to the four-category approach of accountability built on theories.

The observations were assigned to one of the four clusters based on their similarity in the scores on monitoring intensity, discussion quality,

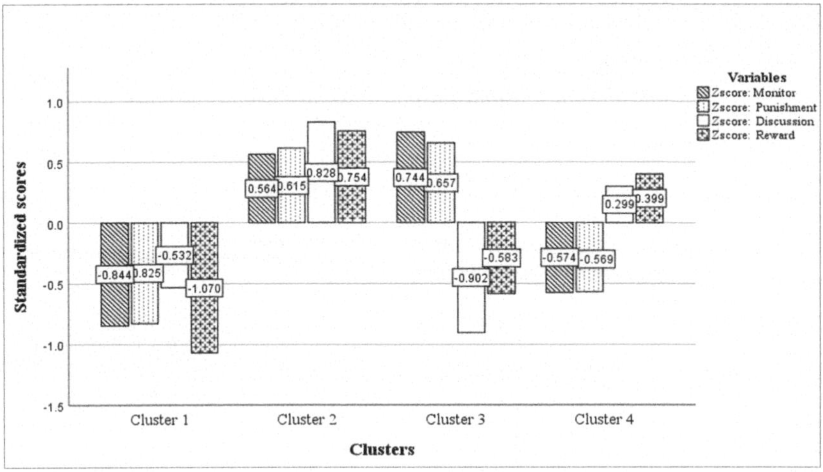

Fig. 5.4 Final cluster centers

reward-based consequences, and punishment-based consequences. A MANOVA using Wilks' Lambda test was performed and indicates that the overall difference between clusters is statistically significant (Wilk's $\Lambda = 0.12$, $F\,(12, 2228) = 222.66$, $p < 0.001$, multivariate $\eta^2 = 0.50$), and the univariate F-tests of the differences between the clusters are also significant ($p < 0.001$). The Wilks' Λ varies from 0 to 1. $\Lambda = 0$ indicates that the groups' mean vectors differ, while $\Lambda = 1$ shows that the groups' means are the same. Thus, minimizing the value of Wilks' Λ means the best distinguishing between groups (Lipovetsky, 2015). Table 5.5 presents the mean scores (both raw and standardized) for the four elements of accountability in each of the four clusters. In general, the four clusters are consistent with the conceptual typology of accountability based on the framework of positive and negative reinforcement.

As shown in Table 5.5, the standardized scores for both negative and positive reinforcement are below the sample average (mean = 0) in cluster 1, which can be considered a "laissez-faire" approach. Conversely, in the second cluster, the standardized scores for all four dimensions are above the sample average, a category that is characterized as the "carrot and stick" approach. In the third cluster, the standardized scores for the negative reinforcement are above average, while the positive reinforcement is below the sample average. This type is the "sanction-based" approach that

Table 5.5 Four clusters of accountability approaches

	Total	*Cluster 1 Laissez-faire*	*Cluster 2 Carrot and stick*	*Cluster 3 Sanction*	*Cluster 4 Trust*
Negative reinforcement					
Monitoring intensity	3.75	2.91 (−0.84)	4.31 (0.56)	4.49 (0.74)	3.18 (−0.57)
Punishment-based	3.52	2.69 (−0.83)	4.13 (0.61)	4.18 (0.66)	2.95 (−0.57)
Positive reinforcement					
Discussion quality	3.12	2.59 (−0.53)	3.95 (0.83)	2.22 (−0.90)	3.42 (0.30)
Reward-based	2.96	1.89 (−1.07)	3.71 (0.75)	2.38 (−0.58)	3.36 (0.40)
Number of observations	849	145	223	209	272

Standardized scores are in parentheses

mainly wields tight monitoring and stern punishment to tighten its grip on bureaucrats. In contrast, the standardized scores for positive reinforcement are above the average, while the scores for negative reinforcement are below the sample average in the fourth cluster. It is entitled to the "trust-based" approach in which discussion, participation, and rewards are the major inducements for public agents.

This study takes a step further to analyze the impacts of the four different accountability configurations on bureaucrats' blame-avoiding tendency. The results in Table 5.6 demonstrate which accountability approach is more likely to inhibit strategic blame containment behavior. Model 8 designates the sanction-based type as the reference group to compare its effects with that of other approaches on ABA, while Model 9 assigns the trust-based type as the reference group.

In Model 7, the respondents who perceive the accountability approach in their organizations to be the sanction-based type have a higher propensity to engage in blame avoidance compared with those who are under the trust-based ($\beta = -0.40$, $p < 0.01$), the carrot and stick ($\beta = -0.37$, $p < 0.01$), and even the laissez-faire ($\beta = -0.16$, $p < 0.1$) types of accountability. However, the trust-based type of accountability is more likely to inhibit bureaucrats' intention of avoiding blame than the laissez-faire type ($\beta = 0.26$, $p < 0.01$) and especially the sanction-based type ($\beta = 0.40$, $p <$

Table 5.6 Different accountability types and ABA

	ABA	
	Model 8	*Model 9*
Independent variables		
Laissez-faire	−0.16*	0.26***
	(0.09)	(0.09)
Carrot and stick	−0.37***	0.04
	(0.09)	(0.08)
Sanction-based		0.40***
		(0.08)
Trust-based	−0.40***	
	(0.08)	
Control variables		
Gender	0.05	0.05
	(0.06)	(0.06)
Age	0.12*	0.12*
	(0.07)	(0.07)
Administrative rank	−0.02	−0.02
	(0.03)	(0.03)
Monthly income	0.03	0.03
	(0.03)	(0.03)
Responsibility clarity	−0.16***	−0.16***
	(0.03)	(0.03)
PSM	−0.10***	−0.10***
	(0.04)	(0.04)
Resource constraint	0.09***	0.09***
	(0.03)	(0.03)
Peer pressure	−0.05	−0.05
	(0.03)	(0.03)
Mid-point responses	−0.75***	−0.75***
	(0.18)	(0.18)
Province fixed effects	Yes	Yes
Constant	4.17***	3.88***
	(0.37)	(0.37)
F	6.627	6.627
Adj R-squared	0.215	0.215

Note *** $p < 0.01$, ** $p < 0.05$, * $p < 0.1$

0.01). The difference between the impacts of the carrot and stick type and the trust-based type on ABA is the smallest and not significant, indicating that negative reinforcement should be accompanied by positive reinforcement to inhibit the potential side effects brought about by the former. In conclusion, in contrast to the sanction-based approach, the trust-based type is effective in reducing bureaucrats' engagement in blame-deflecting activities. Therefore, Proposition 4 is supported.

The reverse causality that ubiquitous blame-avoidance behaviors lead to frequent inspections and sanction-based accountability is unlikely. Being aware of the potential positive effects of sanction-based accountability on blame avoidance, the government is less likely to still impose intense negative reinforcement to curb blame avoidance, which may lead to a vicious circle. The situation in China also suggests that reverse causality is less possible. Realizing the seriousness of blame avoidance brought about by intensified supervision and sanction, the Chinese government established fault-tolerance mechanisms in 2016 to incentivize public officials (Tu & Gong, 2022).

Conclusion

Accountability and blame avoidance are generally considered opposite sides of the same coin. This chapter unpacks the internal mechanism of hierarchical accountability and explores the impacts of its four elements and their configurations on the anticipatory form of blame avoidance. This chapter conceptualizes accountability as a multifaceted and complex cube comprising not only negative reinforcement but also positive incentives.

The research yields two major findings. First, negative reinforcement and positive reinforcement exert opposite effects on bureaucrats' blame-avoiding behavior. Negative reinforcement, including stringent monitoring and excessive punishment, does not necessarily contribute to compliance and good performance. It may provoke defensive emotions and induce bureaucrats to employ various coping strategies to deal with potential blame. This does not mean that monitoring needs to be forsaken. Monitoring plays a prerequisite role in the information phase of the accountability cube to acquire rich performance information. Monitoring should be deployed to promote transparency and be accompanied by dialogue rather than merely be a means of control. Nevertheless, positive reinforcement, comprising discussion and reward-based consequences, is more beneficial in reducing bureaucrats' blame-avoidance intention and in building a participative and inclusive organizational culture that encourages cooperative behavior.

Second, accountability is classified into four types based on the positive and negative reinforcement in the cluster analysis, namely the laissez-faire, carrot and stick, sanction-based, and trust-based types. This study further explores the impacts of different forms of accountability on blame avoidance and solidifies the aforementioned results. The results indicate that the trust-based style of accountability with higher positive reinforcement and lower negative reinforcement is more effective in reducing blame avoidance than the sanction-based approach that relies on higher negative reinforcement and lower positive reinforcement.

This study echoes a burgeoning literature that questions the effectiveness of sanction-based and non-reflective accountability (Ebrahim, 2005; Lewis & Triantafillou, 2012). A growing body of research suggests that accountability centering on instrumentality and fault-finding may undermine public agents' moral reflections and sense of responsibility (Brees & Martinko, 2015; Halachmi, 2014; Jos & Tompkins, 2004; Roberts, 2002). This study adds to this strand of literature by empirically revealing that the appropriate configuration of accountability is essential to effectively managing bureaucrats. Excessive fixation on supervision and sanction may yield unintended negative consequences. This study also contributes to a better understanding of the internal mechanism of accountability and its relationship with responsibility. By adopting the accountability cube, it develops more specific indicators for the empirical measurement of accountability as a mechanism, which supplements the relatively scarce empirical research on accountability.

The mechanism of hierarchical accountability in China and some Western countries may appear to be similar, but the institutional and cultural differences should be considered when testing the external validity of this study. Public agents in Western countries are embedded in a dense "web" of diverse accountability. As a result, bureaucrats adopt blame-avoidance strategies in response to conflicting demands from diverse accountability and external pressures from citizens. Nevertheless, hierarchical accountability dominates the Chinese government with upper-tier authority exercising utmost control over lower-tier agencies, and citizens have few channels to express their expectations (Shi & Ni, 2017). Therefore, the Chinese government is more of an inward-looking hierarchy where blame avoidance is likely to surge when higher-level governments strengthen sanction-based accountability over lower-ranking officials.

Accountability is a multifaceted mechanism, and the government should optimize its configuration rather than simply imposing an arsenal of sanction-based mechanisms. Excessive sanction-based accountability may not contribute to bureaucrats' sense of responsibility and moral deliberation, but instead invoke distrust, fear of being blamed, and gaming strategies. A good accountability system should emphasize how well it fosters a cooperative, reflective, and trusting organizational culture to foster responsible bureaucrats. However, accountability has become a synonym for punishment in many governments that focus on what went wrong and who should be blamed. Given the struggling budget and limited fiscal spaces to offer monetary rewards, monitoring, and punishment are still major strategies to minimize information asymmetry and regulate bureaucrats in many countries. But the negative reinforcement should be exercised without excess, and a truly dialogical mode of communication between superiors and subordinates should be accompanied to prevent bureaucrats' defensive emotions.

A limitation of this study is that blame avoidance is measured by intention instead of actual behavior. Although there is a gap between intention and behavior, the underlying intention is a good predictor of an individual's behavior (Sheeran, 2002). This study calls for more research efforts to expound on the intricate mechanisms of accountability instead of considering it as an abstract term. I also hope to inspire others to reveal the operation of accountability and its impacts on officials' sense of responsibility in different cultural contexts with rigorous methodologies.

References

Acs, A. (2018). Policing the administrative state. *The Journal of Politics, 80*(4), 1225–1238.

Arthur, J. B. (1994). Effects of human resource systems on manufacturing performance and turnover. *Academy of Management Journal, 37*(3), 670–687.

Ashforth, B. E., & Lee, R. T. (1990). Defensive Behavior in Organizations: A Preliminary Model. *Human Relations, 43*(7), 621–648.

Audenaert, M., George, B., & Decramer, A. (2019). How a demanding employment relationship relates to affective commitment in public organizations: A multilevel analysis. *Public Administration, 97*(1), 11–27.

Bartling, B., & Fischbacher, U. (2012). Shifting the blame: On delegation and responsibility. *The Review of Economic Studies, 79*(1), 67–87.

Baumgartner, H., & Steenkamp, J.-B.E.M. (2001). Response styles in marketing research: A cross-national investigation. *Journal of Marketing Research, 38*(2), 143–156.

Baxter, D., Colledge, T., & Turner, N. (2017). A study of accountability in two organizational learning frameworks: Why accountability for learning is critical. *European Management Review, 14*(3), 319–332.

Beck, U. (2009). *World at risk*. Polity.

Beijing News. (2021, March 5). *How to understand this year's GDP targets and macroeconomic policy direction?* Viewed November 10, 2024. https://baijiahao.baidu.com/s?id=1693400068568374021&wfr=spider&for=pc

Blind, P. K. (2014). The accountability cube: Moving from dichotomy to continuity. In P. K. Blind (Ed.), *Policy-driven democratization* (pp. 83–106). Palgrave Macmillan US.

Bovens, M. (2010). Two concepts of accountability: Accountability as a virtue and as a mechanism. *West European Politics, 33*(5), 946–967.

Bovens, M., Schillemans, T., & Hart, P. 'T. (2008). Does public accountability work? An assessment tool. *Public Administration, 86*(1), 225–242.

Brandsma, G. J. (2013). *Controlling comitology*. Palgrave Macmillan UK.

Brandsma, G. J., & Schillemans, T. (2013). The accountability cube: Measuring accountability. *Journal of Public Administration Research and Theory, 23*(4), 953–975.

Brees, J., & Martinko, M. J. (2015). Judgments of responsibility versus accountability. *Journal of Leadership & Organizational Studies, 22*(4), 443–453.

Brehm, J. O., & Gates, S. (1999). *Working, shirking, and sabotage: Bureaucratic response to a democratic public*. University of Michigan Press.

Brodkin, E. Z. (2011). Policy work: Street-level organizations under new managerialism. *Journal of Public Administration Research and Theory, 21*(suppl_2), i253–i277.

Cheng, B., Chou, L., Wu, T., Huang, M., & Farh, J. (2004). Paternalistic leadership and subordinate responses: Establishing a leadership model in Chinese organizations. *Asian Journal of Social Psychology, 7*(1), 89–117.

Chung, J. H. (2016). China's local governance in perspective: Instruments of central government control. *The China Journal, 75*, 38–60.

Corduneanu, R., Dudau, A., & Kominis, G. (2020). Crowding-in or crowding-out: the contribution of selfdetermination theory to public service motivation. *Public Management Review, 22*(7), 1070–1089.

Day, P., & Klein, R. (1987). *Accountabilities: Five public services*. Taylor & Francis.

De Bruijn, H. (2002). Performance measurement in the public sector: Strategies to cope with the risks of performance measurement. *International Journal of Public Sector Management, 15*(7), 578–594.

Dubnick, M. J. (2003). Accountability and ethics: Reconsidering the relationships. *International Journal of Organization Theory & Behavior, 6*(3), 405–441.

Dunn, D. D., & Legge, J. S., Jr. (2001). US local government managers and the complexity of responsibility and accountability in democratic governance. *Journal of Public Administration Research and Theory, 11*(1), 73–88.
Ebrahim, A. (2005). Accountability myopia: Losing sight of organizational learning. *Nonprofit and Voluntary Sector Quarterly, 34*(1), 56–87.
Ehren, M., Paterson, A., & Baxter, J. (2020). Accountability and trust: Two sides of the same coin? *Journal of Educational Change, 21*(1), 183–213.
Eisenberger, R., Rhoades, L., & Cameron, J. (1999). Does pay for performance increase or decrease perceived self-determination and intrinsic motivation? *Journal of Personality and Social Psychology, 77*(5), 1026–1040.
Finan, F., Olken, B. A., & Pande, R. (2017). The personnel economics of the developing state. *Handbook of Economic Field Experiments, 2*, 467–514.
Gamble, A. (2023). Accountability as a democratic virtue. *Political Quarterly, 94*(3), 508.
Gao, J. (2015). Performance measurement and management in the public sector: Some lessons from research evidence. *Public Administration and Development, 35*(2), 86–96.
Gürerk, Ö., Irlenbusch, B., & Rockenbach, B. (2009). Motivating teammates: The leader's choice between positive and negative incentives. *Journal of Economic Psychology, 30*(4), 591–607.
Hafner-Burton, E. M. (2008). Sticks and stones: Naming and shaming the human rights enforcement problem. *International Organization, 62*(4), 689–716.
Halachmi, A. (2014). Accountability overloads. In M. Bovens, R. E. Goodin, & T. Schillemans (Eds.), *The Oxford handbook of public accountability* (pp. 560–573). Oxford University Press.
Han, H., & Wang, J. (2023). Performance management and environmental governance in China. *Journal of Chinese Governance, 8*(4), 498–532.
Harmon, M. M. (1995). *Responsibility as paradox: A critique of rational discourse on government*. Thousand Oaks.
Heinsman, H., de Hoogh, A. H., Koopman, P. L., & van Muijen, J. J. (2006). Competency management: Balancing between commitment and control. *Management Revue, 17*, 292–306.
Herzberg, F. (2008). *One more time: How do you motivate employees?* Harvard Business Review Press.
Hilbe, C., & Sigmund, K. (2010). Incentives and opportunism: From the carrot to the stick. *Proceedings of the Royal Society B: Biological Sciences, 277*(1693), 2427–2433.
Hinterleitner, M., & Sager, F. (2017). Anticipatory and reactive forms of blame avoidance: Of foxes and lions. *European Political Science Review, 9*(4), 587–606.

Hood, C. (2002). The risk game and the blame game. *Government and Opposition, 37*(1), 15–37.

Hood, C. (2010). *The blame game: Spin, bureaucracy, and self-preservation in government*. Princeton University Press.

Hood, C. (2014). Accountability and blame–avoidance. In M. Bovens, R. E. Goodin, & T. Schillemans (Eds.), *The Oxford handbook of public accountability* (pp. 603–616). Oxford University Press.

Howlett, M. (2014). Why are policy innovations rare and so often negative? Blame avoidance and problem denial in climate change policy-making. *Global Environmental Change, 29*, 395–403.

Hupe, P., & Buffat, A. (2014). A public service gap: Capturing contexts in a comparative approach of street-level bureaucracy. *Public Management Review, 16*(4), 548–569.

Jakobsen, M. L., Baekgaard, M., Moynihan, D. P., & van Loon, N. (2018). Making sense of performance regimes: Rebalancing external accountability and internal learning. *Perspectives on Public Management and Governance, 1*(2), 127–141.

Jos, P. H., & Tompkins, M. E. (2004). The accountability paradox in an age of reinvention: The perennial problem of preserving character and judgment. *Administration & Society, 36*(3), 255–281.

Kaufman, L., & Rousseeuw, P. J. (2009). *Finding groups in data: An introduction to cluster analysis*. Wiley.

Koop, C. (2011). Explaining the accountability of independent agencies: The importance of political salience. *Journal of Public Policy, 31*(2), 209–234.

Kung, J., Cai, Y., & Sun, X. (2009). Rural cadres and governance in China: Incentive, institution and accountability. *The China Journal, 62*, 61–77.

Lee, T. C. (2018). Pernicious custom? Corruption, culture, and the efficacy of anti-corruption campaigning in China. *Crime, Law and Social Change, 70*, 349–361.

Leland, S., Mohr, Z., & Piatak, J. (2021). Accountability in government contracting arrangements: Experimental analysis of blame attribution across levels of government. *The American Review of Public Administration, 51*(4), 251–262.

Lewis, J. M., & Triantafillou, P. (2012). From performance measurement to learning: A new source of government overload? *International Review of Administrative Sciences, 78*(4), 597–614.

Li, J., Ni, X., & Wang, R. (2021). Blame avoidance in China's cadre responsibility system. *The China Quarterly, 247*, 681–702.

Lindkvist, L., & Llewellyn, S. (2003). Accountability, responsibility and organization. *Scandinavian Journal of Management, 19*(2), 251–273. Lipovetsky, S. (2015). MANOVA, LDA

Lipsky, M. (2010). *Street-level bureaucracy: Dilemmas of the individual in public service*. Russell Sage Foundation.
Lipovetsky, S. (2015). MANOVA, LDA, and FA criteria in clusters parameter estimation. *Cogent Mathematics, 2*(1), 1071013.
Mansbridge, J. (2014). A contingency theory of accountability. In M. Bovens, R. E. Goodin, & T. Schillemans (Eds.), *The Oxford handbook of public accountability* (pp. 55–68). Oxford University Press.
McCubbins, M. D., & Schwartz, T. (1984). Congressional oversight overlooked: Police patrols versus fire alarms. *American Journal of Political Science, 28*, 165–179.
Meier, K. J., & O'Toole, L. J. (2006). Political control versus bureaucratic values: Reframing the debate. *Public Administration Review, 66*(2), 177–192.
Miller, G. J. (2005). The political evolution of principal-agent models. *Annual Review of Political Science, 8*(1), 203–225.
Mortensen, P. B. (2013). Public sector reform and blame avoidance effects. *Journal of Public Policy, 33*(2), 229–253.
Mulgan, R. (2000). 'Accountability': An ever-expanding concept? *Public Administration, 78*(3), 555–573.
O'Loughlin, M. G. (1990). What is bureaucratic accountability and how can we measure it? *Administration & Society, 22*(3), 275–302.
Orbell, J. M., Van de Kragt, A. J., & Dawes, R. M. (1988). Explaining discussion-induced cooperation. *Journal of Personality and Social Psychology, 54*(5), 811.
Ossege, C. (2012). Accountability—Are we better off without it?: An empirical study on the effects of accountability on public managers' work behaviour. *Public Management Review, 14*(5), 585–607.
Pierre, J., & Peters, B. G. (2017). The shirking bureaucrat: A theory in search of evidence? *Policy & Politics, 45*(2), 157–172.
Podsakoff, P. M., & Todor, W. D. (1985). Relationships between leader reward and punishment behavior and group processes and productivity. *Journal of Management, 11*(1), 55–73.
Rajala, T. (2020). Blame avoidance strategies in governmental performance measurement. *Financial Accountability & Management, 36*(3), 278–299.
Ran, R. (2017). Understanding blame politics in China's decentralized system of environmental governance: Actors, strategies and context. *The China Quarterly, 231*, 634–661.
Rashman, L., & Radnor, Z. (2005). Learning to improve: Approaches to improving local government services. *Public Money and Management, 25*(1), 19–26.
Renmin Luntan. (2024, August 16). *Reducing burdens at the grassroots level! How to solve the 'small horse pulling a big cart' phenomenon?* Viewed November

10, 2024. https://baijiahao.baidu.com/s?id=1807506695583206363&wfr=spider&for=pc

Roberts, N. C. (2002). Keeping public officials accountable through dialogue: Resolving the accountability paradox. *Public Administration Review, 62*(6), 658–669.

Schillemans, T., & Busuioc, M. (2015). Predicting public sector accountability: From agency drift to forum drift. *Journal of Public Administration Research and Theory, 25*(1), 191–215.

Schillemans, T., & Smulders, R. (2015). Learning from accountability?! Whether, what, and when. *Public Performance & Management Review, 39*(1), 248–271.

Sheeran, P. (2002). Intention—Behavior relations: A conceptual and empirical review. *European Review of Social Psychology, 12*(1), 1–36.

Shi, P., & Ni, M. (2017). The allocation mechanism of authority and accountability in Chinese government hierarchies: A case study of the "Earmarked Project System." *The Journal of Chinese Sociology, 4*(1), 4–25.

Shi, T. (2001). Cultural values and political trust: A comparison of the People's Republic of China and Taiwan. *Comparative Politics, 33*, 401–419.

Skarlicki, D. P., & Folger, R. (1997). Retaliation in the workplace: The roles of distributive, procedural, and interactional justice. *Journal of Applied Psychology, 82*(3), 434–443.

Su, Z., Ye, Y., He, J., & Huang, W. (2016). Constructed hierarchical government trust in China: Formation mechanism and political effects. *Pacific Affairs, 89*(4), 771–794.

Sulitzeanu-Kenan, R., & Hood, C. (2005). Blame avoidance with adjectives? Motivation, opportunity, activity and outcome. *ECPR Joint Sessions, Blame Avoidance and Blame Management Workshop, Granada, Spain, 14th-20th April.*

Tian, X. (2023). Supervision Paradox: Blame Avoidance Behaviors of Grassroots Officials. *Seeker*, (05), 159–166 (田先红. 督查悖论: 监督下乡中的基层避责行为. 求索).

Tu, W. (2024a). Unpacking the accountability cube and its relationship with blame avoidance. *Public Management Review, 26*(3), 701–723.

Tu, W. (2024b). The interactive effect of extrinsic controls and public service motivation on blame avoidance. *Public Personnel Management*, 00910260241283549.

Tu, W., & Gong, T. (2022a). Bureaucratic shirking in China: Is sanction-based accountability a cure? *The China Quarterly, 249*, 259–274.

Tu, W., & Gong, T. (2022b). Accountability intensity and bureaucrats' response to conflicting expectations: A survey experiment in China. *Public Management Review, 24*(11), 1779–1801.

Walton, R. E. (1985). *From control to commitment in the workplace: In factory after factory, there is a revolution under way in the management of work.*

US Department of Labor, Bureau of Labor-Management Relations and Cooperative Programs.

Wang, X. (2002). Assessing administrative accountability: Results from a national survey. *The American Review of Public Administration, 32*(3), 350–370.

Wayne, S. J., Shore, L. M., Bommer, W. H., & Tetrick, L. E. (2002). The role of fair treatment and rewards in perceptions of organizational support and leader-member exchange. *Journal of Applied Psychology, 87*(3), 590–598.

Weaver, R. K. (1986). The politics of blame avoidance. *Journal of Public Policy, 6*(4), 371–398.

Wei, W., Wang, C., Zhai, W., & Li, W. (2023). "Honor list" and "shame roll": Quasi-experimental evidence of the effect of performance feedback under political control. *Journal of Public Administration Research and Theory, 33*(1), 122–138.

Zhang, Y., & Mittal, V. (2005). Decision difficulty: Effects of procedural and outcome accountability. *Journal of Consumer Research, 32*(3), 465–472.

Zhong, Y. (2014). Do Chinese people trust their local government, and why?: An empirical study of political trust in Urban China. *Problems of Post-Communism, 61*(3), 31–44.

Zhou, X. (2010). The institutional logic of collusion among local governments in China. *Modern China, 36*(1), 47–78.

Zhou, X., & Lian, H. (2020). Modes of governance in the Chinese bureaucracy: A "control rights" theory. *The China Journal, 84*, 51–75.

Zollo, M., Reuer, J. J., & Singh, H. (2002). Interorganizational routines and performance in strategic alliances. *Organization Science, 13*(6), 701–713.

CHAPTER 6

Accountability Conflicts and Bureaucrats' Working Effort

Although accountability is a "chameleon-like" and "ever-expanding" concept, there is a basic agreement that it revolves around answerability toward significant others who have a legitimate claim to demand an account (Mulgan, 2000; Romzek & Dubnick, 1987). This conceptualization assumes a clear principal-agent relationship, highlighting the importance of controlling bureaucratic agents and ensuring their answerability (Willems & Van Dooren, 2012). When there is a single or limited number of account holders, the expectations imposed on the bureaucracy can be defined more clearly, making it easier to ensure answerability to its primary principals. However, bureaucrats, nowadays, increasingly find themselves embedded in a complicated dense "web" of multiple accountability mechanisms, in which they have to manage the diverse expectations of different stakeholders (Page, 2006; Romzek & Ingraham, 2000). The concept of "answerability" centers on the viewpoint of account holders and their assertion of expectations, while the conceptualization of accountability as managing expectations highlights the proactive role of those being held accountable. It is the account givers who decide how to manage diverse expectations from various stakeholders.

The focus of accountability should center on how public agencies manage "the diverse expectations generated within and outside the organization" (Romzek & Dubnick, 1987, p. 228). There are two reasons underlying this emphasis. First, bureaucrats are often confronted with

W. Tu, *The Accountability Paradox in the Chinese Bureaucracy*,
https://doi.org/10.1007/978-981-96-6392-7_6

diverse expectations imposed by various stakeholders, for example, expectations from immediate superiors, subordinates, constitutions, citizens, and professional norms (Koppell, 2005; Romzek & Ingraham, 2000). The ideal situation is for the expectations to be aligned, so bureaucrats do not need to strike a balance between them. However, this is not necessarily the case in reality. Expectations and policy agendas are often incompatible or undermine each other, making it challenging for the bureaucracy to formulate goals or measures satisfying all stakeholders. Second, even when all parties agree on the overarching goals, the divergence regarding specific performance indicators can lead to significant tensions. When accountability standards are vague, it becomes challenging to hold individuals or organizations responsible for their actions.

Rather than acting as neutral Weberian technocrats, bureaucrats take on the role of network managers, striving to seek viable, practical solutions to policy issues that can satisfy as many stakeholders as possible or balance conflicting expectations (Agranoff & McGuire, 2001; Klijn & Koppenjan, 2012). In this regard, bureaucrats' motivations, preferences, and behavioral choices are of significance in shaping policy agendas and implementation. Viewing accountability as managing expectations offers valuable insights into how bureaucrats address various demands within governance networks.

This chapter examines how local officials manage contradictory expectations from hierarchical account holders and citizens. Underlying the contradictory expectations faced by grassroots bureaucrats is a profound dilemma: as state agents, they are accountable to their superiors in the organizational hierarchy but as citizen agents, they are responsible for what happens to local citizens (Maynard-Moody & Musheno, 2000). Thus, bureaucrats are often caught between top-down pressure and bottom-up expectations. The former holds them accountable to superiors, while the latter requires them to be responsive to local citizens' requests and interests. Therefore, this chapter illustrates the paradox of sources of accountability. Facing contradictory expectations from their superiors and citizens, what choices do grassroots bureaucrats take? Do they work in citizens' interests in defiance of their superiors' instructions, or do they comply with top-down demands regardless of the preferences of local citizens? Does the increase in hierarchical accountability influence how bureaucrats manage these contradictory expectations?

To address these questions, this chapter uses a between-subject experimental design. The findings show that although bureaucrats tend to put more effort into tasks that are aligned with citizens' interests, overly stringent accountability may crowd out their intrinsic motivation to serve the public and push them to follow top-down instructions mechanically. Intensified accountability may therefore not necessarily lead to greater compliance and better policy outcomes. Therefore, this chapter also examines the sub-paradox of responsibility which shows that external controls may threaten to undermine individuals' moral judgment and fail to promote responsible and ethical behavior.

Accountability Expectations in Governance Networks

The political systems gradually evolve from hierarchically structured, unitary forms of government that operate through laws, rules, and order, to more horizontally organized and relatively decentralized governance systems that manage through the self-regulating networks (Torfing & Sørensen, 2014). Democratic or political accountability is facing challenges from self-governing public and semi-public institutions on the right to represent the interest of a "people" (Klijn & Skelcher, 2007; Sørensen & Torfing, 2021). Besides self-governing units, the fragmentation of layered institutional systems complicates governance networks which reshape the sources and nature of accountability (Peters & Pierre, 2001; Schillemans, 2008; Willems & Van Dooren, 2011).

In governance networks, two forms of accountability interact with each other to hold bureaucrats accountable: horizontal accountability and hierarchical accountability. Horizontal accountability as new forms of accountability arrangements complement traditional, hierarchical accountability (Bovens, 2007; Grigorescu, 2008; Reddick et al., 2020), while they cannot replace hierarchical accountability and still operate "in the shadow of hierarchy" (Schillemans, 2008).

Hierarchical accountability operates as a top-down "chain of command" and control system (Jarvis, 2014). It is characterized by a principal-agent relationship that establishes a delegating chain extending from citizens to elected and appointed officials, and down to the street-level bureaucrats responsible for supporting public policy development and implementation (Romzek & Dubnick, 1987). This obligation often implies a formal relationship between the superior–subordinate relationships, suggesting that account holders could directly sanction account givers based on their performance (Schillemans, 2016). Typical hierarchical accountability derives from the political, administrative, and legal directions (Bovens, 2007).

Nevertheless, horizontal accountability normally pertains to non-hierarchical forms of accountability and entails no full principal-agent relationships between account givers and account holders (O'Donnell, 1998; Schillemans, 2011). Therefore, many horizontal accountability arrangements possess limited formal sanctioning authority and depend more on public expression and voices within policy networks (Schillemans, 2008) or on reputation mechanisms where account givers seek to fulfill the demands of societal actors to uphold their good reputation (Busuioc & Lodge, 2017). Based on the principle of affected rights and interests, semi-autonomous agencies, independent evaluators, stakeholder boards, commissioners, the media, interest groups, and the public (including citizens or clients) can all serve as horizontal account holders (Reddick, Demir, & Perlman, 2020). Different from the compliance chain embedded in hierarchical accountability, deliberation, bargaining, compromise, and collaboration are the primary operating mechanisms of network-based governance (Sørensen & Torfing, 2009).

Fragmented Governance Networks in the Chinese Bureaucracy

The governance structure in China is characterized by lines and blocks, which includes a five-tier hierarchy from the central government to provincial-level, prefecture-level, county-level, and township-level administration and multiple functional divisions at each level. Policy-making and implementation necessitate collaboration among various levels of government and diverse functional agencies. In this regard, local authorities at each level need to deal with multiple higher-level account holders imposing various task objectives that may conflict with each other, be independent, or complement one another. In China, local authorities are primarily responsible for three principals at higher levels: Party committees, government, and functional departments, whose goals and interests are often in conflict with each other. Given the constraints on time and attention, local authorities must prioritize or strike a balance among diverse tasks assigned by different superiors. They may tend to place more attention and effort on the expectations from the superior who possesses greater authority to enforce formidable consequences on them. In the

Chinese government, there are significant differences in the authoritative status among the three account holders based on their extent of control over important resources such as personnel, finance, and other assets. As to local governments and departments, the higher-level Party committees hold the most substantial authority, while higher-level governments possess formal authority, and higher-level functional departments only have symbolic authority over them (Jaros, 2016). The SC system is a significant addition to the group of account holders.

Hierarchical accountability enforced by the higher-level Party committee, government, functional departments, and SC plays a dominant role in Chinese governance networks (Hu, 2017; Li, 2024). Upper-level authorities wield various sorts of checks and balances, such as public budgets and audits, cadre responsibility contracts, performance appraisals, promotion, and codes of conduct, to hold lower-level officials accountable for their demands (Hu, 2017). For example, the higher-level Party committee imposes close supervision on lower-level officials by periodically launching inspections. Furthermore, the higher-level Party committee possesses substantial organizational and personnel authority that determines the career advancement of lower-level officials. By signing cadre responsibility contracts with their lower-level government, the higher-level government lays out specific performance goals and indicators, holding their subordinates accountable through the application of rewards and penalties. Upper-level functional departments primarily influence lower-level officials by using honor lists and shame rolls based on their performance in specific areas, thereby affecting their reputations.

Compared to the dominant hierarchical accountability, social organizations are relatively small in scale with limited influence, and citizens have restricted channels to hold public employees accountable. By investigating rural governments, Tsai (2007) reveals that informal norms of accountability generated from encompassing and embedding solidary groups in villages may help to hold local officials accountable in rural China. Ma (2012) illustrates that the development of Chinese social accountability is an essential way to hold officials accountable by promoting citizens' participation in the process of governing. However, hierarchical accountability, compared to the horizontal accountability exerted by the public, media, and social organizations, plays a much more critical role in affecting bureaucratic decisions and behaviors within the Chinese government. The pressure exerted by superiors is disproportionately larger than that imposed by citizens. Without an independent press and a genuine civil society, ordinary citizens find it difficult to hold government officials formally accountable for their interests (Almén & Burell, 2018). In recent years, citizens have exerted increased on bureaucrats through public opinions, petitions, and social protests (Wedeman, 2016). Chinese citizens gain more channels, such as government hotlines at different levels, online government platforms, and social media, to express their requests and concerns. However, citizens' constraints over bureaucrats are soft because their influence largely depends on whether their protests attract the attention of higher-level authorities, whether the higher-level officials prioritize public opinion, and whether corresponding punishment would be enforced on malfeasance.

Under the disproportionate accountability intensity, research finds that some grassroots officials ignore citizens' interests and even resort to illegal administrative strategies or harsh measures to force citizens' compliance in order to accomplish tasks assigned by their superiors (Cai, 2014). The existing research has graphically documented grassroots bureaucrats' detrimental subversion, including selective, symbolic, and violent policy implementation, severely undermining citizens' interests (Göbel, 2011; O'Brien & Li, 1999). Scant attention has been paid to the constructive role of local authorities in minimizing inconsistencies between upper-level policies and local conditions to boost citizens' interests.

Conflicts of Expectations Between Hierarchical and Horizontal Accountability

Both hierarchical and horizontal forms of accountability play crucial roles in policy choices and implementation of bureaucrats. In this chapter, hierarchical accountability primarily involves responsiveness to superiors' commands and expectations, while horizontal accountability focuses on the demands of citizens.

State Agents VS Citizen Agents

The traditional view of bureaucracy considers it to be a neutral instrument whose primary responsibility is to implement public policies promulgated by elected officials (McCubbins et al., 1987). The bureaucracy is seen as an organizational apparatus whose members are accountable only to their superiors along the hierarchical chain (Olsen, 2006). In recent decades, the increased orientation toward customers and the emphasis on the centrality of citizens under the framework of the NPM and the NPA has resulted in substantial changes to the traditional understanding of accountability relationships (Jos & Tompkins, 2004; Osborne, 2006). Bureaucrats are not only "state agents" who act in response to politicians but also "citizen agents" who use their expertise to serve the public (Maynard-Moody & Musheno, 2000).

The ideal situation is that expectations from superiors and citizens are aligned, so bureaucrats do not need to make a choice between them. In theory, a principal should be a benevolent leader who cares about citizens' interests and acts on behalf of them (Lupia & McCubbins, 1994; McCubbins & Schwartz, 1984). Principals are usually portrayed as seeking improved policy outcomes. Previous work has elaborated at great length on agents' violation of legal authority and agency drifting that undermine good policies promulgated by principals. Problems deriving from the principal side have been largely ignored (Schillemans & Busuioc, 2015; Tu & Gong, 2022). An increasing number of studies reveal that principals' opportunism and exploitation are detrimental and that the policies promulgated by them are not always in line with clients' interests (Sobol, 2016). The national or upper-level governments have less information than local bureaucrats about actual conditions and public preferences; as a result, policies formulated by the principals may fall short of citizens' expectations (Hawkins & Jacoby, 2006; Lipsky, 2010). This means that hierarchical accountability and horizontal accountability may conflict with each other.

Furthermore, the centralization of decision-making power may play a major role in the inconsistency of expectations between superiors and citizens or between the principal and the clients. On the one hand, the principal attempts to prevent the power delegated to the agent from being abused and guarantee that policies will be implemented rigorously rather than being sabotaged or aborted by the agent (Calvert et al., 1989; Johnson, 2013). Thus, the principal tries to centralize the policy formulation and squeeze the agents' discretionary power in the implementation of policies in the prevention of behavioral deviation among subordinates. On the other hand, the policies made by the upper-level governments and uniformly imposed on diverse regions are sometimes at odds with the local situation and may have adverse effects on citizens' well-being (Gao, 2015; Huang & Kim, 2020). As a result, bureaucrats frequently face a conflict of expectations between upper-level authorities and citizens.

Local bureaucrats, as bridges between upper-level officials and citizens, are usually aware of the conflicting expectations of superiors and citizens when they implement policies. Bureaucrats, especially those at street level, are likely to be more familiar with local situations and citizens' needs and thus able to amend flaws in top-down policies to better serve the interests of the public (Pepinsky et al., 2017). However, it is sometimes not clear what the public interest is and whether bureaucrats are able to uphold it. The concept of public interest reflects the well-being of the general public and society but is often abstract and even elusive. Critics may question bureaucrats' discretionary power unless the public interest can be clearly articulated (Jos & Tompkins, 2004). "Since there seem to be many 'publics' with different interests and demands, administrators must interpret and reconcile competing claims" (Jos, 1990, 229). For these reasons, the importance of the concept of public interest for bureaucrats does not lie in its clarity but in its function as a reminder to them of the need to consider the genuine public interest in policy implementation instead of mechanically following the principal's commands. "A term that plays this role, even though it lacks precision, is as valuable as it is inescapable" (Pennock, 1962, p. 182).

Furthermore, although the concept of public interest may sound vague in the abstract, bureaucrats who have close contact with the public know citizens' specific needs in particular contexts (Brodkin, 2011; Lipsky, 2010). Scholars suggest that, instead of struggling to clarify what the public interest is, clear and well-developed ethical and justice guidelines should be developed to resolve ethical dilemmas and help promote an "ethical consensus" on how to exercise administrative discretion responsibly to serve the public interest (Hart, 1974, p. 9; Jos, 2016).

Bureaucratic Choices Under Conflicting Expectations

Bureaucrats may face a dilemma; that is, carrying out superiors' ill-informed decisions as state agents may deviate from the interests of the public, while acting on behalf of local citizens may be deemed as disloyal or incompetent by their superiors. In either case, the bureaucrat has to betray someone's trust and interests. The behavioral choices of bureaucrats when facing divergent or convergent expectations between superiors and citizens are illustrated in Fig. 6.1.

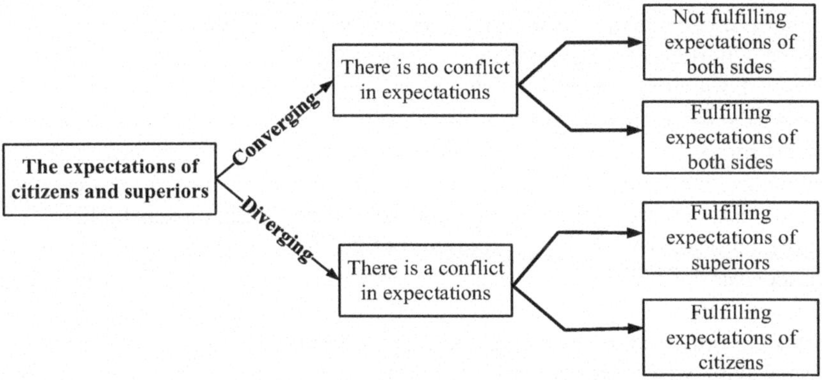

Fig. 6.1 Bureaucratic choices under conflicting expectations

If there is no conflict of expectations between superiors and citizens, bureaucrats may choose to work by fulfilling the expectations of both sides, and those with higher PSM may be more devoted to the project because it is in line with citizens' interests. However, some bureaucrats may choose to shirk by failing to meet the expectations of both sides in order to create more leisure time. If there is a conflict of expectations between superiors' policies and citizens, bureaucrats may need to choose between fulfilling the expectations of superiors and meeting those of citizens. Specifically, when the expectations of the principal and the citizen are consistent, the citizen desires a more obedient bureaucrat who strictly follows the principal's order (Prendergast, 2007). In many circumstances where the interests of the clients and the principal are in conflict, citizens benefit from bureaucrats who can (at least partially) bend rules that harm them and exert less effort in the policy implementation. Whether public officials choose to behave in accordance with the interests of superiors or citizens under divergent expectations may largely hinge on the accountability intensity imposed on them and bureaucrats' intrinsic motivations.

Accountability Intensity and Public Service Motivation

Assuming that bureaucrats act as rational economic individuals who are primarily self-interested and opportunistic, if accountability from higher-level governments is weak, they may opt to shirk their responsibilities to gain more leisure time, given the low risk of punishment, regardless of whether the expectations of their superiors and citizens align or differ. If the top-down supervision and punishment are stringent while the public has difficulty voicing their opinions or exerts little influence on government decisions, bureaucrats may passively place more emphasis on superiors' demands, which is especially destructive when there is a conflict in expectations from the citizens and superiors. In this regard, there is a high likelihood that bureaucrats may behave in accordance with the preferences of their superiors under the pressure of hierarchical monitoring and sanctions.

Some bureaucrats in China actively respond to upper-level governments even when policies conflict with citizens' interests, as it benefits them to cater to their superiors. For example, despite the actual conditions of local economic development and the public's opposition, some township governments carry out luxury infrastructure projects at will and engage in repeated and wasteful constructions in response to upper-level governments' target of boosting economic development (Zhou, 2010). Although bureaucrats meet the demands of their superiors, they fail to fulfill their responsibility to serve citizens and undermine public interests.

However, an increasing number of scholars disagree with the description of bureaucrats as rational economic men and believe that bureaucrats' prosocial values make them work in citizens' interests. Although public administration is often thought to be an instrument for achieving political ends, administrators shape ends in practice (Cook, 2014; Harmon, 1995). Scholars of the NPA disagree on the economic man hypothesis of the public choice approach. Frederickson (1980, p. 9) is opposed to public choice theory, which presents a "particularly unflattering image of public officials and portrays public administration in a spirit of self-service and greed." Conversely, public agents are not a tool of politicians or their superiors and instead are expected to exhibit loyalty to the office, not to the person or party (Cooper-Thomas & Wright, 2013; Friedrich, 2000).

The public sector can foster bureaucrats' prosocial values and altruistic behaviors, rather than promoting a rational choice calculation (Ritz et al., 2016; Vandenabeele et al., 2014). Numerous empirical studies evidence the presence of PSM or prosocial motivation in the public sector (Houston, 2000; Perry & Vandenabeele, 2015; Tu, 2024a; Tu et al., 2024). Thus, bureaucrats may not act merely in response to superiors' pressure and instead prioritize citizens' interests by committing prosocial rule breaking (Dahling et al., 2012; Fleming, 2020).

Some bureaucrats are found to wield their discretionary power to implement perfunctorily, bend, or adjust a policy to make it less pernicious to citizens or beneficial to them when the policy does not fit the local conditions (Fleming, 2022; Potipiroon, 2022). Although this behavioral choice is contrary to the principal's short-term preference, it is beneficial to clients or citizens in the long run. Some officials may work in citizens' interests and risk breaching their superiors' authority due to their high PSM, while others choose to do so because of realistic considerations. Bureaucrats need to be very cautious about a burst of public protests if they impose strictly unpopular policies on citizens. The occurrence of public protests or skip-level petitions imposes a negative impact on their political career. Given the foregoing discussion, I put forth the following proposition.

Proposition 1 Bureaucrats tend to put more effort into a task when it is consistent with citizens' interests than when it deviates from them.

Proposition 2 Bureaucrats with higher PSM are more likely to put effort into a task that is consistent with citizens' interests than those with lower PSM.

Scholars contend that over-stringent accountability may give a negative signal to bureaucrats and is likely to crowd out their intrinsic motivation (Tu, 2024a). In contrast to extrinsic motivation, intrinsic motivation arises from within the individual and occurs when one performs an activity without the need for any obvious external intervention, such as monetary rewards or potential punishment (Deci, 1972). When individuals perceive that they are being compelled to behave in a certain way by external forces, their sense of self-determination and esteem is undermined, and their intrinsic motivation may be overshadowed or even replaced by extrinsic incentives or disincentives; this has been referred to as the "crowding-out effect" (Deci & Ryan, 2008; Frey & Jegen, 2001). In other words, stringent accountability may suppress public servants' intrinsic motivation to work hard on a task.

In contrast to the crowding-out effect, there is a disciplining effect; that is, sanction mechanisms may raise performance by imposing higher costs on bureaucratic shirking (Bowles & Polania-Reyes, 2012). While the crowding-out effect reduces bureaucrats' intrinsic motivation to work hard, the disciplining effect of sanctions boosts their extrinsic motivation to perform (Frey & Jegen, 2001). The rise or fall in agents' performance levels depends on the relative strength of these two countervailing effects of accountability.

Scholars argue that public sector employees are generally prosocial and are motivated to serve the public more by intrinsic reward than extrinsic control (Banuri & Keefer, 2013; Perry et al., 2010). Thus, I assume that when bureaucrats face accountability pressure, the crowing-out effect may have a greater impact on their performance than the disciplining effect. The more they consider a task to be prosocial, the more likely they are to have a strong intrinsic motivation to perform it well, and the more likely an intensive external intervention is to impair that intrinsic motivation. Therefore, it is possible that if a task is in the interest of citizens, the intensification of accountability may not necessarily increase bureaucratic effort because the crowding-out effect is larger than the disciplining effect. Thus, my third and fourth propositions are:

Proposition 3 When a task is aligned with citizens' interests, intensified accountability may be counterproductive and lead to reduced bureaucratic effort.

Proposition 4 When a task is aligned with citizens' interests, intensified accountability tends to have a stronger crowding-out effect on grassroots bureaucrats with higher PSM than those with lower PSM.

However, when a task deviates from the interests of citizens, grassroots bureaucrats have no intrinsic motivation to work hard. In such cases, the disciplining effect exerted by extrinsic control may play a more important role in determining the level of bureaucratic effort. It is likely that grassroots bureaucrats will consider the task a "must-do" and put in more effort under increased accountability intensity so as to avoid being blamed or punished. They may respond opportunistically to accountability; that is, they may put less effort into a task when top-down accountability is less severe but more effort if it is intensified. This leads to our fifth proposition.

Proposition 5 When a task deviates from citizens' interests, the intensification of accountability may force grassroots bureaucrats to put in more effort.

Bureaucrats' Choices Between State Agents and Citizen Agents in China

It is observed that the power and policy-making in the Chinese government have become increasingly centralized in recent years (Schubert & Alpermann, 2019). An increasing number of policies are uniformly formulated by the central government or upper-level governments that demand sweeping conformity across different localities in implementation, characterized by "one-size-fits-all" (*yidaoqie*, 一刀切) approach. This approach imposes policies uniformly or indiscriminately regardless of local differences (Gao, 2015). The centralization of policy formulation and implementation cannot consider the differences across divergent regions and evaluate the plausibility of the policies in diverse places. Thus, although officials at the central or upper level may possess sufficiently good intentions, the unintended consequence is that there is a gap or inconsistency between the policy and the actual conditions of local places, which may cause detrimental effects on citizens' interests if bureaucrats strictly implement an inappropriate policy.

Consequently, grassroots bureaucrats often face a conflict between the expectations derived from top-down directives and those based on local citizens' needs. For example, an official in the village administration of Jiangxi province complained, "instructions from superiors often contradict the actual situation. In our village, we have only four low-income households, which means we do not qualify as an impoverished village. However, we are still required to attend frequent poverty alleviation meetings and submit related reports and data. This takes up a significant amount of time and prevents us from dedicating our energy to the real development of our village" (CB-2023-32). A resident of a town in a central province criticized that, "when the city was tasked with promoting a National Sanitary City, the municipal government mandated that all shop signs along the streets be painted red. This included China Mobile's longstanding blue sign and even the signs of funeral-related businesses, which are traditionally black. The standardized requirement is quite absurd" (The China Comment, 2019). According to an official, the irrigation facilities in their town, designed by a higher-level department, were built without steel reinforcements, rendering them vulnerable to damage and obstructing proper water flow. Many villagers have raised this concern, and their department has also brought it up with their superiors. However, the superiors have refused to listen. "The superior department possesses advanced technology, using satellite remote sensing to capture images of the farmland while refusing to conduct on-site investigations to assess the actual conditions" (CB-2019-3).

The decisions made by grassroots bureaucrats during policy implementation remain significant. Given China's vastness with substantial regional differences, local governments have more information about citizens' preferences in public services and a deeper understanding of local needs (Gong, 2006). Despite the trend toward centralized policy formulation, the fragmented authoritarian nature of the Chinese bureaucracy still endows local officials with considerable discretion in shaping public policies, especially during implementation (Brødsgaard, 2017). While authoritarianism guarantees top-down authority and induces a general allegiance among low-level officials, the fragmentation of power provides substantial latitude and leverage for local officials to bargain, muddle through, and even resist upper-level policies (Mei & Pearson, 2014; Zhou et al., 2013). The multiple-tier hierarchy and various horizontal agencies make the administrative structure segmented and the policy process disjointed, exacerbating information asymmetry and the incongruence of goals between the central and local governments.

Indeed, centralization of power greatly diminishes the discretionary authority of local officials; however, the fragmented structure and information asymmetry allow them to navigate policies with subtle maneuvers. Thus, the interests and decisions of local officials, especially those at the grassroots level who are primarily tasked with the enforcement of public policies, are essential and have to be taken into account in the policy process. Local bureaucrats' detrimental subversion, such as selective enforcement of tasks and aggressive policy implementation to accomplish performance indicators at the expense of citizens' interests, has been well documented in a large body of research (Cai, 2014; O'Brien & Li, 1999).

While it is true that local officials will yield more to vertical than to horizontal accountability in China, a burgeoning strand of literature suggests that grassroots bureaucrats seek to facilitate government responsiveness to local citizens (Mattingly, 2020). In China, local government leaders are tasked not only with executing higher-level policies but also with handling local civil matters and upholding social stability. Furthermore, grass roots officials who are deeply involved in township and village matters may become more "embedded" in local society and develop a strong desire to produce better policy outcomes for local citizens. They establish close relationships with local people and engage with solidarity groups, such as temple and lineage organizations, to provide high-quality public services (Tsai, 2007). Ideally, by serving as "cooperative gatekeepers," they adjust institutional constraints to satisfy the demands of both the rural populace and upper authorities through strategic policy implementation (Schubert & Ahlers, 2012, p. 69). Bureaucratic responses to accountability pressure are multifaceted, and the underlying rationale is more complex than conventionally believed.

A Survey Experiment

This chapter adopts a survey experiment to seek a more accurate analysis of the causal relationship between accountability and bureaucratic behavior. The survey experiment is an effective, low-cost, and widely applicable method to study human preferences and decision-making (Hainmueller et al., 2015). A survey experiment combines the merits of survey research and experimental methodology. By administering large samples, survey research tends to yield high external validity. However, surveys are limited in their ability to make causal predictions because cross-sectional data cannot guarantee that the variation in the dependent variable is solely due to the variation in the explanatory variable.

In contrast, experiment is the prime method of inquiry in science due to its advantage in causal predictions. The word experiment "implies the random assignment of respondents to control and treatment conditions" (Gaines et al., 2007, p. 182). The experimental method is characterized by careful control over variables and the manipulation of variables to test a hypothesis. In an experiment, an independent variable is manipulated and the change in the dependent variable is measured to explore the causal relations between them while controlling any extraneous variables.

There are three types of experiments that researchers typically employ. The first is a lab experiment, conducted in the artificial and highly controlled setting of a laboratory. This method allows for precise control over the location, time, circumstances, participants, and especially the extraneous and independent variables of the experiment. However, the disadvantage of this approach is that the high level of artificiality may not accurately reflect real-life situtations (Slack & Draugalis Jr., 2001). The second type is a field experiment, which is conducted unobtrusively in a real-world setting. Researchers can still manipulate the independent variables, but, in contrast to lab experiments, it is more difficult to control extraneous variables in a real-life situation. The third type is a natural experiment, in which researchers cannot interfere with the independent variable, as it occurs in real-life settings (Leatherdale, 2019). The comparative advantages of experiments lie in their high degree of internal validity, providing strong support for causal inferences due to effective control of variables. However, the external validity (the generalizability of the results) of experiments is often limited because the controlled conditions of a laboratory cannot fully simulate the complexity of reality (Jimenez-Buedo & Miller, 2010).

Therefore, a survey experiment combines the benefits of survey research, which offers relatively strong external validity, with the advantages of experimental methods, which provide high internal validity. A survey experiment involves the deliberate manipulation of explanatory variables within a survey instrument (Gaines et al., 2007). Survey experiments "seek to establish causal relationships that are generalizable—that is, they try to maximize internal and external validity" (Barabas & Jerit, 2010, p. 226). The advantages of survey experiments include contributing to accurate causal inferences due to the adoption of an experimental design and the ability to generalize findings to a broad population through a large survey sample.

The two major types of survey experiments adopted by scholars are between-subjects and within-subjects designs. In a between-subjects design, two or more subject groups experience unique conditions, with each respondent confronted by only one treatment or vignette (Charness et al., 2012). In contrast, the within-subjects design exposes the same subject to all conditions or vignettes. The advantages of the within-subjects design include minimizing the confounding of observed differences among treatments with individual differences, thereby reducing random noise and requiring fewer participants (Charness et al., 2012).

This study adopts a between-subjects randomized survey experiment in which each respondent is confronted with only one treatment or vignette. This design was selected for two reasons. Firstly, subjecting respondents to a single treatment reduces the likelihood that they will grasp the intention of the experiment and choose the most desirable answer, which could lead to biased results. Secondly, it has been suggested that studies in areas such as social psychology, personality, and decision-making should consider using a between-subjects design. Given that this research concerns personal opinions and decision-making, such a design is appropriate.

Vignette Design

Vignettes are designed to integrate explanatory factors into a description of scenarios that should be realistic to respondents. A vignette is a "short, carefully constructed description of a person, object, or situation, representing a systematic combination of characteristics" (Atzmüller & Steiner, 2010, p. 128). The experimental design of this study is shown in Table 6.1. The design manipulates the setting for the two explanatory factors: expectation and accountability intensity. The vignettes vary in terms of whether the expectations of supervisors and local citizens for a task are convergent or divergent and in terms of the level of hierarchical accountability. Thus, the experiment has a 2 (expectation: convergent, divergent) by 3 (accountability intensity: low, moderate, high) factorial design and thus specifies six experimental conditions, namely vignettes.

The six vignettes are distinct and concise, to avoid loading them with too much information and confusing respondents. Nor do they involve confounders to influence respondents' choices. Because the participants come from different government posts and have diverse backgrounds, they have administrative expertise in different areas. Thus, I did not relate the task to any specific area but instead made it general and applicable to each respondent. Vignette 1 states: "Suppose that you are asked by your upper-level superiors to take charge of a specific task. This task is beneficial to citizens and popular with them. Your superiors impose little supervision and few checks on the process and results of the task. There

Table 6.1 Visualization of the six vignettes

		Expectation	
		Convergent	*Divergent*
Accountability intensity	Low	(V1) Convergent expectation & low accountability	(V2) Divergent expectation & low accountability
	Moderate	(V3) Convergent expectation & moderate accountability	(V4) Divergent expectation & moderate accountability
	High	(V5) Convergent expectation & high accountability	(V6) Divergent expectation & high accountability

is also little reward or punishment for the results." In Vignette 2, the intensity of hierarchical accountability is low but it describes a situation in which the task does not benefit citizens and even has some adverse impact on them. Similar to Vignette 1, the task benefits citizens in Vignettes 3 and 5, but accountability intensity is moderate and high, respectively. Vignette 3 states that "your upper-level superiors impose moderate monitoring on you and offer appropriate rewards or penalties based on the success or failure of the task." Vignette 5 states that "your upper-level superiors carry out strict supervision and frequent inspection of the task, and severe punishment will be imposed if you make mistakes." Similar to Vignette 2, the task exerts an adverse impact on citizens in Vignettes 4 and 6, but the accountability intensity differs. Respondents are presented with a scenario of moderate-intensity accountability in Vignette 4 and high-intensity accountability in Vignette 6. After reading the scenario, respondents are asked about the level of effort that they are willing to spend on the task. A 5-point Likert scale is used to measure their responses, ranging from "very little effort" to "very much effort." I emphasized in the questionnaire that the vignettes were hypothetical and general scenarios and did not target any organizations or individuals, so that the respondents would be more likely to share their true views.

Participants

I included the vignette experiment within the survey discussed in the third chapter. Among the survey participants, most of the respondents are at relatively low administrative ranks. The Chinese government has a strictly hierarchical structure with a heavy workload being transferred downward to the county and township officials, who are expected to serve as a bridge between the higher administrative echelons and the populace (Heberer, 2019). More specifically, local officials should not only implement upper-level policies in accordance with central guidelines but also solve local problems and maintain social stability. Thus, although the respondents in the sample do not hold senior administrative posts, they still have discretionary power in local affairs, just like their counterparts, street-level bureaucrats, in Western countries. They face top-down accountability pressures while directly interacting with citizens.

Power analysis referring to Cohen's (2013) criteria is run in *R* to determine the sample size of each group. We used the pwr.anova.test command in *R* and set a significance level of 0.01, statistical power of 0.9, and an

Table 6.2 Statistical description of relevant variables

Variables	*Mean*	*SD*	*Min*	*Max*
Working efforts	3.89	0.88	1	5
Expectation	0.52	0.50	0	1
Accountability intensity	2.02	0.82	1	3
Gender	0.54	0.50	0	1
Age	1.62	1.02	1	6
Monthly income	2.38	1.15	1	5
Administrative rank	1.44	0.79	1	6
PSM	3.87	0.84	1	5

effect size of 0.25. The result indicates that the minimum sample size should be 60 for each group. Based on this calculation, each respondent was randomly assigned a questionnaire embedded with one of the six vignettes, and the six versions of the questionnaire were distributed almost evenly among the participants. We approached about 1100 public officials and obtained 868 valid questionnaires, of which 136 included Vignette 1, 150 Vignette 2, 143 Vignette 3, 139 Vignette 4, 137 Vignette 5, and 163 Vignette 6, all of which meet the minimum sample size requirement. The respondents came from 19 different provinces, with 46.07% male and 53.93% female.

I included PSM as a moderating variable so as to explore the interactions among PSM, accountability intensity, and expectations in driving grassroots bureaucrats' motivations and preferences. Experiments can not only shed light on treatment effects but also assess the interaction between the treatment variables and relevant individual difference factors. This study also controls for basic demographic information, such as gender, age, and income, as well as the respondent's administrative rank. To account for all observed and unobserved time-invariant province-level confounders, province-fixed effects are included in all models. The descriptive analysis of the key variables is shown in Table 6.2.

Descriptive Analysis

Figure 6.2 shows the respective means of the six vignettes. When a task is in line with citizens' interests, the average scores representing respondents' effort on the task are 4.13, 4.40, and 4.04 for low, moderate, and high accountability intensity, respectively. When a task deviates from citizens' interests, the corresponding effort scores are 3.37, 3.52, and 3.86 respectively for low, moderate, and high accountability intensity. This indicates that respondents facing convergent expectations from citizens and superiors are more willing to put in effort than those who are confronted with divergent expectations. When the level of accountability intensity is taken into consideration, respondents make the most effort (scored at 4.40) on a task if it meets the expectations of both supervisors and citizens and the level of accountability intensity is moderate. They make the least effort (scored at 3.37) if the task does not respect citizens' preferences and accountability intensity is low.

Table 6.3 presents the descriptive results of the statistical tests of the six vignettes based on the variation of the two factors. The t-test results show that if the task is aligned with citizens' interests, the respondents are willing to put more effort into it ($t = 11.19$, $p < 0.01$). Regardless of whether the accountability intensity is low, moderate, or high, the respondents show stronger willingness ($p < 0.01$) to make an effort to carry out a task when it benefits citizens than when it does not. The average score

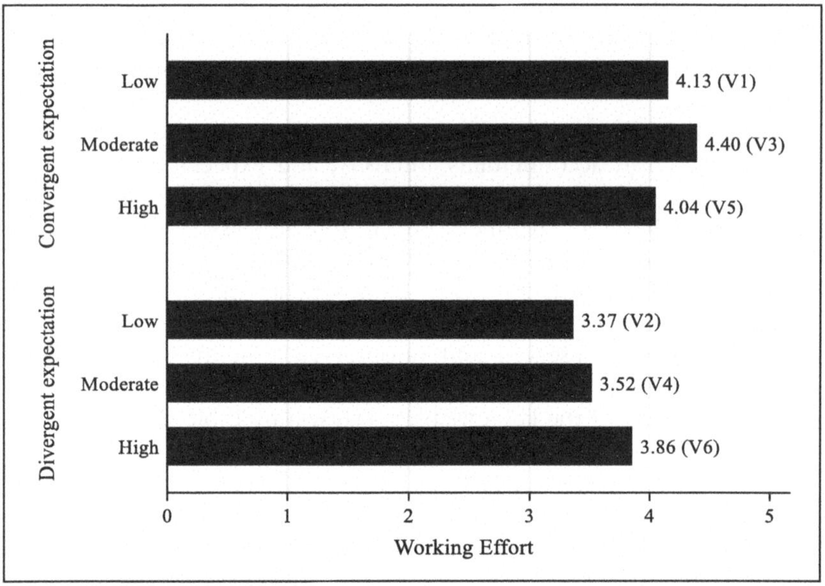

Fig. 6.2 Mean value of the six vignettes

across the three levels of accountability intensity is 4.20 for the former and 3.59 for the latter.

The post-hoc tests reported in Table 6.4 demonstrate that when a task is in the interest of citizens, respondents are more likely to work hard on it under the condition of moderate (M = 4.51, SD = 0.83) than low (M = 4.14, SD = 0.77) or high (M = 4.04, SD = 0.68) accountability intensity, while there is no statistical difference in scores between the low and high accountability groups. However, when the task is contrary to citizens' interests, respondents may put more effort into it if accountability intensity is high (L-H***, M-H**). This implies an undesirable situation; that is, greater accountability may compel grassroots bureaucrats to act in a manner inconsistent with citizens' well-being and simply to meet the preferences of their superiors.

Table 6.3 Differences under convergent and divergent expectations

	Convergent expectations	*Divergent expectations*	D-*value*	t-*test*	p-*value*
Low accountability intensity (L)	4.13	3.37	0.76	7.51	0.00
Moderate accountability intensity (M)	4.40	3.52	0.88	10.95	0.00
High accountability intensity (H)	4.04	3.86	0.19	2.30	0.02
Overall	4.20	3.59	0.61	11.19	0.00

Table 6.4 Differences under different levels of accountability intensity

	Low accountability intensity (L)	*Moderate accountability intensity (M)*	*High accountability intensity (H)*	*Post-hoc tests*
Convergent expectations	4.13	4.40	4.04	L-M***, L-H, M-H***
Divergent expectations	3.37	3.52	3.86	L-M, L-H***, M-H***
Overall	3.74	3.96	3.94	L-M***, L-H**, M-H

Regression Results

I used OLS regression methods to further explore the impact of accountability intensity, expectation, and their interaction effect on grassroots bureaucrats' efforts. The results are reported in Table 6.5. Expectation is a dummy variable indicating whether the task is in line or in conflict with citizens' interests, while accountability intensity, as a ranked variable, indicates the level of accountability imposed by superiors (low = 1, moderate = 2, high = 3). Model 1 only includes the control variables, and Model 2 contains both independent and control variables. The interaction terms between the explanatory variables are included in Model 3. The regression results indicate that after the interaction items are introduced, the coefficient of expectation and its respective interactions with accountability intensity and PSM demonstrate significant effects.

The effects of conflicting expectations. Model 3 shows that when other variables are held constant, expectation is negatively related to the effort put into a task by grassroots bureaucrats ($\beta = 0.59$, $p < 0.01$). That is, if the task is in line with citizens' interests, bureaucrats' effort will increase by 0.59 points (on a 5-point scale) relative to their effort in a task that is not in the public interest. Thus, Proposition 1 is supported. As for the underlying reasons why bureaucrats are more willing to make an effort when their task is in line with citizens' interests, the effects of the interaction terms provide some answers.

The interaction between expectation and PSM is significantly associated with effort ($\beta = -0.24$, $p < 0.01$), as shown in Model 3. The interaction effect is presented in Fig. 6.3. Figure 6.3a plots two regression lines for high and low PSM, indicating that the impact of expectation on effort is heightened when respondents have high PSM. We follow Hainmueller, Mummolo, and Xu's (2019) interaction model to further test the impact of the interaction term between expectation and PSM on grassroots bureaucrats' efforts. Figure 6.3b presents the marginal effect of expectation on effort under different levels of PSM. PSM as a moderator variable is discretized into three bins labeled L, M, and H. The marginal effect is below zero, showing that bureaucrats' effort decreases when a task is contrary to citizens' interests, but the marginal effect is smaller for people with low PSM than for those with high PSM. This indicates that the decreasing effect of expectation on effort is stronger for officials with higher PSM.

Table 6.5 Regression results for working efforts

	Effort			*Effort under convergent expectations*	*Effort under divergent expectations*
	Model 1	*Model 2*	*Model 3*	*Model 4*	*Model 5*
Gender	−0.07	−0.03	−0.00	−0.12	0.06
	(0.06)	(0.06)	(0.06)	(0.08)	(0.09)
Age	−0.04	−0.01	0.00	0.04	0.01
	(0.04)	(0.03)	(0.03)	(0.06)	(0.04)
Administrative rank	−0.09*	−0.07	−0.05	−0.06	−0.07
	(0.05)	(0.05)	(0.05)	(0.07)	(0.06)
Monthly income	−0.01	−0.01	−0.00	0.02	−0.03
	(0.03)	(0.03)	(0.03)	(0.04)	(0.05)
PSM	0.10***	0.12***	0.24***	0.24***	−0.01
	(0.04)	(0.04)	(0.05)	(0.05)	(0.05)
Independent variables					
Expectation		−0.59***	−0.59***		
		(0.07)	(0.07)		
Accountability intensity		0.10**	−0.09	−0.13**	0.29***
		(0.04)	(0.05)	(0.05)	(0.06)
Interaction effects					
Expectation* Accountability intensity			0.37***		
			(0.08)		
Expectation*PSM			−0.24***		
			0.07		
Accountability intensity *PSM			0.01	0.05	−0.04
			(0.04)	(0.06)	(0.07)
Province fixed effects	Yes	Yes	Yes	Yes	Yes
F	2.624***	5.824***	6.627***	2.532***	2.032***
Adj R-squared	0.052	0.150	0.186	0.088	0.060

Note Standard errors in parentheses, * $p < 0.05$, ** p < 0.01, *** $p < 0.001$ (two-tailed test)

Specifically, respondents with high PSM tend to make more effort than those with low PSM when a task is in line with citizens' preferences. Thus, Proposition 2 is confirmed. A possible explanation is that respondents with higher PSM are more concerned about citizens' interests than those with lower PSM. Bureaucrats with "the general altruistic motivation to serve the interests of a community of people" are more likely to be concerned about citizens' interests (Rainey & Steinbauer, 1999, p. 20).

(a)

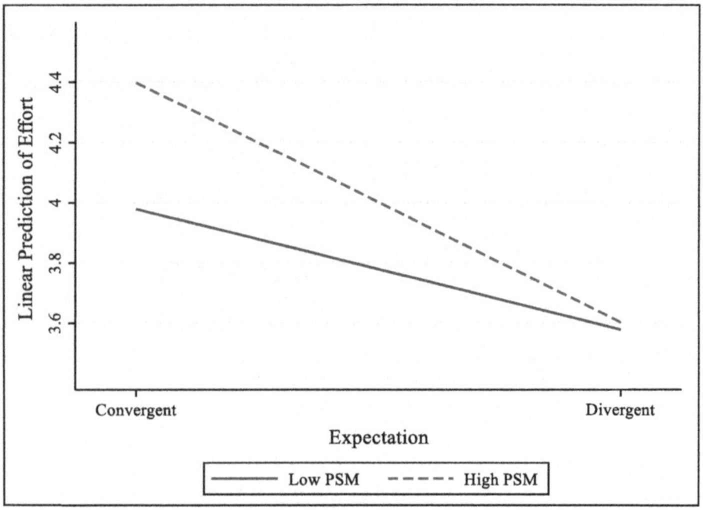

(b)

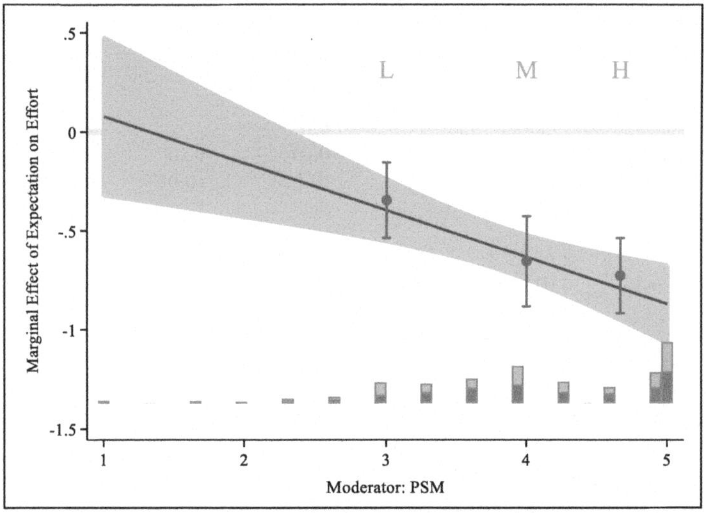

Fig. 6.3 Interaction effect of expectation and PSM on efforts

Furthermore, the interaction between expectation and accountability intensity is positively associated with effort ($\beta = 0.37$, $p < 0.01$) in Model 3. The interaction effect is presented in Fig. 6.4. Figure 6.4a plots three regression lines indicating low, moderate, and high accountability intensity based on the vignettes. The three lines show that the negative impact of expectation on effort is weakened under high accountability intensity. The effects of low and moderate accountability intensity on effort are similar because the two lines are almost parallel, indicating no interaction between them. The line of high-intensity accountability runs across those of low and middle accountability, demonstrating interaction effects. However, it is rather flat, meaning that the difference in bureaucrats' efforts arising from convergent or divergent expectations is weaker under the condition of high accountability intensity.

Figure 6.4b presents the marginal effect of expectation on effort under different levels of accountability intensity. It confirms the results presented in Fig. 6.4a and indicates that bureaucrats' effort decreases when a task adversely affects citizens' interests, but that this marginal effect is smaller for people under high than those under low or moderate accountability intensity. These results demonstrate that the decreasing effect is weaker for officials experiencing high accountability intensity. This implies that grassroots bureaucrats facing intensified accountability will be less concerned about whether their task is aligned with citizens' interests. As mentioned above, high accountability intensity is likely to suppress bureaucrats' intrinsic motivation to behave in accordance with their own values. Facing intensified accountability, bureaucrats may replace extrinsic with intrinsic motivation and see the task as a "must do," putting in the effort necessary to avoid sanction. As a result, they become less sensitive to citizens' interests and so the difference in effort between convergent expectation and divergent expectation is small under the high accountability condition.

The effects of accountability intensity. When accountability intensity is treated as a ranked variable, its main effect on effort is not statistically significant ($\beta = -0.09$, $p > 0.1$) in Model 3. However, its interaction with expectation demonstrates a significant correlation with effort ($\beta = 0.37$, $p < 0.01$), indicating that the effect of accountability intensity on effort depends on whether or not the task is aligned with the interests of citizens. Hence, we further explore the effects of accountability intensity on bureaucrats' efforts under the scenarios of convergent and divergent expectations in Models 4 and 5, respectively. In Model

(a)

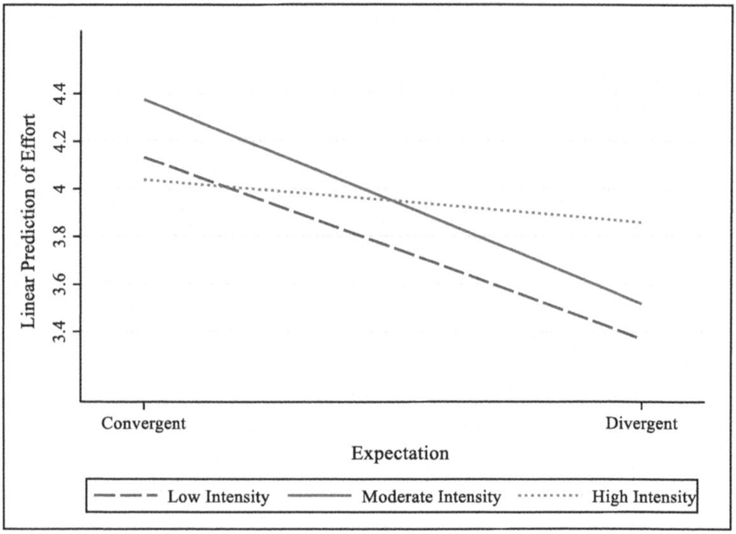

(b)

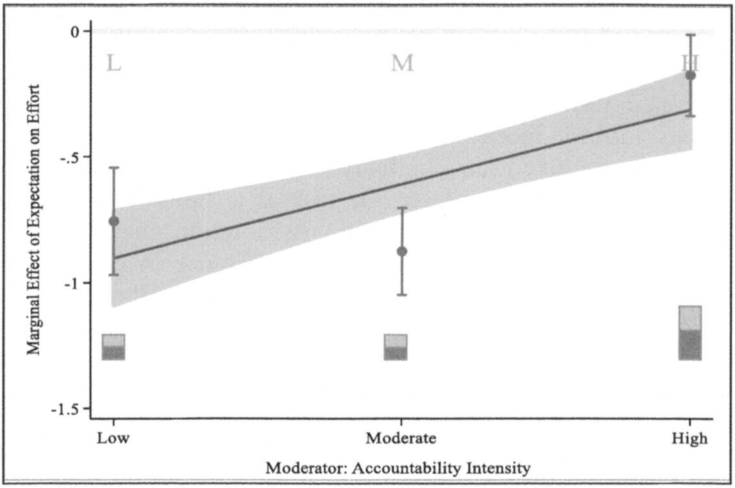

Fig. 6.4 Interaction effect of expectation and accountability intensity on efforts

4, the relationship between accountability intensity and effort has negative statistical significance ($\beta = -0.13$, $p < 0.05$) when the task is in line with citizens' interests, while there is a positive and significant association between them ($\beta = 0.29$, $p < 0.01$) when the task is not so aligned. This implies that when the task is in line with citizens' interests, a higher level of accountability intensity leads to lower bureaucrats' effort, indicating a crowding-out effect. Conversely, when the task deviates from citizens' interests, a higher level of accountability intensity tends to compel respondents to put in more effort than when accountability is low.

To explore the specific effect of the three levels of accountability intensity on grassroots bureaucrats' efforts, we go one step further by treating the former as a categorical variable in Table 6.6. The expectations of citizens and superiors are convergent in Models 6 and 7. Moderate and high accountability intensity, respectively, are treated as the reference group in the two models. Model 6 shows that compared with those who face moderate accountability, respondents experiencing low ($\beta = -0.26$, $p < 0.01$) or high ($\beta = -0.55$, $p < 0.01$) intensity accountability are more likely to put less effort into a task.

These results indicate that a moderate level of accountability intensity is more likely to motivate bureaucrats to work hard if a task is in line with citizens' interests, while high accountability intensity induces the least effort. It is certainly still important to enforce accountability because "a few individuals behaving badly with impunity can weaken the commitment of many others to moral principles, or to conscience, or to habits of generosity" (Payne, 1981, p. 190). Therefore, moderate accountability may be necessary to keep bureaucrats' behaviors under control. Appropriate punishments based on bureaucrats' performance will give them a sense of justice, with their efforts being fairly assessed by the principal.

Scholars suggest that setting performance-contingent incentives appropriately is a good way to sustain PSM (Corduneanu et al., 2020; Tu, 2024b). Proper reward and punishment mechanisms based on grassroots bureaucrats' performance will not make them feel pressured or controlled but rather will yield a sense of justice because their effort is being acknowledged and respected by others. Moderate accountability intensity may crowd in bureaucrats' intrinsic motivation instead of crowding it out, because they perceive the appropriate evaluation as being supportive and enhancing their self-esteem.

Table 6.6 Regression results under convergent and divergent expectations

	Effort under convergent expectations		*Effort under divergent expectations*	
	Model 6	*Model 7*	*Model 8*	*Model 9*
Gender	−0.11	−0.11	0.05	0.05
	(0.08)	(0.08)	(0.09)	(0.09)
Age	0.01	0.01	0.01	0.01
	(0.05)	(0.05)	(0.04)	(0.04)
Administrative rank	−0.04	−0.04	−0.08	−0.08
	(0.06)	(0.06)	(0.06)	(0.06)
Monthly income	0.03	0.03	−0.03	−0.03
	(0.04)	(0.04)	(0.05)	(0.05)
PSM	0.35***	0.21***	−0.06	−0.01
	(0.07)	(0.08)	(0.09)	(0.10)
Low accountability intensity	−0.26***	0.29***	−0.21*	−0.57***
	(0.10)	(0.11)	(0.12)	(0.12)
Moderate accountability intensity		0.55***		−0.37***
		(0.10)		(0.12)
High accountability intensity	−0.55***		0.37***	
	(0.10)		(0.12)	
Low accountability intensity*PSM	−0.24**	−0.10	0.12	0.07
	(0.10)	(0.11)	(0.13)	(0.13)
Moderate accountability intensity*PSM		0.14*		−0.05
		(0.08)		(0.14)
High accountability intensity*PSM	−0.14*		0.05	
	(0.08)		(0.14)	
Province fixed effects	Yes	Yes	Yes	Yes
F	3.621	3.621	1.913	1.913
Adj R-squared	0.152	0.152	0.058	0.058

Note Standard errors in parentheses, *** $p < 0.01$, ** $p < 0.05$, * $p < 0.1$

To examine the aforementioned argument, I explore the impact of interaction between PSM and accountability intensity on bureaucrats' working effort when the task benefits citizens in Fig. 6.5. It shows that when a task benefits citizens, and accountability intensity increases from low to moderate, respondents with high PSM tend to put in more effort than those with low PSM. The interaction is significant ($\beta = -0.24$, $p < 0.05$) in Model 6, demonstrating the crowding-in effect of moderate accountability. However, when accountability intensity goes from moderate to high, respondents with high PSM tend to put in less effort than those with low PSM. This interaction is also significant ($\beta = -0.14$, $p < 0.1$) in both Models 6 and 7, revealing the crowding-out effect of high accountability intensity. Thus, both Propositions 3 and 4 are partially confirmed.

Models 8 and 9 examine situations in which the expectations for a task diverge between citizens and superiors. Under such conditions, high accountability intensity tends to compel respondents to put more effort into a task than low ($\beta = -0.57$, $p < 0.01$) and moderate ($\beta = -0.37$, $p < 0.01$) accountability, as shown in Model 9. This means that when a task is contrary to citizens' interests, high accountability intensity is more likely to force bureaucrats to follow their superiors' instructions than low or moderate intensity. When a task deviates from the interests of citizens, bureaucrats may have no intrinsic motivation to work hard, thus the disciplining effect exerted by extrinsic control may play a more important role in determining the level of bureaucratic effort. It is likely that grassroots bureaucrats will consider the task a "must-do" and put in more effort under increased accountability intensity so as to avoid being blamed or

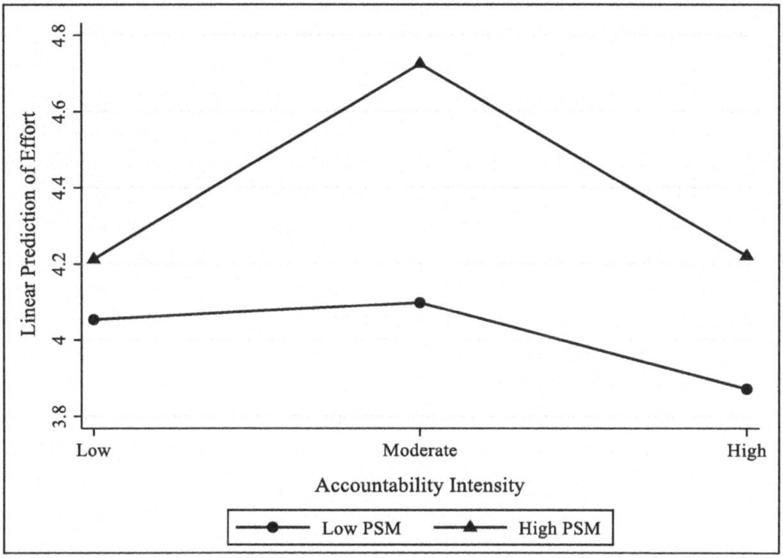

Fig. 6.5 Interaction effect of PSM and accountability intensity on effort when the task benefits citizens

punished. They may respond opportunistically to accountability; that is, they may put less effort into a task when top-down accountability is less severe but more effort if it is intensified. Proposition 5 is thus supported.

An interesting finding concerning PSM is that respondents with higher PSM are more likely to work hard on a task only when it is in line with citizens' interests (Models 6 and 7); this relationship is statistically insignificant when the task is contrary to the interests of citizens (Models 8 and 9). This may be because when they face divergent expectations from citizens and superiors, bureaucrats feel confused about which direction to take. This can happen in China because upper-level officials may present their policies as being in the best interest of the public, even though in reality the policies only serve their own political advancement, and frame different views as shortsighted and ignorant.

Conclusion

This chapter examined how public officials respond to different levels of accountability intensity when they face convergent and divergent expectations from supervisors and citizens. it yields two major findings. First, when an assigned task is aligned with citizens' interests, bureaucrats tend to put more effort into it than when it is not, regardless of whether they are subject to low, moderate, or high levels of accountability intensity. This indicates that grassroots bureaucrats do not mechanically implement policies enacted by upper-level authorities but care at least to some extent about local citizens' needs. Bureaucrats with higher PSM are more concerned about whether their tasks are in line with the public interest and are less likely to follow top-down instructions passively. However, under more intense accountability pressure, bureaucrats may become less concerned about whether a task is in the interest of citizens and more likely to obey their superiors blindly in order to avoid punishment.

Secondly, bureaucrats respond to accountability intensity in different ways when the expectations of local citizens and superiors diverge or converge. When a task is aligned with citizens' interests, moderate accountability intensity is the most effective way to motivate bureaucrats and crowd in their prosocial values. Over-stringent accountability, however, may crowd out their intrinsic motivation while not necessarily inducing greater compliance. When a task is not in line with citizens' interests, increased accountability may compel bureaucrats to put more effort into it to avoid censure. This implies that although grassroots bureaucrats generally tend to put less effort into those tasks that do not serve citizens' interests, intensified accountability may force them to comply with top-down instructions that do not suit local situations.

The findings suggest that when agents act against principals' expectations, they are not necessarily driven by self-interests. Their predisposition and judgment about whether policies are in line with citizens' interests play a pivotal role in promoting social well-being. In the mainstream literature, the Chinese bureaucracy is often portrayed as a political cog to support the party-state's control over society. However, the findings demonstrate the constructive role of lower-level local officials in China working for citizens. While bureaucrats enjoy some leverage to shape the policy process, many of them are able and willing to exercise their discretion to amend policy flaws and benefit the populace.

This study contributes to a better understanding of the role of grassroots bureaucrats in policy implementation. In line with the literature that disputes the effectiveness of coercive supervision of bureaucrats and underscores their discretionary authority (Tummers & Bekkers, 2014), my analysis highlights the fact that grassroots bureaucrats are not passive agents who succumb to intensified top-down accountability pressure and act solely in accordance with their superiors' preferences. Over-stringent accountability does not necessarily result in more compliance and better policy outcomes. To achieve the desired policy objectives and long-term social goals, bureaucrats should be encouraged to exercise responsible professional judgment when handling matters concerning local needs.

On a practical level, the study shows the importance of strengthening the consistency between public policies and citizens' interests. Policymakers may not be entirely familiar with local conditions and needs, so their policies may not always reflect citizens' interests. As a result, the expectations of superiors and local citizens may come into conflict, leading to confusion and poor policy implementation by grassroots bureaucrats. Thus, such officials should be encouraged to make responsible interpretations of top-down instructions based on their expertise and knowledge of local conditions. Grassroots bureaucrats in an administrative system with ambiguous expectations should not simply mechanically comply with superiors' directives, use external requirements as an excuse for not exercising their own judgment, or abandon moral reflection (Cooper, 2012). Exercising responsible personal judgment to meet broader obligations in a bureaucratic hierarchy is challenging, and organizational values and mechanisms should be developed to facilitate it.

In short, the findings indicate that accountability is not a panacea for regulating bureaucratic behavior, despite the fact that it has often been used as a control mechanism to urge officials to perform as expected. Imposing an arsenal of control-oriented accountability measures may provoke undesirable defensive behaviors from bureaucrats, leading to unintended negative consequences. Thus, an appropriate configuration of accountability should be explored to foster moral reflection and a strong inner sense of responsibility among bureaucrats.

References

Agranoff, R., & McGuire, M. (2001). Big questions in public network management research. *Journal of Public Administration Research and Theory, 11*(3), 295–326.

Almén, O., & Burell, M. (2018). Social accountability as social movement outcome: Protests in a Chinese city. *Social Movement Studies, 17*(6), 716–735.

Atzmüller, C., & Steiner, P. M. (2010). Experimental vignette studies in survey research. *Methodology, 6*(3), 128–138.

Banuri, S., & Keefer, P. (2013). *Intrinsic motivation, effort and the call to public service*. World Bank Policy Research Working Paper, 6729.

Barabas, J., & Jerit, J. (2010). Are survey experiments externally valid? *American Political Science Review, 104*(2), 226–242.

Bovens, M. (2007). Analysing and assessing accountability: A conceptual framework. *European Law Journal, 13*(4), 447–468.

Bowles, S., & Polania-Reyes, S. (2012). Economic incentives and social preferences: Substitutes or complements? *Journal of Economic Literature, 50*(2), 368–425.

Brodkin, E. Z. (2011). Policy work: Street-level organizations under new managerialism. *Journal of Public Administration Research and Theory, 21*(suppl_2), i253–i277.

Brødsgaard, K. E. (2017). *Chinese politics as fragmented authoritarianism*. Routledge New York.

Busuioc, M., & Lodge, M. (2017). Reputation and accountability relationships: Managing accountability expectations through reputation. *Public Administration Review, 77*(1), 91–100.

Cai, Y. (2014). *State and agents in China: Disciplining government officials*. Stanford University Press.

Calvert, R. L., McCubbins, M. D., & Weingast, B. R. (1989). A theory of political control and agency discretion. *American Journal of Political Science, 33*, 588–611.

Charness, G., Gneezy, U., & Kuhn, M. A. (2012). Experimental methods: Between-subject and within-subject design. *Journal of Economic Behavior & Organization, 81*(1), 1–8.

Cohen, J. (2013). *Statistical power analysis for the behavioral sciences*. Routledge.

Cook, B. J. (2014). *Bureaucracy and self-government: Reconsidering the role of public administration in American politics*. JHU Press.

Cooper, T. L. (2012). *The responsible administrator: An approach to ethics for the administrative role*. Wiley.

Cooper-Thomas, H. D., & Wright, S. (2013). Person-environment misfit: The neglected role of social context. *Journal of Managerial Psychology, 28*(1), 21–37.

Corduneanu, R., Dudau, A., & Kominis, G. (2020). Crowding-in or crowding-out: The contribution of self-determination theory to public service motivation. *Management Review, 22*(7), 1070–1089.

Dahling, J. J., Chau, S. L., Mayer, D. M., & Gregory, J. B. (2012). Breaking rules for the right reasons? An investigation of pro-social rule breaking. *Journal of Organizational Behavior, 33*(1), 21–42.

Deci, E. L. (1972). The effects of contingent and noncontingent rewards and controls on intrinsic motivation. *Organizational Behavior and Human Performance, 8*(2), 217–229.

Deci, E. L., & Ryan, R. M. (2008). Self-determination theory: A macrotheory of human motivation, development, and health. *Canadian psychology/Psychologie canadienne*, 49(3), 182–185.

Fleming, C. J. (2020). Prosocial rule breaking at the street level: The roles of leaders, peers, and bureaucracy. *Public Management Review, 22*(8), 1191–1216.

Frey, B. S., & Jegen, R. (2001). Motivation crowding theory. *Journal of Economic Surveys, 15*(5), 589–611.

Friedrich, C. J. (2000). Public policy and the nature of administrative responsibility. In Miyakawa, T. (Ed.)., *The Science of Public Policy: Policy analysis II (Vol. 2)*. Taylor & Francis.

Frederickson, H. G. (1980). *New public administration*. The University of Alabama Press.

Gaines, B. J., Kuklinski, J. H., & Quirk, P. J. (2007). The logic of the survey experiment reexamined. *Political Analysis, 15*(1), 1–20.

Gao, J. (2015). Pernicious manipulation of performance measures in China's cadre evaluation system. *The China Quarterly, 223*, 618–637.

Göbel, C. (2011). Uneven policy implementation in Rural China. *The China Journal, 65*, 53–76.

Gong, T. (2006). Corruption and local governance: The double identity of Chinese local governments in market reform. *The Pacific Review, 19*(1), 85–102.

Grigorescu, A. (2008). Horizontal accountability in intergovernmental organizations. *Ethics & International Affairs, 22*(3), 285–308.
Hainmueller, J., Hangartner, D., & Yamamoto, T. (2015). Validating vignette and conjoint survey experiments against real-world behavior. *Proceedings of the National Academy of Sciences, 112*(8), 2395–2400.
Hainmueller, J., Mummolo, J., & Xu, Y. (2019). How much should we trust estimates from multiplicative interaction models? Simple tools to improve empirical practice. *Political Analysis, 27*(2), 163–192.
Harmon, M. M. (1995). *Responsibility as paradox: A critique of rational discourse on government*. Sage.
Hart, D. K. (1974). Social equity, justice, and the equitable administrator. *Public Administration Review, 34*(1), 3–11.
Hawkins, D. G., & Jacoby, W. (2006). How agents matter. *Delegation and Agency in International Organizations, 1*, 199–228.
Heberer, T. (2019). Representation in a context across political orders and the Chinese case. *Journal of Chinese Governance, 4*(4), 339–361.
Houston, D. J. (2000). Public-service motivation: A multivariate test. *Journal of Public Administration Research and Theory, 10*(4), 713–728.
Huang, X., & Kim, S. E. (2020). When top-down meets bottom-up: Local adoption of social policy reform in China. *Governance, 33*(2), 343–364.
Hu, C. (2017). Accountability of public servants under dominant political settlements of China: Effects, challenges, and issues. *International Journal of Public Administration, 40*(3), 240–255.
Jaros, K. (2016). Rethinking subnational government capacity in China. *Journal of Chinese Governance, 1*(4), 633–653.
Jarvis, M. D. (2014). Hierarchical accountability. In Bovens, M., Goodin, R. E., & Schillemans, T. (Eds.), *The Oxford Handbook of Public Accountability* (pp. 405–420). Oxford University Press.
Jimenez-Buedo, M., & Miller, L. M. (2010). Why a trade-off? The relationship between the external and internal validity of experiments. *Theoria. Revista de Teoría, Historia y Fundamentos de La Ciencia, 25*(3), 301–321.
Johnson, T. (2013). Institutional design and bureaucrats' impact on political control. *The Journal of Politics, 75*(1), 183–197.
Jos, P. H. (1990). Administrative responsibility revisited: Moral consensus and moral autonomy. *Administration & Society, 22*(2), 228–248.
Jos, P. H. (2016). Advancing social equity: Proceduralism in the new governance. *Administration & Society, 48*(6), 760–780.
Jos, P. H., & Tompkins, M. E. (2004). The accountability paradox in an age of reinvention: The perennial problem of preserving character and judgment. *Administration & Society, 36*(3), 255–281.
Klijn, E., & Skelcher, C. (2007). Democracy and governance networks: Compatible or not? *Public Administration, 85*(3), 587–608.

Klijn, E.-H., & Koppenjan, J. (2012). Governance network theory: Past, present and future. *Policy & Politics, 40*(4), 587–606.
Koppell, J. G. (2005). Pathologies of accountability: ICANN and the challenge of "multiple accountabilities disorder." *Public Administration Review, 65*(1), 94–108.
Leatherdale, S. T. (2019). Natural experiment methodology for research: A review of how different methods can support real-world research. *International Journal of Social Research Methodology, 22*(1), 19–35.
Li, Y. (2024). Is hierarchy the only answer? The accountability preferences of Chinese public employees in public service delivery. *Review of Policy Research, 41*(3), 531–549.
Lipsky, M. (2010). *Street-level bureaucracy: Dilemmas of the individual in public service.* Russell Sage Foundation.
Lupia, A., & McCubbins, M. D. (1994). Who controls? Information and the structure of legislative decision making. *Legislative Studies Quarterly, 19*, 361–384.
Ma, J. (2012). The rise of social accountability in China. *Australian Journal of Public Administration, 71*(2), 111–121.
Mattingly, D. C. (2020). Responsive or repressive? How frontline bureaucrats enforce the one child policy in China. *Comparative Politics, 52*(2), 269–288.
Maynard-Moody, S., & Musheno, M. (2000). State agent or citizen agent: Two narratives of discretion. *Journal of Public Administration Research and Theory, 10*(2), 329–358.
McCubbins, M. D., Noll, R. G., & Weingast, B. R. (1987). Administrative procedures as instruments of political control. *The Journal of Law, Economics, and Organization, 3*(2), 243–277.
McCubbins, M. D., & Schwartz, T. (1984). Congressional oversight overlooked: Police patrols versus fire alarms. *American Journal of Political Science, 28*, 165–179.
Mei, C., & Pearson, M. (2014). Diffusion of policy defiance among Chinese local officials. In J. C. Teets & W. Hurst (Eds.), *Local Governance Innovation in China* (pp. 25–41). Routledge.
Mulgan, R. (2000). 'Accountability': An ever-expanding concept? *Public Administration, 78*(3), 555–573.
O'Brien, K. J., & Li, L. (1999). Selective Policy Implementation in Rural China. *Comparative Politics, 31*(2), 167–186.
O'Donnell, G. A. (1998). Horizontal accountability in new democracies. *Journal of Democracy, 9*(3), 112–126.
Olsen, J. P. (2006). Maybe it is time to rediscover bureaucracy. *Journal of Public Administration Research and Theory, 16*(1), 1–24.
Osborne, S. P. (2006). The new public governance? *Public Management Review, 8*(3), 377–387.

Page, S. (2006). The web of managerial accountability: The impact of reinventing government. *Administration & Society, 38*(2), 166–197.
Payne, B. L. (1981). *Devices and desires: Corruption and ethical seriousness* (pp. 175–203). Public Duties.
Pennock, J. R. (1962). "Responsible government", separated powers, and special interests: Agricultural subsidies in Britain and Americal. *American Political Science Review, 56*(3), 621–633.
Pepinsky, T. B., Pierskalla, J. H., & Sacks, A. (2017). Bureaucracy and service delivery. *Annual Review of Political Science, 20*(1), 249–268.
Perry, J. L., Hondeghem, A., & Wise, L. R. (2010). Revisiting the motivational bases of public service: Twenty years of research and an agenda for the future. *Public Administration Review, 70*(5), 681–690.
Perry, J. L., & Vandenabeele, W. (2015). Public service motivation research: Achievements, challenges, and future directions. *Public Administration Review, 75*(5), 692–699.
Peters, B. G., & Pierre, J. (2001). Developments in intergovernmental relations: Towards multi-level governance. *Policy and Politics, 29*(2), 131.
Prendergast, C. (2007). The motivation and bias of bureaucrats. *American Economic Review, 97*(1), 180–196.
Potipiroon, W. (2022). Rule Formalization, Bureaucratic Red Tape, and Prosocial Rule Breaking Among Street-Level Bureaucrats: A Citizen-Centered Perspective. *Public Performance & Management Review, 45*(3), 638–671.
Rainey, H. G., & Steinbauer, P. (1999). Galloping elephants: Developing elements of a theory of effective government organizations. *Journal of Public Administration Research and Theory, 9*(1), 1–32.
Reddick, C. G., Demir, T., & Perlman, B. (2020). Horizontal, vertical, and hybrid: An empirical look at the forms of accountability. *Administration & Society, 52*(9), 1410–1438.
Ritz, A., Brewer, G. A., & Neumann, O. (2016). Public service motivation: A systematic literature review and outlook. *Public Administration Review, 76*(3), 414–426.
Romzek, B. S., & Dubnick, M. J. (1987). Accountability in the Public Sector: Lessons from the Challenger Tragedy. *Public Administration Review, 47*(3), 227–238.
Romzek, B. S., & Ingraham, P. W. (2000). Cross pressures of accountability: Initiative, command, and failure in the Ron Brown plane crash. *Public Administration Review, 60*(3), 240–253.
Schillemans, T. (2008). Accountability in the shadow of hierarchy: The horizontal accountability of agencies. *Public Organization Review, 8*(2), 175–194.
Schillemans, T. (2011). Does horizontal accountability work?: Evaluating potential remedies for the accountability deficit of agencies. *Administration & Society, 43*(4), 387–416.

Schillemans, T. (2016). Calibrating public sector accountability: Translating experimental findings to public sector accountability. *Public Management Review, 18*(9), 1400–1420.

Schillemans, T., & Busuioc, M. (2015). Predicting public sector accountability: From agency drift to forum drift. *Journal of Public Administration Research and Theory, 25*(1), 191–215.

Schubert, G., & Ahlers, A. L. (2012). County and township cadres as a strategic group: "Building a new socialist countryside" in three provinces. *The China Journal, 67*, 67–86.

Schubert, G., & Alpermann, B. (2019). Studying the Chinese policy process in the era of 'top-level design': The contribution of 'political steering' theory. *Journal of Chinese Political Science, 24*, 199–224.

Slack, M. K., & Draugalis, J. R., Jr. (2001). Establishing the internal and external validity of experimental studies. *American Journal of Health-System Pharmacy, 58*(22), 2173–2181.

Sobol, M. (2016). Principal—Agent analysis and pathological delegation: The (Almost) Untold Story. *Governance, 29*(3), 335–350.

Sørensen, E., & Torfing, J. (2009). Making governance networks effective and democratic through metagovernance. *Public administration, 87*(2), 234–258.

Sørensen, E., & Torfing, J. (2021). Accountable government through collaborative governance? *Administrative Sciences, 11*(4), 127.

The China Comment. (2019, July 31). *Why is 'one-size-fits-all' so difficult to eradicate?* Viewed December 15, 2024. http://www.banyuetan.org/jrt/detail/20190731/1000200033134991564534134984741697_1.html

Torfing, J., & Sørensen, E. (2014). The European debate on governance networks: Towards a new and viable paradigm? *Policy and Society, 33*(4), 329–344.

Tsai, L. L. (2007). Solidary groups, informal accountability, and local public goods provision in rural China. *American Political Science Review, 101*(2), 355–372.

Tu, W. (2024a). The interactive effect of extrinsic controls and public service motivation on blame avoidance. *Public Personnel Management*, 00910260241283549.

Tu, W. (2024b). Unpacking the accountability cube and its relationship with blame avoidance. *Public Management Review, 26*(3), 701–723.

Tu, W., & Gong, T. (2022). Accountability intensity and bureaucrats' response to conflicting expectations: A survey experiment in China. *Public Management Review, 24*(11), 1779–1801.

Tu, W., Hsieh, C.-W., Chen, C.-A., & Wen, B. (2024). Public service motivation, performance-contingent pay, and job satisfaction of street-level bureaucrats. *Public Personnel Management, 53*(2), 256–280.

Tummers, L., & Bekkers, V. (2014). Policy implementation, street-level bureaucracy, and the importance of discretion. *Public Management Review, 16*(4), 527–547.

Vandenabeele, W., Brewer, G. A., & Ritz, A. (2014). Past, present, and future of public service motivation research. *Public Administration, 92*(4), 779–789.

Wedeman, A. (2016). Corruption and collective protest in China. In T. Gong & I. Scott (Eds.), *Routledge handbook of corruption in Asia* (pp. 195–211). Routledge.

Willems, T., & Van Dooren, W. (2011). Lost in diffusion? How collaborative arrangements lead to an accountability paradox. *International Review of Administrative Sciences, 77*(3), 505–530.

Willems, T., & Van Dooren, W. (2012). Coming to terms with accountability: Combining multiple forums and functions. *Public Management Review, 14*(7), 1011–1036.

Zhou, X., Lian, H., Ortolano, L., & Ye, Y. (2013). A behavioral model of "muddling through" in the Chinese bureaucracy: The case of environmental protection. *The China Journal, 70*, 120–147.

CHAPTER 7

Fault-Tolerance Mechanism: A Compromise Between Outcome-Based Accountability and Process-Based Accountability

The accountability paradox arises not only from excessive accountability intensity and an imbalance in its components but also from the conflicting expectations imposed by diverse accountability. Chapter 6 scrutinizes the conflicts between hierarchical and horizontal accountability. This chapter delves into the conflicts between process-based accountability and outcome-based accountability within the Chinese bureaucracy. In addition, it examines the fault-tolerance mechanism, an innovative institution initiated by the Chinese government to reconcile the collision between process-based and outcome-based accountability and therefore to attenuate the accountability paradox.

The fault-tolerance mechanism refers to the exemption from punishment or lenient handling of deviations, faults, or failures committed by relevant public organizations or bureaucrats in fulfilling their duties or initiating reform and innovation. This mechanism was triggered in a context where intensified process-based accountability, emphasizing rule compliance and procedural obedience, increasingly undermines outcome-based accountability, which focuses on administrative performance since Xi took office. Faced with strengthened process-based accountability, Chinese public officials rationally choose to shirk responsibilities and avoid blame (Li et al., 2021; Tu, 2024; Wang, 2022; Wang & Yan, 2020). In this circumstance, the fault-tolerance mechanism was established to motivate cadres at all levels to take the initiative and strive

W. Tu, *The Accountability Paradox in the Chinese Bureaucracy*,
https://doi.org/10.1007/978-981-96-6392-7_7

for performance. This chapter scrutinizes the characteristics, conditions, and implications of the fault-tolerance mechanism in China. It examines a sub-dimension of the accountability paradox—specifically, the paradox of sources—where multiple logics of accountability impose conflicting expectations on bureaucrats.

Differences Between Process-Based Accountability and Outcome-Based Accountability

The traditional public administration tends to promote process-based accountability to strengthen politicians' control over the bureaucracy, while the NPM advocates outcome-based accountability within the bureaucracy to promote efficiency (Christensen & Lægreid, 2015; Jos & Tompkins, 2004; Patil et al., 2014). Process-based accountability typically employs input, processes, protocols, and rules to constrain bureaucrats' discretion and strictly hold them accountable (Balla, 1998; McCubbins et al., 1989). It is an effective mechanism for the principals or politicians to control the bureaucracy. By applying strict control, process-based accountability indeed alleviates public power abuse, various malfeasance, and corruption issues within the bureaucracy. However, heightened process-based accountability may contribute to red tape, risk aversion, and rigidity.

Outcome-based accountability (similar to managerial accountability) emphasizes neutral and technical assessment of whether output, performance, or ultimate goals are achieved (Ji, 2022; Page, 2006). Outcome-based accountability is promoted by the NPM paradigm. The NPM paradigm lays out specific principles and strategies to boost the economy, effectiveness, and efficiency of the public sector (Fatemi & Behmanesh, 2012). NPM considers that the government should not focus its attention on strict procedures, processes, and regulations in management, but rather on the outputs and performance of management activities, the efficiency and quality of service delivery, and the ability to proactively, flexibly, and cost-effectively respond to changes in the external environment (Dunleavy & Hood, 1994; Osborne, 2002). Thus, it advocates for decentralizing decision-making authority to local governments or autonomous agencies in a bid to improve managerial performance and enhance responsiveness and accountability to citizens (Andrews & Van de Walle, 2013; Barberis, 1998). Process-based accountability and

Table 7.1 A comparison between political-based and outcome-based accountability

	Process-based accountability	*Outcome-based accountability*
Power distribution	Power centralization: restrict discretion	Power decentralization: make the most of discretion
Objective	Compliance with rules and input: curb agency problem	Performance and results-oriented: Economy, effectiveness and efficiency
Tools	Administrative procedures	Performance management
Advantages	Ensure the fairness, legality, and predictability of policy implementation	Ensure professionalism and accountability in responding to specific contexts or public demands

outcome-based accountability differ in four significant ways, as shown in Table 7.1.

First, the major difference between process-based accountability and outcome-based accountability lies in their attitudes toward power distribution and discretionary authority. Process-based accountability seeks to alleviate agency problems embedded within a principal-agent relationship by restricting bureaucrats' "unbridled" discretionary power (Balla, 1998). The delegation process intrinsically suffers from both divergent interests and information asymmetries between political principals and public agents (Bendor et al., 2001). Process-oriented accountability requires bureaucratic agents to execute policies in accordance with established procedures, thereby ensuring the fairness, legality, and predictability of administrative decisions and actions, which effectively curbs agency problems.

In contrast, outcome-based accountability advocates decentralization to allow managers to handle operational issues and emphasizes the benefits derived from the proper exercise of discretionary power (Lægreid, 2014; Wynen & Verhoest, 2016). Decentralization can offer advantages such as access to local specialized knowledge, responsiveness to local conditions and client expectations, and efficient utilization of the expertise and professionalism of the public bureaucracy (Faguet, 2014). Since street-level bureaucrats are more familiar with local circumstances and citizens' demands, they are well-positioned to determine the best approaches for solving public problems (Hill, 2003).

Second, the objectives of process-based accountability and outcome-based accountability differ significantly. To ensure that the remainder of the political system adheres to policies enacted by legislatures or politicians, process-based accountability is often applied by politicians to emphasize inputs, processes, procedures, hierarchical control, and legality (Christensen & Lægreid, 2001). In order to curb agency problems such as bureaucratic drift and corruption within the power delegation structure, process-based accountability primarily focuses on monitoring the processes or procedures to assure fairness and legitimacy in decisions made by administrators (Moncrieffe, 1998). On the other hand, outcome-based accountability prioritizes performance over compliance with rules and inputs. While granting managers considerable autonomy, outcome-based accountability simultaneously holds them directly responsible for achieving measurable outcomes. Under NPM, outcome-based accountability emphasizes outputs, competition, and contractual relationships (Christensen & Lægreid, 2015). By adopting for-profit concepts from the private sector, NPM reforms aim to improve the efficiency, effectiveness, and economy of the entire public sector (De Vries & Nemec, 2013; Nõmm & Randma-Liiv, 2012).

Third, process-based accountability and outcome-based accountability differ in the tools they use to achieve their respective goals. Oversight and ex-ante administrative procedures are typically employed to ensure process-based accountability. McCubbins et al. (1989) consider ex-ante administrative procedures the most effective instruments wielded by Congress to ensure political control and accountability. Procedural requirements constrain discretionary latitude and induce compliance through two mechanisms. First, procedures integrate rules into agencies' decision-making, effectively limiting their independence and protecting against autocratic and capricious decisions by government officials. Second, administrative procedures increase the likelihood that bureaucrats incorporate the preferences of important constituents into agency policies.

In contrast, outcome-based accountability relies on neutral and technical performance management systems to evaluate whether performance is achieved efficiently and effectively (Christensen & Lægreid, 2021). Performance management within organizations may enhance their performance by establishing clear organizational goals, monitoring and measuring results, and using performance information for compensation and accountability (Fryer et al., 2009; Holzer & Yang, 2004). It requires unambiguous objectives, measurable outputs, incentivizing performance contracts, and merit-based compensation (Propper & Wilson, 2003; Verbeeten & Speklé, 2015).

The conflict between process-based accountability and outcome-based accountability may place bureaucrats in dilemma. Political principals desire to ensure that the remainder of the political system aligns with their policies, while simultaneously, they need to leverage the knowledge and expertise of the professional bureaucracy in formulating and implementing public policies. Therefore, intensified process-based accountability, intended to prevent bureaucratic drift, may produce the unintended consequences of restricting the agency's expertise and valuable information in formulating and implementing public policies (Bawn, 1995; Weingart, 1999). On the other hand, the discretion and independence necessary for objective expertise may lead to the agency's political responsiveness being hampered by the personal preferences of the public agents (Mashaw, 2005). Specifically, strong outcome-based accountability, prioritizing bureaucrats' professionalism, effectiveness, and the achievement of organizational goals, may undermine political control over the bureaucratic entities (Christensen & Lægreid, 2001). Reconciling the outcome-based accountability and process-based accountability of the public bureaucracy presents an ongoing challenge for many political systems (Christensen & Lægreid, 2015).

Conflicts Between Process-Based Accountability and Outcome-Based Accountability in China

The interplay and collision between process-based accountability and outcome-based accountability significantly influence bureaucratic behaviors in China. Xi's administration emphasizes the prominence of process-based accountability, valuing process, rule compliance, and strict responsiveness to the central authority.

Shift from Outcome-Based Accountability to Process-Based Accountability

After ending the planned economy that lasted almost 40 years in 1992, the CCP leaders started to embrace a socialist market economy, marking a shift from power centralization around the central authority to power devolution to local governments. In fact, since the reform and opening up, a series of reforms were initiated to unleash the entrepreneurship spirits of local governments. The political loyalty-based competition gave way to economic performance-based competition under Deng's administration. At this stage, outcome-based accountability emphasizing efficiency, output, and goal attainment dominated.

Fiscal decentralization, characterized by the fiscal contracting system from the reform and opening up until 1993, provided local officials with substantial discretion and resources to improve the provision of public services and preserve the market in their jurisdictions (Ding, 2007; Lin & Liu, 2000). The Chinese government at this stage is considered a de facto fiscal federalism, where local officials or bureaucracies enjoy the most discretionary latitude (Weingast, 2009). Local governments were depicted as "local state corporatism" or "local state-led developmental capitalism," with significant discretionary power over the economy being endowed to local governments (Walder, 1995).

Although the tax-sharing system replaced the fiscal contracting system in 1994 to recentralize fiscal management, local governments still enjoy substantial discretionary power in managing local affairs, dealing with various top-down tasks, and determining specific approaches to policy implementation. Subordinate governments decide whether and how much information to disclose to higher authorities. As a result, upper levels often depend on final outcomes for evaluation. Tasks and goals set by higher authorities are frequently assessed solely on outcomes, without considering whether lower-level officials have the necessary skills or circumstances to meet them, or if the execution follows established procedures and rules.

In addition to power devolution, performance measurement systems in the form of cadre responsibility contracts were established in the 1980s to hold local governments accountable to specific performance indicators. The winds of global NPM reforms have swept across China as well. Outcome-based accountability prevailed. At this stage, central power set macro plans or objectives, political intervention, and concrete plans were constrained, and local officials' entrepreneurship was unleashed. Central power served as a role of "steering," but this does not mean that the central authority is weak.

In a nutshell, before Xi came to power, local governments enjoyed considerable discretion in managing territorial affairs, and outcome-based accountability dominated. Process-based accountability was less effective in constraining bureaucrats' discretion, only becoming relevant when social unrest erupted due to local officials' malfeasance or when bureaucrats significantly deviated from the Party's directives. Both the central and local governments made significant efforts to boost the economy, using incentive contracts rather than political control as the primary instrument to regulate bureaucrats. Although this management model led to rapid economic development, it also resulted in rampant corruption and other notorious malfeasance among local officials.

Corruption has become one of the major agency problems and the most severe "tumor" threatening the rule of the CCP. Gong (2006) identifies local officials' predatory practices to expand extra- or off-budgetary funds through, for example, arbitrary fees, arbitrary fines, and arbitrary apportionment. In addition, highly individualized and covert corruption in China has evolved into more organized, destructive, and large-scale collective corruption, wherein Party and government officials in local governments colluded skillfully with each other on a massive scale, as seen in the notorious Zhanjiang smuggling case and the Xiamen smuggling case (Shieh, 2005). Zhu (2008) reveals shocking office-selling chains within the Heilongjiang provincial government, involving a provincial leader, with billions of RMB transacted among office sellers and buyers; this was just one of numerous office-selling cases in China. Rampant corruption and various types of misconduct among local authorities have caused growing social tensions.

When Xi came to power, the Chinese government was plagued more by corruption than by performance issues. It is not surprising, therefore, that the first words uttered by Xi Jinping upon his appointment as the Party's General Secretary in November 2012 were about the urgent to address the widening gap between the ruling elite and the people by combating officials' malfeasance and corruption. Party building and its subsequent enforcement of discipline through the anti-corruption campaign became the immediate means of achieving this (Brown & Bērziņa-Čerenkova, 2018). In fact, Xi's predecessors were aware that endemic corruption plagued the country and that systemic corruption could undermine the Party's legitimacy. However, the emphasis on economic growth outweighed officials' integrity at that stage. Therefore, although campaign-style anti-corruption drives were continuously launched, they were periodic, inconsistent, and compromising.

A considerable degree of centralization has been reinforced. The centralization of power is usually accompanied by strengthened inspections, monitoring, assessments, and directives, which reduce the discretionary power of local authorities. Initially, some people believed that Xi's anti-corruption campaign was no different from previous political campaigns and would be halted after "killing the chicken to frighten the monkey" (*shaji jinghou*, 杀鸡儆猴), a Chinese idiom meaning to punish a few to frighten the many. However, the ongoing effort is far more ambitious and systematic than before, aiming to build legal and institutional foundations for the discipline of bureaucracy and political control. Specifically, political control and accountability are no longer in the form of campaign-style mobilization initiated periodically; instead, process-based accountability is embedded in institutions and can be initiated routinely and frequently. Municipal and county Party committees regularly carry out inspection tours to monitor lower-level Party and government organs.

The central and local inspection tours mainly revolve around four areas: the implementation of the Party's theoretical line, policies, and the decisions and directives from the Central Committee and higher authorities; corruption issues and malfeasance affecting the public; the capacity building of grassroots party organizations; and the rectification of problems identified through inspections and other supervisory checks (Sohu News, 2024). Political supervision primarily focuses on officials' discipline problems and the rectification of malfeasance among party members and organizations. The cost of conducting frequent political inspections is high. An official revealed that "currently, political inspections are more frequent than government inspections. Our auditing department often needs to allocate personnel to participate in inspections. Since grassroots units are already short-staffed and overworked, this has caused some disruption to our daily operations and increased our burden" (CB-2024-33). In a nutshell, process-based accountability in China has strengthened through centralization and formalization, predominantly targeting violations of specific rules and procedures.

Political Control and Effective Governance

By analyzing the changes in governance and accountability models, we can observe that the ruling party alternates between power centralization and decentralization in response to the state's most urgent challenges, which leads to changes in emphasis between process-based accountability and outcome-based accountability. Bureaucrats also strategically adjust their behaviors to adapt to the institutional environment. According to Zhou (2022), a profound conundrum in China's political system is the conflict between a unified system and effective governance. The unified system grants the central government the highest and final decision-making authority over its vast territory, population, and various fields, leading to a concentration of power and resources. This, in turn, weakens the ability of local governments to address practical issues across different areas, thereby diminishing the effective governance of the system. However, power devolution to promote effective governance can lead to agency drift and various forms of malfeasance, posing a threat to the unified system (Mei & Pearson, 2014).

When effective governance or performance is the priority, the central authority tends to decentralize power to motivate the entrepreneurship of local governments and boost economic development. Nevertheless, when ruling risks become urgent, the central authority is more likely to centralize power to curb local authorities' malfeasance, which causes serious tension between the people and the state (Zhou, 2022). The conflict between political control and effective governance is vividly captured by a widespread saying in China: "*yizhua jiusi, yifang jiuluan*" (一抓就死, 一放就乱). This indicates a vicious cycle in which centralization leads to rigidity, rigidity leads to complaints, complaints lead to decentralization, decentralization leads to disorder, and disorder leads back to centralization. In fact, the governance issue in China is not new; rather, it is a classic problem rooted in the principal-agent relationship. The intensified principal's control can effectively suppress the agent's misconduct and corrupt practices, but excessive control can hinder the agent's administrative capacity and efficiency (Mei & Pearson, 2014). The core of this relationship lies in striking a balance between the principal's control and the agent's autonomy (Christensen & Lægreid, 2021).

Why is it especially difficult for the Chinese government to strike a balance between political control and agents' managerial discretion? This vicious cycle seems particularly prominent in the Chinese government. Some scholars claim that officials' heavy dependence on informal institutions to strategically accomplish tasks leaves the bureaucracy vulnerable to process-based accountability that emphasizes discipline and rigid adherence to formal rules (Wang, 2022; Wang & Yan, 2020). First, a structured system of laws and courts has yet to be fully entrenched to play a prominent role in the nation's institutional systems, rendering law-related activities often connected to informal rules and rule-bending (Peerenboom, 2002). In addition, China is vast with a large population, and the resource endowments and development levels vary greatly across different regions. For example, among 361 prefectural cities (including leagues, regions, and autonomous prefectures), Shanghai recorded the highest GDP at 47,218.66 billion yuan, whereas Changbai Mountain in Jilin Province had the lowest GDP at just 1.742 billion yuan in 2023 (Netease News, 2024). This means that Shanghai's GDP is 2711 times greater than that of Changbai Mountain. Therefore, local officials, especially those at the grassroots level, often need to implement policies based on local conditions.

To address the differences between unified policies and local conditions and achieve a satisfactory outcome for both upper-level government and citizens, grassroots officials need to flexibly implement policies to accomplish top-down tasks (Yang et al., 2022; Zhang et al., 2021). This flexible implementation often relies on some informal rules or even violates formal regulations. Power centralization and intensified accountability since Xi came to power imposed harsh punishments on local officials who violate central directives and rules. Intensified process-based accountability triggers bureaucrats' risk aversion, causing them to prioritize self-preservation and rationally avoid political risks and uncertainty by rigidly adhering to upper-level policies and formal rules, even when some of them are outdated and at odds with reality (Li et al., 2021; Tu & Gong, 2022b). Consequently, local officials tend to adopt a "one size fits all" approach for policy implementation to avoid making mistakes and being blamed.

Additionally, although there is a differentiation between the Party's power and the government's power, the scope and boundaries of the two forms of power are not clearly defined, and bureaucrats' expertise and professionalism are not well established in China. Local officials tend to push pressure downward and magnify the central government's directives through the administrative hierarchy. Thus, when the central government decentralizes power, local officials may impose looser supervision on lower-level officials and encourage them to make the most of their discretion. Conversely, when the central government centralizes power, local governments tend to impose stricter supervision on their subordinate officials.

A Compromise Scheme: The Fault-Tolerance Mechanism

Although the intensified process-based accountability has effectively constrained bureaucrats' flagrant abuse of power and malfeasance, it has a downside, as it undermines bureaucrats' entrepreneurship and efficiency (Li et al., 2021; Tu & Gong, 2022b). Facing intensified accountability, local bureaucrats strategically shift their motivations from credit claiming to blame avoidance by shunning risky tasks, stifling innovation and policy initiatives, and over-conforming to rigid regulations (Tu, 2024; Wang & Yan, 2020).

The stringent adherence to rules and regulations has resulted in some sensational social issues sparking widespread discussion within society. For example, in 2024, at a subway station in Wuhan city, a man without arms attempted to use the disabled access passage but was denied by the staff because he forgot to bring his disability certificate. Mr. Li showed his amputated arms and questioned the staff, asking if that was enough to prove he was disabled. However, the staff insisted that he must present the disability certificate; without it, he would have to use the regular paid passage. The staff even offered to buy him a ticket but could not violate regulations to let Mr. Li use the disabled passage. In an interview with a journalist, the staff still insisted that disabled individuals must show a disability certificate to use the disabled passage, and even if there is a visible disability, the certificate is still required; this is the rule (Pengpai News, 2024). This case shows that strict accountability on compliance with regulations among front-line workers may lead to negative social feedback.

The central government has gradually come to recognize the problems of intensive accountability and public officials' defensive responses toward monitoring pressure. It has acknowledged the potential dilemma faced by local cadres, who are caught between demands for taking initiatives for managerial performance and the risks of being blamed for violating regulations or making unintended mistakes. This situtation may render them incapable of taking any action and lead to systemic bureaucratic slack or standstill at the local level. The director of the Construction Bureau of a county in Guangdong Province stated at a seminar: "Our laws, regulations, and institutional rules are continually being refined, which imposes greater restrictions on our actions. While some leaders aim to take the initiative and expedite progress, numerous administrative regulations have to be adhered. These laws and regulations have become obstacles for us to carry out tasks effectively" (Lian, 2023).

In September 2019, the CCP central committee amended the *Chinese Communist Party Regulations on Accountability* issued in 2016. In this version of accountability regulation, two principles were added. First, power and responsibilities should be aligned, and negligence and punishment should be proportional (*quanze yizhi cuoze xiangdang*, 权责一致、错责相当). This principle aims to address the problem of "power overload" or "responsibility overload" and to prevent high-level officials from passing the buck to lower-rank officials. Second, strict control and sufficient organizational support should be integrated, with a balance between incentives and constraints (*yanguan he houai jiehe jili he yueshu binghzong*, 严管和厚爱结合、激励和约束并重). This principle reflects that the CCP has recognized the unintended negative effects of stringent accountability and has started to emphasize positive incentives and organizational support for bureaucrats.

In addition, the General Office of the CPC Central Committee issued the *Circular on Overall Specification for Inspection, Check, and Assessment* (《关于统筹规范督查检查考核工作的通知》) in August 2018 to deal with the excessive supervision of grassroots officials. The circular stated that the number of inspections, checks, and assessments of county and township governments should be significantly decreased. After the promulgation of the circular, local governments responded to it by reducing redundant inspections and conferences. A district in Changsha City reduced the 132 performance assessments that it had planned to conduct among the lower-level government at the end of 2018 to 25 (The China Comment, 2018).

Former Premier Li highlighted the fault-tolerance mechanism in his report on the work of the government in 2016, emphasizing the need to enhance mechanisms for incentives and fault tolerance to encourage public officials to be proactive, take initiative, and make accomplishment (Chinese Government Website, 2016). In 2018, the General Office of the CPC Central Committee issued *Opinions on Further Encouraging Cadres to Embrace a New Era, Take on New Responsibilities, and Make New Achievements*, which makes deployment for fault-tolerance mechanisms. Since then, almost all provinces and a considerable number of cities and counties have developed local measures for the fault-tolerance mechanism, including specific provisions to facilitate their effective operation and outlining certain circumstances under which public officials can be exempt from accountability or face a lighter punishment.

The fault-tolerance mechanism was established in the context where intensified process-based accountability emphasizing rule compliance and procedure obedience increasingly overweighs outcome-based accountability focusing on administrative performance since Xi took office. Faced with strengthened process-based accountability, Chinese public officials rationally choose to shirk responsibilities and avoid blame (Wang & Yan, 2020). Consequently, the fault-tolerance mechanism was initiated to encourage cadres to be willing to take initiative and achieve performance.

In 2016, President Xi proposed "three separations" as the guidance for the application of the fault-tolerance mechanism. First, a distinction should be made between mistakes and errors made by officials due to a lack of experiences or attempts to promote reforms, and willful violations of discipline and law. Second, a distinction should be made between mistakes and errors in policy experimentation where there are no clear directives from higher authorities, and violations of discipline and law despite explicit prohibitions from superiors. Third, a distinction should be made between unintentional mistakes made in the pursuit of development and disciplinary or legal violations committed for personal gains (Chinese Government Website, 2024).

The Tradeoff Between Performance and Rule Compliance

According to Willems & Van Dooren (2011), accountability tools serve three key purposes. First, they aim to ensure that public authorities adhere to established rules and procedures to prevent unfairness and misuse of power. Second, citizen—either directly or through their elected representatives—seek to maintain ultimate control, as sovereignty resides with the populace. Therefore, accountability mechanisms are instruments to fulfill citizens' expectations. Third, there is also a concern about the actual outcomes or achievements of government actions. While the ultimate objective of rule compliance is to protect citizens' interests and achieve satisfactory outputs, these three expectations can sometimes be at odds with one another. Excessive rule compliance or outdated red tape may undermine citizens' interests and the final outcomes.

When bureaucrats are held accountable by process-based accountability, they tend to emphasize rules, regulations, procedures, and Party disciplines while refraining from exercising their expertise and making initiatives based on local contexts to accomplish tasks. In contrast, when bureaucrats are more responsive to outcome-based accountability, they pay more attention to organizational performance and the attainment of tasks while are more likely to neglect regulations and procedures. The newly established SC system, a typical political organ in China, primarily emphasize compliance with rules and procedures. The crucial role that local SCs play in monitoring local officials makes them pay more attention to rules and procedures, which sometimes in the cost of managerial performance. Fault-tolerance mechanism can be considered an innovative institution to reconcile the tension between rule compliance and managerial performance.

Based on whether bureaucrats fulfill expectations exerted by process-based accountability or outcome-based accountability, this study classifies four bureaucratic practices (Table 7.2). The first form is when bureaucrats meet the expectations of both process-based accountability and outcome-based accountability (Type 1). This means that bureaucrats implement policies effectively while strictly adhering to the rules and specified procedures, representing the ideal type of practice. The second type occurs when bureaucrats meet the expectations of process-based accountability while failing to fulfill outcome-based accountability (Type 2). In this circumstance, bureaucrats strictly follow regulations and procedures but fail to produce satisfactory results and performance. Type 2 has been prevalent within the Chinese bureaucracy since the process-based accountability was strengthened. Facing political risks and uncertainty, bureaucrats tend to over-conform to regulations, standard operating procedures, established precedents, and so forth, leading them to apply rules mechanically rather than flexibly (Lipsky, 2010). Some officials even deliberately turn important or emergent affairs into routines, burying them in red tape to minimize the need for discretionary decision-making. The prevalence of Type 2 is a major trigger for the introduction of fault-tolerance mechanisms.

Table 7.2 Four forms of bureaucratic practices

		Fulfill process-based accountability	
		Yes	*No*
Fulfill outcome-based accountability	Yes	Ideal administration (Type 1)	Tolerable faults (Type 3)
	No	Ineffective administration (Type 2)	Intolerable faults (Type 4)

The third type occurs when bureaucrats meet the expectations of outcome-based accountability while failing to meet process-based accountability (Type 3). In this case, bureaucrats produce satisfactory results and effectively resolve problems based on local contexts while failing to strictly follow particular procedures or regulations, which is the primary type of practice that the fault-tolerance mechanism seeks to target. The central government is aware that requiring local officials to strictly comply with rules may undermine their initiatives and entrepreneurship, which are essential for local development. The lengthy and complicated principal-agent chains between the central and local governments means that the former is heavily reliant on the latter to effectively enforce central policies, directly interact with citizens, and address local problems. The fourth form occurs when bureaucrats fail to meet the expectations of both outcome-based accountability and process-based accountability (Type 4), which is unacceptable and necessitates accountability. This chapter focuses on Type 3. By exempting officials from punishment for deviations or faults that benefit the final results or performance, the fault-tolerance mechanism attempts to uphold bureaucrats' initiative and morale.

Collision Between Process-Based Accountability and Outcome-Based Accountability

To identify patterns and characteristics of tolerable faults, this study collected 66 cases that received the fault-tolerance mechanism and were publicly reported by official media and websites from 2012 to 2023. These cases were identified by searching two terms that have been officially used to describe the fault-tolerance mechanism in China: "fault tolerance and error correction" (*rongcuo jiucuo anli,* 容错纠错案例) and "fault tolerance and liability exemption" (*rongcuo mianze anli,* 容错免责案例). I searched for these terms in Baidu Information, which provides comprehensive coverage publicized by central and local official media and websites. Content analysis was applied to the 66 cases to scrutinize the characteristics, conditions, and implications of the fault-tolerance mechanism in China. This study identified four types of conditions that can receive the fault-tolerance mechanism. To unpack the characteristics of each type of condition, I employed typical case studies to elaborate on the contexts, processes, and mechanisms that trigger the fault-tolerance mechanism.

The necessity to initiate the fault-tolerance mechanism primarily stems from the conflicts between rule compliance and managerial efficiency. Although the efficacy of the rules in achieving functional objectives is undeniable, scholars notice the compliance burden coming with rule compliance (Borry, 2016; Bozeman & Feeney, 2014; Coursey & Pandey, 2007). Public employees may feel burdened in complying with the rule when it demands excessive time or energy, or it is overly complex and frustrating (Pandey & Scott, 2002). Van Loon et al. (2016) classify rules into four types based on two dimensions: perceived lack of functionality and compliance burden. A rule perceived as imposing a significant compliance burden while lacking functionality is considered red tape. Rules that impose a high compliance burden but still fulfill their intended purpose can be termed necessary bureaucracy. Those that do not impose a heavy compliance burden yet fail to serve a functional purpose can be classified as unnecessary rules. Conversely, rules that have a low compliance burden and effectively achieve their goals are regarded as high-quality rules.

This classification is insightful and sheds light on different types of rules. However, the static classification of a rule into a specific type suffers from some flaws as the functionality of a rule heavily depends on the specific contexts. In some situations, a rule may be viewed as high-quality, while in others, it might be seen as unnecessary or as red tape. Furthermore, the standards for the assessment of rules vary across different stakeholders and perspectives. Through the analysis of 66 cases, I classified the cases into four categories that involve different forms of conflict between rule compliance and managerial efficiency, resulting in the trigger of the fault-tolerance mechanism. I illustrate the four conflicts below.

The Conflict Between Compliance Time and Objective Outcomes

The time required for compliance with rules mandated by process-based accountability can sometimes impede administrative efficiency and delay timely responses to emergencies. Compliance time refers to the duration that public projects spend meeting the qualifications, requirements, and other conditions outlined by relevant laws, regulations, and policies. If this compliance time is rigidly defined, failing to complete a particular procedural step can bring the entire project to a standstill. In instances where timely production is essential or there is a need to address emergencies, a rigid compliance timeframe can impede developmental opportunities or delay the prompt management of urgent issues. The tendering system for public projects is a crucial regulation to ensure integrity, and if designed effectively, it can be considered a high-quality rule that facilitates the smooth execution of a project. However, in some situations or from certain actors' perspectives, it may be viewed as red tape.

For example, in April 2018, during a routine inspection, the River Management Bureau of a certain city in Hubei Province discovered that a reservoir's spillway gate was leaking, posing a safety hazard. The bureau decided to implement maintenance and repair projects for the reservoir gates and the spillway gate's waterproofing, in response to the upcoming flood season. After investigation, they found that the construction period was relatively short and that the work needed to be completed before the water level rose. Given the urgency, the bureau's party secretary and director, Huang, bypassed the government procurement procedures and arranged for a hydropower company with relevant project experience to commence construction. This approach of starting construction first and completing the procurement procedures later violated the procedural regulations of the *Government Procurement Law* and its implementation regulations. However, Huang's breach of procedure aimed to effectively handle an emergency situation. After deliberation, the local SC decided that while Huang violated relevant procedural regulations, his subjective intention was to safeguard the public interest; therefore, he was granted leniency and exempted from punishment.

In another case, Chi, the party secretary and director of a city's administrative approval bureau, was overseeing the approval of five key construction projects related to economic and social development. He noticed that these projects were lacking relevant approval documents. Considering that the approval process for these documents was complex and time-consuming, and that the actual situation for project construction in the city was urgent, Chi decided to accept the applications with deficiencies and issued the administrative license and related permits for these projects first, while later urging the completion of the necessary procedures. Although Chi violated relevant procedural regulations, his intention was to advance the progress of significant projects, and ultimately, he was also exempted from punishment.

Both of these cases reflect officials' good intentions to achieve overall social benefits by breaking the rigid constraints on rule compliance.

Generally speaking, when officials violate formal organizational policies and regulations to fulfill their responsibilities more efficiently or to achieve public interests and social benefits, this can be regarded as prosocial rule breaking (Morrison, 2006). During the policy implementation process, bureaucrats often feel like a "mouse" in a bellows, caught between the dual pressures of being "prosocial" and adhering to "rules." If they act prosocially for the interests of citizens or the ultimate outcomes, they may risk violating relevant rules. However, strict compliance with regulations may lead to delays in the timely management of urgent situations.

The Conflict Between Compliance Burden and Administrative Efficiency

Without considering whether the rules or procedures align with actual circumstances and require updating, merely urging bureaucrats to follow the rules may result in a high compliance burden, leading to rigidity and inefficiency within the bureaucratic system. While rules can bring stability and order, organizations should constantly examine whether these rules have devolved into red tape and outdated practices that hinder administrative efficiency. "Rule-evolved red tape occurs when a once-functional rule loses effectiveness over time" (Borry, 2016, p. 3). Bozeman and Feeney (2014) identified six situations in which rules can evolve into red tape: "rule drift," where the original intent of a rule becomes unclear over time; changes in implementation that make a rule ineffective and necessitate updates; shifts in a rule's purpose that make it less relevant or ineffective for its intended function; changes in ecology affecting its applicability and effectiveness; "rule strain," where an overload of rules can lead to conflicts; and incompatibility, which occurs when old rules and new ones do not align well together. The fault-tolerance mechanism can provide an opportunity for the elimination of red tape and the updating of rules. When officials are held accountable for breaching unreasonable rules, the government should closely examine and evaluate the relevance of those rules in relation to their intended purpose and context.

For example, in January 2019, a service center in a certain city held a training course on the management of fruit trees for people with disabilities. Among the 153 participants, 79 were over 60 years old, which did not meet the requirement in the documents stating that "participants must be of working age." However, this violation was due to the consideration of the actual demographic structure in rural areas of the city, where the majority of fruit farmers are elderly individuals over 60 years old. The training proved to be very effective, and the local CDI granted the center immunity from accountability for the violation of regulations.

The Conflict Between Process Compliance and Policy Innovation

The pursuit of certainty emphasized by process-based accountability often entails a profound contradiction with the need for flexibility in innovation. Specifically, process-based accountability may, to some extent, suppress the motivation for reform and innovation among local officials. Innovation involves creating something from nothing or transforming the existing into something new, which requires breaking through traditions, changing established practices, and disrupting existing procedures (De Vries et al., 2016). As a result, it often involves experimentation, trial, and error. The legal and regulatory framework in China is not well established, leading to significant uncertainty and ambiguity. Without concrete support from higher-level authorities, local officials may hesitate to launch innovation due to the high risk of violating existing rules and procedures. Facing increased process-based accountability, local officials have a strong motivation to adhere strictly to regulations and inhibit innovation as a means of avoiding blame.

For example, in June 2023, Changyang Tujia Autonomous County implemented an innovative reform to simplify the non-notarized inheritance procedures for real estate. For applicants who, due to the passage of time, missing files, or other reasons, are unable to obtain proof of kinship, personal commitments can be accepted in place of kinship certificates. This reform lowers the proof standards for property rights registration and addresses the difficulty for citizens to provide evidence. Many news reports indicate that citizens take great trouble visiting local police departments or residents' committees many times to obtain proof of a "parent–child relationship" or to verify their identity during inheritance procedures. Although benefiting citizens, this policy innovation may entail the risks of erroneous transfer registrations, which leads to the reluctance of many local governments to launch the reform. Changyang government also submitted a risk reporting document to the local SC to disclose potential risks associated with the reform. This policy innovation means that the local government needs to break the existing regulations related to non-notarized inheritance procedures and may endure the risks of making mistakes in the process of transfer registrations. If accountability prioritizes excessively strict adherence to rules and procedures, it may potentially reduce officials' motivation to innovate.

The Conflict Between Formal Procedures and Informal Practices

Grassroots officials, especially at the village level, often rely on informal rules to flexibly handle tasks, which can conflict with formal regulations. In China, local culture and customs in villages play an important role in managing local affairs. These informal practices can sometimes provide significant support to formal authorities in addressing social issues and alleviating the government's burden, but they can also act as a resistance against the implementation of state policies. Over the last decade, the Chinese government has launched numerous programs to alter customs and rituals in various villages, extending state power to the farthest reaches of society. However, local officials may be accustomed to relying on local informal practices to address problems, leading to violations of formal rules.

For example, in 2018, approximately 30 teachers, represented by a person named Ma, gathered at the Binjiang County People's Government to petition, and their emotions were quite agitated. Officials from the Binjiang County Education Bureau attempted to clarify policies and persuade the petitioners to go home. To conciliate the petitioners and calm their anger, Lihong Luo, an official from the Binjiang County Education Bureau, privately invited Ma to have a meal for in-depth communication. Ma agreed and invited several other teachers to join them at a restaurant in the county town. During this meal, Luo and the petitioning representatives ate and drank for nearly three hours, violating the eight-point code. Considering Luo's intention was to address significant petitioning incidents and prevent the escalation of public sentiment, the local CDI issued a warning as a form of lenient disciplinary punishment.

Alcohol consumption is a key aspect of traditional Chinese culture and serves as a primary facilitator for social interactions and bonding. In China, drinking culture is deeply embedded in social customs and traditions, often acting as a means to show respect and strengthen relationships (Tu & Guo, 2023). For a long time, extravagant hospitality and drinking—integral to position-related consumption within the government—have been commonly employed to foster interpersonal relationships, creating a fertile ground for power abuse and corruption

(Gong & Xiao, 2017). The issue of the eight-point code in late 2012 strictly prohibits luxury banquets and excessive alcohol consumption, thereby helping to limit the culture of eating, drinking, and corruption. However, drinking still enjoys high social acceptance across the country and is considered an effective way to facilitate relationships. In rural areas, government officials particularly need to cultivate close relationships with citizens to advance their work, and drinking or other informal practices are key methods for them to connect with the general public. Xi's anti-corruption initiatives aim to alter certain social customs that facilitate corruption. However, this is a long-term transformation that may involve resistance and dilemmas in the short-term, requiring coordination between formal rules and informal norms.

Between Process and Outcome: Movable Accountability Risk Frontier

Public officials, particularly those at the grassroots level, often find themselves in a difficult position due to the tension between rule compliance and the need for effective management. Strict adherence to regulations may not lead to satisfactory results, which could leading to blame from higher-ups or the public. Conversely, a more flexible approach to policy enforcement aimed at achieving better outcomes might incur punishment from SCs or frequent top-down inspections from the Party. For example, simplifying administrative approval procedures can enhance administrative efficiency and seize development opportunities, but it may also lead to accountability risks for violating relevant regulations. Strictly adhering to public project approval procedures can ensure the legality of the process; however, neglecting timely responses to emergencies may trigger larger disasters, resulting in a loss of overall social benefits and ultimately more stringent punishment. "To improve efficiency, some of my colleagues did not fully adhere to specific rules. After being punished for rule violations, they chose to be slack, but then received complaints from the public" (CB-2024-34). Therefore, officials find themselves in a dilemma: by evading process-based accountability, one may face outcome-based accountability, whereas steering clear of outcome-based accountability could result in process-based accountability.

The Model of Accountability Risk Frontier

Based on the "risk protection frontier" model (Graham & Weiner, 1995; Weiner, 1998), Hood (2010) proposed the "blame avoidance frontier" (BAF) model. The assumption of the BAF model is that for each source of blame, there exists a corresponding form of counter-blame (for example, being held accountable for violating procedures is countered by being held accountable for poor outcomes). The BAF reflects a zero-sum game in a risk society, where either taking action or inaction may lead to the risk of being blamed. It places bureaucrats in a dilemma of being "damned if you do" (doing something may lead to blame) and "damned if you don't" (not doing something may also lead to blame), creating a push-and-pull dynamic that shaped bureaucratic behavior (Hood, 2010, p. 108).

I refer to the BAF model to construct an accountability risk frontier (ARF) around process-based and outcome-based accountability (Fig. 7.1). On this arc-shaped accountability risk frontier, the two types of accountability risks faced by bureaucrats exhibit an inverse relationship. As one moves along the frontier from point P on the 45-degree diagonal line to the vertical axis, the perceived risk being blamed by process-based accountability gradually increases while the risk of outcome-based accountability decreases. Conversely, when point P moves along the arc toward the horizontal axis, the perceived risk of outcome-based accountability becomes stronger while the risk of process-based accountability diminishes. In this light, officials may discreetly select policy strategies to identify the optimal position along the frontier. They must conduct a comprehensive assessment by weighing the severity of punishment, the likelihood of being blamed, and other environmental factors of the two forms of accountability risks in order to make the "best" choice. However, no matter what decision is made, there is no optimal solution or true no-blame option available on the frontier (no-blame option). Bureaucrats can only select the option that minimizes the potential blame by weighing different risk factors. The logic of blame avoidance implies a search for the least blame policy option.

The model reflects that in a risk society, bureaucrats often face conflicts arising from multiple accountability risks or expectations. They must make decisions that best align with their own interests amid these multiple conflicts. Figure 7.1 only illustrates the conflict between outcome-based

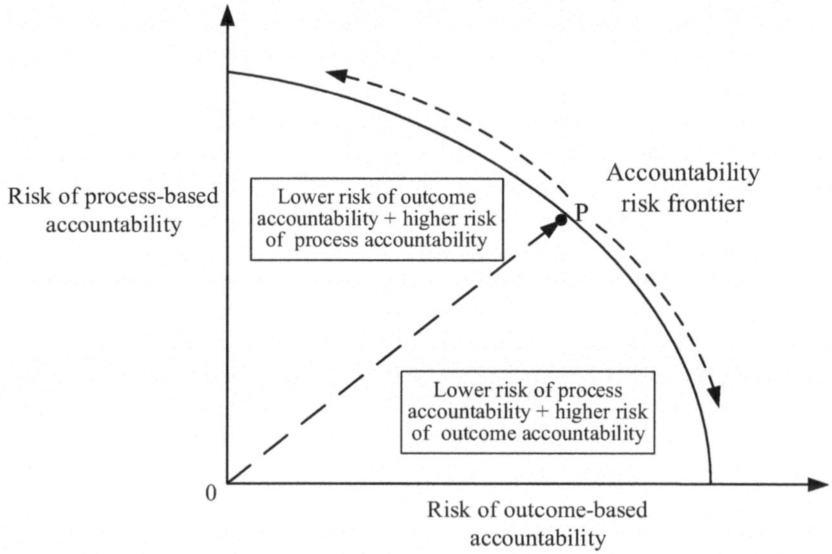

Fig. 7.1 Accountability risk frontier (*Source* Adapted from Hood [2010, p. 105], Graham & Weiner [1995], Weiner [1998])

and process-based accountability, whereas, in practice, bureaucrats may confront more multidimensional risks and conflicts at play.

How Does the Fault-Tolerance Mechanism Change the ARF

Hood (2010) argues that if more efficient or productive management methods are developed, it could change the entire BAF curve, allowing for the reduce in one type of blame without increasing another type of blame, or vice versa, thereby making blame trade-offs less restrictive. This study argues that an appropriately designed fault-tolerance mechanism can, to some extent, narrow the accountability risk frontier and mitigate the "no-win point" situation. Figure 7.2 illustrates the movable ARF, demonstrating how the fault-tolerance mechanism and sanction-based accountability shape the frontier of accountability risk. The fault-tolerance mechanism narrows the ARF from Frontier 1 to Frontier

2, while sanction-based accountability, characterized by stringent supervision and punishment, expands the ARF from Frontier 1 to Frontier 3.

Stringent sanction-based accountability undermines trust between superiors and subordinates, hindering the development of mechanisms for adaptability, flexibility, and mutual support (Tu & Gong, 2022a). Sanction-based accountability, which emphasizes fault-finding and punishment, may expand the ARF and expose bureaucrats to higher risks of being blamed. Specifically, if the balance point between process-based accountability and outcome-based accountability at ARF1 is M1, it will shift to M3 by sanction-based accountability at ARF3. This means that while the risk of being punished by process-based accountability remains unchanged, the risk of receiving outcome-based accountability becomes stronger, thereby exposing bureaucrats to greater accountability risks when making trade-offs between procedural compliance and managerial efficiency.

The movable frontier helps us to understand how sanction-based accountability shapes the motivations and behavior of bureaucrats. The

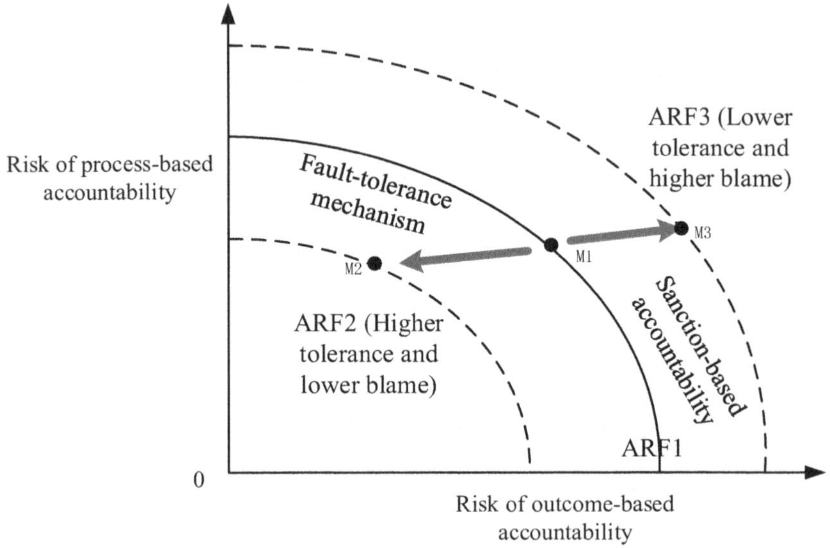

Fig. 7.2 Movable accountability risk frontier

sanction-based accountability tends to connotate a binary logic of "either/or," "right or wrong," and "black or white," leaving narrow latitude for complexity, alternatives, and gray areas. When organizations strengthen sanction-based accountability, bureaucrats tend to prioritize either outcomes over processes, or processes over outcomes, showing no incentive to mitigate their conflicts. In the face of stringent sanction, officials' attempts to make modifications and reconcile conflicts between different expectations may incur higher costs to justify the legitimacy of their behavior to the accountability forum that requires absolute obedience. Therefore, as sanction-based accountability intensified, all stakeholders sought to protect themselves and pass the buck, escalating the trust crisis. In this situation, individual interests, organizational interests, and social interests will be in a zero-sum game and cannot be reconciled. The majority of bureaucrats may choose practices aligned with the rational actor hypothesis, opting for blame-avoiding strategies including abstinence (just say no) and herding (stay with the group). Specifically, bureaucrats may minimize decision-making or conform to their peers in order to avoid the risks of making mistakes and being blamed. This low-trust, sanction-based form of accountability may undermine bureaucrats' moral deliberation and decision-making, causing them to mechanically focusing on fulfilling the requirements of the most stringent account holder. If strict adherence to rules shields them from being blamed, they will no longer be responsible for outcomes and performance. Consequently, they become mere blame-avoiding machines.

The fault-tolerance mechanism, to a certain extent, conveys a higher level of trust and a lower tendency to blame. It can be seen as a mechanism that is oriented toward individual and organizational learning. By encouraging officials to innovate and experiment while tolerating their mistakes during exploration, adjustment, and innovation, the fault-tolerance mechanism fosters a more inclusive and supportive organizational environment. The fault-tolerance mechanism may reduce the risk of accountability, causing M1 on ARF1 to shift to M2 on ARF2. It indicates that while the risk of being punished by process-based accountability remains unchanged, the risk of receiving outcome-based accountability decreases. Consequently, bureaucrats may perceive a lower level of accountability risk when reconciling the conflicts between procedural compliance and managerial performance. When the frontier of accountability risk is narrowed, officials have greater motivation to make context-appropriate adjustments between procedure compliance and managerial outcomes to achieve maximum social benefits. The fault-tolerance mechanism allows street-level bureaucrats to implement policies based on specific circumstances and local conditions, and this latitude allows them to better respond to complex and dynamic environments, coordinate conflicting expectations, and take innovative measures to address challenging social issues. Unlike sanction-based accountability that operates on binary opposition logic, by allowing officials to make mistakes during processes of exploration, adaptation, and innovation, it grants them greater discretion to thoughtfully balance various expectations and makes the trade-offs between rule compliance and managerial performance less constraining.

Bureaucrats' Choices Between Process and Outcome

In certain circumstances, public officials find themselves in a dilemma: they can either be blamed for rule violations or for poor performance. As the Chinese government places increasing emphasis on rule compliance, this conflict intensifies, especially for grassroots officials who tend to rely on informal practices or social customs to flexibly complete tasks and engage with citizens. When confronted with the conflicts between rule compliance and managerial effectiveness, local officials may adopt three strategies.

First, officials may weigh which accountability forum has greater authority to impose sanctions and might prioritize the expectations of the more powerful forum. Specifically, one expectation may totally substitute other expectations, and reconciliation will not be pursued to attain a potential balance. Prior to the establishment of SCs, the upper-level government exerted the strongest impacts on the lower-level officials, and more attention was paid to the attainment of goals and effectiveness set by the higher-level government. With the establishment of the system of SCs as specialized supervisory organs, more focus is on the violations of rules, regulations, and administrative procedures. As local SCs gain momentum and the central government emphasizes rule compliance, some local officials blindly follow the rules without considering the actual conditions. Such an approach often results in policies that fail to meet public needs, stifle innovation, and contain adaptability in local administration. In this regard, the emphasis on rule compliance substitutes the pursuit of managerial effectiveness without a conciliation.

There are various strategies for navigating the regulatory landscape, including strictly adhering to rules, establishing additional regulations and procedures, and frequently seeking permission and guidance from superiors, which can limit discretionary decision-making. Qizheng Zhao, who once served as the Director of the State Council Information Office, has a famous saying: "If you want to make something won't get done, simply keep requesting approvals from your superiors…… For decisions I can make on my own, I won't seek approval. By asking for permission, you're shifting the responsibility up the chain. If you seek their agreement and they approve but something goes wrong, doesn't that place the blame on them?" (Sina Finance, 2024). Therefore, superiors can only be cautious; either they delay or refuse to approve to avoid taking responsibility. Seeking permission from superiors frequently seems like adherence to work discipline, it's actually a strategy to avoid responsibility.

Second, some public officials may tend to achieve managerial effectiveness without being blamed for violating regulations. In this regard, they need to cautiously strike a balance between rule compliance and goal achievement. It is no longer practical to prioritize output and performance without considering procedures and rules, as was common in the past when economic development is the priority. Previously, it was quite common to push forward projects first and then complete the necessary procedures afterward, often summarized by the saying "getting on the bus first and then buying the ticket" (*xian shangche hou bupiao,* 先上车后补票). Officials now need to make compromises and discreetly deal with divergent expectations. Some officials rely on derived rules as an alternative basis for decision-making. Specifically, by creating sub-rules from official meetings, oral instructions, or supplementary documents, they create a procedural basis for issues that fall outside the legal framework or established regulations, ensuring that tasks can be enforced with textual and procedural support (Lian, 2023). For example, one reason some cases are exempted from punishment by SCs is that they adhere to other sub-rules or procedures.

In September 2022, the Committee of Shenshui Village in Hubei Province managed to apply for an approved budget of 155,000 yuan to carry out an environmental improvement project designated for building a greenbelt. In November, during the construction of the project, nearby residents reported that the roads in the rural community were too narrow and that the construction of a greenbelt would affect vehicle access, posing safety hazards. Xu, the Party secretary, and village head, conducted a field investigation, gathered opinions from nearby residents. After a discussion and agreement in a meeting with the village's "two committees" (the Party committee and the village committee), he decided to change the original project plan from constructing a greenbelt to building a pedestrian pathway. Due to the short project timeline of less than a month, Xu verbally reported this change to the relevant personnel in the town (who have since been held accountable) and, with their consent, instructed the construction team to replace the originally designed greenbelt with crushed stone pavement. Xu was investigated for unauthorized change of project construction plan by the inspection team dispatched by the county's Party committee. However, Xu was exempted from disciplinary punishment by the Party, and instead received oral criticism. The fact that Xu discussed with two committees and made an oral report to the upper-level superior becomes one of the reasons why the fault-tolerance mechanism was applied in this case.

Yuxi City in Yunnan province regulates that if a decision is made through collective research, democratic discussion, and transparent processes with relevant written records, faults related to this decision can be tolerated. It seems that using derived rules from democratic decisions as the basis for policies provides a procedural foundation for matters that fall outside the legal framework or established rules, ensuring that tasks can be pushed forward with textual and procedural support. This stipulation gives local governments the opportunity to navigate one "procedure" by employing another "procedure." The first "procedure" refers to higher-level laws and regulations, while the latter "procedure" refers to the procedures of collective discussion and democratic decision-making (Lian, 2023). It, to some extent, endows local officials certain latitude to solve problems as their discretionary power has been highly impaired since 2012.

Besides resorting to deriving sub-rules, more and more officials apply for exemption from liability for faults (risk reports) from local SCs when they encounter conflicts between rule compliance and managerial effectiveness. For example, the Housing and Urban–Rural Development Bureau of Xiaoting District, Hubei Province, planned to grant the construction permit to a major energy storage with some items that have not been stamped in order to expedite the construction and production. However, this move bypasses the current housing and construction regulations and administrative oversight procedures. The bureau reported the potential risks of this move to the local SC and gained approval for issuing a permit with deficiency (Pengpai News, 2023). Currently, it has become a typical move for local officials to reconcile the conflicts between procedure compliance and managerial performance. For example, in July 2021, Jieshou City, Anhui province, launched the approval with "deficiency" (*rongque shenpi*, "容缺"审批) for construction projects, allowing projects with missing minor supporting materials to get production permits after signing a written commitment. By 2022, 31 construction projects in the city had obtained permits through this process (People's News, 2022). The risk reporting mechanism or deficiency approval process under the fault-tolerance system is an elastic design to give local officials a certain discretion to strike a balance between procedure requirements and the desire to promote development, softening the rigid institutional framework.

Third, the ideal result is to promote a reassessment of the rules and update obsolete regulations that have lost their original functionality and become red tape. The transformation of regulations is normally initiated by higher-level organizations or local SCs. When I conducted fieldwork in Sichuan province, the secretary of a city's CDI shared a case to illustrate the challenges encountered by grassroots officials. There is a pond that was deserted for many years. The village head viewed it as a waste, so he cleaned the pond and introduced fish, which not only rejuvenated the pond but also created a source of income for the village. However, some villagers reported it to the local CDI, accusing the village head of embezzling public assets for private gains. The accusation isn't entirely baseless, as the village head indeed used the public pond for his own fish business, but punishing him seems unfair, given that his actions ultimately benefited the village. This case led to a clarification and refinement of the regulations concerning the contracting of collective assets by the local CID. It is a typical case where the assessment of conflicts between rule compliance and managerial effectiveness drives transformation and enhancements of regulations. Table 7.3 illustrates the three choices made by bureaucrats.

Sanction-based accountability is more likely to force bureaucrats to adopt the substitution strategy, where the priority of one expectation crowds out other expectations. However, the fault-tolerance mechanism encourages officials to adopt measures of compromising or rule transformation to mitigate conflicts between outcomes and procedures. Local SCs or related organizations should help examine the underlying reasons behind rule violations, determining whether it is due to intentional misconduct or the difficulty in coordinating the conflicts between rigid

Table 7.3 Three choices of bureaucrats between process and outcome

Institutional contexts	*Bureaucrats' choices*	*Thinking logic*	*The paradox of responsibility*
Sanction-based accountability	Substitution	A binary opposition logic: the most powerful account holder forces out expectations of other holders; unable to make trade-offs between different procedures and outcomes	Rational actor: mechanically follows the most stringent holder; becomes a mere blame-avoiding machine
Fault-tolerance mechanism	Compromise	An integrative logic: Strike a balance between different expectations; mitigate the conflicts between rule compliance and goal achievement	Moral actor: capable of making ethical decisions instead of mindless compliance
	Transformation	Systematic thinking: Reflect on the reasons underlying the conflicts; update regulations	Moral organization: build a culture of support and learning for bureaucrats

procedures and managerial effectiveness. If it is determined that once-effective rules have turned into bureaucratic red tape, prompt adjustments should be made to improve organizational procedures. This involves the timely establishment, amendment, or repeal of policies and regulations to maintain the effectiveness and continuity of rules, ensuring a close connection between regulations and social development.

Who Can Tolerate Officials' Faults

Another important issue related to the fault-tolerance mechanism is who possess the authority to decide when the fault-tolerance mechanism can be initiated. While the central government proposes "three separations," and numerous local governments have issued regulations to guide the application of the fault-tolerance mechanism, there are no clear standards regarding "which faults to tolerate," "how to tolerate faults," and "who can tolerate officials' faults." When accountability is heightened, few officials are willing to initiate the fault-tolerance mechanism because they also fear that issuing leniency may be incorrect, and they also encounter difficulties in implementing such a mechanism.

Currently, local SCs and CDIs play a major role in deciding whether a fault should be tolerated and how to tolerate it. However, in some places, local SCs involve more stakeholders in the discussion of the initiation of the fault-tolerance mechanism. For example, in one case, the local SC organized a joint meeting with the local People's Congress, the Political Consultative Conference, and the Organization Department to discuss whether the faults of an official can be tolerated. In another case, the local SC held a meeting assembling public officials in leadership positions, Party representatives, representatives of the People's Congress, members of the Political Consultative Conference, and industry experts to discuss whether the fault-tolerance mechanism should be applied in the case.

While it may be a strategy for local SCs to use collective decision-making to disperse the risk of making decisions, it is beneficial to aggregate diverse stakeholders with unique experiences and viewpoints, both within and outside the government, to discuss cases. First, collective discussions facilitate communication and understanding across different groups, reducing misunderstandings and conflicts. In particular, they provide account givers with a chance to explain their actions and share the challenges they encountered. Second, a diverse group is more likely to represent the interests and needs of the broader community, ensuring that decisions are inclusive. This inclusivity is essential for enhancing network governance, which requires compromises among diverse expectations. Third, dialogues that incorporate diverse insights leads to a more comprehensive understanding of issues and challenges. Varied perspectives can foster creative solutions by merging ideas and approaches, facilitating reflection on the underlying reasons for the conflict between rule compliance and managerial performance. This process may help address loopholes in regulations or transform outdated or unsuitable rules.

Conclusion

Bureaucrats, especially the street-level ones, often face complex contexts for policy implementation, reflected in the ambiguity and uncertainty of issues, as well as the diverse expectations. In such complex situations, bureaucrats frequently need to navigate multiple, even conflicting, accountability expectations and requirements. This chapter outlines two types of accountability encountered by bureaucrats: process-based accountability and outcome-based accountability. Currently, the Chinese government imposes higher demands for the legitimacy and standardization of policy processes, while also expecting local officials to initiate reforms and innovation to promote overall social benefits. Officials tend to make rational decisions along the frontier of accountability risks, taking into account the institutional and organizational factors, in order to minimize the risks of being blamed. This chapter offers the following considerations for effectively bridging accountability and the fault-tolerance mechanism.

First, it is crucial to create a systematic framework that allows for the concurrent launch of accountability investigations and the fault-tolerance mechanism. The typical process begins with the initiation of an accountability mechanism, which usually imposes sanctions on individuals or organizations. It is only after the account givers seek leniency that the fault-tolerance mechanism is initiated to thoroughly assess the issues. This sequence places the burden on the account giver to bear the risks and costs associated with making adjustments, initiating innovations, and launching reforms. In other words, they must face the potential negative consequences of their actions without any guarantee that their cases will be evaluated fairly and granted leniency afterward. Furthermore, China's accountability mechanism continues to intensify, marked by rigidity in execution and a lack of flexibility, while the fault-tolerance mechanism remains ambiguous and uncertain, undermining bureaucrats' confidence in its effectiveness. Although most provinces and cities have issued documents related to the implementation of the fault-tolerance mechanism, only a few cities have effectively applied it in practice. "Since the introduction of the fault-tolerance mechanism, it has only been applied to one case" (CB-2024-35). As a result, local officials tend to avoid tasks that involves the risk of violating potential regulations and are reluctant to dedicate time and resources to justify their actions, particularly when there is no assurance of leniency.

Accountability and the fault-tolerance mechanism should not be viewed as two separate, mutually exclusive institutional arrangements; rather, they should be interconnected and collaboratively integrated into a holistic system. Simultaneously initiating accountability investigations and the fault-tolerance mechanism can encourage a comprehensive analysis of the institutional, procedural, and contextual factors regarding a particular administrative fault. This approach allows for a more holistic understanding of officials' "malfeasance" and helps balance fault-finding with learning from systemic problems. Additionally, it can foster an organizational culture that nurtures trust, reducing fear and defensive behaviors stemming from punitive measures.

Second, the boundaries of accountability and the fault-tolerance mechanism should be established through discussions among diverse stakeholders. Both accountability mechanisms and fault-tolerance mechanisms should not become a tool for a small number of politicians and high-level officials to arbitrarily exert power over bureaucrats, whether by punishing or granting leniency. Furthermore, it is impossible to create a standard template for fault tolerance, as each case involves intricate contextual information. This necessitates that local governments, after establishing basic protocols for the mechanism, analyze each specific case and context during the application.

In complicated networks of governance, decision-making and execution need to involve collaboration and discussions among multiple stakeholders. Different types of accountability inherently represent the diverse expectations of these stakeholders. Therefore, the process of examining specific cases should include negotiations among various parties; only through genuine and contextually relevant dialogues can the interests of all parties be comprehensively considered. Cases can be analyzed from different and comprehensive perspectives, allowing for a deeper and more nuanced understanding. Additionally, public disclosure of the cases receiving tolerance, along with the remedial measures taken, should be further strengthened to check the power of those able to initiate the fault-tolerance mechanism while safeguarding the rights of those subjected to it.

Finally, while regulating the exercise of power, it is essential to provide bureaucrats, especially the street-level ones, with a certain degree of latitude. A combination of a flexible accountability mechanism and a credible fault-tolerance mechanism is crucial for constructing a more resilient governance system. A sanction-based accountability does not necessarily enhance the sense of responsibility among bureaucrats; instead, it may lead them to constrain moral deliberation regarding their responsibilities and fall into a pattern of blame avoidance.

The nature of grassroots officials' work requires them to exercise discretion and make compromises between complex situations and diverse demands. Street-level bureaucrats are close to the problems and citizens, they are in a good position to decide when rules should be strictly followed and when they may not align with the actual circumstances. This does not imply that front-line officials can misuse their power or disregard rules at will; rather, they should be granted the latitude to make moral judgments. The cornerstone of an effective accountability system is to ensure that bureaucrats have the essential autonomy to make decisions that serve the public interest in complex situations, while ensuring that this discretion is legally regulated.

References

Andrews, R., & Van De Walle, S. (2013). New public management and citizens' perceptions of local service efficiency, responsiveness, equity and effectiveness. *Public Management Review, 15*(5), 762–783.

Balla, S. J. (1998). Administrative procedures and political control of the bureaucracy. *American Political Science Review, 92*(3), 663 673.

Barberis, P. (1998). The New Public Management and a new accountability. *Public Administration, 76*(3), 451–470.

Bawn, K. (1995). Political control versus expertise: Congressional choices about administrative procedures. *American Political Science Review, 89*(1), 62–73.

Bendor, J., Glazer, A., & Hammond, T. (2001). Theories of delegation. *Annual Review of Political Science, 4*(1), 235–269.

Borry, E. L. (2016). A New Measure of Red Tape: Introducing the Three-Item Red Tape (TIRT) Scale. *International Public Management Journal, 19*(4), 573–593.

Brown, K., & Bērziņa-Čerenkova, U. A. (2018). Ideology in the Era of Xi Jinping. *Journal of Chinese Political Science, 23*(3), 323–339.

Chinese Government Website. (2016, March 5). *Premier's report on government work*. Viewed November 15, 2024. https://www.gov.cn/xinwen/2016-03/05/content_5049531.htm

Chinese Government Website. (2024, November 16). *How to understand the implementation of the 'three separations' to encourage officials to be proactive and entrepreneurial*. Viewed November 15, 2024. https://www.gov.cn/zhengce/202411/content_6987534.htm

Christensen, T., & Lægreid, P. (2001). New public management: The effects of contractualism and devolution on political control. *Public Management Review, 3*(1), 73–94.

Christensen, T., & Lægreid, P. (2015). Performance and Accountability—A Theoretical Discussion and an Empirical Assessment. *Public Organization Review, 15*(2), 207–225.

Christensen, T., & Lægreid, P. (2021). The Demise of an Agency Director—A Puzzling Saga of Political Control and Professional Autonomy. *International Journal of Public Administration, 44*(3), 250–261.

De Vries, M., & Nemec, J. (2013). Public sector reform: An overview of recent literature and research on NPM and alternative paths. *International Journal of Public Sector Management, 26*(1), 4–16.

De Vries, H., Bekkers, V., & Tummers, L. (2016). Innovation in the public sector: A systematic review and future research agenda. *Public Administration, 94*(1), 146–166.

Ding, Y. (2007). Fiscal decentralization and economic growth in China, 1994–2002. *Journal of Chinese Economic and Business Studies, 5*(3), 243–260.

Dunleavy, P., & Hood, C. (1994). From old public administration to new public management. *Public Money & Management, 14*(3), 9–16.

Faguet, J.-P. (2014). Decentralization and governance. *World Development, 53*, 2–13.

Fatemi, M., & Behmanesh, M. R. (2012). New public management approach and accountability. *International Journal of Management, Economics and Social Sciences (IJMESS), 1*(2), 42–49.

Fryer, K., Antony, J., & Ogden, S. (2009). Performance management in the public sector. *International Journal of Public Sector Management, 22*(6), 478–498.

Gong, T. (2006). Corruption and local governance: The double identity of Chinese local governments in market reform. *The Pacific Review, 19*(1), 85–102.

Gong, T., & Xiao, H. (2017). The Formation and Impact of Isomorphic Pressures: Extravagant Position-Related Consumption in China. *Governance, 30*(3), 387–405.

Gong, T., & Tu, W. (2022). Fighting corruption in China: Trajectory, dynamics, and impact. *China Review, 22*(2), 1–19.

Graham, J. D., & Baert Wiener, J. (1995). Confronting Risk Tradeoffs. In J. D. Graham & J. B. Wiener (Eds.), *Risk vs. Risk* (pp. 1–41). Harvard University Press.

Hill, H. C. (2003). Understanding implementation: Street-level bureaucrats' resources for reform. *Journal of Public Administration Research and Theory, 13*(3), 265–282.

Holzer, M., & Yang, K. (2004). Performance Measurement and Improvement: An Assessment of the State of the Art. *International Review of Administrative Sciences, 70*(1), 15–31.

Hood, C. (2010). *The Blame Game: Spin, Bureaucracy, and Self-Preservation in Government*. Princeton University Press.

Ji, S. (2022). Role of managerial and political accountability in improving performance of local governments. *Public Performance & Management Review, 45*(3), 499–531.

Jos, P. H., & Tompkins, M. E. (2004). The accountability paradox in an age of reinvention: The perennial problem of preserving character and judgment. *Administration & Society, 36*(3), 255–281.

Lægreid, P. (2014). Accountability and new public management. In M. Bovens, R. E. Goodin, & T. Schillemans (Eds.), *The Oxford handbook of public accountability* (pp. 324–338). Oxford University Press.

Li, J., Ni, X., & Wang, R. (2021). Blame avoidance in China's cadre responsibility system. *The China Quarterly, 247*, 681–702.

Lian, H. (2023). Navigating between procedure and efficiency: A study on the multiple rule of local governments. *Society*, (06), 181–208 (练宏. 游走在程序与效率之间: 地方政府的多重规则运作研究. 社会)

Lin, J. Y., & Liu, Z. (2000). Fiscal Decentralization and Economic Growth in China. *Economic Development and Cultural Change, 49*(1), 1–21.

Lipsky, M. (2010). *Street-level bureaucracy: Dilemmas of the individual in public service*. Russell sage foundation.

Mashaw, J. L. (2005). Judicial review of administrative action: Reflections on balancing political, managerial and legal accountability. *Especial 1 DIREITO GV L. Rev.*, 153.

McCubbins, M. D., Noll, R. G., & Weingast, B. R. (1989). Structure and process, politics and policy: Administrative arrangements and the political control of agencies. *Va. L. Rev., 75*, 431–481.

Mei, C., & Pearson, M. M. (2014). Killing a Chicken to Scare the Monkeys? Deterrence Failure and Local Defiance In China. *The China Journal, 72*, 75–97.

Moncrieffe, J. M. (1998). Reconceptualizing political accountability. *International Political Science Review, 19*(4), 387–406.

Morrison, E. W. (2006). Doing the Job Well: An Investigation of Pro-Social Rule Breaking. *Journal of Management, 32*(1), 5–28.

Netease News. (2024, October 24). *2023 China GDP rankings of 361 prefecture-level cities*. Viewed November 12, 2024. https://www.163.com/dy/article/JF8UGFVG0556AAQQ.html

Nõmm, K., & Randma-Liiv, T. (2012). Performance measurement and performance information in new democracies: A study of the Estonian central government. *Public Management Review, 14*(7), 859–879.

Osborne, S. P. (2002). *Public Management: Policy making, ethics and accountability in public management* (Vol. 5). Taylor & Francis.

Page, S. (2006). The web of managerial accountability: The impact of reinventing government. *Administration & Society, 38*(2), 166–197.

Patil, S. V., Vieider, F., & Tetlock, P. E. (2014). Process versus outcome accountability. In M. Bovens, R. E. Goodin, & T. Schillemans (Eds.), *The Oxford handbook of public accountability* (pp. 69–89). Oxford University Press.

Peerenboom, R. (2002). *China's long march toward rule of law*. Cambridge University Press.

Pengpai News. (2023, November 17). *Yichang city releases six typical cases of fault tolerance and risk reporting*. Viewed November 20, 2024. https://m.thepaper.cn/baijiahao_25330815

Pengpai News. (2024, March 22). *An armless men was asked to show his disability certificate to ride the subway for free; Wuhan Metro Company has apologized*. Viewed November 12, 2024. https://www.thepaper.cn/newsDetail_forward_26773951

People's News. (2022, November 16). *Jieshou, Anhui: 'approval with deficiency' accelerates project construction*. Viewed November 20, 2024. https://baijiahao.baidu.com/s?id=1749636371406871677&wfr=spider&for=pc

Propper, C., & Wilson, D. (2003). The use and usefulness of performance measures in the public sector. *Oxford Review of Economic Policy, 19*(2), 250–267.

Shieh, S. (2005). The Rise of Collective Corruption in China: The Xiamen smuggling case. *Journal of Contemporary China, 14*(42), 67–91.

Sina Finance. (2024, August 11). *A former ministerial official reveals the hidden rules of bureaucracy: If you want to prevent something from being accomplished, just keep asking for approvals from the high-ups*. Viewed November 15, 2024. https://finance.sina.com.cn/roll/2024-08-11/doc-incietww4290170.shtml

Sohu News. (2024, May 21). *Jieshou, Anhui: 'approval with deficiency' accelerates project construction*. Viewed November 25, 2024. https://www.sohu.com/a/780450265_121365034

The China Comment. (2018, December 27).*The China Comment revisits one of the top ten problems in grassroots governance: Frequent inspections and checks*. Viewed November 12, 2024. https://www.sohu.com/a/284839565_120026231

Tu, W. (2024). Unpacking the accountability cube and its relationship with blame avoidance. *Public Management Review, 26*(3), 701–723.

Tu, W., & Gong, T. (2022a). Accountability intensity and bureaucrats' response to conflicting expectations: A survey experiment in China. *Public Management Review, 24*(11), 1779–1801.

Tu, W., & Gong, T. (2022b). Bureaucratic shirking in China: Is sanction-based accountability a cure? *The China Quarterly, 249*, 259–274.

Tu, W., & Guo, X. (2023). Gendered clientelism and corruption: Are women less corrupt than men in China? *International Feminist Journal of Politics, 25*(2), 223–243.

Van Loon, N. M., Leisink, P. L. M., Knies, E., & Brewer, G. A. (2016). Red Tape: Developing and Validating a New Job-Centered Measure. *Public Administration Review, 76*(4), 662–673.

Verbeeten, F. H. M., & Speklé, R. F. (2015). Management control, results-oriented culture and public sector performance: Empirical evidence on new public management. *Organization Studies, 36*(7), 953–978.

Walder, A. G. (1995). Local Governments as Industrial Firms: An Organizational Analysis of China's Transitional Economy. *American Journal of Sociology, 101*(2), 263–301.

Wang, E. H. (2022). Frightened mandarins: The adverse effects of fighting corruption on local bureaucracy. *Comparative Political Studies, 55*(11), 1807–1843.

Wang, P., & Yan, X. (2020). Bureaucratic slack in China: The anti-corruption campaign and the decline of patronage networks in developing local economies. *The China Quarterly, 243*, 611–634.

Weingart, P. (1999). Scientific expertise and political accountability: Paradoxes of science in politics. *Science and Public Policy, 26*(3), 151–161.

Weingast, B. R. (2009). Second generation fiscal federalism: The implications of fiscal incentives. *Journal of Urban Economics, 65*(3), 279–293.

Wiener, J. B. (1998). Managing the iatrogenic risks of risk management. *Risk, 9*, 39.

Willems, T., & Van Dooren, W. (2011). Lost in diffusion? How collaborative arrangements lead to an accountability paradox. *International Review of Administrative Sciences, 77*(3), 505–530.

Wynen, J., & Verhoest, K. (2016). Internal performance-based steering in public sector organizations: Examining the effect of organizational autonomy and external result control. *Public Performance & Management Review, 39*(3), 535–559.

Yang, F., Zhang, Z., & Wang, S. (2022). Enlisting citizens: Forging the effectiveness of policy implementation in local China. *Journal of Chinese Governance, 7*(3), 400–417.

Zhang, L., Zhao, J., & Dong, W. (2021). Street-level bureaucrats as policy entrepreneurs: Action strategies for flexible community governance in China. *Public Administration, 99*(3), 469–483.

Zhou, X. (2022). *The logic of governance in China: An organizational approach*. Cambridge University Press.

Zhu, J. (2008). Why are offices for sale in China? A case study of the office-selling chain in Heilongjiang province. *Asian Survey, 48*(4), 558–579.

CHAPTER 8

Promoting Good Accountability: What Should Be Done

This book delves into the dynamic interaction between individual bureaucrats and accountability structures in the Chinese bureaucracy. It taps into how bureaucrats respond to heightened accountability and how their actions, in turn, shape the development of accountability. It also investigates the accountability paradox within the Chinese bureaucracy by unpacking the structure of accountability and the conflicts arising from various accountability forms.

In this concluding chapter, I summarize the main arguments and examine in detail the factors contributing to the accountability paradox. Furthermore, this chapter explores the contentious effects of accountability on three concepts: sense of responsibility, trust, and organizational learning. Whether and how the configuration of accountability reinforces or undermines them is highly debated. Next, I analyze two emerging forms of accountability: felt accountability and dialogue accountability. By outlining some characteristics of innovative accountability as opposed to the traditional form of accountability, I propose three criteria for good accountability. Last but not least, I examine emerging manifestations of accountability in the evolving landscape of network governance and digital governance. I discuss the potential accountability paradoxes that may arise with the growing networks of stakeholders and the increasing application of Information and Communication Technologies (ICTs).

W. Tu, *The Accountability Paradox in the Chinese Bureaucracy*,
https://doi.org/10.1007/978-981-96-6392-7_8

The Accountability Paradox in the Chinese Bureaucracy

This book delves into an accountability paradox, demonstrating how intensified accountability fails to bring about more effective governance within the Chinese bureaucracy where a variety of accountability mechanisms have been significantly strengthened under Xi's administration. Accountability is typically viewed as a powerful means of achieving virtuous social outcomes, such as improved performance and ethical behavior. However, it can sometimes backfire, leading to decreased motivation, innovation, or even ethical lapses.

The book unpacks the accountability paradox from three perspectives: the intensity of accountability, the dimensions of accountability, and the conflicts arising from different sources of accountability. Accountability intensity describes levels ranging from deficit to overload. The exercise of audits, investigations, monitoring, and punishments for rule violations or unsatisfactory performance increases accountability intensity (Dubnick, 2005; Jos & Tompkins, 2004). However, the intensification of accountability in China since 2012 has led bureaucrats to strategically cope with their responsibilities. Bureaucrats tend to reframe from overt shirking activities, such as idling or surfing the Internet during working hours, which are easily detected by close monitoring. Instead, they subtly reframe their responsibilities by rigidly adhering to regulations and gaming the system to avoid blame. The accountability paradox illustrates that the intention to control bureaucrats is subtly subverted by the bureaucrats themselves.

I further explore the dimensions of accountability. Accountability is a multifaceted mechanism with various elements, and a poor configuration may lead to an unintended increase in bureaucrats' malfeasance. It consists of negative reinforcements, which primarily use monitoring and sanctions to ensure compliance, and positive reinforcements, which aim to motivate employees by offering rewards and encouraging job participation. Sanction-based accountability, featuring intensive monitoring and punishment, may deter bureaucrats from evading responsibility, but may backfire and induce bureaucrats to employ some subtle coping strategies to deal with potential blame, a demanding workload, and significant pressure. Trust-based accountability characterized by high discussion quality and reward-based consequences, on the other hand, is beneficial for building a more participative, cooperative, and trusting organizational culture that discourages defensive blame-avoiding strategies. Furthermore, discussion quality moderates the impact of monitoring intensity on blame-avoiding propensity by impairing their positive relationship. The findings indicate that effective discussions between subordinates and superiors may mitigate the tension and defensive emotions caused by intensive monitoring. By unpacking the internal mechanism of accountability, the book unveils the factors underlying the accountability paradox. A bad accountability configuration with an unbalanced combination of different components may lead to unintended negative consequences.

Conflicts arising from different sources of accountability act as another factor contributing to the accountability paradox. The Chinese bureaucracy constantly faces divergent expectations from upper-level authorities and local citizens. Bureaucrats need to be responsive to both top-down accountability from their superiors and bottom-up expectations from citizens. However, the policies promulgated by upper-level authorities are not always in line with citizens' interests due to their lack of information and unfamiliarity with local conditions. Local governments in China must navigate a complex law enforcement landscape, characterized by varied local circumstances with differing resources and endowments, as well as a range of diverse public demands. In this light, local officials need to implement or adapt policies according to local circumstances and citizens' demands. However, power centralization under Xi's administration advocates top-down policy-making and one-size-fits-all implementation, leaving insufficient latitude for local officials to amend the gap between policies and local circumstances. The intensified top-down accountability may crowd out local officials' intrinsic motivation to serve the public and make them mechanically follow top-down instructions and be less concerned about whether a project is in citizens' interests or not, ultimately leading to poor policy outcomes.

Furthermore, the conflict between intensified process-based accountability and undermined outcome-based accountability aggravates the accountability paradox. A series of transformation in anti-corruption agencies and supervision systems substantially reinforce process-based accountability which emphasizes rule and procedure compliance. An excessively rigid adherence to rules and the intentional concealment of actions behind a facade of regulations greatly diminishes managerial effectiveness.

In conclusion, this book examines bureaucrats' responses to accountability pressures and multiple sources of accountability. It shows that intensified accountability does not necessarily contribute to the high responsiveness of bureaucrats to their superiors' steering or good governance. Discretionary power and information advantage still leave the latitude for bureaucrats to work toward their own preferences, even in the face of increasingly stringent formal legal accountability mechanisms. Individual judgment is necessitated to manage work pressures and navigate multiple, often conflicting expectations. This book also illustrates the recursive interaction between the accountability structure and human agency in the Chinese context. Regardless of the informational advantages and expertise they possess, agents' strategic behaviors are still influenced and limited by existing accountability frameworks (Yang, 2012). In response to heightened accountability, bureaucrats in China rationally opt to limit overt shirking behaviors, instead employing more subtle tactics, such as redefining responsibilities and dodging blame. Simultaneously, accountability structures evolve in response to the strategic actions of agents. Observing that local officials react to strict sanction-based accountability with negative coping and gaming strategies, the central government has made various adjustments, including reducing inspections, placing greater emphasis on incentives and organizational support, and introducing the fault-tolerance mechanism to alleviate the unintended adverse effects of increased accountability. Timely responses and institutional adjustments to bureaucrats' behaviors and reactions are essential for a competent and resilient government.

Does Accountability Boost Sense of Responsibility and Trust?

Accountability is closely linked to two concepts: a sense of responsibility and trust. The accountability paradox partly arises from the erosion of officials' sense of responsibility and organizational trust. The careful handling of the relationship among these three interrelated concepts is crucial for establishing a sound accountability framework.

Accountability and Sense of Responsibility

In the literature, some scholars use the terms responsibility and accountability interchangeably as if they are synonymous. However, responsibility and accountability carry different connotations. Responsibility is normally composed of functional and moral obligations (Bivins, 2006). Functional responsibility is considered a bundle of obligations associated with a person's position, function, or work. Moral obligation extends responsibility to a higher level of morality and denotes that moral agents impose moral laws on themselves to do the right thing (Bivins, 2006). Sense of responsibility is more closely associated with the internal and personal aspects of moral obligation, while accountability often implies a focus on the instrumentality of external controls (Lindkvist & Llewellyn, 2003; Mulgan, 2000).

The debate between Friedrich and Finer might be better understood by reference to the distinction between responsibility and accountability. Some scholars advocate for responsibility, emphasizing internal motivation and self-regulation, while others consider accountability an effective external control of one's actions to another, such as an employee to an employer (Jackson, 2009). The main argument highlights the difference between accountability, which involves following orders, and responsibility, which entails making decisions based on a judgment of the greater good (Jackson, 2009). Friedrich (2000, p. 114) argues that "even under the best arrangements, a considerable margin of irresponsible conduct of administrative activities is inevitable." Thus, intrinsic motivation should not be replaced by restrictive formal legal accountability, and the responsible judgment and moral reflection of bureaucrats should be encouraged (Cooper, 2012; Harmon, 1995; Thompson, 1992).

Accountability mechanisms can be regarded as external controls in a bid to hold public agents accountable to their functional responsibility and, ideally, may promote their moral obligations. However, the instrumentalist logic of some accountability arrangements instead threatens to undermine their moral deliberation (Hatch, 2013; Tu, 2024). Jos and Tompkins (2004) consider that the effective implementation of external accountability requires bureaucrats' exercise of responsible interpretation and moral administrative judgment. However, the institutions and mechanisms that are used to strengthen accountability undermine the very qualities that promote responsible judgment, which constitutes the major cause of the accountability paradox. The connotation of responsibility is central to the capability to manage conflicting requirements and forces. The ability to sustain a dynamic and creative equilibrium among varying expectations, while embracing complexities to find innovative solutions, is a key quality of a responsible administrative expert. Harmon (1995) suggests that depending too much on external standards can undermine an individual's perception of themselves as an active choosing agent, whereas acting based solely on personal values may lead to narcissistic tendencies.

Accountability is normally held through two external standards: compliance with formal legal rules or procedures and performance or outcome-based standards (Jos & Tompkins, 2004; Patil et al., 2014). Neither of the two accountability standards necessarily enhances bureaucrats' sense of responsibility; in fact, they may even undermine it. Compliance with rules ensures that bureaucrats strictly follow prescribed procedures when implementing policies, thereby guaranteeing the fairness, legality, and predictability of administrative decisions and actions, which effectively curbs a variety of agency problems, such as corruption and abuse of power. However, it still relies on bureaucrats' sound judgment to ensure that rules and standards are applied reasonably. First, not all rules are considered high-quality rules; those that impose a compliance burden without advancing legitimate objectives are regarded as red tape (Borry, 2016; Pandey & Scott, 2002). Red tape can be further classified as "rule-inception red tape" and "rule-evolved red tape" (Bozeman & Feeney, 2014). Rule-inception red tape occurs when a newly created rule is ineffective from the start due to causes such as rules created for self-interests or the interests of a small group, or rules created with incorrect means-ends assumptions that stray from their original intent (Borry, 2016). Rule-evolved red tape occurs when a once-functional rule loses its effectiveness over time (Bozeman & Feeney, 2014). In this light, strict compliance with rules does not necessarily mean that bureaucrats have exercised moral deliberation regarding the applicability and validity of those rules. Actions that violate established rules or norms but are intended to benefit citizens or serve a greater good are instead praised as prosocial rule breaking (Morrison, 2006). Understanding prosocial rule breaking can help organizations navigate the balance between mechanical compliance and ethical responsibility.

Furthermore, overemphasis on procedures and inputs may contribute to bureaucrats' intentional constraint on their discretionary power by rigorously sticking to bureaucratic practices, stifling innovation, and restricting agendas to mitigate the risks of violating rules and procedures. In China, Local officials depend on extensive paperwork, conferences, responsibility contracts, inspections, and documented records to demonstrate that they have adhered to necessary procedures and put into required efforts, thereby avoiding responsibility for the final outcomes. It ultimately results in a de facto vacuum of responsibility and a state of collective irresponsibility. Some bureaucrats exploit the complexities of regulations and conflicting rules as a shield to avoid functional responsibilities. In China, where laws and regulations are not yet well-established and local disparities are significant, demanding strict adherence to rules may lead to poor managerial performance.

Performance or outcome-based accountability endows bureaucrats more latitude in choosing tools and strategies to achieve expected outcomes compared with the compliance standard. However, when the final goals and corresponding indicators are clearly defined, the latitude for bureaucrats to exercise moral deliberation is limited. Bureaucrats may selectively implement policies that yield easily measurable results over those that are essential but harder to quantify (O'Brien & Li, 1999). Furthermore, organizations or bureaucrats may prioritize immediate results at the expense of long-term objectives, jeopardizing sustainable development and exacerbating deeper systemic problems. Pressure to achieve specific outcomes sometimes encourages unethical behavior, such as data manipulation or "gaming" the system to meet targets (Gao, 2021; Tu & Gong, 2022b).

In conclusion, both compliance with rules and outcome-based standards do not necessarily lead to ethical reflection instead may result in creative subversion of rules or performance assessment. To address the accountability paradox, scholars and practitioners should shift their attention to the process of accountability. Engaging in dialogues, promoting participation, and fostering interactions—rather than viewing bureaucrats as mere passive instruments—may be more effective in alleviating the accountability paradox.

Accountability and Trust

Another major concern related to the accountability paradox is that accountability undermines trust. Trust and accountability are frequently seen as opposites, with the idea that accountability arises from a lack of trust (Ehren et al., 2020; Gundlach & Cannon, 2010). Trust appears to be a crucial element in almost all human interactions, as effective communication, learning, and problem-solving all depend on it (Blomqvist, 1997, p. 283; Tu, 2023). Trust is defined as a trustor's willingness to take a risk based on their evaluation of a trustee's competence, benevolence, and integrity (Mayer et al., 1995; Oomsels & Bouckaert, 2017).

There are three elements in the definitions of trust: benevolence, competence, and risk (Laine, 2008; Poon, 2013). First, the trust relationship is mutual between the principal and the agent based on their evaluation of each other's benevolence and competence. Govier (1998, p. 6) states that a trustworthy person is characterized by both good intentions and adequate competence. For one person to completely trust another, they must recognize the other's good intentions, sound judgment, and competence, believing that the trusted individual will not cause them any harm (Hardin, 2013; Ullmann-Margalit, 2004; Xiao et al., 2024). When a principal places great trust in an agent's competence to perform duties and their integrity to legally exercise the entrusted power, they are more likely to decentralize power to the agent and exercise less oversight, believing that the agent will accomplish tasks even without supervision (Lewicki & Brinsfield, 2015). The agent must also trust the principal, putting faith in her legitimacy and expertise to oversee and evaluate his actions, as well as her good intentions and care for his interests and needs. If the agent lacks trust in the principal, it can lead to a "leakage of authority" and a reduced responsiveness to the accountability forum (Hall et al., 2017; Pérez-Durán, 2024; Schillemans et al., 2021b).

Second, trust inherently entails a degree of risk (Brower et al., 2000). Risk or vulnerability arises when a principal delegates power and grants autonomy to an agent and depends on his skills, knowledge, judgments, or actions to complete tasks (Bachmann et al., 2015). Furthermore, the risk aggravates when there is limited ability to fully understand the agent's motivations and behaviors (Brehm & Gates, 2015). As the principal relies on the agent's expertise and information to implement policies, the principal becomes vulnerable to the agent and feels a strong desire to impose supervision to mitigate this vulnerability. Monitoring or accountability can be viewed as the principal's effort to mitigate her vulnerability to the agent by gathering pertinent information about the agent's abilities, intentions, and behaviors, thereby addressing agency problems. Unless she has high trust in the agent, her anxiety about needing to enforce stricter oversight will persist. However, trust develops not from complete control over another person's actions (Hardin, 2006). Trust is relational and dynamic. The principal and agent reinforce or diminish their trust in each other based on repeated interactions and the behaviors of others.

When the principal imposes frequent and stringent oversight on the agent due to the distrust in the agent, the agent may also accordingly reduce his trust in the principal's good intentions. A lack of trust appears to hinder the effective implementation of accountability (Ehren et al., 2020). Burgeoning studies show how intensive accountability in a low-trust and high-blame situation leads to risk aversion, innovation deprecation, and blame shifting (Dubnick, 2005; Hood, 2010; Jos & Tompkins, 2004). Therefore, the orientation of accountability is significant; the principal should first covey good intentions to show her commitment to providing help and support to the agent. When the agent perceives the accountability mechanism as a means to identify systemic problems, foster dialogues, and resolve conflicts, he may be more likely to accept the principal's authority, share information proactively, and support the implementation of accountability.

In China, the intensified accountability appears to have a damaging effect on the trust between superiors and subordinates, among peers, and between the government and citizens. In the past, the next level up of superiors tended to collaborate with low-level officials to accomplish tasks and even cover up implementation discrepancies, forming an alliance of "collusion" to share risks. However, as accountability increases, high-level superiors and low-level officials strive to clearly outline their own responsibilities, steering clear of any extra or unclear duties that could affect them. "The higher-ups are no longer willing to share responsibility with us as they once did; now we have to confront the risks on our own. In case of being implicated, they simply stand by and let the inspection team hold us accountable without defending us. At times, they even shift the blame onto us, making us scapegoats. We not only have to take on our own faults but also bear the blame for the mistakes of those in higher positions" (CB-2024-34). In this light, low-level officials are less likely to trust the commitment to protection and career advancement offered by higher-ups when they are asked to take on more challenging tasks. They clearly establish the boundaries of their responsibilities with their superiors and may even redirect potential liability upward by refraining from exercising discretion and consistently seeking approval from higher-ups. "Now, superiors can no longer motivate their subordinates through intimate conversations or mobilizing conferences, as the subordinates are primarily concerned with protecting themselves" (CB-2024-33). Even worse, heightened accountability leads low-level officials to conceal information from higher-ups, as they believe that if the truth comes to light, the superiors are more likely to punish them instead of helping to resolve the problems and provide support (CB-2024-36). In this regard, while accountability mitigates some destructive collusion, it erodes trust between superiors and subordinates, making it challenging for them to share information for genuine conversations and collaborate to solve problems.

Furthermore, accountability undermines trust among peers or agencies at the same levels. Each official and department aims to safeguard its own interests and is wary of the punishment that accountability may bring. The growing complexity of contexts and tasks often necessitates collaboration among various officials or departments. When problems arise, officials frequently turn to group discussions to mitigate the risks of making decisions alone. However, they often struggle to reach a unified opinion, as each individual approaches the situation from a self-protective standpoint, prioritizing their own concerns and interests over collective solutions. Their unwillingness to compromise further complicates the situations, leading to fragmented dialogues where everyone presents their own views without intentions of finding common ground. The prolonged collective decision-making has become a tactic to shift responsibility instead of a way to find common ground to solve problems. "The police want to close cases quickly, while the inspectors want to conduct a more thorough review. Discussions will not reach a consensus as both parties seek to safeguard their own interests to avoid being blamed" (CB-2024-34). The paradox is that on the one hand, officials or departments tend to engage in collective decisions and collaborations to disperse risks; on the other hand, they firmly guard their interests and are unable to reach a consensus.

Accountability may also undermine trust between the government and citizens. As the central government places greater emphasis on citizens' voices and complaints, citizens are given more channels to lodge complaints and express their views. The Chinese government established mayoral hotlines, citizen inquiry websites, and "Internet + monitoring" platforms, allowing citizens to report misconduct committed by local officials. When higher-level agencies or local SCs receive complaints from citizens, they will conduct investigations and may initiate accountability measures. It's promising that citizens now have a greater voice in the decision-making process. However, as the constructive legal interactions between the government and citizens are not yet fully established, social accountability appears to undermine trust between officials and citizens rather than foster it. Some citizens opportunistically create ruckus to pressure local officials, who prioritize "maintaining stability" (*weiwen,* 维稳), into meeting their unreasonable demands. Chinese netizens have coined the term "ruckus-based distribution" (*annao fenpei, 按闹分配*) to describe a system that favors those who are bold, energetic, and capable of creating confrontational scenes, while penalizing those who do not engage in such behavior (Li, 2019). Ruckus-based distribution is quite common at the grassroots level where those who make the most noise, and do so more aggressively, gain more advantages in the resolution of conflicts and disputes. As a result, local officials' trust in citizens diminishes, causing them to perceive citizens as disruptive. Consequently, they may choose to withhold information from the public to avoid complaints and prevent escalated petitions.

It appears that heightened external accountability brings unintended risks or vulnerabilities in China. However, burgeoning research indicates that when oversight aligns with initial positive perceptions of someone's trustworthiness, it can actually strengthen trust (Mills & Reiss, 2017). Scholars suggest that when structuring the interaction around a clear set of standards and stabilizing the relationship in repeated games, an external accountability framework may help mitigate risks and enhance trust (Ehren et al., 2020). In this light, the mindset that accountability will undoubtedly destroy trust need to be transformed. Accountability cannot be forsaken, but the configuration of accountability should be improved to reshape the hostile relationship between the supervisors and supervisees. Formal control can enhance trust when those being regulated view the monitoring and sanction/reward processes as a signal of the regulator's good intentions and can feel supervisors' genuine concern and support (Näslund & Hallström, 2017). In a collaborative environment, accountability safeguards cooperation by containing opportunistic behaviors, which strengthens the interplay between trust and collaboration; whereas, the implementation of a control system in distrustful settings is more likely to result in an escalation of distrust.

Accountability and Organizational Learning

One of the controversial issues related to accountability is its potential contribution to organizational learning (OL) (Baxter et al., 2017; Schillemans & Smulders, 2015). While some scholars suggest that accountability can enhance organizational learning (Bovens et al., 2008; Greiling & Halachmi, 2013), others claim that the punitive nature of accountability undermines learning (Gersen & Stephenson, 2014; Ossege, 2012). It is highly significant for the public sector to learn from previous experiences and others and adjust to environmental changes (Currie & Suhomlinova, 2006; Greiling & Halachmi, 2013). Therefore, as a significant institution, whether the configuration of accountability can lead to OL decides the effectiveness of accountability.

Argyris and Schön (1997) define organizational learning as a process of detecting and correcting errors, emphasizing the importance of double-loop learning, where organizations not only adjust actions but also modify underlying values and policies. Although there is no consensus on the definition of organizational learning, scholars agree that OL is closely related to learning from past experiences and errors, collective learning, systems thinking, organizational adaptation, and knowledge generation (Basten & Haamann, 2018; Fiol & Lyles, 1985; Sun & Scott, 2003).

As to the level of learning, scholars are divided on whether OL is an individually based phenomenon or a collective process. Some scholars suggest that all learning occurs within the minds of individuals, meaning that the process of learning is fundamentally within the individual. Organizations learn and retain knowledge through their present members, who acquire insights through experiential learning, problem-solving, experimentation, collaboration, and various others (Herriott et al., 1985). However, a large number of scholars consider organizations to possess specific goals, the capacity to learn, and the ability to retain memories (Popova-Nowak & Cseh, 2015; Schilling & Kluge, 2009). Learning resides within individuals but is ultimately transferred to the organization's systems, structures, and procedures (Chen, 2005; Chiva et al., 2014). Hedberg (1981) suggests that "although organizational learning occurs through individuals, it would be a mistake to conclude that organizational learning is nothing but the cumulative result of their members' learning …… Members come and go, and leadership changes, but organizations' memories preserve certain behaviors, mental maps, norms, and values over time" (p. 6). Therefore, I analyze the relationship between accountability and OL from individual and organizational perspectives.

The role of the accountability process in organizational learning can vary significantly, serving either as a facilitator or a barrier. Referring to some dimensions of barriers to OL proposed by Schilling and Kluge (2009), Table 8.1 outlines potential barriers or facilitators of accountability mechanisms for learning, as well as the learning objectives from both individual (actional) and organizational (structural) aspects.

Table 8.1 How does accountability facilitate learning

Units	*Barriers/facilitators*	*Learning objects*
Actional- individual	• Level of trust toward the account holder; • Level of stress and fear of blame; • Degree of openness to new ideas; • Ability of deep learning and systematic failure analysis	• Acquiring skills; • Accumulating experiences; • Generating knowledge; • A change in behavior
Structural-organization	• Level of blame culture or tolerance for errors; • Degree of rigid hierarchical structure; • Level of restrictive, controlling management; • Degree of disproportion between power and responsibilities	• Integrating shared understanding and knowledge; • Institutionalizing systems, structures, and procedures; • Adapting organizational culture and values

From the perspective of individual members in an organization, individuals' cognition, motivation, and personality may exert significant impacts on whether accountability can facilitate learning. First, the level of trust toward the account holder plays a crucial role. When individuals have high trust in their superiors' sincere concern and support, they are more likely to engage in open dialogue and share insights without withholding information. Conversely, a low level of trust can lead to defensiveness and thus hinder learning (Laine, 2008). Thus, trusting someone involves the belief that they will not harm the person who trusts them, and a superior who shifts blame and takes credit for their subordinates' efforts will not earn that trust (Poon, 2013). Second, the level of stress and fear of blame significantly impacts individuals' willingness to consider accountability a learning process. High levels of stress and the fear of negative repercussions make individuals reluctant to admit mistakes or share failures. Detecting and correcting errors is an indispensable part of learning (Argyris & Schön, 1978). The reluctance to share errors blocks the first step of learning.

Third, the degree of openness to new ideas among team members influences the effectiveness of accountability processes in fostering learning. If individuals are set in their way and are unwilling to accept any new ideas, accountability may not encourage reflection; instead, it might lead them to seek strategies to preserve their way (Sun & Scott, 2005). Bureaucrats in a rigid hierarchical system are more likely to wrap themselves in a shell of regulations. Lastly, individuals' ability to engage in deep learning and systematic failure analysis is essential. When individuals approach mistakes with a comprehensive mindset, they focus on understanding the underlying systematic factors contributing to the failure. The ability to identify systematic factors—such as structures, processes, or environmental influences—leads to a more comprehensive understanding of what went wrong, as opposed to superstitious learning (Cannon & Edmondson, 2001).

From the perspective of structural organization, an organization's culture, structure, management style, and resource allocation may determine whether the accountability process promotes or hinders learning. First, the level of blame culture or tolerance for errors is crucial. Scholars consider that effective organizational learning requires a safe atmosphere where reporting does not lead to punishment, since a punitive environment can hinder organizational learning (Bapuji & Crossan, 2004). When accountability with punitive measures is in place, it may inadvertently create a culture of fear, discouraging individuals from reporting issues to avoid being blamed (Jos & Tompkins, 2004; Morris & Moore, 2000). Individuals may be eager to avoid being associated with concrete instances of failure, as they otherwise risk being stigmatized as incompetent and cut off from potential organizational rewards (Cannon & Edmondson, 2005). A moderate level of sanctions may be necessary to push actors to change and be responsible for their negligence, whereas the threat of severe sanctions probably leads to gaming behaviors (De Bruijn, 2002). Furthermore, the degree of rigid hierarchical structure plays a crucial role in learning from accountability. A rigid hierarchical structure that prioritizes overspecialization and formalization can hinder communication and collaboration. The presence of standard operating procedures, detailed job descriptions, and overarching layers of supervision can lead bureaucrats to overly adhere to established protocols, making them resistant to change (Ashforth & Lee, 1990).

Third, the level of restrictive, controlling management style may exert an impact on organizational learning. Accountability in a management style that emphasizes control often inhibits creativity and risk-taking, which are essential for learning. A controlling management style that relies on oversight and punishment can strengthen defensive behaviors, leading to psychological unsecurity, feelings of hopelessness, and organizational cynicism among team members (Berthoin-Antal et al., 2019). Finally, the degree of disproportion between power and responsibilities, as well as resources and workload, can create imbalances that affect accountability and learning. The grassroots or street-level bureaucrats are often assigned with heavy workload while granted limited resources, leading to the overload of responsibility (Lipsky, 2010). When they are struggling to complete tasks with insufficient resources, it is challenging for them to make time and energy to learn. Collectively, the individual factors and organizational factors can reinforce each other to contribute to an accountability system that facilitates or inhibits learning.

An individual's learning objectives derived from the accountability process can encompass four dimensions: skills, experiences, knowledge, and behavior. First, acquisition of skills enables individuals to enhance their competencies and expertise. Accountability requires individuals to take ownership of their tasks and responsibilities, motivating them to pursue and hone the skills or knowledge they need, which in turn enhances their expertise in their roles. Second, the process encourages the accumulation of experiences, allowing individuals to learn from past successes and failures. Engaging in an accountability framework often involves facing challenges and navigating through various situations and expectations, which offers officials rich experiences. Accountability mechanisms should allow officials to take a systematic and constant assessment and reflection on past experiences, deepening their understanding of what works and what doesn't. In addition, the generation of knowledge is a critical objective of learning through accountability. Knowledge is an organized combination of ideas, experiences, procedures, and information (Tsoukas & Vladimirou, 2001) and is professional intellect (Bhatt, 2002). Dialogues, collaborations, and experimentation contribute to the amplification and development of new knowledge (Bhatt, 2002). Finally, a change in behavior often emerges as a result of these learning experiences, leading individuals to adopt more effective practices and approaches in their work. A change in cognition translates into a noticeable change in behavior is a critical step of learning (Crossan et al., 1995). Collectively, these objectives highlight the transformative potential of accountability in promoting personal and professional growth.

An organization's learning objectives arising from the accountability process are more comprehensive than individual learning. Duncan (1979) argue that learning must be "shared, evaluated, and integrated with that done by others" (p. 89). "Organizational learning must be viewed as a series of interactions between adaptation at the individual or subgroup level and adaptation at the organizational level" (Cangelosi & Dill, 1965). First, the accountability process should help integrate shared understanding and knowledge among organization members. Conversion of individual knowledge and insights into a systematic organizational knowledge base which informs decision-making is significant of OL (Shrivastava, 1983). In the accountability process, written, oral, and visual reports, along with discussions and collaboration, serve as effective tools for knowledge transfer among individuals or small groups within the organization, fostering a collaborative learning environment (Basten & Haamann, 2018). Successful and failed lessons learned need to be stored and openly accessible to the members of the organization (Crossan et al., 1995).

Second, some learning and knowledge that are successfully embedded in the systems, structures, and procedures of the organization, in turn, guide the future interactions and learning of organizational members (Crossan et al., 1995). This is the key distinction between organizational learning and individual learning that only exists within the minds of individuals. Through evaluations, the accountability process can reveal weaknesses in existing structures and practices, such as information asymmetry, communication breakdowns, or outdated regulations. Some accountability measures that emphasize openness to learning and adaptation enable organizations to address shortcomings and incorporate best practices into their systems, ensuring that successful initiatives are recorded and repeated. Last but not least, the ideal situation is that the accountability process ultimately fosters a culture of trust and continuous improvement by learning. If accountability mechanisms can help create a culture that promotes transparent and honest communication, prioritizes psychological safety, encourages collaborations, and embraces change and new ideas, then the learning objectives can be achieved. Together, these learning objectives underscore the importance of accountability in enhancing organizational effectiveness and resilience. The structure of accountability should enhance a double-loop learning process, where "the win/lose, low-trust, low-risk-taking behaviors are replaced by cooperative, high-trust, inquiry-oriented processes" (Argyris, 1982, p. 106).

Learning from Emerging Forms of Accountability

In order to mitigate the accountability paradox, it is crucial to change how we view and understand accountability itself. Emerging forms of accountability, such as felt accountability and dialogue accountability, give us insight of the alternative connotations of accountability and better configuration of accountability. By exploring these alternative perspectives, we can reshape our understanding of accountability, making it more effective and responsive to the complexities of modern governance and relationships.

Felt Accountability

As previous chapters demonstrate, even under the most stringent accountability mechanisms, bureaucrats manage to manipulate formal controls. Therefore, it is logical to consider accountability from the viewpoint of those being held accountable. Accountability can be conceived as bureaucrats' management of diverse expectations exerted by different stakeholders. Specifically, account holders may have their strategic mechanisms or schemes to convey their demands and divert bureaucrats' attention to their expectations. However, facing diverse and usually conflicting expectations, bureaucrats also develop their own coping strategies to manage conflicts. Examining accountability through the lens of expectation management alters the traditional views that primarily concentrate on formal accountability mechanisms and perceive bureaucrats as passive participants. By recognizing bureaucrats as proactive agents who choose how to prioritize their attention and handle various expectations, the perspective shifts the focus from external accountability controls to bureaucrats' internal controls. The effectiveness of formal public sector accountability mechanisms is largely predicated on individuals' perceptions of accountability and their responses to diverse accountability expectations.

Scholars are increasingly acknowledging that there are several intermediate steps in the causal relationship between formal accountability mechanisms and the ultimate organizational outputs or outcomes (Overman et al., 2021). One of the most important steps is how account givers perceive accountability and then take corresponding actions to respond to the mechanisms (Hall et al., 2017; Overman & Schillemans, 2022).

They propose that individuals interpret and respond to identical accountability environments in varied ways, and that these individual perceptions are vital for understanding when and how formal accountability mechanisms take effect (Bovens et al., 2008; Dubnick & Frederickson, 2011). An innovative and emerging concept sheds light on the importance of individuals' perceptions of accountability mechanisms, known as felt accountability (Hupe & Hill, 2007; Thomann et al., 2018). Felt accountability is commonly conceived as "the 1) implicit or explicit expectation that one's decisions or actions will be subject to evaluation by 2) some salient audience(s) with the belief that there exists the potential for one to receive either rewards or sanctions based on this expected evaluation" (Hochwarter et al., 2007, p. 227). This definition primarily focuses on bureaucrats' anticipation of future accountability. Overman et al. (2021) suggest that besides individuals' expectation of accountability, felt accountability also connotates individuals' perception of the account holder's ability to hold them accountable. This ability includes two core elements: (1) the perceived legitimacy to exercise authority and (2) the perceived expertise to do so effectively.

Forum legitimacy refers to whether the account giver perceives that an account holder possesses legitimacy to oversight and mete consequences on their behavior (Carpenter & Krause, 2015). They consider the account holder's scrutinizing role to be "desirable, proper, or appropriate within some socially constructed system of norms, values, beliefs, and definitions" (Suchman, 1995). This legitimacy is fundamentally normative, affecting actors' respect for and acceptance of the account holder's authority, which in turn influences their responsiveness to accountability measures (Schillemans et al., 2021). Lerner and Tetlock (1999) derived their conclusions from an analysis of the empirical literature, stating that "when people perceive accountability as illegitimate, such undesired effects as attitude polarization away from advocated positions, decline in intrinsic motivation, and excessive stress are all possible responses" (p. 259).

Forum expertise pertains to the account giver's perception of the forum's ability to effectively monitor and advise their actions (Schillemans et al., 2021). The account holder must have a certain level of expertise to understand the nature of tasks and effectively monitor and evaluate the tasks assigned to the agent, as this understanding is crucial for establishing a strong foundation for any effective accountability relationship (Overman et al., 2021). Interventions imposed by superiors who lack legitimacy and expertise are unlikely to encourage subordinates to engage in self-reflection and reexamination of their behavior; instead, gaming and defensive behaviors are more likely to be triggered.

In the Chinese bureaucracy, both the perceived legitimacy and expertise of the account holder are insufficient to foster an effective accountability relationship. Firstly, the legitimacy of these holders is weakened by their tendency to shift blame onto lower-level officials within the hierarchical structure. The fragmented governmental structure, characterized by lengthy hierarchical chains, obscures the principal-agent relationship. The county-level government is viewed as a principal by the village-level government, while serving as an agent for the municipal-level government. As a result, there is no genuinely benevolent or responsible principal; each level of government or agency attempts to evade responsibility and shift blame both downward and upward.

Second, local officials question whether the newly established SC system possesses the capacity and expertise to assess and advise on their administrative actions. The SC system has become an overarching institution specifically tasked with overseeing and ensuring accountability for all individuals exercising public power. Besides corruption prevention and investigation, the agency also looks into violations of rules or procedures and instances of poor administrative performance. As the SC system works jointly with the Party anti-corruption agencies, the expertise of the majority of staff members in the SC system lies in investigating corruption-related malfeasance. Local officials question whether the SC, as a disciplinary inspection agency, has the expertise to thoroughly understand the work of public bureaucracies, which requires specialized knowledge and an understanding of specific circumstances to effectively address tasks. Some local officials may even perceive the monitoring as an intervention that disrupts their routine work. In this light, local officials do not fully recognize the authority of the account holders, leading them to employ various adverse coping strategies, such as shirking and blame avoidance, in response to accountability pressure.

Dialogue Accountability

The concept felt accountability allows us to approach accountability from an innovative perspective. Another term related to accountability may aid us in the specific design of accountability mechanism, that is, dialogue accountability. By reviewing the existing accountability designs, many of them focus on performance information acquisition through reports and monitoring as well as the enforcement of consequences. The discussion or dialogue process between the account holder and the giver or other relevant stakeholders is largely neglected. Harmon (1995) suggests that accountability pathologies can be tackled if accountability is constructed as a process of dialogue to manage conflicting motives and forces. Dialogue represents a flow of meaning in the whole group (Bohm & Nichol, 1996) and "a process of successful relationship building" (Yankelovich, 1999, p. 15).

Different from other forms of communication, dialogue has two unique characteristics. First, all participants should be regarded as equal, despite any status differences they may have outside the dialogue. To uphold this equality and foster mutual respect and trust, they should avoid using coercive tactics to assert dominance in the dialogue (Yankelovich, 1999, pp. 41–46). Second, dialogue is a process of mutual understanding that necessitates participants to genuinely engage, listen empathically to each other's concerns, and examine underlying assumptions (Roberts, 2002). Establishing a shared language and exchanging ideas among participants is the prerequisite of dialogue accountability. Explanation and reasoning play key roles in dialogue, helping to foster a mutual understanding of the opportunities and challenges to reconcile the contradictory expectations from diverse stakeholders (Goretzki & Messner, 2016; Messner, 2009). Constructing accountability as a process of dialogue contributes to learning from each other and, thus a sense of trust and a shared identity.

In the Chinese bureaucracy, while there is a process of inquiry that allows account givers to justify their actions when accountability measures are activated, the status of the account givers and holders remains hierarchical during the dialogue. The account holders serve as powerful judges, while the account givers seek to defend their actions, often hindering genuine dialogue and leading to bureaucratic blame-avoidance strategies, such as denying responsibility, shifting blame, or spreading blame. Sanction-based accountability may diminish mutual understanding and consensus, as everyone seeks to distance themselves from any blame during the inquiry process.

Postmodernism holds that traditional public administration is a system characterized by discourse hegemony, in which top-down instructions and directives must be executed at every level without room for negotiation, and questioning or dissent is not permitted (King, 2005). Public policies generated on the basis of this "monologic dialogue" can only reflect the policy preferences of political and bureaucratic elites, rather than the expectations of low-level officials and citizens. Postmodernism believes that the complexities of contemporary public issues are more likely to be resolved through dialogues than through objective measurements or rational analysis (Bogason, 2001). Fox and Miller (1997) propose a process of "authentic discourse"—a discourse free from the prejudicial and dominant influences, and is based on inclusive, honest, and genuine engagement among some individuals. How to build an authentic discourse in the process of accountability is crucial for the efficiency of accountability. Who should be included in the discourse of dialogue, and how to design the mechanism of dialogue to ensure mutual understanding and genuine communication are the questions that require further exploration.

Promoting Good Accountability: What Should Be Done?

After a thorough examination of how accountability mechanisms can enhance bureaucrats' sense of responsibility, trust, and organizational learning, along with insights gained from felt and dialogue accountability, this section introduces an innovative form of accountability that contrasts with the characteristics of traditional accountability and outlines three criteria for good accountability.

Characteristics of Innovative Accountability

Table 8.2 presents an innovative accountability form and compares it with traditional forms of accountability in four dimensions. First, the account giver under the innovative accountability form is obliged to exercise moral deliberation to manage and coordinate diverse accountability relationships in a network relationship. It is an unstoppable trend that bureaucrats are facing increased stakeholders in governance networks when delivering public services. In these network relationships, public projects often necessitate collaboration among various organizations or agencies to achieve shared objectives.

Furthermore, bureaucrats are subject to increasing horizontal accountability imposed by media, non-profit organizations, or citizens (Romzek & Dubnick, 1987). Under thick public networks, the proper

Table 8.2 A comparison between traditional and innovative forms of accountability

	Traditional accountability	*Innovative accountability*
Obligation	Vertical principal-agent relationship	Network collaboration
Culture	Low trust	High trust
Process	Focus on information acquisition	Focus on dialogues
Orientation	Control	Organizational learning

exercise of responsible judgment is essential and serves as a crucial indicator of a bureaucrat's competence. The innovative form of accountability is a dynamic, flexible, and mutual relationship between a network of account holders and givers. It constructs a stark contrast with traditional accountability that is characterized by a vertical principal-agent mechanism. This obligation implies a formal relationship between superiors and subordinates, which is often equipped with top-down monitoring and sanction mechanisms to protect the authority of the principal-agent framework.

The organizational culture and accountability process are mutually reinforced. Under the innovative form of accountability, the accountability process is featured by genuine dialogues among different stakeholders and opens up the opportunity for reflective discussion on fundamental issues underlying social problems and how policies can be further improved. In the dialogue process, stakeholders can primarily focus on discussions of three aspects. First, account holders and givers summarize the good implementation strategies and the lessons learned from failures. Second, they analyze whether the established policies and regulations are at odds with the actual circumstances and meet the demands of citizens. Third, after a careful discussion of the case, it may be easier to clarify the roles and responsibilities of the relevant bureaucrats who also get a better understanding of his power and duties and when and how discretion can be exercised.

Such dialogue processes can only be implemented in organizations with a high-trust culture that is featured by open communication, constructive feedbacks, recognition and appreciation for employees, and a supportive environment. The dialogue process also further solidifies the inclusive organizational culture. In contrast, premised on low trust, traditional accountability seeks to alleviate information asymmetry by strengthening monitoring, work reports, and citizens' whistle-blowing. The reinforcement of various monitoring mechanisms is typically derived from, but also alternatively solidifies, an organizational culture characterized by low trust. If account holders display distrust and control, bureaucrats tend to prioritize risk aversion, self-preservation, information hoarding, and blame shifting over engagement, sincere dialogue, and collaboration (Greiling & Spraul, 2010; Hood, 2010). It contributes to a cycle of distrust, further entrenching the low-trust culture and making it difficult for organizations to innovate or adapt (Tetlock et al., 1989).

Third, the innovative accountability is oriented to facilitate organizational learning. The dialogue process allows for retrospective examinations of past performance, decisions, and practices (Schillemans et al., 2013). Organizational learning denotes detection and correction of errors, and gaining lessons from past experiences in order to guide and improve prospective behavior (Schillemans & Smulders, 2015). Learning-oriented accountability requires a certain level of tolerance for errors and a commitment to learning, which makes bureaucrats feel safe to discuss and reflect on their experiences and errors (Baxter et al., 2017). Traditional accountability is often viewed as a control mechanism featured by intensive monitoring and sanctions and focuses on what went wrong and who should be blamed. Premised on the assumption that bureaucrats are opportunistic and self-interested beings, intensive monitoring and sanction mechanisms should be in place to control bureaucrats (Wood & Waterman, 1991). An increasing number of scholars argue that sanction-oriented accountability cannot produce responsible bureaucrats and instead may lead to an increase in ethical problems (Jos & Tompkins, 2004; Lewis & Triantafillou, 2012). When the account holder primarily emphasizes regularity and control, the fear of being blamed and sanctioned may lead to a range of counterproductive reactions from bureaucrats, discouraging fundamental forms of learning and change (Ebrahim, 2005; Schillemans et al., 2013).

What Constructs a Good Accountability

I propose three tentative criteria for good accountability. First, a good accountability system should help to generate commitment and a sense of responsibility from bureaucrats and, at the same time, curb their defensive emotions and behaviors. An imposing arsenal of sanction-based mechanisms may invoke all sorts of undesirable defensive behaviors among bureaucrats. It will not lead them to reflect on their responsibilities but may induce fear of punishment and strategies to escape blame (Brees & Martinko, 2015). For example, bureaucrats may respond to intensive accountability with quick wits, creative subversion, or other defensive strategies to mitigate pressure and deflect criticism (Bowman & Williams, 1997). Bureaucrats' information advantages over their superiors and the difficulty and cost of monitoring make it possible for them to manipulate policies and public authority. Thus, bureaucrats always find ways to subvert external pressures unless they recognize the values behind accountability mechanisms. It is important to avoid triggering bureaucrats' defensive emotions and to induce cooperative spirits. Feldheim and Wang (2002) consider that ethics enhancement strategies, such as role modeling, ethics development, and ethics enforcement and review, can promote public officials' willingness and support for accountability mechanisms. Furthermore, an accountability mechanism should concentrate more on discussion and rewarding good behaviors to generate mutual understanding and collaboration. Even punishment for deviations should ultimately serve to reinforce the attachment to those shared norms and values and the reaffirmation of personal responsibility rather than assigning blame.

Second, good accountability should be judged on how well it fosters the capacities for moral judgment and reflection on multiple accountability demands (Jos & Tompkins, 2004). Responsible bureaucrats should possess good judgment and moral deliberation on ambiguity and conflicting expectations. It is essential to promote responsible choices, as the working context is increasingly filled with diverse obligations and demands from social, political, and organizational actors (Jos & Tompkins, 2009). Bureaucrats should develop the capacity for thoughtful moral reflection on the ambiguity and conflicts of demands. Encouraging blind and uncritical compliance with authority can lead to the adoption of unethical policies and negatively impact citizens' well-being. As mentioned earlier, the preferences of higher-level authorities do not always align with those of the public. Although bureaucrats, as agents, should be responsive to their superiors' commands, they also need to consider their broader obligations, have a particular concern about the attainment of social equity, and use their expertise, professionalism, and common sense to protect the needs and rights of the disadvantaged people (Frederickson, 1980). Public administration should not be considered a threat to citizens or a scapegoat for upper-rank politicians and officials. Exercising responsible individual judgment in bureaucratic settings is challenging, and good accountability should be designed to support reflective administrative judgment.

Third, good accountability should promote deliberation and foster the learning ability of bureaucrats. An excessive focus on control and sanctions is found to undermine the fundamental forms of change and innovation (Hood, 2010). Learning-oriented accountability may convey bureaucrats what is expected from them, what works, and what does not work rather than focusing on allocating blame to them (Bovens et al., 2008). Accountability mechanisms should enhance openness and reflection in political and administrative systems to promote actors' learning from insiders and outsiders in case of being primarily inward-looking (Bovens et al., 2008). A one-way (hierarchical) flow of communication is inadequate, and a truly dialogical mode of communication between superiors and subordinates is important if learning is to take place (Lewis & Triantafillou, 2012). Accountability should be designed to lead to the learning and improvement of bureaucrats, which may be achieved through participatory decision processes, dialogue, and consultation to make civil servants feel empowered.

In short, there is nothing wrong with imposing accountability, but the question is how to impose it to foster responsible bureaucrats who are committed to their jobs, possess moral reflection, and are eager to learn. The enforcement of accountability should help to build a participative, cooperative, and trusting organizational culture to nurture a sense of responsibility among bureaucrats. Responsible bureaucrats should actively assume their responsibility rather than adopt various adverse coping strategies to evade responsibility in response to accountability pressure. Responsible bureaucrats can impose moral law on themselves and self-regulate to maintain adherence to appropriate moral standards of action rather than passively respond to external pressures (Bivins, 2006). Responsible bureaucrats can play an important role in amending policy flaws and ensuring policies' alignment with citizens' interests.

A New Environment for Accountability

In the future, bureaucrats may have to operate within expanding networks of stakeholders and a more open and transparent environment, facilitated by ICTs. Network governance and digital governance are transforming the structures and processes of accountability. Network governance requires bureaucrats to navigate various accountability forums and processes, making their judgment increasingly important. Meanwhile, digital governance can greatly reduce information asymmetry between the principal and the agent, leading to less dependence on incentive mechanisms for the principal to regulate their agents.

Accountability under Network Governance

Over the recent two decades, public administration has been undergoing a transformation as our societies have become more multi-centered, the political and administrative authority is increasingly fragmented, and societal problems are increasingly complex and dynamic (Ansell & Gash, 2008; Emerson et al., 2012; Peters & Pierre, 2000). Scholars argue that a transition occurs from hierarchical, unitary government to horizontal, fragmented network governance with joint public and private involvement and collaborations (Agranoff & McGuire, 2003; Klijn & Koppenjan, 2004). Networks are viewed as an innovative and beneficial approach to coordination that aims to resolve the shortcomings of both markets and hierarchical structures (Provan & Kenis, 2008).

In networks, diverse stakeholders, including government agencies, the private sector, social organizations, and citizens, need to collaborate on public affairs, establishing vertically and horizontally interconnected network governance structures. Thick governance networks modify the way of decision-making processes and interactions, shaping the Weberian's command-and-control hierarchy chain where authority and directives flow in a defined, hierarchical manner. Specifically, bureaucrats must continuously engage with semi-public and private actors, collaborating within multi-level, multi-agency networks (Klingner et al., 2002; Koppell, 2005). The principal-agent relationship has grown more intricate due to the presence of multiple principals, various agencies, and informal accountability connections, suggesting the inadequacy of agency theory to effectively explain the evolving dynamics of accountability. The erosion of traditional boundaries complicates and obscures the accountability relationship. These shifts may shape accountability structures and bring about new accountability paradoxes from three different perspectives.

First, bureaucrats face varying expectations from multiple stakeholders and different norms in dense networks. At times, they act as agents of high-level government, focused on fulfilling policy commitments; at other times, they serve as citizen representatives, working to connect policy directives with public needs. Additionally, they may function as members of collaborative partnerships aiming for long-term cooperation, or as organizational leaders accountable to the interests of their staff and the organizations (Schillemans et al., 2021a; Tu & Gong, 2022a). In addition, bureaucrats often encounter conflicting demands, such as the need to achieve results and meet targets versus adhering to process-oriented regulations. They also grapple with the tension between government control and public participation in establishing local priorities, as well as the pressure to prioritize organizational learning from mistakes while simultaneously striving to avoid blame. Each of these creates distinct logic for appropriate action, making it challenging for bureaucrats to develop their own ethical understanding of accountability (Newman, 2004).

Numerous studies highlight detrimental effects resulting from conflicting expectations within multiple accountability relationships (Koppell, 2005). Various and contradictory expectations from the public, superiors, organizations, and the media create accountability disorder, leading to disasters such as the Challenger tragedy and the crash of Ron Brown's plane (Romzek & Dubnick, 1987). In dense governance networks, bureaucrats have to routinely cooperate with multiple stakeholders and manage various accountability demands, a reality they cannot escape in the future. Simplifying complex accountability frameworks does not appear to be a viable solution given the trend of multi-centered and fragmented collaborative networks. Instead of being viewed as a dilemma and a source of chaos, conflicts stemming from diverse expectations may be beneficial for achieving good policy outcomes (Willems & Van Dooren, 2012). In networks, stakeholders engage in dialogue, negotiate, make compromises, and ultimately deepen their understanding of the issues while reaching a consensus on differing expectations. Network governance offers an opportunity to expand beyond narrowly defined traditional accountability relationships, fostering a broader and more balanced form of accountability known as holistic accountability (Cordery et al., 2010; Pellinen et al., 2018).

Due to the complexity of accountability itself, over-reliance on certain types of accountability can lead to many problems: excessive legal accountability and hierarchical accountability undermine professional accountability and political accountability; excessive political accountability and hierarchical accountability undermine professional accountability (Kim, 2005; Romzek & Ingraham, 2000). This implies that bureaucrats need to apply their expertise, information, and judgment to balance and coordinate different forms of accountability, preventing any one type from dominating or infringing on the interests of other stakeholders. Negotiating diverse, even conflicting, demands creates opportunities to systematically analyze social problems and identify policy options that comprehensively address the needs of various stakeholders. "Networks create the space for the active, creative subject able to negotiate their way through dilemmas but also requires them to perform multiple identities in different contexts" (Newman, 2004, p. 20). Developing bureaucrats' moral judgment regarding diverse demands and establishing a platform for genuine dialogue to facilitate negotiations are crucial for addressing multiple accountability disorders.

Second, in networks, accountability as a mechanism involves managing various processes of information, discussion, and consequences imposed by different public forums that may utilize a range of tools to compete for attention from the agent (Willems & Van Dooren, 2012). The shift from single-centered to multi-centered authority signifies greater participation by various public and private actors in public decision-making. However, this does not equate to the establishment of network governance or collaborative governance, which necessitates principles of trust, reciprocity, negotiation, and mutual interdependence among the actors (Provan & Kenis, 2008). In many instances, multiple stakeholders are reluctant to share information, engage in discussions, or make compromises. Instead, they impose accountability processes on the agent separately, which requires additional time and efforts from the account giver to prepare and report repeated information, leading to disjointed and redundant work.

This situation is particularly pronounced in the Chinese government, where bureaucrats spend significant time in preparing overlapping information for various high-level departments. "The most overwhelming task is filling out various forms and preparing for inspections from superiors. The work of rural cadres involves daily filling out a large number of repetitive forms and responding to various inspections from different higher-ups. Much of the information required in the forms is redundant, yet different superior functional departments require us to fill them out" (CB-2019-3). Intensified accountability leads multiple superior principals to place a greater pressure on bureaucrats to avoid being blamed by their higher-ups. Therefore, besides conflicting expectations, multiple uncoordinated accountability processes may also be a significant contributor to accountability disorder. Within networks, various principals fail to cooperate with one another to provide bureaucrats with consistent, clear, and non-redundant tasks. Additionally, multiple agents tend to compete rather than collaborate, leading to redundant efforts and a waste of administrative resources. Network governance is an institutional framework that brings together different stakeholders, various organizations, and their resources within a network structure, creating an organized governance system characterized by mutual interdependence, negotiation, collective action, and shared risks. However, the ability to establish effective network governance from fragmented and disconnected networks may impact the effectiveness of accountability and vice versa.

Third, while networks may engage multiple stakeholders in decision-making, they also dilute responsibility among a considerable number of actors, creating a "paradox of shared responsibility" (Papadopoulos, 2007). Hood (2010) noted that identifying the right person responsible for a problem in complex public organizations can be challenging. A shared understanding of accountability is essential for constructive dialogues and network governance. This includes clear expectations for individuals or organizations, as well as the ethical principles and norms that shape behavior and decision-making (Roberts, 2009). However, rather than creating a shared understanding of accountability, bureaucrats may utilize networks to disperse responsibilities and potential blame. For example, to avoid responsibility and potential liability, some departments in the Chinese government depend on collective discussion to make decisions on the majority of issues. "Each staff member in the department must take a position, and each representative from the involved agencies must cast a vote when multiple agencies are part of the decision-making process" (CB-2024-35). Furthermore, the unequal distribution of resources within networks suggests that members with greater power or resources have more strategies at their disposal to deflect blame. Therefore, a poorly structured accountability framework within networks may lead to greater fragmentation and segmentation of interests rather than fostering an equal and genuine dialogue.

Accountability under Digital Governance

In recent decades, the rapid development of ICTs has dramatically reshaped various aspects of life and work. The emergence of new ICTs such as mobile internet, big data, blockchain, and artificial intelligence (AI) has significantly impacted how information is structured and flows. It has transformed the ways in which information is acquired, stored, and disseminated. These changes may, in turn, reshape organizational structures, incentive mechanisms, and the behavior of officials. The application of ICTs in the public sector also significantly influences the structure of accountability mechanisms.

ICTs significantly improve the efficiency of collecting and processing information, thereby reducing the problem of information asymmetry between superiors and subordinates, or between principals and agents. Three forms of changes in accountability may be brought about by enhancing information symmetry. First, with access to more information, principals may shift their assessment of agents from emphasizing outcomes to prioritizing compliance with procedures (Li & Nie, 2024). In situations of information asymmetry, it is difficult for principals to observe agents' behavior and can only infer their effort levels based on outputs or outcomes, which often results in a preference for results or performance-based evaluation methods. As information asymmetry decreases due to ICTs, principals can not only observe outputs but also even obtain information related to agents' specific behavior, procedural compliance, and rule adherence. This enables principals to implement process-based evaluation and impose stricter control over the agent's behavior.

Second, there is a shift from emphasizing incentives to monitoring. When principals are unable to observe agents' specific behaviors and, consequently, their effort levels, they must rely on material and promotional incentives to align agents' interests with their own. If designed effectively, incentive contracts can encourage agents to act in the interests of principals even in the absence of supervision. The advent of ICTs has reduced the costs of acquiring and processing information, thereby allowing principals to monitor agents' behaviors and efforts at a lower cost. As a result, principals are more likely to rely on supervision rather than incentives to mitigate agency problems, lowering incentive costs. Third, performance assessment may broaden to include a wider range of indicators. Information that was previously difficult to be obtained can now be acquired with the assistance of advanced digital technologies. It enables governments to move their focus from more quantifiable targets to evaluating overall performance by incorporating some qualitative indicators as well. However, it may lead to stress if the attainment of diverse indicators is perceived as overly demanding.

The three shifts have become evident in China since Xi took power. There is a noticeable transition from a focus on results or performance to an emphasis on compliance with procedures and regulations through enhanced monitoring and frequent top-down inspections. The results-oriented approach centered on GDP or fiscal revenue is evolving toward a multidimensional evaluation framework that incorporates indicators related to environmental protection, party building, rule of law, and public safety. Consequently, local officials' behavior has also experienced a great shift to adapt to the new institutional framework. Officials now put great emphasis on procedure compliance, paperwork, and Party construction, often refraining from taking initiatives and making innovations. For metrics that cannot be quantified, grassroots officials are required to take work photos and upload them to government applications or WeChat job groups (CB-2024-32).

The development of ICTs also brings about transformative changes in the interactions between the government and citizens. It is expected to promote the disclosure of government-related information and the involvement of citizens in monitoring and evaluating the performance of public services and officials, thereby strengthening social accountability. However, scholars are divided on whether ICTs serve to reinforce traditional institutional structures or act as a transformative force that changes the government and its accountability systems. Some people see ICTs as a catalyst for the transformation of accountability, allowing for a move away from a limited financial accountability where only a few institutions, like audit offices, hold governments and public officials responsible, often leaving citizens in the dark. ICTs foster a wider understanding of accountability that promotes direct and open communication with citizens, requiring officials to clarify and justify their actions (Fan & Ma, 2024; Lindquist & Huse, 2017; Pina et al., 2007). ICTs render financial or administrative practices, such as detailed budgets and expenditures, policy decisions, and organization performance, accessible and traceable over time, allowing citizens to be informed about public policies and to exercise monitoring (Elbahnasawy, 2014). Furthermore, the government's proactive information disclosure and citizens' active request for information disclosure allow public collaboration in the analysis of information and the monitoring of government practices, which turns the public into thousands of auditors and generates collaborative transparency (Tu et al., 2024; Wu et al., 2022).

However, a burgeoning literature cautions against the overly optimistic views regarding the positive effects of ICTs on openness, transparency, and accountability of public administrations (Halachmi & Greiling, 2013; Wong & Welch, 2004). Bauhr and Grimes (2017) suggest that transparency is sensitive to who the intended principals and agents are. If the flow and content of information are subject to the manipulation of the government agency, it is agent-controlled transparency (Lindstedt & Naurin, 2010). When a government agency seizes the predominant authority in information disclosure, it may publish information selectively or deny requests for additional documentation release from citizens (Lindstedt & Naurin, 2010). Some public agencies strategically refrain from disclosing information related to officials' malfeasance; others may deliberately overwhelm citizens by disclosing a flood of useless information (Ejiogu et al., 2019; Strathern, 2000). As a tool at the disposal of the government, transparency promoted by ICTs is largely an agent-controlled transparency in many countries, especially in the non-democratic ones. By making certain issues visible, new forms of closure and self-censorship may occur through the maneuvering of government agencies (Ejiogu et al., 2019; Fenster, 2010; Shkabatur, 2012). Some scholars even suggest that e-government tends to exacerbate the inherent characteristics of public bureaucracies and the patterns of politics rather than technology per se (Wong & Welch, 2004).

The use of ICTs in China reinforces existing institutional structures while also enhances social accountability. With the rise of web-based technologies, the e-government movement has become a global trend in public administration since the early 21st century (Wong & Welch, 2004). The widespread adoption of digital technologies by governments worldwide, along with the encouragement from the international community for countries to strengthen digital governmence to promote openness and transparency, impose pressure on countries, especially those who seek to integrate into the international world. Since joining WTO, the Chinese government has accelerated the applications of ICTs in public management and public service delivery, making information publicly accessible via official portals (Ma et al., 2005).

A series of "Informatization" (*Xinxihua*, 信息化) plans and the "National Informatization" plans were launched by the Chinese State Council in 1997 (Ma et al., 2005). The year 1999 was known as the "inaugural year of government internet access" in China, marking the initial stage of e-government portal construction, and the construction of provincial-level government portal websites was fully completed in 2007 (Wu & Bauer, 2010). China enacted the *Regulations on the Disclosure of Government Information of the People's Republic of China* (《中华人民共和国政府信息公开条例》) in 2008 (amended in 2019) to require that governments at all levels proactively disclose government information to the public. Since Xi took office, a strong emphasis has been placed on the development of digital governance, leading to the introduction of several key policies and initiatives aimed at creating a "powerful cyber nation" and "digital China." At the 25th Meeting of the Central Committee for Deepening Overall Reform in 2022, President Xi emphasized the need to "fully implement the strategy of becoming a strong cyber power, widely applying digital technology in government management and public services, promoting the digital and intelligent operation of the government, and providing strong support for the modernization of the national governance system and governance capabilities."

It is undeniable that e-government substantially enhances social accountability by facilitating government openness, societal engagement, and public monitoring. The *Notice from the General Office of the State Council on Regulating Matters Related to Government Information Disclosure Platforms* (《国务院办公厅政府信息与政务公开办公室关于规范政府信息公开平台有关事项的通知》) stipulates that the government information disclosure platforms should publish 15 types of government information, including administrative regulations, rules, and normative documents; agency functions, organizational structure, office addresses, office hours, contact information, and names of responsible persons; fiscal budget and final accounts information; catalog, standards, and implementation status of government procurement projects, approval and implementation status of major construction projects, etc. Official portals encompass various functional modes, including the disclosure of policies and regulations, the delivery of public services, and interactive communication between the government and citizens, aiming to provide the public with comprehensive, timely, and accurate information services. Government websites have become the major outlets for citizens to acquire government-related information in China.

Furthermore, e-government transforms the relationship between the government and citizens by establishing interactive virtual interfaces that provide additional channels for citizens to express their demands and engage with the government. The Chinese government is committed to creating "Internet + Monitoring" platforms, allowing the public to provide feedback and suggestions on government work and report improper administrative practices through online platforms, thereby establishing effective social supervision mechanisms. As of September 2024, a total of 405 websites publicly disclosed reporting and complaint procedures (Chinese Government Website, 2023).

Nevertheless, we still see strategies of manipulation by the government beneath a seemingly open, transparent, flexible virtual government. The Chinese government asserts its bureaucratic privilege over important government decisions and actions when fulfilling transparency obligations. Although the government allows citizens' criticisms of local officials and is willing to respond to their grievances, public opinion remains under government control. There was a period when online public opinion was out of the control of the government and led to the downfall of a considerable number of corrupt officials. The year 2009 is recognized as "the inaugural year of internet anti-corruption" (*wangluo fanfu yuannian, 网络反腐元年*), marked by widespread netizens' criticism of corruption related to earthquake relief funds following the Wenchuan earthquake. Since then, netizens have flooded various social platforms with reports of corrupt officials, exposing many notorious cases. This includes a director of the Real Estate Management Bureau caught smoking expensive cigarettes, a tobacco director whose sensual diary depicting his inappropriate relationship with several female subordinates was exposed online, and a director of the Safety Production Supervision and Administration Bureau filmed wear expensive watch and smile at an incident scene. During this time, the public tended to publicly expose official misconduct and place more trust in online exposure than in official reporting channels. The procedure of "online exposure - public discussion - media involvement - official investigation" became the pathway for investigating officials, depicted as an anti-corruption campaign driven by the public.

The online anti-corruption campaign indicates the intense level of criticism that the populace places on the government. The long-pressed frustration with corrupt officials has found an outlet for expression, leading to citizens' frenzied enthusiasm to hold them accountable by publicly exposing them. Every netizen has taken on the role of a "disciplinary auditor." However, this public-driven campaign was short-lived, as it generated chaos and a loss of control, leaving the government feeling passive and embarrassed. In September 2013, the official website of the CCDI was established alongside an online reporting channel, marking a shift toward an official-led model for online anti-corruption. It results in a sharp decline in online exposure of corrupt officials on social platforms. In 2014, the total number of posts from influential Weibo users who play a significant role in triggering public opinion dropped to 121,199 from 205,222 in 2013, a decrease of 40%. Only 51 corruption cases were exposed through online reporting in 2014, fewer than the number of cases in a single quarter of the "peak period" of online anti-corruption, which saw 90 cases in the first quarter of 2013 (Pengpai News, 2023). Since then, social accountability has operated within the government's institutional framework in a structured and orderly manner. However, the interactions between citizens and the government are dynamic. Whether citizens turn to online public exposure or official reporting channels depends on the efficacy of the anti-corruption agency and citizens' trust in the government. When their reports get no feedback from the government, they may lose confidence in the official authority and tend to online exposure to exert pressure on the government. However, we see some internet users publicly identify and expose corrupt officials by their real names online in recent years. Before 2012, citizens typically did not dare to report corrupt officials using their real names for fear of retaliation. Xi's firm determination to fight corruption may bolster citizens' courage to expose corrupt officials publicly by real name.

Furthermore, although numerous regulations on information disclosure were enacted, some local governments failed to comply with them. The *2024 Report on the Development of Government Disclosure in China* (*《中国政务公开发展报告(2024)》*) shows that only 10 State Council departments, 19 provincial governments, 84 municipal governments, and 23 county (city, district) governments published the handling of suggestions from representatives of the People's Congress for the year 2023 on their official websites, accounting for 20.83%, 61.29%, 79.25%, and 19.17%, respectively. Additionally, 3 provincial governments, 40 municipal governments, and 51 county (city, district) governments did not disclose the rules, methods, and processing timelines for complaints from foreign-invested enterprises, which accounted for 9.68%, 37.74%, and 42.50%, respectively.

In conclusion, the relationship between e-government and social accountability is conditional on the context and characteristics of the formal institutional framework. In China, e-government indeed promotes openness, transparency, public engagement, and thereby social accountability. However, the nature and extent of social monitoring is still tightly regulated and controlled by the government. Specifically, the government decides what information to disclose, when and how the information is publicized, and how long the information can be traced online. Furthermore, citizens' online exposure of corrupt officials has also been incorporated into formal institutions.

A Final Thought

In Western countries, accountability has long been a well-established system that plays a crucial role in regulating official behavior and ensuring government transparency and integrity. In contrast, China's accountability system has been formally established until 2003 and suffered from relatively underdeveloped mechanisms. However, the accountability system has undergone profound transformation since Xi came into office. The establishment of the SC system and the strengthened accountability mechanisms signify a shift in China's accountability framework from a fragmented and weak form to a systematic and comprehensive approach, fundamentally altering the motivation and behaviors of officials. Nevertheless, the practices of some accountability mechanisms has revealed deep-seated paradox and challenges. How to address these issues will determine the future trajectory of the accountability system.

The intensification of accountability has brought about significant changes in bureaucratic motivation and behavior. The motivation of bureaucrats has shifted from maximizing performance to minimizing blame. The "promotion tournament" mechanism was once the primary driver of Chinese officials, who sought promotion through visible achievements such as economic growth. Accountability now has become the major "constraint" looming over officials, leading them to focus more on blame avoidance and procedure compliance. While this shift may contribute to a decrease in the abuse of power and corruption, it could also stifle the innovative vitality of local governments. Future research needs to further explore how to uphold officials' entrepreneurship and innovation within the framework of accountability.

The paradox of accountability requires a balance between incentives and constraints. The intent of the accountability system is to strengthen supervision to constrain official behavior and ensure their fulfillment of duties. On one hand, enhancing the accountability system encourages local officials to prioritize legality and procedure compliance in decision-making, thereby reducing the abuse of power. However, in practice, intensive accountability has also led to some unexpected paradoxes. For instance, the ambiguity of accountability standards and the rigidity in their enforcement provoke dissatisfaction and resistance among officials, fostering a propensity of blame avoidance and even inaction within the Chinese bureaucracy. The fear of accountability has, to some extent, dampened officials' drive for innovation and sense of responsibility. Therefore, finding a balance between accountability constraints and incentives has become a key focus for future system design.

Dynamic adjustment is essential in the interaction between the accountability structure and human agency. The accountability system is not static; it requires dynamic adjustments based on officials' behavioral responses. For instance, when excessive accountability pressure leads to widespread blame avoidance and shirking among officials, upper-level authorities may need to introduce more positive incentive measures, such as fault-tolerance mechanisms and performance rewards, to mitigate the negative effects of accountability. Additionally, the accountability system should place greater emphasis on transparency and consistency to avoid provoking dissatisfaction and resistance among officials.

The future development of China's accountability system can be explored through several key directions. First, fault-tolerance mechanisms need to be further improved to provide officials with certain latitude for trial and error, thereby motivating them to take initiative and be innovative. Second, public participation should be enhanced to increase the transparency and credibility of the accountability process. The accountability mechanism should not merely function as a closed, top-down control system within the government. Instead, it should incorporate a broader range of social stakeholders. By fostering extensive participation and dialogues among both internal and external actors, the mechanism can explore the proper ways to fulfill responsibilities, thereby enhancing the capacity for reflection and mutual learning. Finally, technology empowerment, such as the application of big data and artificial intelligence, can significantly improve the precision of information and change the structure of accountability. These aspects will not only shape the future of China's accountability system but also serve as critical topics for further research.

References

Agranoff, R., & McGuire, M. (2003). Inside the matrix: Integrating the paradigms of intergovernmental and network management. *International Journal of Public Administration, 26*(12), 1401–1422.

Ann Feldheim, M., & Wang, X. (2002). Accountability through ethics enhancement strategies: Empirical evidence from American cities. *International Review of Public Administration, 7*(1), 77–84.

Ansell, C., & Gash, A. (2008). Collaborative governance in theory and practice. *Journal of Public Administration Research and Theory, 18*(4), 543–571.

Argyris, C. (1982). *Reasoning, learning and action.* Jossey-Bass.

Argyris, C., & Schön, D. A. (1978). *A theory of action perspective.* Addison-Wesley Publishing Company.

Argyris, C., & Schön, D. A. (1997). Organizational learning: A theory of action perspective. *Reis, 77*(78), 345–348.

Ashforth, B. E., & Lee, R. T. (1990). Defensive behavior in organizations: A preliminary model. *Human Relations, 43*(7), 621–648.

Bachmann, R., Gillespie, N., & Priem, R. (2015). Repairing trust in organizations and institutions: Toward a conceptual framework. *Organization Studies, 36*(9), 1123–1142.

Bapuji, H., & Crossan, M. (2004). From Questions to Answers: Reviewing Organizational Learning Research. *Management Learning, 35*(4), 397–417.

Basten, D., & Haamann, T. (2018). Approaches for organizational learning: A literature review. *SAGE Open, 8*(3), 2158244018794224.

Bauhr, M., & Grimes, M. (2017). Transparency to curb corruption? Concepts, measures and empirical merit. *Crime, Law and Social Change, 68*(4), 431–458.

Baxter, D., Colledge, T., & Turner, N. (2017). A study of accountability in two organizational learning frameworks: Why accountability for learning is critical. *European Management Review, 14*(3), 319–332.

Berthoin Antal, A., Debucquet, G., & Frémeaux, S. (2019). When Top Management Leadership Matters: Insights From Artistic Interventions. *Journal of Management Inquiry, 28*(4), 441–457.

Bhatt, G. D. (2002). Management strategies for individual knowledge and organizational knowledge. *Journal of Knowledge Management, 6*(1), 31–39.

Bivins, T. H. (2006). Responsibility and accountability. In K. Fitzpatrick & C. Bronstein (Eds.), *Ethics in Public Relations: Responsible Advocacy* (pp. 19–38). Sage.

Bogason, P. (2001). Postmodernism and American public administration in the 1990s. *Administration & Society, 33*(2), 165–193.
Bohm, D., & Nichol, L. (1996). *On dialogue*. Routledge.
Borry, E. L. (2016). A new measure of red tape: Introducing the three-item red tape (TIRT) scale. *International Public Management Journal, 19*(4), 573–593.
Bovens, M., Schillemans, T., & Hart, P. 'T. (2008). Does public accountability work? An assessment tool. *Public Administration, 86*(1), 225–242.
Bowman, J. B., & Williams, R. L. (1997). Ethics in government: From a winter of despair to a spring of hope. *Public Administration Review, 57*, 517–526.
Bozeman, B., & Feeney, M. K. (2014). *Rules and red tape: A prism for public administration theory and research: A prism for public administration theory and research*. Routledge.
Brees, J., & Martinko, M. J. (2015). Judgments of responsibility versus accountability. *Journal of Leadership & Organizational Studies, 22*(4), 443–453.
Brehm, J., & Gates, S. (2015). Bureaucratic politics arising from, not defined by, a principal–agency dyad. *Journal of Public Administration Research and Theory, 25*(1), 27–42.
Brower, H. H., Schoorman, F. D., & Tan, H. H. (2000). A model of relational leadership: The integration of trust and leader–member exchange. *The Leadership Quarterly, 11*(2), 227–250.
Cangelosi, V. E., & Dill, W. R. (1965). Organizational learning: Observations toward a theory. *Administrative Science Quarterly, 10*, 175–203.
Cannon, M. D., & Edmondson, A. C. (2001). Confronting failure: Antecedents and consequences of shared beliefs about failure in organizational work groups. *Journal of Organizational Behavior, 22*(2), 161–177.
Cannon, M. D., & Edmondson, A. C. (2005). Failing to learn and learning to fail (intelligently): How great organizations put failure to work to innovate and improve. *Long Range Planning, 38*(3), 299–319.
Carpenter, D., & Krause, G. A. (2015). Transactional authority and bureaucratic politics. *Journal of Public Administration Research and Theory, 25*(1), 5–25.
Chen, G. (2005). Management practices and tools for enhancing organizational learning capability. *SAM Advanced Management Journal, 70*(1), 4–21.
Chinese Government Website. (2023, September 19). *405 websites disclose their reporting and complaint procedures*. Viewed November 15, 2024. https://www.gov.cn/zhengce/jiedu/tujie/202309/content_6904939.htm
Chiva, R., Ghauri, P., & Alegre, J. (2014). Organizational Learning, innovation and internationalization: A complex system model. *British Journal of Management, 25*(4), 687–705.
Cooper, T. L. (2012). *The responsible administrator: An approach to ethics for the administrative role*. Wiley.

Cordery, C., Baskerville, R., & Porter, B. (2010). Control or collaboration? Contrasting accountability relationships in the primary health sector. *Accounting, Auditing & Accountability Journal, 23*(6), 793–813.

Crossan, M. M., Lane, H. W., White, R. E., & Djurfeldt, L. (1995). Organizational learning: Dimensions for a theory. *The International Journal of Organizational Analysis, 3*(4), 337–360.

Currie, G., & Suhomlinova, O. (2006). The impact of institutional forces upon knowledge sharing in the UK NHS: The triumph of professional power and the inconsistency of policy. *Public Administration, 84*(1), 1–30.

De Bruijn, H. (2002). Performance measurement in the public sector: Strategies to cope with the risks of performance measurement. *International Journal of Public Sector Management, 15*(7), 578–594.

Dubnick, M. (2005). Accountability and the promise of performance: In search of the mechanisms. *Public Performance & Management Review, 28*(3), 376–417.

Dubnick, Melvin and Frederickson, H. George, Public Accountability: Performance Measurement, the Extended State, and the Search for Trust (June 1, 2011). National Academy of Public Administration & The Kettering Foundation, June 2011, Available at SSRN: https://ssrn.com/abstract=1875024

Duncan, R. (1979). *Organizational learning: Implications for organizational design. Research in organizational behavior*, 1, 75–123.

Ebrahim, A. (2005). Accountability myopia: Losing sight of organizational learning. *Nonprofit and Voluntary Sector Quarterly, 34*(1), 56–87.

Ehren, M., Paterson, A., & Baxter, J. (2020). Accountability and trust: Two sides of the same coin? *Journal of Educational Change, 21*(1), 183–213.

Ejiogu, A., Ejiogu, C., & Ambituuni, A. (2019). The dark side of transparency: Does the Nigeria extractive industries transparency initiative help or hinder accountability and corruption control? *The British Accounting Review, 51*(5), 100811.

Elbahnasawy, N. G. (2014). E-government, internet adoption, and corruption: An empirical investigation. *World Development, 57*, 114–126.

Emerson, K., Nabatchi, T., & Balogh, S. (2012). An integrative framework for collaborative governance. *Journal of Public Administration Research and Theory, 22*(1), 1–29.

Fan, Z., & Ma, L. (2024). E-government, anticorruption, and citizens' use of personal connections: evidence from Chinese municipalities. *Journal of Chinese Governance, 9*(3), 372–395.

Fenster, M. (2010). Seeing the state: Transparency as metaphor. *Administrative Law Review, 62* (3), 617–672.

Fiol, C. M., & Lyles, M. A. (1985). Organizational learning. *The Academy of Management Review, 10*(4), 803–813.

Fox, C. J., & Miller, H. T. (1997). The depreciating public policy discourse. *American Behavioral Scientist, 41*(1), 64–89.
Frederickson, H. G. (1980). *New public administration*. University Alabama Press.
Friedrich, C. J. (2000). Public policy and the nature of administrative responsibility. In Miyakawa, T. (Ed.), *The Science of Public Policy*: Policy analysis II (114–132). Taylor & Francis.
Gao, J. (2021). Mitigating pernicious gaming in performance management in China: Dilemmas, Strategies and Challenges. *Public Performance & Management Review, 44*(2), 321–351.
Gersen, J. E., & Stephenson, M. C. (2014). Over-accountability. *Journal of Legal Analysis, 6*(2), 185–243.
Goretzki, L., & Messner, M. (2016). Coordination under uncertainty: A sensemaking perspective on cross-functional planning meetings. *Qualitative Research in Accounting & Management, 13*(1), 92–126.
Govier, T. (1998). *Dilemmas of trust*. McGill-Queen's Press-MQUP.
Greiling, D., & Halachmi, A. (2013). Accountability and organizational learning: Introduction. *Public Performance & Management Review, 36*(3), 375–379.
Greiling, D., & Spraul, K. (2010). Accountability and the challenges of information disclosure. *Public Administration Quarterly, 34*(3), 338–377.
Gundlach, G. T., & Cannon, J. P. (2010). "Trust but verify"? The performance implications of verification strategies in trusting relationships. *Journal of the Academy of Marketing Science, 38*, 399–417.
Halachmi, A., & Greiling, D. (2013). Transparency, e-government, and accountability: Some issues and considerations. *Public Performance & Management Review, 36*(4), 572–584.
Hall, A. T., Frink, D. D., & Buckley, M. R. (2017). An accountability account: A review and synthesis of the theoretical and empirical research on felt accountability. *Journal of Organizational Behavior, 38*(2), 204–224.
Hardin, R. (2006). *Trust* (Vol. 10). Polity.
Hardin, R. (2013). Government without trust. *Journal of Trust Research, 3*(1), 32–52.
Harmon, M. M. (1995). *Responsibility as paradox: A critique of rational discourse on government*. Sage.
Hatch, T. (2013). Beneath the surface of accountability: Answerability, responsibility and capacity-building in recent education reforms in Norway. *Journal of Educational Change, 14*, 113–138.
Hedberg, B. (1981). How organizations learn and unlearn. In W. H. Starbuck & P. C. Nystrom (Eds.), *Handbook of Organizational Design: Remodeling organizations and their environments* (pp. 3–37). Oxford University Press.
Herriott, S. R., Levinthal, D., & March, J. G. (1985). Learning from experience in organizations. *The American Economic Review, 75*(2), 298–302.

Hochwarter, W. A., Ferris, G. R., Gavin, M. B., Perrewé, P. L., Hall, A. T., & Frink, D. D. (2007). Political skill as neutralizer of felt accountability—Job tension effects on job performance ratings: A longitudinal investigation. *Organizational Behavior and Human Decision Processes, 102*(2), 226–239.

Hood, C. (2010). *The blame game: Spin, bureaucracy, and self-preservation in government*. Princeton University Press.

Hupe, P., & Hill, M. (2007). Street-level bureaucracy and public accountability. *Public Administration, 85*(2), 279–299.

Jackson, M. (2009). Responsibility versus accountability in the Friedrich-Finer debate. *Journal of Management History, 15*(1), 66–77.

Jos, P. H., & Tompkins, M. E. (2004). The accountability paradox in an age of reinvention: The perennial problem of preserving character and judgment. *Administration & Society, 36*(3), 255–281.

Jos, P. H., & Tompkins, M. E. (2009). Keeping It Public: Defending Public Service Values in a Customer Service Age. *Public Administration Review, 69*(6), 1077–1086.

Kim, S.-E. (2005). Balancing competing accountability requirements: Challenges in performance improvement of the nonprofit human services agency. *Public Performance & Management Review, 29*(2), 145–163.

King, C. S. (2005). *Postmodern public administration*: In the shadow of postmodernism. *Administrative Theory & Praxis, 27*(3), 517–532.

Klijn, E., & Koppenjan, J. F. (2004). Institutional design in networks: Elaborating and analysing strategies for institutional design. *Vezetéstudomány-Budapest Management Review, 35*(7–8), 84–98.

Klingner, D. E., Nalbandian, J., & Romzek, B. S. (2002). Politics, administration, and markets: Conflicting expectations and accountability. *The American Review of Public Administration, 32*(2), 117–144.

Koppell, J. G. (2005). Pathologies of accountability: ICANN and the challenge of "Multiple Accountabilities Disorder." *Public Administration Review, 65*(1), 94–108.

Laine, N. (2008). *Trust in superior-subordinate relationship—An empirical study in the context of learning*. Tampere University Press.

Lerner, J. S., & Tetlock, P. E. (1999). Accounting for the effects of accountability. *Psychological Bulletin, 125*(2), 255.

Lewicki, R. J., & Brinsfield, C. (2015). Trust research: Measuring trust beliefs and behaviours. In F. Lyon, G. Mšllering, & M. N. Saunders (Eds.), *Handbook of research methods on trust* (pp. 46–64). Edward Elgar Publishing.

Lewis, J. M., & Triantafillou, P. (2012). From performance measurement to learning: A new source of government overload? *International Review of Administrative Sciences, 78*(4), 597–614.

Li, J., & Nie, H. (2024). National governance mechanisms in the digital age: Balancing development and security. *Economic Theory and Business Management* (07), 119–136 (李靖,聂辉华. 数字时代的国家治理机制: 发展和安全的权衡. 经济理论与经济管理).

Li, X. (2019). Understanding *nao*: A Chinese, "image event." *Communication and Critical/cultural Studies, 16*(4), 370–381.

Lindkvist, L., & Llewellyn, S. (2003). Accountability, responsibility and organization. *Scandinavian Journal of Management, 19*(2), 251–273.

Lindquist, E. A., & Huse, I. (2017). Accountability and monitoring government in the digital era: Promise, realism and research for digital-era governance. *Canadian Public Administration, 60*(4), 627–656.

Lindstedt, C., & Naurin, D. (2010). Transparency is not enough: Making transparency effective in reducing corruption. *International Political Science Review, 31*(3), 301–322.

Lipsky, M. (2010). *Street-level bureaucracy: Dilemmas of the individual in public service*. Russell Sage Foundation.

Ma, L., Chung, J., & Thorson, S. (2005). E-government in China: Bringing economic development through administrative reform. *Government Information Quarterly, 22*(1), 20–37.

Mayer, R. C., Davis, J. H., & Schoorman, F. D. (1995). An integrative model of organizational trust. *The Academy of Management Review, 20*(3), 709.

Messner, M. (2009). The limits of accountability. *Accounting, Organizations and Society, 34*(8), 918–938.

Mills, R. W., & Reiss, D. R. (2017). The role of trust in the regulation of complex and high-risk industries: The case of the US Federal Aviation administration's voluntary disclosure programs. In *Trust in regulatory regimes* (pp. 37–59). Edward Elgar Publishing.

Morris, M. W., & Moore, P. C. (2000). The lessons we (don't) learn: Counterfactual thinking and organizational accountability after a close call. *Administrative Science Quarterly, 45*(4), 737–765.

Morrison, E. W. (2006). Doing the job well: An investigation of pro-social rule breaking. *Journal of Management, 32*(1), 5–28.

Mulgan, R. (2000). 'Accountability': An ever-expanding concept? *Public Administration, 78*(3), 555–573.

Näslund, L., & Hallström, K. T. (2017). Being everybody's accomplice: Trust and control in eco-labelling. In Six, F., & Verhoest, K.(Eds.), *Trust in regulatory regimes*, 145–180.

Newman, J. (2004). Constructing accountability: Network governance and managerial agency. *Public Policy and Administration, 19*(4), 17–33.

O'Brien, K. J., & Li, L. (1999). Selective policy implementation in Rural China. *Comparative Politics, 31*(2), 167–186.

Oomsels, P., & Bouckaert, G. (2017). Interorganizational trust in Flemish public administration: Comparing trusted and distrusted interactions between public regulatees and public regulators. In F. Six & K. Verhoest (Eds.), *Trust in regulatory regimes* (pp. 80–114). Edward Elgar Publishing.

Ossege, C. (2012). Accountability—Are we better off without it?: An empirical study on the effects of accountability on public managers' work behaviour. *Public Management Review, 14*(5), 585–607.

Overman, S., & Schillemans, T. (2022). Toward a public administration theory of felt accountability. *Public Administration Review, 82*(1), 12–22.

Overman, S., Schillemans, T., & Grimmelikhuijsen, S. (2021). A validated measurement for felt relational accountability in the public sector: Gauging the account holder's legitimacy and expertise. *Public Management Review, 23*(12), 1748–1767.

Pandey, S. K., & Scott, P. G. (2002). Red tape: A review and assessment of concepts and measures. *Journal of Public Administration Research and Theory, 12*(4), 553–580.

Papadopoulos, Y. (2007). Problems of democratic accountability in network and multilevel governance. *European Law Journal, 13*(4), 469–486.

Patil, S. V., Vieider, F., & Tetlock, P. E. (2014). Process versus outcome accountability. In M. Bovens, R. E. Goodin, & T. Schillemans (Eds.), *The Oxford handbook of public accountability* (pp. 69–89). Oxford University Press.

Pellinen, J., Mättö, T., Sippola, K., & Rautiainen, A. (2018). Blame game or dialogue? Financial, professional and democratic accountabilities in a complex health care setting. *Accounting, Auditing & Accountability Journal, 31*(2), 626–650.

Pengpai News. (2023, September 19). The public sentiment around anti-corruption has entered an officially led mode, resulting in a dramatic decrease in online revelations. Viewed November 20, 2024. https://www.thepaper.cn/newsDetail_forward_1288952

Pérez-Durán, I. (2024). Twenty-five years of accountability research in public administration: Authorship, themes, methods, and future trends. *International Review of Administrative Sciences, 90*(3), 546–562.

Peters, B. G., & Pierre, J. (2000). Citizens versus the new public manager: The problem of mutual empowerment. *Administration & Society, 32*(1), 9–28.

Pina, V., Torres, L., & Acerete, B. (2007). Are ICTs promoting government accountability?: A comparative analysis of e-governance developments in 19 OECD countries. *Critical Perspectives on Accounting, 18*(5), 583–602.

Poon, J. M. (2013). Effects of benevolence, integrity, and ability on trust-in-supervisor. *Employee Relations, 35*(4), 396–407.

Popova-Nowak, I. V., & Cseh, M. (2015). The meaning of organizational learning: A meta-paradigm perspective. *Human Resource Development Review, 14*(3), 299–331.

Provan, K. G., & Kenis, P. (2008). Modes of network governance: Structure, management, and effectiveness. *Journal of Public Administration Research and Theory, 18*(2), 229–252.

Roberts, J. (2009). No one is perfect: The limits of transparency and an ethic for 'intelligent' accountability. *Accounting, Organizations and Society, 34*(8), 957–970.

Roberts, N. C. (2002). Keeping public officials accountable through dialogue: Resolving the accountability paradox. *Public Administration Review, 62*(6), 658–669.

Romzek, B. S., & Dubnick, M. J. (1987). Accountability in the public sector: Lessons from the challenger tragedy. *Public Administration Review, 47*(3), 227–238.

Romzek, B. S., & Ingraham, P. W. (2000). Cross pressures of accountability: Initiative, command, and failure in the Ron Brown plane crash. *Public Administration Review, 60*(3), 240–253.

Schillemans, T., et al. (2021a). Conflictual accountability: Behavioral responses to conflictual accountability of agencies. *Administration & Society, 53*(8), 1232–1262.

Schillemans, T., et al. (2021b). Understanding felt accountability: The institutional antecedents of the felt accountability of agency-CEO's to central government. *Governance, 34*(3), 893–916.

Schillemans, T., & Smulders, R. (2015). Learning from accountability?! Whether, what, and when. *Public Performance & Management Review, 39*(1), 248–271.

Schillemans, T., Van Twist, M., & Vanhommerig, I. (2013). Innovations in Accountability: Learning Through Interactive, Dynamic, and Citizen-Initiated Forms of Accountability. *Public Performance & Management Review, 36*(3), 407–435.

Schilling, J., & Kluge, A. (2009). Barriers to organizational learning: An integration of theory and research. *International Journal of Management Reviews, 11*(3), 337–360.

Shkabatur, J. (2012). Transparency with (out) accountability: Open government in the United States. *Yale Law & Policy Review, 31*, 79–120.

Shrivastava, P. (1983). A typology of organizational learning systems. *Journal of Management Studies, 20*(1), 7–28.

Strathern, M. (2000). The tyranny of transparency. *British Educational Research Journal, 26*(3), 309–321.

Suchman, M. C. (1995). Managing legitimacy: Strategic and institutional approaches. *The Academy of Management Review, 20*(3), 571–610.

Sun, P. Y., & Scott, J. L. (2003). Exploring the divide–organizational learning and learning organization. *The Learning Organization, 10*(4), 202–215.

Tetlock, P. E., Skitka, L., & Boettger, R. (1989). Social and cognitive strategies for coping with accountability: Conformity, complexity, and bolstering. *Journal of Personality and Social Psychology, 57*(4), 632.

Thomann, E., Hupe, P., & Sager, F. (2018). Serving many masters: Public accountability in private policy implementation. *Governance, 31*(2), 299–319.

Thompson, D. F. (1992). Paradoxes of government ethics. *Public Administration Review, 52*(3), 254–259.

Tsoukas, H., & Vladimirou, E. (2001). What is organizational knowledge? *Journal of Management Studies, 38*(7), 973–993.

Tu, W. (2023). Trust and corruption: How different forms of trust interact with formal institutions. *Global Public Policy and Governance, 3*(2), 160–179.

Tu, W. (2024). The Interactive Effect of Extrinsic Controls and Public Service Motivation on Blame Avoidance. *Public Personnel Management*, 00910260241283549.

Tu, W., & Gong, T. (2022a). Accountability intensity and bureaucrats' response to conflicting expectations: A survey experiment in China. *Public Management Review, 24*(11), 1779–1801.

Tu, W., & Gong, T. (2022b). Bureaucratic shirking in China: Is sanction-based accountability a cure? *The China Quarterly, 249*, 259–274.

Tu, W., Gong, T., & Li, H. (2024). The divergent effects of agent-controlled transparency on corruption latency: Evidence from China. *Government Information Quarterly, 41*(2), 101942.

Ullmann-Margalit, E. (2004). *Trust, distrust, and in between.* Russell Sage Foundation.

Willems, T., & Van Dooren, W. (2012). Coming to terms with accountability: Combining multiple forums and functions. *Public Management Review, 14*(7), 1011–1036.

Wong, W., & Welch, E. (2004). Does e-government promote accountability? A Comparative analysis of website openness and government accountability. *Governance, 17*(2), 275–297.

Wood, B. D., & Waterman, R. W. (1991). The dynamics of political control of the bureaucracy. *American Political Science Review, 85*(3), 801–828.

Wu, Y., & Bauer, J. M. (2010). E-government in China: Deployment and driving forces of provincial government portals. *Chinese Journal of Communication, 3*(3), 290–310.

Wu, Y., Xiao, H., & Yang, F. (2022). Government information disclosure and citizen coproduction during COVID-19 in China. *Governance, 35*(4), 1005–1027.

Xiao, H., Gong, T., & Tu, W. (2024). Why trust weighs more? Investigating the endogenous relationship between trust and perceived institutional effectiveness. *Administration & Society, 56*(5), 602–627.

Yang, K. (2012). Further understanding accountability in public organizations: Actionable knowledge and the structure–agency duality. *Administration & Society, 44*(3), 255–284.

Yankelovich, D. (1999). The Magic of Dialogue: The Art of Turning Transactions into Successful Relationships. New York: Simon and Schuster.

Yih-Tong Sun, P., & Scott, J. L. (2005). An investigation of barriers to knowledge transfer. *Journal of Knowledge Management, 9*(2), 75–90.

Appendix A: Lists of Rules or Regulations Issued by the Central Organs

No.	Chinese title	English title	Date
1	《国务院办公厅关于推行行政执法责任制的若干意见》	*Several Opinions of the State Council on Pushing Forward the Administrative Law Enforcement Responsibility System*	2005
1	《关于实行党政领导干部问责的暂行规定》	*Interim Provisions on the Implementation of Accountability of the Party and Government leading cadres*	2009
2	《中国共产党党内法规制定条例》	*Chinese Communist Party Regulations on the Draft of Laws and Regulations within the Party*	2012
3	《党政领导干部选拔任用工作条例》	*Regulations on the Selecting and Appointing of Party and Government Leading Cadres*	2014
5	《领导干部"为官不为"五个一律问责实施细则》	*Implementation Rules for Accountability of Leading Cadres' Five Types of Shirking Behaviors*	2014
6	《党和国家工作人员履职不力行为问责暂行办法》	*Interim Measures for the Accountability of the Party and State officials for Improper Performance of Duties*	2014
7	《中国共产党巡视工作条例》	*Chinese Communist Party Regulation Regarding On-Site Inspections*	2015

(continued)

W. Tu, *The Accountability Paradox in the Chinese Bureaucracy*,
https://doi.org/10.1007/978-981-96-6392-7

(continued)

No.	*Chinese title*	*English title*	*Date*
8	《中国共产党廉洁自律准则》	*Chinese Communist Party Principles on Integrity and Self-discipline*	2015
9	《中国共产党纪律处分条例》	*Chinese Communist Party Regulation on Party Discipline*	2015
10	《中国共产党党内监督条例》	*Chinese Communist Party Regulation on Inner-party Supervision*	2016
11	《中国共产党问责条例》	*Chinese Communist Party Regulation on Accountability*	2016
12	《领导干部报告个人有关事项规定》	*Provisions on the Reporting of Individual Matters of Leading Cadres*	2017
13	《党政领导干部选拔任用工作条例》	*Regulations on the Selecting and Appointing of Party and Government Leading Cadres*	2002, 2019 (amend)
15	《关于进一步激励广大干部新时代新担当新作为的意见》	*Circular on Further Encouraging the Cadres to Take Initiatives in the New Era*	2018
16	《关于统筹规范监督检查考核工作的通知》	*Circular on Overall Specification for Inspection and Assessment*	2018
17	《中国共产党问责条例》	*Chinese Communist Party Regulations on the Draft of Laws and Regulations within the Party*	2016, 2019 (amend)
18	《中华人民共和国监察法》	*Supervision Law of the People's Republic of China*	2018
19	《中华人民共和国政府信息公开条例》	*Regulations on the Disclosure of Government Information of the People's Republic of China*	2008, 2019 (amend)

Appendix B: Basic Information of Interviews

The coding format (e.g., CB-2019-1) utilized in this study consists of three levels of information. The prefix "CB" stands for "the Chinese bureaucrat," followed by the year the interview took place ("2019"). The last number, "1," signifies that this is the first interview.

No.	*Code*	*Interviewee*
1	CB-2019-1	An official from a township government in Guangdong Province
2	CB-2019-2	An official from a township government in Guangdong Province
3	CB-2019-3	An official from a township government in Guangdong Province
4	CB-2019-4	An official from a township government in Guangdong Province
5	CB-2019-5	An official from a township government in Guangdong Province
6	CB-2019-6	An official from a municipal department in Guangdong Province
7	CB-2019-7	An official from a municipal government in Jiangsu Province
8	CB-2019-8	An official from a provincial department in Jiangsu Province
9	CB-2019-9	An official from a municipal department in Jiangsu Province
10	CB-2019-10	An official from a township government in Jiangsu Province
11	CB-2019-11	An official from a municipal department in Guizhou Province
12	CB-2019-12	An official from a county government in Anhui Province
13	CB-2019-13	An official from a municipal department in Jiangsu Province
14	CB-2019-14	An official from a township government in Jiangsu Province
15	CB-2019-15	An official from a township government in Jiangsu Province
16	CB-2019-16	An official from a township government in Anhui Province
17	CB-2019-17	An official from a township department in Jiangsu Province
18	CB-2019-18	An official from a township department in Jiangsu Province
19	CB-2019-19	An official from a township department in Anhui Province

(continued)

W. Tu, *The Accountability Paradox in the Chinese Bureaucracy*,
https://doi.org/10.1007/978-981-96-6392-7

(continued)

No.	*Code*	*Interviewee*
20	CB-2019-20	An official from a township department in Jiangsu Province
21	CB-2019-21	An official from a township government in Hunan Province
22	CB-2019-22	An official from a municipal department in Hunan Province
23	CB-2019-23	An official from a municipal department in Hunan Province
24	CB-2019-24	An official from a township government in Hunan Province
25	CB-2019-25	An official from a township government in Hunan Province
26	CB-2019-26	An official from a municipal department in Hunan Province
27	CB-2019-27	An official from a municipal department in Hunan Province
28	CB-2019-28	An official from a township government in Hunan Province
29	CB-2019-29	An official from a municipal department in Jiangxi Province
30	CB-2019-30	An official from a municipal department in Jiangxi Province
31	CB-2019-31	An official from a municipal department in Sichuan Province
32	CB-2019-32	An official from a village government in Jiangxi Province
33	CB-2024-33	An official from a county department in Jiangsu Province
34	CB-2024-34	An official from a county department in Jiangsu Province
35	CB-2024-35	An official from a county department in Hubei Province
36	CB-2024-36	An official from a state-owned enterprise in Shanghai City

Appendix C: Measurement Scale of Key Variables

Monitoring intensity:

1. Upper-level departments impose strict supervision on my work.
2. I need to report my work to upper-level departments frequently.
3. Upper-level departments check and evaluate my work frequently.
4. Any detail of the tasks must be recorded in the paperwork.

Discussion quality:

1. The higher authorities will listen to my explanations if my performance is not satisfying.
2. The upper authorities are willing to listen to our suggestions on work.
3. The higher authorities communicate with me regularly.

Reward-based consequence:

1. Performance evaluation in our department is fair.
2. Chances for getting a promotion or better transfer is large if I perform well.
3. Good performance will be rewarded with incentive material gains.

W. Tu, *The Accountability Paradox in the Chinese Bureaucracy*,
https://doi.org/10.1007/978-981-96-6392-7

Punishment-based consequence:

1. Poor performance will be severely criticized.
2. The possibility of being punished is very high if I do not perform well

Evade responsibility:

1. It is no big deal to delay tasks for two or three days.
2. It is fine to surf the internet or watch videos occasionally during working hours.
3. One does not have to handle work with great care.

Shift responsibility:

1. More responsibilities lead to more mistakes, so one should get involved as little as possible.
2. One should avoid risk and give difficult tasks to others.

Reframe responsibility:

1. Well-written reports are more important than well-done jobs.
2. Trophy projects demonstrate good political performance and please superiors.
3. One should comply strictly with written rules, even though they are not in line with reality.
4. One should stick to routines and do not want to make any change or innovation.

Anticipatory blame avoidance:

1. More responsibilities lead to more mistakes, so one should get involved as little as possible.
2. One should avoid risk and give difficult tasks to others.
3. One should stick to routines and avoid making any change and innovation.

Survey experiment design

Vignette 1: Suppose your superior orders you to take charge of a specific project. This project is beneficial to citizens and popular among them. Your superior imposes almost no supervision or checks on the process and results of the project's implementation.

Vignette 2: Suppose your superior orders you to take charge of a specific project. This project does not benefit citizens and may even have adverse consequences for them. Your superior imposes almost no supervision or checks on the process and results of the project's implementation.

Vignette 3: Suppose your superior orders you to take charge of a specific project. This project is beneficial to citizens and popular among them. Your superior imposes moderate monitoring and offers appropriate rewards or penalties based on the project's implementation.

Vignette 4: Suppose your superior orders you to take charge of a specific project. This project does not benefit citizens and may even have adverse effects on them. Your superior imposes moderate monitoring and offers appropriate rewards or punishments based on the project's implementation.

Vignette 5: Suppose your superior orders you to take charge of a specific project. This project is beneficial to citizens and popular among them. Your superior implements strict supervision and frequent inspections, and severe punishment will be imposed if you make mistakes.

Vignette 6: Suppose your superior orders you to take charge of a specific project. This project does not benefit citizens and may even have adverse effects on them. Your superior implements strict supervision and frequent inspections, and severe punishment will be imposed if you make mistakes.

Question: How much effort are you willing to make to implement the project?

The manufacturer's authorised representative in the EU is Springer Nature Customer Service Centre GmbH, Europaplatz 3, 69115 Heidelberg, Germany. If you have any concerns regarding our products, please contact ProductSafety@springernature.com

Printed and bound by CPI Group (UK) Ltd, Croydon, CR0 4YY
01/10/2026
02225912-0011